"Cynthia has presented in pedantic detail the daily experiences of her mother during her mandatory service in the Hitler Youth in the most compelling and easy to read way. From the time of her initiation until her completed training at Landjahr Lager Seidorf, the book brings to the reader new perspectives and an intimate first-hand accounting of the purpose, ideology, and daily routines of the Hitler Youth Movement as experienced by Gertrude Kerschner. These details will dispel many possible misconceptions or skewed perspectives of the League of German Girls."

~ Paul E. Fischer, President ~
The German Cultural Society of Erie, PA

"Through Innocent Eyes" is the fascinating biography of Gertrude Kerschner and her time as a BDM girl in the elite rural educational program called Country Service Year Camp. I was captivated by the steady indoctrination of Gertrude as she progressed from her time in the Young Girls League, to becoming a "Girl in Service" for her country. The reader is given a chronological account into the progress of what the BDM girls learned every step of the way. Every chapter builds upon the prior, giving an insightful look into Gertrude's personal world."

~ Jeanne M. Onuska ~
CEO – European Military Historical Society, Conneaut, Ohio
Previous Sponsor & Promoter of D-Day Conneaut, Conneaut, Ohio

Through Innocent Eyes

Through Innocent Eyes

THE CHOSEN GIRLS OF
THE HITLER YOUTH

Cynthia A. Sandor

BDM
History

Library of Congress Control Number: 2017918820

Published by:

BDM
History

BDM History
427 Oakleaf Blvd.
Oldsmar, FL 34677
(813) 895-2516
www.bdmhistory.com

ISBN: 978-0-578-17724-3 (paperback)
ISBN: 978-0-999-75500-6 (hardback)
ISBN: 978-0-999-75501-3 (E-Book)

Copy Editor: Jeanne M. Onuska
Design: BDM History

First Printing in the United States of America – 2012 – Balbo Press
Revised Edition – April 20, 2018
10 9 8 7 6 5 4 3 2 1

ALSO BY THE AUTHOR

"Europe to New York City on the United States—July 6, 1957" as contained in the 50th Anniversary Maiden Voyage Edition–S.S. United States: Fastest Ship in the World by Frank Braynard and Robert Hudson Westover, published by Turner Publishing Company.

This book is dedicated to my parents.

"Gertrude and Robert"

Contents

"The task of our Girls League is to raise our girls as torch bearers of the National-Socialist world. We need girls who are at harmony between their bodies, souls, and spirits. In addition, we need girls who, through healthy bodies and balanced minds, embody the beauty of divine creation. We want to raise girls who believe in Germany and our leader, and who will pass these beliefs on to their future children."[2]

Dr. Jutta Rüdiger
German Psychologist
Reich's Deputy of the Bund Deutscher Mädel
(Reichsreferentin des BDM)
1937–1945

---

[1] Photo: André Huesken, Germany
[2] Bund Deutscher Mädel

PREFACE

Four months before Gertrude Kerschner passed away from bone cancer her daughter, Cynthia, found her mother's personal hand-written green cloth journal. A faded and torn red cloth emblem of a sword piercing an Odal rune is glued to the right-hand, lower corner. The journal is bound together on the left with a simple green string.

When Cynthia opened the journal, she noticed her mother's name written in the upper left hand corner of the first page. She delicately turned each well-worn page, examining the writings and studied each black and white photo. There are photos of a very large house and teenage girls wearing uniforms, standing at attention, playing with children, and taking care of farm animals. The most remarkable photo shows the Hakenkreuz flag, known to the world as the swastika.

The journal is written with black ink in a style called "Sütterlin" while the poems are written using a dip pen in "Fraktur." This style of cursive writing was taught in all German and Austrian schools from 1935 until 1941. Gertrude's journal contains chapter headings, stories, poems, songs, and pictures.

Instantaneously, a million questions raced through Cynthia's mind. Where's this house? Who are these girls in the photos? When was this written? What's written here? Why did my mother write this book? Many more questions raced through her mind as she drove to the hospital in anticipation of eagerly showing her mother the journal. She knew only her mother could give her the answers to the meaning of this priceless historical treasure.

Cynthia quietly walked into the hospital room and with a great big smile and softly said, "Hi, Mom! I'm here!"

Gertrude greeted her daughter with a weak smile and responded with a soft "Hello." Cynthia walked to the side of her bed, stroked her mother's thick black hair, and kissed her forehead. No longer being able to contain her excitement, she pulled the book out from behind her back and said "Mom! Look what I found!"

"Where did you find this?" Gertrude gasped in disbelief.

"I found this when I was cleaning your bedroom. It was next to the nightstand. What is this? Did you write this? Can you read this?" Cynthia asked as she handed her mother the journal.

Gertrude's hand pierced with an intravenous needle reached out. Within an instant, the epoch of time passed from the daughter to the mother. Carefully, Gertrude opened the journal and started turning the pages. Cynthia pulled a chair up next to the hospital bed and sat watching her mother compose her thoughts.

Then, Cynthia noticed her mother's entire disposition change. She adjusted herself and sat upright in bed. It seemed as if Gertrude had gained an inner sense of hidden strength. It looked as if she was silently reminiscing about a time in her life that made her very happy. Then, in a vigorous voice, Gertrude proudly responded, "Of course I can read it. I wrote it. I was in the Hitler Youth."

Cynthia could not believe what she was hearing! Her mother was in the Hitler Youth. She was in shock! More questions raced through her mind as she continued to watch her mother gingerly turn each page. She noticed how her mother's face relaxed and her brown eyes sparkled with a sense of contentment.

Cynthia thought her mother would tell her another one of her picturesque stories about growing up on her beautiful farm in Kleinzell, hiking the mountains in Tirol, or walking along the Mirabel Palace Gardens in Salzburg where the "Sound of Music" was filmed. The places her mother told her about in her stories would eventually become the places she would visit on the many family trips to Gertrude's homeland, Austria. However, the next sentence would put a screeching halt to her daughter's fairytale dreamlike state of mind and instead, awaken her consciousness to question her own identity every time she researched this topic.

Gertrude closed the journal, placed both hands on the book, and looked her daughter straight in her eyes. In a very stern voice, she pointed her finger at her daughter and said, "Do *not* show this book to anyone because they will kill you."

Cynthia felt a deep sense of electrified foreboding vibrate through her body which immediately permutated into a sense of adventure. "Well, all right then!" she said as she clapped and rubbed her hands together wanting to find out more. "What's in the book? What does it say?" Cynthia asked. Gertrude always had a hard time understanding her daughter's curious sense of extreme adventure especially when she was twenty years old and jumped out of a perfectly good airplane, twice.

For the remainder of their short time together Gertrude opened up and shared her entire life story with her daughter, growing up in Kleinzell, and the time she was in the Hitler Youth.

Cynthia's mother never did answer all of her questions. After her mother's passing, she began her research project on her life and the girls in the League of German Girls (Bund Deutscher Mädel - BDM).

Her Aunt Mitzi from Kleinzell helped her to decipher her mother's journal. It would be some years before declassified information became available by England's Counter Intelligence, and until Chris Crawford and Stephan Hansen would present valuable information about the League of German Girls on their website "Bund Deutscher Mädel — A Historical Research Page and Online Archive" (bdmhistory.com). Cynthia's neighbor, Irma Nagengast-Rosich spent an entire year working alongside her to translate hundreds of pages of German documents.

Back in Europe, Gertrude's friends called her Trudel. In America, everyone called her Trudy. Cynthia's mother learned the American lifestyle and raised her children with integrity, strong principles, and with a strong European work ethic, she learned while serving in the BDM.

Cynthia has based this book on Gertrude's personal Landjahr Lager Journal, together with original JM/BDM Leadership documents, declassified wartime records, family discussions, Internet research, books, and personal interviews with German and Austrian women. She had the fortunate opportunity to communicate with the last four surviving members of Landjahr Lager – Seidorf: Ellie, Nelly, Steffi, and Marie. They were all roommates in the elite rural educational camp Gertrude had attended in Sosnówka, Poland.

Cynthia believes there comes a time in life when we question our identity and family roots. The vicissitude of this journey parallels Cynthia's personal self-development. The principles by which she lives today were taught to her by her mother that she wrote about in her journal and what she had learned during her time in the BDM.

The full extent of the American term coined after WWII, "Nazi Ideology," did not permeate her mother's being. Instead, she extrapolated the good from a horrific period in human history and continually strived to become a better human being, wife, and mother, devoting her entire life to her husband, children, friends, and within her community.

At times, Cynthia was left wondering about some of her mother's principles. For example, when Trudy said, "Don't stop because you will die," left Cynthia searching for its true meaning for years.

Children born before and during WWII lived this part of their lives through their own innocence. They were not aware of the atrocities that were secretly occurring around them, nor were they politically aware of their government's internal actions. Gertrude was never taken in by the racial ideology. She treated everyone with respect, without judgment, and she lived her life with absolute integrity.

This is not a book analyzing the Hitler Youth. This is a biography about an Austrian girl named Gertrude Kerschner and her life in the BDM, based upon her handwritten journal entitled "Landjahr Lager—Seidorf."

This book is my mother's story.

Acknowledgment

It takes a creative and dedicated group of individuals to bring a book to life. I am grateful to Irmgard M. Nagengast-Rosich, for translating hundreds of pages of German documents. A special thank you goes to Randall Bytwerk, Professor of Communication Arts, and Sciences at Calvin College for his valuable contribution and permission to reference his material.

I am appreciative to Chris Crawford and Stephan Hansen for their historical documentation on the website, bdmhistory.com, "Bund Deutscher Mädel—A Historical Research Page and Online Archive." Permission to cite their material has been graciously received by Mrs. Crawford and Mr. Hansen.

I gratefully acknowledge Winfried Schön for his contribution of historical research material and to Arek Kubala for locating the manor home in Sosnówka, Poland. I would like to thank Malgorzata Jackiewicz, the current owner of Landjahr Lager—Seidorf, now called Monte Cassino, for taking her valuable time to show me the home and the many places my mother wrote about in her journal.

I also want to thank Lotte Landl, Ernst Birke, Peter Dubiel, Dennis Weidner, and my family, Tante Mitzi, Uncle Franz, and Tante Anita. I would also like to thank my friend, Elin Toona Gottschalk, and especially my editor, Jeanne Onuska, CEO – European Military Historical Society.

Finally, to the BDM women who shared their remarkable stories with me including Hedwig Kraushofer-McLeod, Gertrude Lippenberger, Gertrude Hödlmaier, Gretel Reisinger, Gertrude Niederhuber, and the Landjahr Seidorf Girls including Marie Mikolasz-Dubiel, Eleanor Mohler, Steffi Pucks, and Elli Musial. I thank them for their valuable historical contribution.

Gertrude's home was in Region (Gebiet) # 28 – Niederdonau
Landjahr Lager Seidorf was in Gebiet # 4 – Schlesien

[1] Arvo Vercamer

Part One

Preparing to Become a Hitler Youth

**"You are the future of Germany.
Where you are now, you will be.
You are the future of Germany.
It will be and it must be!"**

~ Gertrude Kerschner ~

1931

IN KLEINZELL, AUSTRIA, a little girl looks down at her baby sister sleeping in the straw crib. She pulls back the white down quilt and picks up her younger sister. Even though Anita is dressed warmly, her little sister is not. Wearing only cloth panties, the child shivers in the chill that consumes the daytime air. Anita does not realize how deathly ill her sister is as she removes her from the comfort of her crib. Diagnosed with tuberculosis Gertrude does not have long to live.

Anita wraps Gertrude in a thin blanket. Gently, she holds her dying sister in her arms and tiptoes to the front door. She is wearing her winter clothes and heavy wool jacket. She reaches for the red crochet hat that her mother knitted and places it on her head. After taking a few steps forward, she stops for a moment, stands still, and contemplates whether she should leave her father alone even for a moment. He lies seriously ill in his bed.

Anita looks toward the bedroom and sees her father's body beneath a white goose down comforter. Heavy, dark curtains drape over the window to keep out the sunlight. He coughs. She peers around the room and watches the flames from the fireplace illuminate the large main room of their wooden farmhouse. Anita's father, Emmerich, a middle-aged father of five, appears old and brittle. His once beautiful brown eyes are now red and sensitive to bright light. His black hair is aged with grey streaks. His frail body shakes with sweat and fever. He was once a brave, strong, and dependable Austrian soldier in WWI. Now he holds his chest with every bloody cough. Blood stains the beautiful embroidered quilt made by his wife.

Anita places her hand gently on the iron knob of the heavy oak entry door. Feeling anxious and scared she quietly turns the handle so as not to awaken her father. The doorknob clicks twice before it releases from its latch. The door creeks open and sunlight blinds her for a moment. She glances back at her father to make sure she did not wake him. Holding her sister's body close to her chest Anita turns to the door, shades her eyes to regain her sight, and steps outside onto the front porch. Once through she closes the creaking door behind her.

Standing on the front hand-hewn porch Anita looks around the farm for the rest of her family. The snow forms a breathtaking landscape as it hangs delicately onto the pine needles and blankets the ground like a thick carpet. Under the limbs of a nearby tree stands a family of reindeer. The doe and her two small calves lick the salt blocks while the bull stands at attention looking for predators.

The snow-covered Reisalpe Mountain stands majestically in the distance giving Anita a feeling of strength. She steps from the porch onto a well-worn path of snow. "What a beautiful day it is to go skiing", she thinks to herself.

Anita walks past the large woodpile remembering how her father chopped it earlier in the spring. Her brown knee-high suede boots crunch the iced-over snow underfoot as she walks toward the barn. On the ground, the sun's rays capture the crystal-like rainbow colors of each snowflake that fell the night before. "I wonder why the snow sparkles," she thinks to herself.

Her foot hits a snow-covered log and she trips dropping her sister in the snow bank. The child begins to cry. Reactively, Anita rescues Gertrude from the ground and wipes the snow away from her half-naked body. Anita places her sister back inside the blanket and strokes her frigid body to keep her warm. Looking up toward the deep blue sky Anita prays, "Oh God, please let my sister live. I didn't mean to drop her. I don't want her to die."

Anita sits down on the stable steps and gently rocks her crying sister back and forth, singing an old Austrian folk lullaby: "Hush, hush, hush! Behold the wondrous Light! Who will appear? The Christ-child, dear, for this, you know, is Holy Light, for this, you know, is Holy Light."

Gertrude's cry turns into a gentle whimper and then stops altogether. The child is content with the love she receives from her sister. Anita gives Gertrude another heartfelt hug, kisses her on her head, and pulls the blanket tightly to warm her tiny body. As Anita stands up, she is unaware of the thick icicles hanging from the eave as they drip from the warm winter's sun leaving droplets in the snow below.

With one great shove, Anita uses her entire body to slide open the barn door. This time the darkness inside the building blinds her and everything seems black. As she waits for her eyes to adjust, she can hear her mother, Josefa, giving orders in her Austrian Austro-Bavarian dialect. Because Anita's father is deathly ill her family including her two older brothers, Hans and Emmerich, along with her younger brother, Franzel, must take over the farm responsibilities.

"Hans remove the old hay and lay down fresh bedding for the cows. Move it. This place is a pigsty! Emmerich, go upstairs, throw the bale of hay down, and be careful! I don't want you falling through the ceiling! And once you are finished you can clean out the chicken coop. Schnell, schnell!" Josefa commands of her children while milking their last dairy cow.

Anita stands in the doorway listening and watching as her brothers' hurry through their chores. Her mother did not hear the barn door open. Instead, Josefa's mind is distracted with thoughts about her husband's illness. How is she going to care for her home, the finances, the farm, the animals, and feed her five children if her husband passes away?

Josefa is a well-worn woman who was born and raised in Kleinzell. Her strong muscular build gives her the ability to handle the laborious farm chores while her strong will and determination help sustain the family nucleus. She is an intelligent woman for her age and has borne five children before reaching the age of thirty-one. When she was eighteen, she had survived the Great War. She witnessed drastic political, cultural, and socio-economic changes. She learned about new countries forming and new ideologies that replaced the old. She has lived a lifetime and wishes for her children not to experience the same.

4

Anita watches her family soundlessly so as not to disturb them. Suddenly, Josefa stops milking the cow, turns her head, and notices her daughter holding the young child in her arms. Josefa jumps from her milking stool, knocking it over, takes two steps toward Anita, and backhands her hard across the face.

"What do you think you are doing bringing your little sister out here in this cold?" Josefa yells at her daughter.

"Mother, I—" Anita cries as she clutches her little sister closer to her breast.

"What right in God's mind are you thinking bringing your little sister out here in this cold? Do you want her to die?" Josefa screams waiting for a response.

"I ... I need," Anita sniffs, "some ... help in the kitchen. I can't lift the ... the kettle from the fire," Anita says sobbing. "Oh, please forgive me, Mother! I didn't mean to make you angry!" Anita's tears fall upon her baby sister's face. The child begins to cry again.

"Hans!" Josefa yells. "Get Trudel inside this very second and help your sister with the cauldron."

A loud *thump* sounds behind Anita as she looks up to see Emmerich peering down through the opening in the attic floor. Pieces of straw and dust gracefully fall from above to the floor. Hans places the pitchfork against the wall and quickly runs to Anita. He gently takes his sister from Anita's arms, opens his wool coat, and wraps her inside. Anita runs from the barn crying. Hans is not too far behind.

Anita scurries down the path forgetting about how the sun's rays make the snow sparkle. Tears swell up in her eyes making it difficult to see. She trips and falls hard onto the front porch and lets out another cry. Her older brother helps her to her feet. With compassion, Hans speaks softly. "Listen, Mom's going through a lot right now and we'll need to help her the best way we can." Anita shakes her head up and down fighting back the tears. Hans puts his finger under her chin and lifts her head up. "I think it would have been better if you left Trudel inside the house and just came out to get me. Think the next time before you do something like this again, okay?"

"Uh, huh," Anita says, feeling a little bit better. They stomp the snow from their feet before entering their home.

"Here, take Trudel and put her back into bed," Hans says as he leans over to remove his sister from inside his jacket. "I'll get the kettle." He takes off his coat, hangs it on the wooden peg next to the front door, and then walks to the fireplace.

Anita holds her sister in her arms and strokes her head affectionately. She walks to the far side of the room and carefully places her sister onto the hay mattress. She continually caresses her head wiping back the tears from her own swollen face.

Fifty-seven years later, Anita stands over Trudel's bed once more caressing her thick, black, wavy hair and fighting back the tears. She has just arrived moments earlier from the airport. She has traveled fourteen hours from Linz, Austria to pay her last respects to her dying sister. Anita is emotionally dying while her sister lies in the hospital bed dying from bone cancer. Anita feels as if she has no soul as if everything and every moment in her life has been nothing but a dream. Fifty-seven years ago, Anita took her sister outside in a cloth diaper. Anita did not know that the shock from the frigid temperature would break her sister's fever, saving Trudel's life. That same winter night Death took their father's life instead.[1]

Trudel's eldest daughter Cynthia watches as her mother opens her eyes to gaze upon Anita for the first time in over four years.

"I can't believe you are here," she whispers in her Austrian dialect. Cynthia watches as the two sisters hug each other. They quietly converse in their native Austrian dialect. With all her strength Trudel reaches underneath the sheets, pulls out her journal, and shows it to Anita.

"Do you remember these days?" Trudel asks.

"Oh my God!" she exclaims remembering her time in the Bund Deutscher Mädel. "I cannot believe you still have your journal. They'll kill you if anybody finds out about this."

"I'm dying anyway. It doesn't matter anymore."

For the last time, the two sisters begin sharing their intimate moments and reminisce about their time growing up in the League of German Girls.

---

[1] Anita Leugner

Trudel Prepares for Service

"Our flag flutters high before us
We are the future man for man
We are marching for Hitler by night and by necessity
With the banner of the youth for freedom and for bread
Our flag flutters high before us
Our flag represents the new era
And, our flag leads us to eternity!
Our flag means more to us than death."

APRIL 1941 - It is 7:00 am on this beautiful morning in Niederschlesien, Germany. Three County Service Year Leaders stand at attention in the courtyard, their right arms stretch out in salute to the Hakenkreuz flag. Forty adolescent girls including Gertrude Kerschner, otherwise known by her friends as Trudel, proudly wears her BDM uniform for the morning flag greeting ceremony. These young girls have been specially chosen to participate at this state-run educational facility called Landjahr Lager. They are responsible young German women who are prepared physically, mentally, and intellectually to serve their country. Conscription into Landjahr Lager is a great honor. [1]

Twenty-one year old troop leader, Fräulein Dieter, recites the morning decree. Her voice strongly commands their oath: "You are the future of Germany and where we are now, you will be! You are the future of Germany. It will be and it must be!"

Fräulein Dieter and the Camp and Economics Assistant Leaders are wearing their federally regulated BDM uniform. It is widely recognizable by the black neckerchief clasped together by a woven leather knot, resembling a necktie in the front and worn underneath the collar of their white blouse. The distinguishing green and white triangle patch inscribed with the word "Landjahr" is worn on the upper left sleeve, centered between the shoulder and the elbow. Over her blouse, the leader wears the traditional buttoned-up fawn-colored knit sweater. She wears a green lanyard around her neck underneath the black neckerchief that loops through the leather slide knot at the front. The silver clasp end is tucked into the left chest pocket. Fräulein Dieter's rank as troop leader is signified by the green lanyard, which is the highest position for this camp. The dark blue knee-high wool skirt, a black buckled belt, white socks, and black flat sole laced shoes complete the leader's service uniforms. The young girls wear the identical uniform without the lanyard and sweater.

---

[1] Annemarie Leppien, p. 50

The camp leader, Fräulein Albrecht, strives to keep a touch of glamour by wearing her shoulder-length blonde hair in the popular rolled hairstyle. A slight hint of makeup outlines her eyelashes. The economic assistant leader, Fräulein Grüber, emulates Fräulein Dieter's vintage finger-wave hairstyle.

The troop leader was selected into her position based upon her personal skills and loyalty in addition to her training and disciplined attitude. Her steady climb began seven short years ago when she was thirteen and held the lowest rank as a girl's appellant in Schleswig-Holstein. Once Fräulein Dieter proved herself as an appellant, she became a leader candidate and received one year of training prior to holding her current position. Once she attained this rank, it was mandatory for her to continue her education by participating in a six-weekend long course. There, she received further instructions about her leadership role and duties including how to conduct afternoon sports meetings and hold weekly evening social events. Prior to completing this training, she was allowed to discuss her future ambitions and intentions for being in service for the Fatherland.

Fräulein Dieter was highly recommended by her fellow peers to head her own camp. She requested to transfer to Niederschlesien a year ago. This is her second year teaching at Country Service Year Camp - Seidorf. She is an aspiring leader hoping to move into the highest regional position as long as the war does not invade the area. Her goal is to serve in Seidorf, continue her education, and eventually move up into a regional leadership position. However, she must work her way up the ranks accordingly to the hierarchy.

Her plan is to become a Group Leader next year and then become a Township Leader within the next two years. She has registered to train at the Regional Leadership School for three weeks at the end of the year. Once her training is complete, she will be able to oversee and manage four squads holding one-hundred and sixty members. Once she becomes a Township Leader, she will have over eight hundred girls under her direct supervision.

To head up the Lower District Leader position she will have to attend the National Leadership School in Potsdam, Germany. From there, she will attend one annual leadership conference at the Sports Academy in Weimar. Leading individuals from within the party, state, and administrative branches will give presentations, and they will lecture on topics including politics, changes in rules and regulations, or other happenings pertaining to the HJ. Since this is such a large conference, she will have the opportunity to become acquainted with other BDM leaders from the various forty-two districts within the Reich. Once she completes her requirements, Fräulein Dieter will be in charge of five regional circles containing over three-thousand members.

The prestigious Regional Leader position is the highest position attainable for her before heading to the nationals. In this position, she will oversee seventy-five thousand girls and will attend quarterly training conferences held by the head of the National Speaker of the BDM or the overall National HJ Youth Leader if the conference is held for both men and women. Their respective peers will give lectures, discuss their work, and current issues will be some of the topics addressed.

Along with Fräulein Dieter, any young BDM woman aspiring to become a leader will be educated in all aspects of character building. This includes sports, particularly gymnastics, philosophy, and culture. She will become adept in German traditions, classical composers, arts and crafts, songs, and folk art. She will attend various lectures within her region in addition to joining various work groups pertaining to the specific aspects of her desired level of service.[2] Learning the physical, socio-emotional, and cognitive development of middle to adolescence girls helps these future leaders train the young future mothers of the state in discipline, obedience, and loyalty.[3] These skills prove valuable while working with the parents to obtain the common goal of being in service for the Führer.

This morning, Fräulein Dieter examines the girls standing in formation. She must become quickly acquainted with the young girls' conduct, disposition and aptitude. She thinks back to when she met them for the first time yesterday afternoon after their overnight train excursion from St. Pölten.

The camp leader, Fräulein Albrecht, arrived with twenty girls. Together with their luggage, they walked two and a half miles to their new home up on the hill overlooking Seidorf. Since the girls were already acquainted with one another on the train all they needed to do was to become acquainted with the daily chores and routines before settling into their assigned shared dormitories. At 6:00 am, their morning ritual at Camp Seidorf begins with the sharp blow of the whistle. By 7:00 a.m., they are in the courtyard for the morning flag ceremony.

As Trudel gives her morning greeting, she remembers back to the day of the Anschluss, March 12, 1938, when her country, Austria, ceased to exist. She is ten years old on the day she walked through the front door and sees her mother, Josefa, sitting down at the kitchen table at their home in Kleinzell, crying. In the background, the radio is playing the traditional Austrian folk song, "Aus Grauer Städte Mauern."[4] "What is it, Mama?" Trudel asks as she walks into the room. She removes her coat and places it on the chair beside the fireplace. Then, she places her arms around her mother and gives her a loving hug. "Don't cry, Mama. I love you. Is there something I did to make you cry?"

"Trudel, please sit down." Josefa removes the handkerchief from her pocket, wipes her eyes, blows her nose, and places the handkerchief back into her apron pocket. She regains her composure before speaking with her daughter.

Trudel sits down on the chair next to her mother be-wildered by her state.

"I just heard a very special announcement on the radio. Our beloved homeland is no more. We have now become a part of Germany and the new name of our country is Ostmark. Do you know what that means?"

"No, I don't, Mama. What does it mean?"

"It means that we will have many changes in the future. Let's just hope that these changes are for the better and not for the worse," Josefa said as she tries to explain the situation to her daughter.

---

[2] Bund Deutscher Mädel - Becoming a Leader
[3] Jungmädel Führerinnen Dienst – January 1941
[4] From Gray City Walls

Austria is currently in a very deep recession. The people have little food to eat, practically no money, and unemployment is rampant. Hyperinflation has set in and the interest on bank loans start at twenty-five percent. Every day another farmer or business declares bankruptcy and there simply are not enough jobs. Josefa helps as many people as she can when they come knocking on her door.

Looters are vandalizing city blocks in Vienna, Linz, and Graz. Unlike the country people, the city people have no food. They are desperate and petitioned the government to stabilize the economy.

The Chancellor of the former Federal State of Austria, Kurt Schuschnigg, despises Hitler and his ambition of absorbing Austria into the Third Reich. In an attempt to calm turbulent waters, Schuschnigg met with Hitler at the Eagle's Nest in Berchtesgaden. Their negotiations failed and their political relations worsened. Hitler presented Schuschnigg with a set of ultimatums. Schuschnigg had to hand over his powers or die. Schuschnigg was then coerced into signing an agreement between both countries, thereby relinquishing his command, without a fight to resolve the political uncertainty of Austria. Schuschnigg wanted his people of Austria to remain Austrian and independent of Hitler and the Third Reich.[5] In turn, Schuschnigg was forced to resign his position. He was arrested and sent to a labor camp.

The people of Austria are desperate. They want so much to be like their neighbors in Germany. The Austrian people were told that Germany has no unemployment, no crime, and that they have a higher standard of living. Rumors spread that everyone has work. Everyone is happy in Germany and Austria wants the same. However, Austria wants the same without giving up her sovereignty. Austria wants to stay independent and guarantee the best interests of its citizens.

Germany's Führer, Adolf Hitler, has re-awakened industry and set his people on a path of prosperity. When Hitler annexes Austria into the Third Reich, he promises assistance to the businesses just as he had done for Germany. Farmers will receive lands taken away from them and the first autobahns in Austria will be constructed. Everyone is guaranteed work and because of this, ninety-eight percent of the people voted for the annexation. The people of Austria voted for National Socialism and not Communism. Josefa wants her country to remain independent.

For three days, the people in Kleinzell celebrate and dance in the streets. The beer garden at Rupert Scheicl's Gasthaus is overflowing with beer, song, and food. Candlelight parades light up the streets in celebration and before everyone knows it, the little village of Kleinzell has food and work again.

German SS officers come into town and oversee law and order. Within a few short weeks, everyone in Kleinzell is employed. The timber company hires most of the men. Most of the women are hired by the Salzerbad Hotel that is known for its refreshing, spring bathing waters that cater to the tourists and the German troops stationed within the area. Life in Austria is changing and it is changing fast.

---

[5] Kurt Schuschnigg

Even life in the school is changing. A portrait of Adolf Hitler and the swastika replaces the crucifixes that once hung on every classroom wall. No longer do they begin class with a prayer. Instead, children sing the new canticle to their Führer. It is now mandatory for all children over the age of ten to register in the Hitler Youth.

Compulsory attendance is required by all Austrian children. If a child does not attend, the parents receive a very stern warning letter from the Reich Ministry of Education, Science, and Culture. Josefa is not pleased with this arrangement because her children must devote at least one full day of work on the farm. Rumors spread that if the parents refuse a second time, a fine equivalent to $300 must be paid. If the parents do not comply with the orders a third time, they are subject to jail and interrogated for at least three days.

Josefa does not like the idea of sending her children into the Hitler Youth. She does not believe in National Socialism and she does not believe that anyone besides her own chancellor should rule the policies of her country. Josefa has a feeling that National Socialism will come with a steep price.

The next day, while Trudel attends school, Josefa walks to the local store, purchases white flax cloth and blue wool and spends the entire day tailoring a uniform for her daughter. By the time Trudel comes home, her mother presents her with the surprise.

"It's not much, but here's a little something I made for you," Josefa says. She hands her daughter the package she had hidden on the chair underneath the kitchen table.

Giddy with excitement, Trudel accepts the package from her mother, slips off the red ribbon, and pulls back the white crêpe paper from the garment. "It's a BDM uniform!" Trudel exclaimed with excitement.

"Do you like it?" Josefa asks.

"I love it, Mama! Thank you!" Trudel gives her mother a loving hug.

"Why don't you try it on and make sure it fits. Tomorrow you can wear it when we walk over to the BDM office and get you registered into the Young Girls' League."

Trudel cannot contain her enthusiasm. She jumps up and down holding her shirt close to her chest before wrapping both arms around her mother. She gives her mother big hug and a kiss on her cheek.

"Everybody's been talking about joining the League, Mama. They were passing out flyers in town and talking to us at school today. They look so smart in their uniforms and they were all having a good time too. I met this one girl and her name is Erika. She's a little older than I am and she told me that they hiked all the way here from Lilienfeld," Trudel excitedly tells her mother.

"Imagine that, walking all the way over here from Lilienfeld. That is a long walk," Josefa compassionately comments.

"Oh yeah or ... maybe she told me that they came over here on a truck. I forgot. Anyway, they are going around the area to tell all the kids what they do and how to join them. They were telling us about their camping trips, their weekly meetings, and all the songs they are learning. Before they left, they even

11

marched and sang a song for us. They sounded so beautiful, Mama. They look so smart! I am so excited! I can't wait to tell all my friends!"

"Why don't you go upstairs and try on your new uniform and come back to show Mommy, won't you?"

"Oh, Mother!" Trudel exclaims. "I'll wear this with all my heart and I will be the best youth girl for the Father Country. You'll see!"

With great honor, Trudel salutes her mother and excitedly runs upstairs to her attic bedroom.

Josefa feels a sense of helplessness and anxiety in her heart. On April 20th, it will be an absolute requirement for all Austrian children of the age of ten to join the Hitler Youth. Josefa stands and turns on the radio to hear the voices of the crowd shouting, *"Heil, Hitler! Heil, Hitler!* Then he speaks.

"You belong to me. We will learn to stand together in my Reich. You are the flesh of our flesh, the blood of our blood, and the same spirit that possesses me drives your young minds! Before us lies Germany. In us marches Germany! Those behind us will follow Germany! Germany's future belongs to you youths!"[6]

The crowd roars over the radio, as Josefa listens to the re-broadcast from the original speech given on September 5, 1934 from Nuremberg. Josefa shuts off the radio, silencing the seventy-thousand voices from her mind. She is appalled that her children have become the property of the state. Her kitchen is now quiet. She leans against the counter and places her hand across her heart. Deep in thought, she contemplates her young daughter's future. Her intuition screams at her. She does not like Hitler or his ideology. Most of all, she does not trust him.

Josefa's eldest son Emmerich is sixteen years old and her second eldest son, Hans, is fourteen. They are training in the HJ Proper. Her eldest daughter, Anita, is twelve and is training for the Young Girls' League in Heinfeld. Anita does not live at home. For the past three years, Anita has been living with her grandparents in Halbach, the next village over from Kleinzell. At thirty-eight years old, Josefa does not have the means to support her five children. She thought it would be best to send Anita to live with her parents, Johann and Anna Kandlhofer, on their farm. Her youngest son, Franzel, is eight years old and two years away from serving in the German Youth.

Trudel is unable to sleep the night before she registers in her new group. All night long, she tosses and turns for fear of not being able to wake up in time for the appointment. She gingerly rises from bed, tiptoes to the window, pulls back the curtains, and unlatches the lock on the window. With confidence, she pushes the window open to get a breath of fresh air. "I wish today were here already," she sighs. As she leans on the windowsill, she curls her hand and places it underneath her chin. She lets out another sigh as she looks up to the first quarter moon. Trudel imagines the fun she will have and the new friends she will meet.

---

[6] Triumph of the Will

Early the next morning Josefa rings the cowbell, and with a bit of humor hollers, "Awake you sleepyheads!" from the bottom of the stairs.

"Coming, Mother!" Trudel shouts back. Exhaustion will not stop her from this day. Sitting on the edge of the bed, she stretches her arms out wide, arching her back. She takes a deep breath of fresh air, clasping her hands over her head, and stretches her body upward. She rubs her eyes for a second, jumps off the bed, and dashes to her pine wardrobe. She opens the closet doors and looks for her best day dress to wear. She pulls her dress out from the closet and hangs it on the hook. Then, she bends over, grasps the bottom of her handmade white nightdress, and pulls it over her head throwing it on the bed. Trudel feels proud when she slips on her red and white checkered dress with short sleeves and white lace trim that her mother made for her. The dress hangs to her knees. She reaches into the wardrobe, grabs a pair of white socks and her church shoes from the bottom drawer. She quickly jumps back, sits on the bed, bends over, puts on her socks and shoes, and then ties her laces. Once dressed, she runs down the stairs and embraces her mother with a big hug.

"Good morning, Mother."

"Good morning, Trudel. Do you not want to wear your new uniform today? Josefa asks her daughter.

"No. I would rather wait until my first official meeting. I don't want it to get dirtied," Trudel replies.

"Ok. Let's get you some breakfast. Did you wash your face and brush your teeth?" she asks.

Trudel runs into the washroom adjacent to the kitchen. She grabs her cup off the shelf and places it next to the white porcelain washbasin and pitcher. She picks up the pitcher with both hands, pours the warm chamomile-mint tea solution into the washbasin and fills her cup. She quickly washes her face using the homemade lye soap and rinses her face in the washbasin. She grabs the towel, dries her face. She hurries to brush her teeth, spits the paste into the basin, rinses, and then dries her mouth. She races back into the kitchen.

"Where's Franzel?" Trudel asks as she sits down on the corner bench seat.

"Your little brother is out in the chicken coop gathering some fresh eggs and goat milk for your breakfast this morning," Josefa responds.

Franzel opens the back door to the washroom and walks into the kitchen with a basket full of fresh eggs and a tin full of warm goat milk. He is dressed warmly in his hand-me-down winter jacket. His trousers are tucked inside his winter boots. He does not realize it, but one of the chickens has followed him into the house. Josefa's concentration is on the speck cooking in the cast iron skillet. She turns her head to ask Franzel a question when suddenly she sees a chicken strutting on her clean kitchen floor. Without a moment's hesitation, she grabs a dishcloth, and starts waiving it to scoot the white rock hen out of her house.

"Phew deivy! Shoo! Shoo!" Josefa shouts as she waves the towel at the bird. It takes a startled leap in the air, lands on the floor, and then darts under the table between the chairs, bumping Trudel's leg. Startled, she jumps in her seat and laughs. Franzel places the eggs and milk on the countertop, removes his jacket and starts chasing the chicken around the floor. Together, the family is in a frenzy as Franzel dashes around the room trying to catch the chicken. The chicken is quick and smart too, for every time the boy gets close, it flies away leaving a few small feathers behind. Franzel takes aim at the bird and with all his might, he leaps onto the floor and throws his jacket over the chicken.

"Gotcha" Franzel exclaims as he carefully wraps the chicken in his jacket and stands up. The fowl struggles to release itself from the clutches of the boy.

"Franzel" Josefa yells as she catches her breath walking back toward the stove. "Get that chicken out of here right now! How many times have I told you to close that door behind you when you come into the house?"

Franzel walks to the door, throws the chicken out into the yard, and closes the door. As he is walking back into the kitchen, he turns to Trudel and with a smirk on his face says, "So, today's the big day for my older sister."

"That's right!" Trudel mocks back as she adjusts her dress and sits back down in the chair. "I am going to be loyal to my Führer and I will be obedient to him at all times, not like you!"

"What did you just say?" Josefa scornfully questions as she turns her head away from the stove and looks at her daughter.

"I am going to be loyal to my Führer," Trudel bashfully repeats. "That's what we've been taught in school."

Franzel starts marching around the room and makes believe he is leading the brigade while swinging a baton. Josefa stops preparing the morning meal, turns and squats down close to Trudel. She looks directly into her daughter's eyes. "Learn whatever they teach you, but always remember, my little one, that family always comes first. Do not ever forget that. You need your family and your family needs you. You cannot be one without the other." Josefa's love can be felt through the gaze in her eyes and her reassuring words.

"Yes, Mama," Trudel replies as she puts down her head in embarrassment.

Josefa takes her index finger and places it underneath her daughter's chin. Trudel raises her head and looks at her mother.

"Now, let's get you some breakfast and sign you up into the league.

Trudel Registers for Service

JOSEFA STANDS UP kisses her daughter on the forehead and returns to prepare the morning meal. Franzel finishes his march and sits down waiting for his breakfast to be served. The children do not see Josefa take her apron and wipe the tears from the corner of her eyes. After breakfast the family leaves together to register Trudel in the Young Girls League of the Hitler Youth.

Holding her mother's hand, Trudel skips down the gravel road. Four days ago, Trudel was an innocent child, happily playing and tending to the chores on the family farm, while her world is evolving around her. On this beautiful spring day, she is walking innocently toward a threshold to uphold the beliefs of a man she does not know, someone whom she will never meet, and for whom she will dedicate her life. She does not understand the meaning of National Socialism, political strategies, or being politically correct. She is not aware of right-wing socialism that rejects egalitarianism and instead supports a stratified economy with classes based on merit and talent.[1] All she knows is that her friends are in the Jungmädelbund and she wants to be with them in this exciting new group.

Franzel is on his mother's left side practicing his goose-step.

The family turns the corner by the grocery store then walks past the mayor's office and up the stairs into the local HJ building located in the Kleinzell School.[2] As they walk into the main entrance, Josefa takes a moment to review the notices on the bulletin board and to see which room the registration is taking place. They walk down the hall to the main office where the Young Girls' League den leader, Fräulein Schmidt, greets them.

Her simple BDM uniform lacks jewelry and yet portrays a strong image of power. She is a tough-looking BDM head leader with black, rolled up hair, dark brown eyes, and a pale white complexion that is more prominent behind her heavy, black-rimmed glasses. She does not depict the blonde hair, blue-eye Aryan race. She is, however by birthright, German and is under the strict guidance of the Reich's Ministry for Science, Education, and Culture.

"Good morning," she starts. "May I help you?"

"Yes, I am here to register my daughter," Josefa says.

"What is her name?" Fräulein Schmidt asks.

"This is my daughter, Gertrude Kerschner. Here …" Josefa pauses as she pulls the letter out from her pocket ordering her daughter to register. "I received this in the mail." Josefa hands the letter to the BDM leader.

"You should be very proud, Frau Kerschner. Today, Gertrude's life will be changed forever. From now on, she will be serving in the League of German

---

[1] George Bailey, pg. 399
[2] Franz Kerschner

Girls. As her leader, I am directed by the Führer to instruct all girls and to awaken in them their responsibility toward the community of our great nation."

Fräulein Schmidt takes the letter from Josefa and reads it closely. She marks Gertrude's name in the registration book, stamps the letter, and then hands it back to Josefa.

"After we finish registering your daughter, the doctor will give her a full medical examination. Once completed, you and Gertrude will take a seat and wait for further instructions." Fräulein Schmidt asks Josefa a few more questions, documenting her answers in the registration book. "Now, follow me, Heil, Hitler!"

Fräulein Schmidt salutes the parent, snaps her heels, and turns about face in a military fashion. Her military disposition commands authority. She leads Josefa and her children into the examination room. She stands by the door and watches as the family walks into the room. Fräulein Schmidt exits completely closing the door behind her.

Trudel looks around the sterilized room. In the center is an examination table and on the wall is an eye chart. Next to the chart is a scale. She becomes hesitant when she sees scary looking metal instruments on the counter top next to the sink.

Josefa bends down, turns to Franzel, and says, "Please sit and wait in the chair in the hall. We'll be out in a little while." She opens the door and encourages Franzel to leave. Franzel walks out, sits down, and starts fidgeting. "Now, don't go anywhere and I mean it!" Josefa says. She returns to the room and waits for the doctor to enter.

"Mama," Trudel innocently starts.

"Yes, Gertrude?" her mother asks.

"Who is that lady?" Trudel questions pausing trying to find the right words. "She seems so strict. Why is that, Mommy?"

"Shhh … be quiet. Don't say that about her," Josefa orders.

"I don't understand, Mama." Trudel seems confused.

"That's because you must respect your elders. Even I must listen to the authorities and do what they say. Just as you must now listen to your instructors and do exactly as they say. Do you understand now dear?" Josefa explains.

"I'm afraid," Trudel whispers under her breath.

"What are you afraid of my little one?" Josefa asks.

"What are those things on the counter?"

"That's so the doctor can examine you properly. There is no reason to be afraid," Josefa says reassuring her daughter.

"I guess so. I don't know. Things seem different now," Trudel says, shaking her head in bewilderment. Together, Josefa and Trudel wait for another moment before the doctor enters the room.

When he enters, Trudel runs and hides behind her mother.

"Good day, ladies. I am Doctor Herbermeyer, and you must be Gertrude," the doctor says as he beams a smile to the little girl.

He is a handsome man with high cheekbones, standing six feet-two with thick, black hair and deep blue eyes. He is wearing a white collared shirt and a black tie underneath his white medical overcoat. A stethoscope hangs around his neck. His black wool trousers and highly polished black leather shoes distinguishes him from this provincial woman.

"This is my daughter, Gertrude," Josefa declares with pride and honor. "Trudel, now come out from behind and let the doctor take a look at you."

Trudel bashfully steps out from behind her mother and looks up at the doctor towering upon her. Immediately, her face beams with a smile at the doctor's handsome physique. "This is my mother, Frau Kerschner, but she's not a Frau anymore because my father died when I was only four years old," Trudel impulsively responds, wanting to show her mother off to the doctor.

Not wanting the doctor to find out that her husband died from tuberculosis, Josefa thinks quickly. "Yes, my husband died in a hunting accident when Trudel was very young. We are of pure German blood. My parents are the Kandlhofer's of Halbach. My grandfather is from the Bernhard family line, distant cousins to the Hapsburgs, and my mother is from the Sulzer family line." Josefa quickly recites her family heritage as far back as she can remember.[3]

"Don't worry about that, Frau Kerschner. We will trace your family records and make sure your daughter is of pure German descent," the doctor calmly says. "Now, let's proceed with Gertrude's medical examination." The mother stands by and observes.

After the examination, Josefa and Trudel finish the registration process with Fräulein Schmidt. Franzel impatiently sits in the hall listening to the women speak.

"I see you have completed the physical examination very well. Here is your required paperwork. It contains the instructions for you to follow in the next step in your child's development. Starting Monday, March 21st, all new members will attend a formal Preparatory Service that will be held here at the school.[4] The lecture will commence at 3:00 p.m. Each girl will be informed about her tasks, duties, and responsibilities. On Saturday, March 26th, the sporting event will be held in the sport's field. At that time, we will test your daughter's abilities, courage, and agility. On Wednesday, March 30th, the social evening meeting will be held. At the end of that meeting, the young girls will be told whether or not they have passed the requirements to become members of the Hitler Youth. Finally, on our Führer's birthday, April 20th, all Jungmädels will meet in the HJ hall for the official membership ceremony. At that time, all new members will be sworn in and will be presented with their membership identification certificates.[5] We expect all new members to arrive on time and be dressed in their new uniforms." Fräulein Schmidt hands Josefa some paperwork. "Here is a complete list of the required attire and equipment for your daughter. All items can be purchased

---

[3] Franz Kerschner
[4] Bund Deutscher Mädel
[5] Ibid

from the Reich's Quartermaster Store (RMZ) in Rohrbach. Do you have any questions?"

Josefa has nothing to say.

"Good. Meeting dismissed. Heil, Hitler!" Fräulein Schmidt declares as she proudly raises her arm in salute to the Führer.

Josefa warily raises her arm in salute as the children look on. "Heil, Hitler."

Trudel can hardly contain herself she is so elated! She does not notice her mother's concern as she is contemplating her children's fate, nor does she know how much her life will change after today. With the medical examination over Josefa takes her children's hands, and together they walk from the building, down the street to their little farm home. Josefa hears a female voice calling to her from behind. "Frau Kerschner! Frau Kerschner!"

Josefa turns around and sees Frau Bauer her neighbor, hurrying towards her.

Josefa's Painful Past

IN THE VILLAGE, The Bauer Family owns the largest farm. Frau Bauer is a sturdy, hard-working woman of thirty-five years. She is known in the village for wearing the prettiest homemade dirndls. The cold weather does not seem to bother her. Frau Bauer and Josefa are childhood friends. Before the Great War, the women attended school together, played in the forests, and helped each other on their family farms. After the Great War, the Austrian economy did not stabilize. Austria experienced drastic political, cultural, and social changes. The Habsburg Empire collapsed and Austria became a component of the German Republic. This unification was forbidden due to the Treaty of Saint-Germain-en-Laye. The first Austrian Republic was then established in 1919.

By 1922, consumer prices were fourteen-thousand times greater than before the start of the war eight years earlier.

By 1924, severe hyperinflation set in rendering the Austrian-Hungarian Krone worthless. The Austrian's lost faith in their country and in their currency. International organizations gained control and many new ideologies took a firm hold in the people's minds. To stabilize the economic devastation, one new Austrian Schilling replaced ten-thousand Kronen. During these severe economic times, these women remained true to their culture, their heritage, and to their traditional family values.

When they were in their early twenties, they married, gave birth, and raised their children. Frau Bauer and her husband were able to buy a large piece of property on the outskirts of the village. Together they worked very hard to build their farm until it became the largest in the area. They own over six hundred heads of livestock, including cattle, sheep, goats, pigs, and chickens. The Bauer family and their employees are never without food, working from dawn until dusk to manage the overall daily farm operations.

When Josefa and her husband, Emmerich, lost their own farm during the depression, they rented a small home on the outskirts of Kleinzell. The backyard vegetable garden was large enough to support them. A small barn housed their milk cow, two pigs, a goat, and their many chickens. Back then, Josefa taught her eldest daughter, Anita, the daily management of the household. By the time Anita was seven years old, she was cleaning, washing the laundry, ironing, cooking, and canning vegetables to store for the winter months.

Whenever Papa Emmerich was not working in the forest, he would teach his eldest sons, Hans and Emmerich, how to milk the cow, clean the stalls, butcher the livestock, and smoke the meat. In 1931, Emmerich became severely ill. Josefa was thirty-one years old when she became a widow.

Summoning all her determination and strength, Josefa would rise early in the morning to pack the oldest children off to school and start her daily laborious farm chores. At night, she would fall into bed absolutely exhausted, pray to God, and ask him for help. No help came. Within a few months of her husband's passing, she exhausted her financial reserves and was no longer able to provide for her children. When the property owner demanded the rental payment, she was forced to give him her last cow. When the cow was gone, he took all the goats. When the goats were gone, he claimed the pigs, and then the chickens. When all the animals were gone, the proprietor threw Josefa and her children out into the streets.

Josefa refused to besmirch her character in exchange for accommodations. Homelessness was a terrible blow to her self-esteem. Desperate and in fear of her future, she packed all their belongings in a hand-held wooden wagon. With her youngest children clutching tightly to her overcoat, the family proceeded to walk down the road.

On that day, Frau Bauer happened to look out her front window and saw Josefa and her five children pushing the heavy wooden wagon down the street. Quickly, she ran outside and invited Josefa and her family to live with her. Josefa bartered for a place to stay in return for working on the farm. Appreciative of Frau Bauer's kindness, Josefa vowed to work hard, take care of the animals, and help with the household chores. Subsequently, Josefa would be in the barn before sunrise milking the cows. By the afternoon, she would help Frau Bauer with the daily housekeeping.

Josefa's children had to work on the large dairy farm for their free room and board. They were not in the least happy about the extensive, heavy manual labor. Josefa's two eldest sons, Emmerich and Hans, eventually left to work on another farm in the next village over. They met a few local girls and decided to settle close to them.

Her oldest daughter, Anita, was frustrated and ran away on several occasions. Anita believed there was a better life for her besides cleaning pig dung and swatting flies. She despised being poor and had always wanted to live in the glamourous city of Vienna.

The police were sent to look for Anita the last time she ran away. They found her in the woods sitting besides her father's grave crying. From that day on, she was sent to stay with her grandparents on the Kandlhofer's farm in Halbach. Anita did not know that she would work twice as hard on her grandparent's farm. She was too young to understand why her life was changing. Anita's grandfather, Johann, viewed children as burdensome. He demanded the young girl help her grandmother, Anna, with the household and farm chores, while he sat inside and drank his homemade schnapps.

One day, Anita snuck off with her friends to go skiing. She returned home that evening with a broken ankle. As punishment, she was forced to watch her grandfather chop her skis into firewood. This tearful experience left a deep scar in Anita's heart and she never skied another day in her life.[1]

Josefa never knew of the turmoil her daughter was going through because she was raising her two youngest children, Trudel and Franzel, and working six days a week, twelve hours a day, on the Bauer farm. When Josefa had free time, she would ride her bicycle to visit her daughter. Neither Josefa's parents nor her daughter spoke of the punishments. All Josefa wanted for her children were to have a warm bed, a loving family, and food in their stomachs. For eight years, Anita had to work extremely hard for her freedom. Josefa did not understand why her daughter never appreciated that which was given to her so freely. On the other hand, Anita did not know the country was in the midst of a severe economic depression and that her mother could not financially care for her.

After the Anschluss, Hitler ordered the central banks to print additional money. This money would be given to Austrian war widows who were single handedly raising children on their own. The only requirement was that that their husbands fought courageously in World War I. Josefa received an envelope with 1,000 Reich Marks from the new German government.[2] The mayor of Kleinzell also awarded Josefa with the Bronze Cross of Honor of the German Mother. It meant she exhibited probity, exemplary motherhood, and conceived and raised at least four children.[3] Josefa has five children.

With this financial windfall, Josefa was able to move from the Bauer's farm and rent a little home in the village. Instead of working on the farm, Josefa found a position in town as a postal carrier. Delivering the mail on foot was a full-time job. She would start work at six o'clock in the morning, sorting the mail, then walk over twenty miles before returning to drop off her empty mail sack. Due to inclement weather, sometimes she would not come home until very late at night, and by the next morning, she had to start all over again.

The head postmaster was impressed by Josefa's diligence to deliver the mail even in the worst weather conditions. With the new government surplus of money, he bought Josefa a car and helped her get her driver's license. Now with Hitler in power, everyone had money, everyone was working, and Austria's economy was climbing out from the deep depression.[4]

Josefa never forgot how Frau Bauer's helped her in her dire time of need. The two had already lived through one world war and two major depressions. Frau Bauer still lives on the north side of Kleinzell while Josefa was able to build a new home in town.

It was normal for families to stay in their hometowns. Living in a small village, everyone knows each other's business. Frau Bauer and Josefa are known as kind, gentle women, compassionate, and discrete.

Josefa turns to see who is behind her. "Yes, Frau Bauer?" Josefa asks.

---

[1] Anita Leugner
[2] Franz Kerschner
[3] Irmgard Weyrather
[4] Franz Kerschner

"I need to speak with you," Frau Bauer glances nervously both ways to see if anyone is watching and then whispers, "in private."

Josefa wonders what the latest horror could be now that her country has been seduced and raped. She and the children stop walking.

"Go ahead and run home children," she says in her warm, motherly voice. "Get out of your good clothes and start your chores. I'll be home shortly."

"Come on! I'll race you!" Franzel shouts to Trudel as he gets a running start ahead of his older sister.

"Na-ah," Trudel retorts as she takes off running fast behind him.

Frau Bauer and Josefa stroll together talking in a low tone. Every once in a while, one of the women looks over her shoulder to see if anyone else is listening.

The women are rightly concerned. The Third Reich's propaganda continues to gain power over the Austrian people through newspapers, radio broadcasts, and from the posters hanging on their village bulletin board. Frau Bauer has heard from other concerned parents about their sons being forged as hard as steel to fight in future battles.

Josefa shares her worries about the manufacturing plants running day and night. She is deeply upset over hearing the radio broadcasts that said children's lives were no longer as important as their duty to the Führer. Both women see Austrians replace their red-white-red flags with the Swastika. Austria, the motherland that they both love is fast becoming the Fatherland of Germany.

The local townspeople speak their fears in whispers, since neighbors can easily use their words against each other. It is crucial to know whom to trust. The locals can do nothing to stop the silent annihilation being plotted outside their land, behind Hitler's closed doors at Berchtesgaden in Germany's Bavarian Alps.

Just as the women are finishing their conversation, Fräulein Schmidt approaches. The three women come to an abrupt stop.

Fräulein Schmidt looks at Josefa. "May I speak with you Frau Kerschner?"

"Good bye, Frau Kerschner" nods Frau Bauer.

"Good day to you, Frau Bauer," Josefa responds with a warm smile. "Yes, Fräulein Schmidt? How may I help you?"

Preparatory Service

ON MARCH 21, 1938, TRUDEL gives her mother a kiss on the cheek and sprints out from the house to meet up with her friends. The girls walk enthusiastically and promptly arrive at 3:00 pm for their first young girls meeting. Trudel is wearing the uniform her mother made, gray knee-high socks, and black leather shoes. Her plump rosy face smiles as her brown eyes radiates with happiness.

The National Socialistic plan for rearing innocent young girls like Trudel is to capitalize on their natural enthusiasm, their craving for action, and their desire for peer approval. The young ones will be taught that the Jungmädelbund (JM) is their new home away from home.

Trudel enters the building through the same doors she walked through when she was simply a child of Austria. Today, Trudel feels important because she is now a child of the newly formed country Ostmark, which has been annexed into the Third Reich. A sign posted on the doorway leads the girls to their meeting room.

Trudel and her comrades walk into the room. Some of her mates are already present and flipping through their Young Girl's pamphlet. Their new leader, Fräulein Schmidt, sits at her large oak desk patiently waiting for the remaining girls to take their seats.

Rather than individual desks for each child, two rows of five darkly stained wooden desktop benches, not unlike church pews, fill the room. From the aisles, the children can enter by sliding their buttocks along the pew. Desktops run along the backsides of the benches. Down the middle of the room is the main aisle. This single row desk layout is an effective seating arrangement designed to eliminate disruptions in the classroom.

A single large, wood-framed window illuminates the faded, whitewashed stucco walls. A green flowered border is stenciled on the wall beneath the twelve-foot high ceiling. One stark light bulb is suspended from the ceiling fixture in the middle of the room. Hanging on the back wall is a map of Austria prior to the Anschluss. Next to it, a wood frame poster board hangs by a single wire, shows in illustration form how limestone and asbestos are removed from the land and made into cement blocks to build homes. On the front wall is a large slate blackboard. The printed motto above it reads:

"The supreme task of the school is the education of all youths for the service of the Volk and State in the National Socialist spirit."[1]

Next to the blackboard hangs a map outlining the twenty-six regions of Germany together with the new seven regions of Ostmark. A single portrait of the

---

[1] Diane Evans

Führer and two NSDAP flags replace the crucifix on the wall. As a devout Catholic, Fräulein Schmidt is not pleased about the removal of her cross. Her mother had given it to her when she first became a teacher. Now, it is against the law to keep a religious icon hanging in the classroom. Praying in school has been replaced with a political agenda. All JM leaders are now members of the NSDAP Teachers' Association and those regarded as being disloyal would promptly be removed.[2]

Fraulein Schmidt rises from her swivel chair, faces the classroom, and calls the children to attention.

"Welcome to the first part of the Preparatory Service for the Young Girls' League, ladies. My name is Fräulein Erika Baron von Schmidt and I am your den leader." She writes her name on the blackboard and turns back to her students. "I am very happy to have you here." The leader wants to make sure the girls feel welcomed and important. However, this is the Young Girls League and there is a specific agenda to follow. Even if the JM leaders are against the new vocational training material, they cannot voice their dissent. Their job is to teach and the girls have to learn. This is not school. This is the Hitler Youth.

Despite such circumstances, Fräulein Schmidt uses a gentle yet firm tone when speaking to her unit. "This is your first introduction into the League of German Girls (BDM). Before we start, I am going to take roll call." She leans over her desk and picks up the attendance book. "When I call your name, I want you to raise your hand and say here." She recites the names from her attendance book and places a check mark next to each name.

"Gretchen Ackerman, Margarita Bauer, Gretel Fuchs, Hanni Gottlieb, Gertrude Kerschner, Maria Kline, Erika Koch, Mitzi Rotheneder, Helga Schreiber, and Irma Schumacher. Good, everyone is in attendance."

Fräulein Schmidt places the attendance book back on her desk, picks up a pamphlet, and turns back to her class to begin the lecture.

"I have received the very important 'Young Girl's Leadership Pamphlet' which was given to me by the Reich's Ministry for Science, Education, and Culture.[3] This pamphlet is your introduction into the Jungmädelbund. This is our new law, ladies. From now on, we will live by these rules and regulations as if it is your Bible. I expect you to take notes and memorize everything because you will be tested on this material. Now, please open your pamphlets to page one.

The girls open their pamphlets and follow along with the instructor.

"Starting today, all ten-year old girls throughout Ostmark must attend the formal Preparatory Service before being formally inducted into the Young Girl's League on April 20th. During this time, you will have three requirements to fulfill." Fräulein Schmidt walks to the chalkboard and highlights the main points of this evening's lecture.

"The purpose of our meeting today fulfills our first requirement. That means I will educate you about the history of the Young Girl's League, and those tasks

---

[2] Chris Trueman
[3] Jungmädel Führerinnen Dienst – January 1941

and duties that are expected of you to grow up and become proper German women in service for the Reich.

"Secondly, you will participate in the sports afternoon where I will start training you for the Jungmädel Challenge. Your challenge must be completed within the first six months.

"Lastly, you will participate in one social evening meeting. Thereafter, all future meetings will be held on Wednesday after school.

"Now, let's go over everything in more detail. The Young Girls' League (JM) is the first female branch of the League of German Girls' (BDM) in the Hitler Youth (HJ). Its origins date back to the 1920s as the 'Sisterhood of the Hitler Youth.' By 1930, it was founded as the female branch of the Hitler Youth and in 1931 was formerly integrated.[4] Membership in the Hitler Youth has been compulsory since 1936 when it was first signed into law.[5]

"Our National Speaker is Dr. Jutta Rüdiger and she oversees all the girls in the League of German Girls.[6] She reports directly to the Reich Youth Leader, Baldur von Schirach, and he reports directly to our Führer."[7]

"There are thirty-four regions of the Hitler Youth throughout Germany. Each region is divided into districts, lower-districts, townships, groups, troops and a den, like ours is here. We are in region number twenty-eight designated under the Lower Danube (Süd Niederdonau) area. We are in district number twenty. We are located in the lower-district of Lilienfeld and our group number is eleven. Our den number is five-hundred and twenty-seven. Our local headquarters is in Lilienfeld and our main headquarters is in the city of Vienna."[8]

"The purpose of the Young Girls' League is to educate you for companionship, honor, and faith. You will learn about your duties and responsibilities. After serving your first four years, you will automatically advance into the League of German Girls (BDM). There, you will serve for another four years. When your service in the BDM is complete, you will have the opportunity to join the Faith and Beauty Society (Glaube und Schönheit). This voluntary society is for women between the ages of seventeen to twenty-one who aspire to work. Courses range from fashion design to healthy living. However, the overall curriculum is to educate you in properly running your household, cooking well for your families, and caring for your children. When you are twenty-one years old, you can join the National Socialists Women's League where you will be further educated in becoming proper German women.

"As of today, there are over four-million girls who are dedicating their lives to our Führer. Including the boys, there are over eight-million youths serving in the entire Hitler Youth. You should feel very proud. Our Führer wants you to learn because you are destined to become the best! It doesn't matter whether or

---

[4] Dennis Weidner
[5] Bund Deutscher Mädel - "Jungmädelbund"
[6] League of German Girls
[7] Holocaust Education and Archive Research Team
[8] The Hitler Jugend

not you are in school, helping your mother at home or serving in the community. Everywhere you go, you will always have special tasks that you must fulfill that is, and if you want to say that you are a proper German girl. Therefore, the essence of becoming a young girl in service is in your joyful duty. The entire league is based upon two standards and that includes your behavior, and your appearance.

"Now, let us take a moment to learn your First Decree. I have written it here on the board. Please copy it down in your notebooks. When you are done, look up for that will let me know that you are finished." Fräulein Schmidt sits back down at her desk and waits as the girls copy down their first decree. "Okay, everyone, let's recite it together."

"I am the first servant of my State. At all times, I will be obedient, loyal, and disciplined. I happily perform my duties. At all times I am a clean, honest, and a model young German girl."

"Very good, girls, you said that very nicely. You must memorize this first decree. From this moment forward, the Führer demands that you are obedient, loyal, and disciplined. At all times you must obey your leaders. Anyone who speaks out against our Führer or our country must be immediately reported to the nearest authority, whether they are your friend, family, or comrade."

The girls look at each other bewildered. Trudel raises her hand.

"Yes, Trudel, you have a question?" the teacher asks.

"Fräulein Schmidt, does that include everyone?" Trudel inquires cautiously.

"As I said before, if anyone at all should talk badly about our Führer, the Hitler Youth, or the Third Reich, yes, you must report them immediately to the first official you see. Do I make myself perfectly clear?"

"Yes, Fräulein Schmidt," Trudel responds with humility.

"Now let us continue. We have examined your ancestral records and they prove that you are superior because you have pure German blood. The blood inside of you is the blood from your fathers and ancestors. You do not know of your long dead ancestors, but their blood lives in you through your parents. Your parents gave you their blood, thereby giving you your life. To deny your parents' blood is to deny yourself. You cannot change it because it is who you are by nature. You have the honor to pass your pure blood onto your children. Therefore, the pure German bloodline can never be broken because you are the carrier of life. You carry the secret of creation itself. Your blood and body is holy and because of this, God lives through you." Fräulein Schmidt pauses, giving the girls time to digest this crucial information.

"To be in service means that you are expected to perform your duties voluntarily, always with joyful happiness. You will never shirk your obligations. At all times, you will stand firm and upright. You will be held accountable for all your actions and you will always honor and respect your leaders. You will fight against being untrue to yourself. You will always tell the truth. You will not use flattery or bribery to procure your various badges or awards either, because all promotions will be based upon you alone and on your individual competence. The fundamental commands for each young girl are rectitude and honor. It is up to you to know what it means to be in service for the Hitler Youth. You must be in camaraderie with each other. Now, here is your Second Decree that you must learn and memorize. Let's take a moment to write this down in our notebooks and once finished, we will recite it together."

"I am a loyal and obedient young girl in service for the State. I will happily perform my duties and wear my uniform with pride. I am clean, honest and at all times, a young German girl."

"That was very good. Now, during your service you will continually demonstrate your character as if you are constantly being tested. Within the first half of the year, you should be able to show me that you want to be an upright, young girl in service for the Fatherland. This is who you are by serving in this den."

"This Saturday, you will begin training for the Young Girl's Challenge. This challenge has two parts. The first part of the challenge is to begin training you in sports. The second part of the challenge is to begin training you for the monthly hiking trips." Trudel's ears perk up in excitement! She loves the idea of going on a hiking trip.

"We will meet every Saturday afternoon at 2:00 pm and begin practicing for the Young Girl's Challenge. First, you will learn to run one-hundred and ninety-six feet in fourteen seconds or less. Then, you will train to jump a distance of six and one-half feet. Lastly, you will train to throw a leather ball at least forty feet.[9] These challenges will show me your physical abilities, your agility, and your willingness to own up to any task set before you. It will also show me how well you obey my instructions. The results of the tests will be recorded in your Achievement Book. In order to pass the challenge, these minimum requirements must be met during your first six months in the league.

"If you successfully complete the challenge, I will officially award you the black neckerchief and leather knot in a special ceremony. This ceremony will be held on Oct 2nd, the anniversary of the first Youth Congress at Potsdam. Only then, will you be confirmed as a *full* member in the Young Girl's League.[10]

"Any girl who cannot meet the requirements can repeat the challenge at a later point in time. If it turns out that, you are unable to meet these challenges I will defer your service for one year and you will be examined by a doctor.

"The second part of the Young Girl Challenge is your participation in a one day hiking trip. We will go over the hiking trip in more detail during our social evening meeting next week. However, in the meantime, please mark it down in your books that the hike will take place on Saturday, April 9th.

---

[9] Reinhold Sautter, p. 166-167
[10] Bund Deutscher Mädel - "The Jungmädel Challenge"

"Now, pay attention. Next Wednesday, you will fulfill the final requirement for the Preparatory Service. This will be our only evening social meeting. We will meet at 5:00 pm. From then on, all future meetings will take place after school on Wednesday at 2:00 in this room.

"Then, on our Führer's birthday, April 20th, you will be formally inducted into the Hitler Youth. At that time, you will be issued your membership certificate and Hitler Youth pin. Does anyone have any questions?"

Margarita is a young Aryan girl with blond hair, blue eyes, and high cheekbones. She raises her hand. "Where do we get our uniforms?" she asks.

"I'm glad you asked that question Margarita. As described in your pamphlet, your uniforms can be purchased from the Reich's Quartermaster's Office (RZM) in Rohrbach. Your parents should know where the Brown Store is located. All uniforms and equipment, including your haversack, must carry the appropriate RZM identification tag because you cannot possibly wear anything that is a cheap imitation. Your parents are aware of what needs to be purchased. They have been given a complete list of the required items for your uniforms." The den leader pauses for a moment the turns her look toward Trudel.

"Look at Gertrude. She is the only girl in this room prepared to serve for she is dressed in her appropriate uniform. Gertrude, please step up in front of the room and show us your uniform."

Hearing this, Gertrude feels embarrassed for only she knows that her mother made her uniform. She does not mention this to her instructor.

"Very nice Gertrude. Why don't you turn around and show everyone your uniform."

Gertrude does as she is asked.

"Thank you Gertrude. You may now sit down," the leader replies.

"For now, let's take a moment to go over the required uniform."

The instructor flips through the pages of her manual and continues with her lecture.

"Here it is. Your parents will need to buy you the white short-sleeve dual flap-pocket blouse, the dark blue wool skirt with waist belt loops that has a single central pleat in center front from hem to mid-thigh, a plain black belt with a silver buckle, the faux suede climbing jacket, and two "Südost Niederdonau" regional triangles. You will need two because one patch will be sewn onto your blouse and one onto you jacket. Ask your mother to show you where and how to sew the insignia onto your uniform so that you can wear it at the next meeting. In addition, you will need to buy the black scarf and the leather slipknot. You may wear your own white ankle socks and brown or black flat-soled shoes. However, if you do not have the appropriate shoes, they can be purchased from any store that carries the official RZM tag. We recommend that if you purchase brand-new shoes that you start wearing them immediately. This way you can break in the leather and avoid getting blisters on your feet. We want your shoes to be comfortable. In addition, remember to keep them clean at all times. We do not want you running around with dirty shoes because I will inspect them, along with your clothing, prior to every meeting you attend."

The ten-year-old girls follow along in their pamphlets as Fräulein Schmidt continues listing the required purchases.

"Most importantly, you will need your sport uniform by *this* weekend. Your parents will need to buy you the white sports shirt, the cloth HJ insignia, which you will sew onto your sports shirt beforehand, the black sport shorts, and a pair of gym shoes. You cannot wear your uniform shoes with your sport uniform. These are two totally, different shoes and you don't want to stand out and look like a brown duck with white swans now do you? At all times, don't you want to look your best when you are dressed exactly like your comrades?"

The girls respond in unison, "Yes, Fräulein Schmidt."

"Now, make sure your entire uniform is complete when you wear it at our next meeting. In addition, make sure your uniform is pressed to perfection and that there are no dangling strings. From the very first moment you put on your uniform, you must always pay attention to detail. You are a representative for the Young Girls' League and everyone will notice you. Therefore, at all times, your uniform must be in first-rate condition. It must be clean and not have any dirt, food stains, or frayed threads. Your shoes must polish to a shine and the soles must be clean. It goes without saying that a proper young German girl will always will look like a woman and this includes your hairstyle.

"Your hair must be properly brushed and braided. Long hair will be braided on either side of your head so that it can hang down in front of your shoulders. You cannot wear your hair up, as I do. Only after you join the BDM can you change your hairstyle.

"In addition, it is strictly forbidden to wear any jewelry, or charms of any kind, except for your HJ pin. This means you cannot wear a necklace, bracelets, or earrings. And those of us …," Fräulein Schmidt slows down her delivery as she surveys around the room, "who *think* they are little princesses are *not* allowed to wear their tiaras."

The girls giggle and glance at each other in amusement.

Fräulein Schmidt likes to inject a little humor into her scripted lecture. "It is absolutely terrible to see a young girl looking like a colored zebra when she wears a red hat with a green scarf, blue gloves, and yellow socks and clogs while wearing her uniform. This will never be allowed! If you do this, not only will you destroy the image of your group with your sloppiness, you will be severely reprimanded, and I will note it in your attendance book.[11] Is this understood?"

"Yes, Fräulein Schmidt," the young girls reply in unison.

"It is now time for your Third Decree that is written up here on the board. Let's recite it together and then we will write it down in our notebooks. Please repeat after me."

"I am a neat and clean young girl in service to the State. I am at all times, well groomed, and wear my uniform with pride. I am at all times a clean, honest, and a model German girl."

---

[11] Jungmädel Führerinnen Dienst – January 1941

"Good." The den leader smiles in approval. "When you go home this evening, remind your parents to buy your uniforms. You must have them ready by your next meeting. Remember that, in case of war, the procurement of these uniforms, together with their accessories, including the HJ insignias, will comply with all federal regulations."

"Now, I know you have learned this, but let's go over it again to make sure we know how to properly salute. Everyone, stand up!"

In unison, the girls stand.

"At all times, you must have your salute perfected and ready to execute. Pay attention now! During the salute, your right arm is stretched out in front of you until your hand is level with your eyes. Your palm is open, facing downward, and your fingers are together." Fräulein Schmidt demonstrates and all her students follow suit. While everyone stands in this position, Fräulein Schmidt continues with her lecture.

"You will always show your salute this way. It would be an insult to our Führer should you salute with your arms straight up. You are not hanging like a monkey from a branch. You are saluting our Führer, the Father of our country! In this manner, you will salute your acquaintances, relatives, teachers, and your comrades. While you are wearing the federation uniform, you will salute all your leaders above you. This includes your Youth Girl Leaders, the Hitler Youth Leaders, the S.A. Leaders, the local Women's League Leaders, the BDM girls, the Armed Forces, and the police too. You will make it a matter of self-consciousness to salute each other. As being the youngest members in the federation, you must always be the first one to salute. Furthermore, when you greet your flag each morning you must raise your right arm in salute. Every time you sing our national anthem, 'The Flag on High,' and the Hitler Youth flag anthem, 'Our Flag Flutters before Us,' your arm must always be in the salute position.[12] Now everyone arms down and sit."

The young girls obey.

"Does everyone understand when we are to salute?"

The girls nod in agreement.

"Good. Now, let's go on to the membership dues. Each of you must pay your initial one-time membership fee of ten pfennig. Thereafter, the monthly dues are thirty-five pfennig and include accidental insurance coverage. There is no such thing as being unable to make your monthly dues! Each and every one of us must make our own personal financial sacrifice to pay our monthly dues. Do not spend your extra change buying a piece of candy. Instead, save the pfennig and pay your membership dues. Be conscious about saving your change because someone might need your help in paying her dues. From now on, we all work together to help each other.[13] Once you monthly due has been paid, I will place a stamp in your Hitler Youth service card.

---

[12] Bund Deutscher Mädel
[13] Jungmädel Führerinnen Dienst – January 1941

"Your service card is your official identification. Your ID cards contains the most essential information about you including a photo of you in your BDM uniform, your name, date, and place of birth, your home address, and the date you joined the League of German Girls. This document is only valid under the following conditions: First, it must contain the Lower Danube regional stamp; secondly, it must contain a photo of the bearer; third, it must contain the signature of the bearer; forth, it must contain my signature and lastly, it must contain the current membership dues stickers. Protect and carry your service card with you at all times.

"Now, let's talk about attendance. There will be no excuse for you to miss even one day of your service. It is your *absolute* duty to attend every event, every meeting, and every sport afternoon. Your attendance must be punctual, and met with joyful enthusiasm. Under no circumstances will anyone be excused from her duties unless there is an emergency or a severe illness. Even then, I must be notified beforehand. Am I making myself perfectly clear?"

"Yes, Fräulein Schmidt," the girls answer. The immediate response by the girls is pleasing to the leader.

"Your service and your behavior will continually be monitored by everyone including me. How you compose yourself is how everyone will see both you and your den. Therefore, it is your obligation to be on your best behavior at all times. There will be no back talking, no whining, no crying, and no complaining. Your den is your new family, your new home, and together it will shelter you in comradeship. Is this understood?"

"Yes, Fräulein Schmidt," the girls call out in unison.

"Now, we will go over the ten special decrees in our pamphlets. You must memorize and obey these decrees at all times because one day, your life may depend upon it!

"Number one; at all times, you must carry your membership service card, your health pass, writing paper, and a pencil. Is this understood?" Fräulein Schmidt asks.

"Yes!" the girls reply together.

"Number two; although being so young, I don't think you will—The fact is that the high officials want me to tell you that it is forbidden for you to enter into a guesthouse or to be out on the streets after 8:00 o'clock.

"Number three; you are not allowed to wear your uniform to any amusement parks.

"Number four; you are not allowed to be seen begging on the streets for money.

"Number five; bonfires are forbidden without adult supervision.

"Number six; when being transported by bus, ship, or railway, you must always pay attention to the commanding officers.

"Number seven; hitchhiking is against the rules.

"Number eight; swimming is only allowed in designated areas under adult supervision. You must behave according to the rules and regulations and you are not allowed to swim alone. If you are unable to swim, don't worry, because we'll be here to teach you.

"Number nine; you will always obey traffic ordinances when crossing the streets.

"And finally, number ten. You will execute each of these orders competently as if you are being tested. You will always behave as if you could be given a test at any time.[14] Does anyone have any questions?

No one responds.

"Good. Then, let us continue." The den leader stands and walks around to the front of her desk to finish her delivery.

"Now, I happen to have here in my hand the Young Girl's Achievement Badge." Fräulein Schmidt shows the girls the proficiency clasp they are striving to achieve. "This award is made from solid silver. As you can see, the letters JM are within a rectangular frame with a plain red ribbon background. Once you turn twelve years old, you can strive for this badge. In order to earn this, certain tests must be completed within the span of one year. These tests include nursing, first aid, physical and athletic exercises.[15] All tests results will be marked down in the Proficiency Book. Once you have passed all the tests, you will be awarded the JM badge by the National Youth Leader himself! Most importantly, this badge is awarded to you when you complete the worldview educational requirements.[16] The test for the worldview education is in three main parts. This includes learning about our Führer and his movements, the Hitler Youth, and Germandom throughout the world.

"You will learn about our Führer, where he was born and educated. By the time we are finished, you will be able to talk about his life, and how he became our Führer. You will also learn about the history of the entire Hitler Youth, its movement, and the battles of the S.A., and the Hitler Youth.[17] I will teach you how to sing our national anthem, the "Horst Wessel Song," and "Forwards, Forwards." You will learn the meanings of the songs and of our national holidays.

"You will know why we are called the Hitler Youth. You will be able to name those HJ who have died before you and talk about their struggles. I will also teach you how to make our den pennant.

"When we learn about Germandom throughout the world, you will be able to draw from memory a map of the German Reich and talk about its borders. You will learn about the famous men and women in German history, and learn about the Germanic people who are still living outside the Reich, especially those in Sudetenland You will read about those brave people of strong character who shall serve as examples for your own lives.

"You should be proud to prove your physical prowess and proficiencies because you are working towards your awards based upon your own desire and

---

[14] Jungmädel Führerinnen Dienst – January 1941
[15] Bund Deutscher Mädel – Proficiency Clasps
[16] Randall Bytwerk – Worldview Education for Winter 1938/39"
[17] SA - Sturmabteilung a/k/a "Storm Detachments"

worthiness. You are striving to earn these awards not to show them off, but out of the joyful willingness to show your worth as a young girl in the Young Girls League.[18]

"But, we're not done yet! Once you reach the age of thirteen, you can then apply for your first honorary position in becoming my appellant! By starting at the lower organizational level, you can work your way up to one day becoming a leader in your region or district. Isn't that exciting?"[19]

Trudel nods her head in agreement.

"During your first four years, we will teach you the way of becoming the future girl of Germany. We will teach you how to become a self-reliant adult in service to the Fatherland, a task you cannot do alone. Through your formal eight years of education, we will teach you how to become a productive member for society.

"We will share many enjoyable hours together singing, listening to classical composers, and playing our recorders. Aside from learning ten new songs every month, we will be telling stories, acting in plays, and playing fun games. We will also be learning new folk dances for each of the annual festivities such as May Day and Harvest Day. Our meetings are very exciting especially when we go out into the community and perform social work. It is important to place your own needs behind those of others in need. Community work stands first, whether it is for the National Socialist People's Welfare, the Winter Relief, or the German Red Cross. And, we have camping trips planned for you!"

Trudel perks up at the thought of camping, possibly with her sister!

"We'll learn about our region and meet new people. We will learn about nature, plants, and animals. In addition, while at camp, you will be in entirely new surroundings, with new girls from different troops, and competing with them in various sports competitions.

"In the sports program, we will teach you about bravery, agility, and how your body functions. We will perform gymnastics and participate in track and field. You should always strive to achieve good scores, just as you will always strive to become the best. Only then can you call yourself a true young girl.

The den leader checks her watch.

"Our time is coming to an end. This concludes the first young girls meeting for your preparatory service. If nobody has any questions, this meeting is finished." Fräulein Schmidt takes a moment to acknowledge the girl's questions.

"Let us now stand, salute the flag, and sing our national anthem. Everyone, stand up and salute!"

Across the street in front of the WWI memorial, Josefa patiently waits for her daughter. From inside the school, she can hear the children sing their new national anthem, "Deutschland, Deutschland, Uber Alles."

---

[18] Jungmädel Führerinnen Dienst – January 1941
[19] Ibid

Germany, Germany above everything,
Above everything in the world,
When, for protection and defense,
We always takes a brotherly stand together,
From the Meuse to the Mermel,
From the Adige to the Belt,
Germany, Germany above everything,
Above everything in the world![20]

Trudel feels a new sense of pride and joy emerging from her soul. At no other time in her life has she had the desire to learn so much about her duty to her country. She is thinking neither about the future nor the past. She is simply enjoying the present moment, digesting what she has learned in her first Young Girl's Preparatory Service meeting. How can she perfectly execute her requirements with joyful obedience? Trudel is only ten years old, but her imagination ignites with thoughts of becoming a young girl in service for her Führer. She suddenly feels important!

After Trudel and her den are excused from their lesson, they forget their manners and run excitedly from the building. As Trudel dashes from the building, she spots her mother sitting across the street. She runs over and gives her a great big hug, almost knocking her off the bench.

"Oh, my little one," chuckles Josefa hugging her daughter back. "How was your first meeting?"

"It was great, Mother. We learned so much today!"

"What did you learn, my little one?"

"Well, we talked about our Führer and what it means to be a young girl in service to our country, and that our sport event is this Saturday, our uniforms, saluting, dues, our awards, and we even sang a song!" Trudel is talking so fast that her mother is having a hard time following her daughter's excitement.

"Okay, okay. Slow down, Trudel. I'm sure you and the other girls had a nice time. Now, let's get back home. Your JM Leader will be coming over for dinner tonight and we'll have to cook a special meal for her."

Josefa and her daughter walk back hand in hand to their little farmhouse.

In the kitchen, Josefa prepares a Viennese veal cutlet. Trudel walks in with a basket full of vegetables and herbs she picked from their garden.

"Trudel, please go and prepare the vegetables for Mommy."

"Yes, Mother," Trudel affably says with a smile. She places the basket down on the table and goes outside to fetch a pail of water from the hand pump. Back on the kitchen table, she starts cleaning and preparing the vegetables for dinner.

"Why is Fräulein Schmidt coming over this evening and having dinner with us?" Trudel asks. "She's never done that before."

Josefa rubs the schnitzel in flour and dips it into the egg batter. "Well, there are a few things we must discuss about your services."

---

[20] Deutschlandlied

Breaded veal cutlet is a traditional Austrian dinner made with a boneless piece of veal thinned by hammering the meat with a wooden mallet. It is coated with flour, dipped in eggs, breadcrumbs, and then deep-fried in a hot skillet. Lemon and parsley garnish the meal while potato salad is often served as a side dish.

"What are you going to be talking about, Mama?"

"Oh, it's adult talk. It's nothing to be concerned about my dear."

Trudel does not give it a second thought and continues helping her mother. Dinner is almost ready when a knock is heard on the front door.

"Coming," Josefa responds in a lilting tone. She wipes her hands on her apron, slides the iron skillet from the direct heat, and puts the spatula down on the plate. She turns from the stove and hastens through the hall, removing her apron. She hangs it up on the coat rack, looks at the mirror, and calmly fixes her graying hair. After adjusting her housedress, she turns to opens the front door.

"Come in Fräulein Schmidt. Please, do come in," Josefa greets Trudel's den leader formally.

"Thank you, Frau Kerschner, for allowing me to come into your home. I look forward to spending some time with you this evening."

"I have made a nice dinner for us. Please come in. Let me take your coat." Josefa feels honored for this is the first time the respected BDM leader has come to Josefa's home.

Fräulein Schmidt hands over her jacket and Josefa hangs it with care on the coat rack.

"You have such a nice home here. Everything seems to be very neat and organized." Fräulein Schmidt makes a mental note for her records.

"Thank you. Thank you very much, Fräulein Schmidt. I do my best with what little I have," Josefa smiles. "Please, sit down. May I get you something to drink?"

Josefa cannot seem to ease the anxiety she feels about the discussion this evening. Even though she is an honorable, responsible, and hard-working mother who deeply loves her children, she can sense there is an agenda to this meeting. Fräulein Schmidt is an authority of the state. She knows if she implies anything negative about the new régime she could be arrested and taken in for questioning, or worse.

"A cup of coffee would be nice, thank you," requests Fräulein Schmidt in a soothing voice. "Where's Trudel?"

Josefa grabs the apron and proceeds back into the kitchen composing herself. "Trudel is in the kitchen. She is helping me prepare dinner. Do you need to speak with her?"

"No, but I do need to speak with you alone."

"Trudel," Josefa calls to the back of the house.

Her daughter appears in the doorway and salutes the adults.

"Yes, Mama, you called?"

"Be a nice girl and take the vegetables back outside and finish cleaning them up for Mommy, won't you?"

"Yes, Mama, as you wish." Trudel salutes, turns, and leaves the room.

Josefa lets out a deep breath. "And, what would you like to discuss, Fräulein Schmidt?"

"Today, I could not help but notice how impeccably dressed your daughter was for her first meeting. She seems to be very attentive and willing to perform her duties joyfully. Because of this, I would like to discuss with you the possibilities of your daughter serving in Niederschlesien. The Führer has initiated his plans to reorganize the area. Once her service in the Young Girls' League is completed, we will need girls like her to…"

Outside, Trudel is preparing the vegetables for dinner. Her gray kitten walks up and starts rubbing against her ankle. She bends down and pets her. Curious chickens strut up to Trudel hoping for a scrap of food. Trudel plucks a cucumber from her basket, cuts it into quarters, and throws the chunks onto the ground. In a mad dash, the chickens race to peck it apart. Trudel gazes upward and sees her brother, Franzel, in the field with his friends, practicing his salute.

Sports Afternoon

SPRING IS ON THE HORIZON. It is an unusually warm afternoon on this 26th day in March 1938. Trudel arrives at the HJ building a few minutes before-hand and changes into her sports attire. Afterwards, she joins her den in the sports field. She is ready to begin training for her Young Girl's Challenge.

Fräulein Schmidt arrives with another leader, and in synchrony walk towards the girls. This new leader is dressed in her BDM sports uniform. She looks to be in her early twenties.

Fräulein Schmidt blows the whistle. "Everyone, line up," she orders. "This is Fräulein Brückner, your sports instructor. Please give her your full attention and cooperation." Fräulein Schmidt salutes the sports leader and returns to the HJ building.

Fräulein Brückner was educated by the Personnel Office of the National Youth Leadership. She was selected by her peers to lead this group based upon her proficiency and personal character, as well as her education and attitude. She has an enterprising spirit, possesses the ability to assert herself, and has strong leadership skills.[1] The National Youth Leadership recognizes that sport activities are a vital component in educating their youth.

"Listen up, ladies!" commands the instructor. "I am Fräulein Brückner, your sport leader. For the next half hour, we will perform our warm-up and stretching exercises. Then, we will start training for the Young Girls' Challenge. It is very important that you perform these exercises with your entire mind, body, and spirit, because that will make you strong, beautiful, and proud.[2] Let us begin with the warm-up exercises. I want everyone to form a perfectly straight line. Now, backs straight, and chests out!"

Trudel feels validated and a part of her team. Building camaraderie is an important part of being in her den. Little does she know that she is experiencing the socio-emotional development skills through positive interactions with her peers and leaders.[3] Soon, she will be sharing her personal stories, her thoughts and developing her own perception. She will come to trust and support her friends and her leaders.

The positive feedback Trudel receives will help her to solidify her self-image as a competent, worthwhile individual with a purpose in life.[4] Unfortunately, some of the girls do not receive validation from within their family unit. The parents naturally expect the girls to perform daily household chores and help their mothers without question. The new government understands this and by

---

[1] Bund Deutscher Mädel – Becoming a Leader
[2] Mädel im Dienst, p. 8
[3] John W. Santrock
[4] Mädel im Dienst, p. 291

capitalizing on these new experiences, they will be able to direct these young girls accordingly by molding their body, mind, and spirt to become strong, compliant servants for the Third Reich.

"Excellent, girls, you have done your warm-up exercises very well. Now let us stretch our muscles. When we stretch, we send oxygen to our muscles, fibers, and tissues. This greatly reduces injuries such as sprained ankles or pulled muscles. It is very important to always warm up and stretch before performing in any types of sports. Now, let's sit down on the ground and start," she commands.

For the next half hour, the girls perform a variety of stretching exercises before beginning their Young Girls Challenge.

After their warmup session, Fräulein Brückner orders the girls to attention. "During your service, you will have to prove yourself both in character as well as in your physical abilities. You will have six months to prove that you want to become a Jungmädel and that you can fit into the community. Your physical abilities and your willingness to own up to any task set before you are to be tested in the Young Girls Challenge. There are two parts to this challenge. First, we have the performance test. Secondly, we have the agility test. In the performance test, you will be timed in running, trained in the long jump, and you will throw a heavy leather ball. In the agility test, you will perform a series of rolls without your hands touching the ground, and you will jump through a swinging rope.[5] Now, let us begin our challenges.

"In first test, you will learn to run one-hundred and ninety-six feet in fourteen seconds or less. If you make that time, you will receive forty points. If you make it in nine seconds or less, you will receive eighty points."[6]

Fräulein Brückner calls each girl's name in alphabetical order. They line up one behind the other and wait for their names to be called. The sports leader walks to the far end of the field with her whistle and stopwatch. The instant the whistle is blown, each girl sprints the length of the field.

Grooming these girls is important for their physical well-being. Depending upon the tone of their muscles, the strength of their bones, including their weight, height, and stride, these girls will train to run as fast as 14 mph.

Sprinting is a difficult challenge, especially for Trudel. Even though she will use all her strength to exert herself to her maximum performance, she is not a runner. Eight years earlier, Trudel had suffered from a near fatal bout of tuberculosis. Her lungs are not strong and it hinders her ability to breathe.

The sports leader calls Trudel's name. She steps up to the line and crouches down into her starting position. She extends her right leg straight behind her and digs the toe of her sport shoe into the grass. Her left knee touches her chest. Her poised body leans forward. Three fingers on both hands touch the ground and stabilizing her in the ready position. In anticipation, she feels her heart beating in her chest. It seems like she is waiting an eternity for the whistle to blow. The longer she waits, the more her muscle tense up.

---

[5] Bund Deutscher Mädel – The Jungmaedel Challenge
[6] Jungmädel-Dienst im Monat Mai 1939, p.17

Then, the whistle blows!

With all her strength, Trudel takes off and runs down the field. With every pounding stride, the other girls cheer her on to run faster. She can feel the muscles in her legs beginning to burn. The exhilaration of closing in on the finish line keeps her focused. For a brief moment in time, she is the center of everyone's attention.

As Trudel sails across the finish line, the leader stops the timer and smiles. She records twenty-three seconds in the Accomplishment Book.

Grateful that this part of the performance test is over, Trudel stands bent over with both hands on her knees, panting for air. Her comrades rush to her side, pat her on the back, and then give her a high five.

Fräulein Schmidt watches the girls congratulate Trudel. She acknowledges the fact that all her girls put forth their best efforts. Indeed, she believes they are running very well and she feels certain that with enough practice, they will all pass the Young Girls Challenge. This is after all their first attempt.

The group takes a short break before performing the long distance jump. After a running start, the girls will leap in the air, and land in a pit filled with finely ground sand. Jumping at least nine feet will reward them with forty point, whereas jumping thirteen feet will reward them with eighty points.[7] The main requirement is that only their heels will hit the sand. They will be disqualified if their hands or bodies touch the ground.

Trudel wants to do her best. During practice, the girls randomly take turns leaping. Maria and Gretel measure the distance and call out the length of the jump to Fräulein Brückner where she records it in the Accomplishment Book. The girls quickly rake the markings away in the sand and then patiently wait for the next contestant.

The final test in this segment is to throw a heavy leather ball at least forty feet. If the ball reaches the designated distance, they will be awarded with forty points. If the ball goes over forty feet, they will receive eighty points.[8] The girls are allowed to throw the ball any way she pleases.

"How are you going to throw the ball?" Trudel asks Gretchen.

"I am going to run and then throw the ball," she replies.

Trudel turns and whispers to Mitzi, "How are you going to throw the ball?"

"I am going to throw it from a standing position," she says.

Each girl takes her turn. Some hold the ball close to their chin and then throws it as if putting the shot. Others take a running start and then throw it, while others simply lean back and throw the ball as far as possible. They practice until they find the best way to throw the ball. Maria and Gretel measure the distance and call out the length to the sport instructor.

The first training part of the Young Girls Challenge has been completed. Now they can continue to practice on their own and during the Sport Afternoon lessons.

---

[7] Jungmädel-Dienst im Monat Mai 1939, p. 17
[8] Ibid

"Now, let's move on to our agility tests. In the first agility test, you will roll forward once and stand up, then immediately roll backwards twice and stand up, all without using your hands. Falling over is not allowed. Let me demonstrate what I expect from you girls!" Fräulein Brückner demonstrates the procedure. "Ok everyone, got it? Now, let's go!"

Trudel clears her mind and concentrates. She wants to develop a strong will and perform these new challenges. She is determined to perform well. She psyches herself up. *I can do this. I know I can do this,* she thinks to herself as she watches the other girls roll before her.

The girls grow anxious as a silent competition begins to build between them. They pay close attention to how each girl before them rolls and stands without losing her balance or using her hands.

Some of the girls stumble over, lose their balance, and start crying. Other girls put their hands down, while others jump with joy when they completed the rolls and stands successfully. The girls view each other with a fun competitive spirit, yet they warmly console those who failed. Fräulein Brückner marks the scores in the book. Their next test is to run and jump inside a swinging rope.

"Gretchen, grab the rope that is lying on the table over there. You and Mitzi will be the ones to swing it as the girls jump through!" Fräulein Brückner orders.

The two girls happily take the ends of the rope and start swinging it in a circular motion. The sports leader reads the girls' names off the list. Each girl counts to three, runs straight towards the rope, and jumps five times before she exits. Not one of the girls has a problem with this activity because they know how to jump rope. However, according to the Reich's Ministry of Education, the main purpose of this exercise is to determine the girls' agility, eye and body coordination, and balance. It is also a way to improve their cardiovascular and muscular endurance. Each girl receives a passing grade.

"This concludes our sports afternoon," Fräulein Brückner announces. "I am very proud of each and every one of you performing so well. Because of this, we have a special surprise waiting for you inside." Fräulein Schmidt walks over to join the group.

Even though their muscles ache, the sweaty girls run enthusiastically towards the washroom. They fill the white enamel watering containers with cold water. The first group helps bathe the second group of girls. The bathing girls remove their socks and shoes and line them neatly on the floor. They remove their sporting attire, undergarments, and hang them neatly on the hooks next to their small towels. Then they step into their individual aluminum tubs and start cleaning themselves while their assistants' pour small amounts of warm water from the vessels over their bodies. The aluminum tubs capture the runoff. Once the first group is finished bathing, they dry themselves off, get dressed, and assist the next set of girls. Soon, everyone is clean and dressed. In pairs, the girls pick up the washing pails, dump the dirty water outside onto the grass, rinse out the containers, and stack them neatly in their original holding place. They assemble and wait for further instructions.

Gretchen and Mitzi are the first ones to finish. They decide to part from their group and explore the basement of the building. Adventure appeals to them.

They creep quietly down the stairs, through the hallway, testing each door handle to see if it is locked. They soon come upon a sign on one door that reads 'Attention! Keep out!' This warning sign intrigues Mitzi enough that she decides to go against protocol and discover what lies behind the mystery door.

"I don't think we should go in there," Gretchen pleads. "We're going to get into trouble."

"Na-ah, let's check it out! There is something really good inside because that's why they're telling us to stay out," Mitzi whispers. Quietly, she presses down on the aluminum flair handle until the latch pops open. The door creaks open and she begins to salivate from the distinct aromas of freshly baked breads. Once the door is fully open, she can see the assortment breads, pastry, and fruits perfectly lined up in baskets on the table.

"Look at all this food!" Mitzi exclaims.

Gretchen pulls back on Mitzi's arm dragging her away from temptation. "We can't go in there or else we are going to get into trouble. Now, let's go! I mean it—right now, Mitzi, let's go now!"

Mitzi's grumbling stomach, however, supersedes her sense of self-discipline. She inhales the glorious aroma. No longer can she contain herself. She grabs the nearest item.

"Oh my God!" she exclaims in delight as she takes a bite from the butter cookie. "This tastes so good! You've got to try at least one!"

"No, I am not. Are you crazy? Now let's get going!" Gretchen pleads. No sooner does she say that when she hears someone coming down the hall. "I'm getting out of here," Gretchen says as she runs out the back door, leaving Mitzi behind.

"Oh my God, this is so delicious," Mitzi mutters as she finishes off her treat. Ignoring all possible consequences, she snatches another cookie from the table and shoves it into her pocket. It was understandable why she was so hungry. She had not eaten all day. Without guile, she turns around, only to find Fräulein Schmidt standing a few feet away from her, arms crossed, and taping the toe of her shoe. Meanwhile, Gretchen meets with her fellow den mates upstairs near the washroom.

"Where have you been?" Trudel asks Gretchen. "We've been looking all over for you. Come on with us," Trudel says with enthusiasm. "Fräulein Schmidt said she has a surprise waiting for us!"

Without a moment's hesitation, the girls follow Fräulein Brückner in an orderly manner, down the stairs, and into the hallway. The pervasive aroma smells delightful. The girls enter the lunchroom and their eyes open wide as they focus on the amazing spread.

They do not notice the contemptuous expression of Fräulein Schmidt, or the chastised Mitzi standing beside her.

"Here you go, girls!" interrupts the den leader. "Because you've performed so well in your very first sport event, all this was meant for you. However..." She pauses ominously. "Because your comrade, Mitzi, was caught stealing and eating the cookies before everyone else, I am afraid that all these delicious fruits and desserts will be off limits. Blinded by her single-mindedness, she has not proven herself an outstanding and obedient young girl in the league. She is not straight and honest. Nor does she display the unified mind, will, and spirit of her comrades. You will all learn that the greatest goals for Germany can only be achieved together as one! You are thereby instructed to take this food and go to each house in the neighborhood and donate it back to the families instead of eating it yourselves. In addition, if anyone asks you why you are giving this food away, you can explain to them that one of your comrades was caught stealing this food. This will demonstrate to our community that we are honest people in service for the greater good of Germany. Selfish, young girls who only think about their own needs will be severely reprimanded — along with all of her comrades. Now, get going!" retorts the den leader.

The girls are stunned, overwhelmed by a swirl of conflicting emotions. One moment they were feeling proud and cheerful, and then angry and resentment the next. It is against the rules to express negative feelings, so instead, they try to repress them and reluctantly do as they are told. As the girls file past Mitzi to gather their shares of food, they shoot her a scornful look, and some whisper derogatory remarks.

With tears streaming down her cheeks, Mitzi cannot move from Fräulein Schmidt grasp. She feels more than just shame. She feels guilty, stupid, and miserable, but most of all, she feels ostracized. By putting herself first, she has let all of her sisters down.

However, the den leader is implacable. "Perhaps this will teach all of you a lesson in comradeship. When any one of you fails to perform, all of you will fail."

Fear instantly freezes in the hearts of these little girls. Any sense of feeling important was just shattered by one's moment of weakness. They silently vow that this will never happen again. In their minds, each decides to exclude Mitzi from the group.

Gretchen and Trudel are the last two girls to grab their baskets. Just as they are about to exit the lunchroom, Trudel turns back and witnesses Fräulein Schmidt grab Mitzi's arm and backhand her viciously across her face. Disobedience will not be tolerated in the Young Girls League and anyone who is caught stealing will be severely reprimanded.[9]

---

[9] Mitzi Rotheneder

First Social Evening Meeting

FRÄULEIN SCHMIDT BEGINS the first social evening meeting of her Young Girls' den. This is the third and last requirement prior to their formal indoctrination next month into the Hitler Youth organization, which will take place on April 20th, the Führer's birthday. The girls wear their federally required uniforms with the exception of the black tie and leather knot, which they will receive in a special ceremony on October 2nd. By that time, they should be able to meet all the requirements of their Young Girls Challenge and become full members of the Bund Deutscher Mädel.

On the blackboard, their new song is written. This song will be sung prior to every meeting. Two swastika flags stand on either side of the board. A new portrait hanging on the wall depicts the Führer as a knight in silver armor riding a black stallion, holding up a billowing national flag. His stern gaze looks forward into the promising future. This man has come to be revered by his German people as a messianic figure, a savior. He is leading the country with a new set of values into a new era, a new way of life, with a strong will.[1]

Hanging over the blackboard is a large red banner in white Fraktur script that reads, "Today is Germany and tomorrow is the World."

Roll call is taken and every den girl is present and accounted. Fräulein Schmidt orders the girls to stand at attention, raise their right arms in salute, and sing their new canticle to their Führer.

> A drum beats in Germany,
> And the Commission proposes to lead
> Follow him! Follow him!
> We have been chosen by him!
>
> We swear by him and we swear by our flag
> Retinue and court, he whirls his destiny track
> With a brazen face he progresses to the sun
> With a tense hard force, his drum is you, Germany!
> He passionately helps the people[2]

"Everyone may sit down," the den leader begins. "Today's meeting will make us very happy and proud. You are only but a small part of the Reich that has spread all over Germany, but one day you and your comrades will be the mothers of great brave and strong sons. You will have the trust of this great

---

[1] Lanzinger
[2] Wir Mädel Singen, "Der Führer," p. 31

nation buried deep within you. We want one nation. You must therefore educate yourselves and prepare for it. You must practice obedience and discipline, and at all times, you must remain faithful to your country and to your Führer. No matter what we create today, our thousand-year Reich will live on long after we have died. Humanity depends upon us! We can maintain the Reich's dominance only if we retain our purity and our inner drive for self-preservation.[3] Now, in today's meeting, you will first learn your new decrees. Then, we will go over the requirements for becoming a Jungmädel. The rest of this meeting will help you prepare for your formal induction ceremony. So, are you ready to learn your first new decree?" Fräulein Schmidt questions the girls with enthusiasm.

"Is it the one up on the chalkboard next to our Führer's song," Trudel asks.

"Yes, it is, Trudel. That is a very good observation. I would like you to open your notebooks and write down this new decree. Once you are finished please put your pencils down and raise your hand."

A competitive spirit motivates the girls as they quickly write their new commandment in their notebooks. Who is going to be the first girl to raise her hand, Trudel wonders as she writes. One by one, the girls raise their hands.

"Excellent! I see how excited you are. Now, let's say it together." Simultaneously, everyone recites her new decree.

> A will must dominate us,
> We must form a unity,
> We must forge a discipline,
> An obedience, subordination,
> Must fill us all because,
> The nation is in us.[4]

"Terrific, girls, I am very proud of each and every one of you." Fräulein Schmidt is in a very good mood. Over the weekend, she was informed that she is in line for a promotion. Someone from the Ministry of Education will be stopping by for an inspection. Fräulein Schmidt aspires to become a Young Girls' Troop Leader and oversee four squads of girls in the BDM proper. It is her dream to oversee the entire educational training in the Lower Danube district.

The young girls admire their instructor. Fräulein Schmidt holds the first leader position in the BDM organizational structure. The respective red and white lanyard is part of her uniform and signifies her position in the rank of Mädelschaftsführerin.[5]

"Our goal is to become a model German girl and this demands devotion and dedication from each and every one of you." Fräulein Schmidt encourages the girls by guiding them through a clearly articulated national socialistic worldview to follow.

---

[3] Joseph W. Bendersky
[4] Annemarie Leppien, p.44
[5] Bund Deutscher Mädel – Organization of the Hitler Youth

These new tenets are the basis for a greater worldview focused on preparing their minds for obedience, discipline, and loyalty to their country. The strength of the nation starts with educating the children in this new world order. Much of who the girls will become in adulthood is based upon the principles they will learn while serving in the League of German Girls. Millions of young children are being simultaneously conditioned by the social-emotional indoctrination which they innocently find themselves. Their parents are not at liberty to interfere. Hierarchy has to be introduced while the girls are still very young. This new worldview is established by the perfectly scripted guidelines from the book "Mein Kampf," written by Germany's strict but charismatic dictator.

"A less well-educated, but physically healthy individual with a sound, firm character, full of determination and willpower, is more valuable to the *Volkish* community than an intellectual weakling," the den leader continues.[6]

The first and strictest doctrine the girls must learn is the leadership principle emphasizing the den leader's position, and that she is in absolute total control. Each leader is responsible for her own troop and she expects nothing less than absolute obedience and discipline from her own troop.[7]

The second most prominent doctrine the girls must learn are the three Ks— Kinder, Küche, und Kirche (children, kitchen, and church). In the Third Reich, women are subordinate to men. Educating them in obedience, duty, self-sacrifice, discipline, and self-control, they will learn the German woman's value by being the perfect homemaker and mother and passing these virtues on to her children.[8] The highest recognition any woman can receive is the "Cross of Honor of the German Mother," awarded for those who exhibited probity, exemplary motherhood, and who conceived and raised at least four or more children in the role of a parent.[9] It is imperative that these new principals are be introduced when the girls are very young.

Fräulein Schmidt continues with the meeting. "It is for the good of Germany that we all work hard and serve in the people's community. You are starting your new life with honor. Each of you possesses a unique spirit inside of you that you own. It is the spirit of the people! It is our character as a nation. This spirit will teach you to value your duty to your country. We are one people, one empire with one leader.[10] Our great leader solved the most terrible economic crisis we ever had when he ascended into power in 1933. In less than two years, he restored the faith of the people, and he brought work to over twenty million unemployed citizens. Our leader restored the soul of the German people, revitalized industry through the creation of the Volkswagen, and built our new autobahns. He honors our workers with celebrations and festivities. He mobilizes volunteers to assist working-class people who are no longer impoverished

---

[6] Dennis Weidner – "Anti-Intellectualism"
[7] Ibid
[8] Lina Buffington
[9] Cross of Honor of the German Mother
[10] Nazism

through a social welfare program. He has boundless devotion to his people! He is forever in service to his country. Hitler is Germany, and Germany is Hitler. The life skills you learn from this day forward will make our German people strong and pure. For these are our country's values shaped by our Führer.

"You will feel the 'Volkgeist' inside of you when you perform your duties with happiness and joy. It will always be inside of you. Even when you get a bit older and marry, you will pass the people's spirit down to your children. You manifest this spirit through your labor, obedience, and discipline. The people's spirit shows itself when we help one another in community. It demonstrates itself when we keep our homes and bodies clean, healthy, and pure. That is why we are forever loyal to ourselves, to our neighbors, and to our country.

"However, the evil people's spirit called 'Geistreskrank' will make itself known when it wants you to do bad things. If you do bad things, you will become insane and mindless, and you will wander around without a spirit! That is why your education is very important. Always do your best, and obey the rules, girls. Our Führer has given us the people's spirit to use in our mind, body, and soul. Therefore, at all times, you must be physically fit, well groomed, and obedient."

These girls enthusiastically absorb these new basic principles of service. Those who display exemplary skills will be recognized by the Reich's Ministry of Science, Education, and Culture. Some will be specifically chosen to continue their education in the elite rural educational program known as Landjahr Lager. For the foreseeable future, this generation will dedicate their lives to their country, strengthen their character, and help their fellow compatriot, for the overall good of Germany.

"And, there is one final requirement besides this weekly social meeting —" Fräulein Schmidt pauses dramatically before announcing with a smile, "We will participate in a day-long hiking trip!"

Trudel's eyes open wide and her face lights up with glee. She sits up extra attentively in her chair. This will be her very first trek with her den!

"And this is not the only journey you will take, ladies. During your next eight years, we will take many trips. You will have the opportunity to learn firsthand about your homeland, our natural surroundings, and the culture of our people. You will master our traditional German music, its folk songs, and dances. You will even learn the stories and fairytales written by our nation's great authors!"

Trudel feels giddy with anticipation about her adventurous new life! The National Socialist Youth Movement sounds exciting! It provides her with peer camaraderie and personal involvement in various causes to serve the German people. No longer will she be stuck with tedious family chores or bound by the laborious farm work. Instead, she will feel important! She will gain a sense of purpose and inner freedom. She will not be limited by her immediate surroundings. A new vision of the young girl's world is opening up for her. She will become a feminine young woman, well versed in her culture, learning the necessary life skills to prepare her for adulthood. She will master a new behavioral structure and thought process. At age ten, the Third Reich is teaching her how to become a valuable member of society.

Trudel's friend Irmgard, otherwise known to her friends as Irma, raises her hand. Irma is the same age as Trudel. They have been best friends since first grade. They play together, hike the mountain behind their home together, and help each other's mother with various household chores. Irma is a very high-spirited young girl who enjoys life. She is very inquisitive and loves a new adventure. She is strong spirited and does not allow anyone to mock her—or slow her down. "Why are we going on so many trips?" she asks the den leader.

"That is a very good question, Irma," Fräulein Schmidt replies. "Experiencing these trips as a group will teach you to stand in fellowship with each other. In fact, our very first hike will take place this weekend. We will be hiking up the Reisalpe! However, before the group goes anywhere, we will need to learn how to hike together in formation. So right now, I am going to teach you're your formations."

The young girls eagerly start sliding their chairs out from underneath their desks.

"Halt! Wait until I have finished talking girls. I know you are excited about our first trip, however, remember discipline! You need to be patient and follow my exact orders before we go outside to practice."

The girls sit back in their chairs.

"When we line up, I will need the shortest girls to lead the march, with the next tallest girls behind her, and so on, up to the tallest girl in the rear. Okay, now everyone come up to the front of the room, and let's arrange ourselves in the correct positions."

The girls rise in an orderly fashion from their chairs and walk to the front of the room. For the next few minutes, the leader positions the girls in formation according to their height.

"Now, stand at attention facing me, backs straight, and chests out! This posture is how you will always begin your formation." Fräulein Schmidt takes a step back to appraise the girls' stance. "Now, when I say face left, you will turn left. When I say face right, you will turn right. On my command, face right!"

The girls comply. "On command, turn left and face forward. Now, remember your places girls. This is exactly where you will need to stand whenever we march. You may now return to your desks."

For the next half hour, Fräulein Schmidt explains the differences between the single and double-line marching formations. On the blackboard, she draws two horizontal lines, the first being the single-line formation, and the second being the double-line formation. The small circles in each line represent the positions of each girl. A dash connects each circle. The arrow at the end shows the direction the girls are to march. At the end, the line curves showing the girls how to turn in formation. The instructor demonstrates how to march in place, how to turn, and how to stop. Each social meeting will include a marching drill.[11]

---

[11] Mädel im Dienst, p. 21-23

Then, the leader demonstrates the various whistle signals. One shrill means to line up while two shrills means to march. One long blow followed by one short blow means to stop.

Next, the leader instructs the girls in the voice commands. They learn the military drill terms for when to line up, when to start marching, how to march, and when to stop.

After their instructions, they leave the meeting room with their JM banner and head outside into the field to practice.

The whistle blows sharply. "Line up!" Fräulein Schmidt commands. On either side, Trudel stands one arm length apart from her comrades. She snaps to attention facing her leader.

"This is the single-line formation, girls. This is exactly how you will line up and position yourself. You will use this single-line formation when running during our sport afternoons, when marching along busy roadways, and when hiking narrow trails. Now, I will show you the double-line formation. Trudel, count off starting with the number one. After the count, I want each girl with an even number to take one step backwards."

The girls do as they are instructed.

"Very good. Now, I want the girls in the back row to take one-step to your left and line up directly behind the girl in front of you. This is your double-line formation. Remember where you stand. We will use this formation when marching through our village. Now, let me demonstrate how to walk in formation. Face right!" the leader orders.

On command, the girls face right.

The leader walks to the front of the line. "When the command is given, you will start by placing your right foot out in front of you as your left arm swings forward. This is the exact same movement as when we walk. You must pay close attention to your comrade in front of you. Everyone must move in the exact same step. Now, we will take ten steps forward and then stop." Fräulein Schmidt loudly blows her whistle twice and the girls start on their right foot.

Margarita and Helga have a difficult time keeping pace with the other girls in front of them. Margarita starts with her left instead of her right. Helga hesitates just long enough that Erika, who is behind her, steps on her heel.

"Oh, no, girls, not like that," Fräulein Schmidt orders. "We are not walking like a school of geese on a farm," as she imitates a white snow goose waddling from side to side. "Our posture should be like this." She demonstrates the correct procedure by standing upright, pushing her chest out, and raising her chin. "We are marching like the boys for our Führer. Okay, let's practice that again, and this time, we will march and sing our country song.

> In one heartbeat with God, we all step together,
> Marching through our beautiful country land,
> The air that we breathe is refreshing,
> And our bread comes from our farmers,

The water we drink from the mountain is pure,
The columns of our youth stand tall and strong,
We can march all day long,
We are the young girls of Kleinzell.

When Fräulein Schmidt feels the girls are ready, she will march them through the village. Not only will this boost the girls' self-esteem it will show respect among the townspeople.

The commander leads them down the main street. The girls march in high spirits. The townspeople hear the girls singing as they approach. They leave their stores, shops and homes, and walk outside to greet the marchers. The girls are surprised when they see the townspeople greeting them in salute. Old men hold their right arms straight out, smiling. Mothers wave their white handkerchiefs while saluting with their right arm. Some wave from their living room windows while others greet the girls from their front yards.

The girls are quite surprised to see the townspeople saluting and waving to them. They feel proud for they are being recognized for the first time!

Josefa is in her backyard tending to her garden with her son when she hears the sweet voices of the girls singing in the distance. She stops picking the string beans, stands straight, tilts her head toward the cadence of the voices, and listens. She hastily wipes her hands on her apron as she and Franzel hurry through the garden path around to the front of the house. Josefa opens the gate just in time to see Trudel's den marching towards her down the street.

As the girls draw near, Josefa spots her daughter proudly marching at the front of the line, just behind Fräulein Schmidt. Trudel carries the banner and beams a smile in delight toward her mother. Her brown eyes sparkle. Trudel composes her Cheshire grin for she is in service and must act like a dignified young girl in her league. Trudel's little brother stands at attention next to his mother, proudly saluting his sister.

Josefa removes her white handkerchief from her apron and waves it joyously honoring the dignified JM troop with her salute. As the girls file by, Josefa places the handkerchief back into her apron and returns with her son to the garden. She feels disheartened to see Trudel marching.

Route marching helps the girls remain fit and builds their endurance. Singing breaks the monotony, boosts morale, and unites the girls in fellowship. The marching rules are simple: keep the banner raised high, march in perfect formation, and sing joyously.

The group turns right onto the dirt path leading into the park. They march pass the brook long believed to have medicinal curing powers. They march pass a small waterfall and trout farm. Crossing over the narrow wooden-arched bridge, they approach their building. Their practice march ends at the main door, where Fräulein Schmidt blows the whistle loudly and commands them to stop.

The girls relax their positions and relish in the excitement of the moment. They proudly look at each other with glowing smiles. The townspeople had formally acknowledged them!

The local appreciation has also been recognized by their chieftain.

"Girls, you performed exceptionally well on your first march. All the towns-people noticed you and came out to greet you. You marched straight and tall, in perfect formation, and sang beautifully, as true German girls should. I can see that you put your heart and soul into your first march. Congratulate yourselves!"

The girls break formation and hug each other in a spirited embrace.

"Now, let's get back into our room so we may finish our social meeting."

Eager to continue with their lessons, the young maidens enthusiastically skip back to their meeting room. Trudel replaces the banner in its stand, salutes the portrait of the Fuhrer, and returns to her seat. Energized, the young girls discuss their first march. They feel happy and most of all, they feel a strong sense of patriotism. Their magical new belief system is beginning to form as they explore life with new enthusiasm, curiosity, and a sense of adventure.

Fräulein Schmidt takes her time returning to the classroom. She knows how important it is for the girls to talk about this experience among themselves. As she enters the room, the girls immediately stop talking and stand at attention. The leader walks to the front of the room, raises her arm, and greets the students with "Heil Hitler."

The girls raise their arms and respond, "Heil Hitler Fräulein Schmidt."

Their leader slowly walks behind her desk and sits down in her chair. Only then do the girls sit. Even through the room is quiet the air is pierced with excitement.

"I'd like to take a moment to talk about our march. Who would like to start?" She looks around the room and eyes Maria with her arm raised high straight up in the air. "Maria, you may go first. Tell me what you liked the most about our march."

"I really liked it when the villagers saluted us. It makes me feel real important."

"I'm glad you feel important. What about you, Margarita?"

"I feel very proud to wear my uniform. It makes me feel smart too," Margarita says as she sits straight up in her chair.

"We must feel proud when we wear our uniform. You must also take the strictest care to wash and properly iron your uniforms. Our uniforms symbolize the Greater Third Reich." Fräulein Schmidt uses validation as an advance communication skill to emphasize the girls' new responsibilities.

As the girls bond, they naturally develop a stronger interest in learning new activities. Some of the most achievement-oriented children are those who have a high personal standard for achievement and are highly competitive. When a child is not doing competent work, is bored, or has a negative attitude, it may be worthwhile to consider discipline or incentives to improve motivation. Fräulein Schmidt however, understands when to offer an incentive in order to motivate the children to perform. She also realizes that rewards can get in the way of their own personal self-motivation. By allowing the children to learn to attribute to themselves the cause of their own success or failure, implies that internal motivation should be promote and external factors deemphasized.[12]

At this stage in their development, a competitive foundation will aid them in dealing with a variety of life experiences later on, both good and bad. Whenever they witnessed their peers completing assignments, they will sense that they too possessed the ability to master such challenges. Verbal encouragement in the form of validation from their instructor helps the girls overcome self-doubt. The children focus on excellence because they want to be perceived as mature and confident young girls.

Trudel raises her hand as she patiently waits to be called upon.

"And what did you like about our march, Trudel," the leader questions.

"I liked the way we all marched together, and I really enjoyed being in the front holding our flag too! But …," Trudel pauses, not sure, whether or not she should address her real concern.

"Yes?" their leader asks.

"But the flag kind of got heavy after a while. I was having a hard time holding it up." Trudel's voice lowers and her head bows down.

"With that said, this is not the banner we will take on our trips. Oh no, our banner is a symbol of our group. After the lecture, we will learn how to make our new banners!" Fräulein Schmidt stands up from her desk. She walks to the front of the meeting room holding both her hands together behind her back. "Because our hearts are close to our homeland we will take many trips into the countryside and into our neighboring villages. This is why it is very important that we learn how to march together correctly and in formation. By learning how to march, we also learn how to hike together.

"Hiking is important because when we journey into the Fatherland, I will teach you the natural properties of the plants used for medical remedies and those used for cooking. Our Führer wants you to learn how to become a self-sufficient wife, a good mother, and a good homemaker because one day when you grow up, you will become the bearers of the heritage torch, the light that will be passed on to your children and to your children's children. Our great Führer wants me to teach you how to be the best in all your practical skills. He is entrusting in each of us the responsibility of carrying out his duties. Most importantly, you will never betray the trust that our great Führer has placed into your hearts and minds. You will be met with very strict discipline if you betray that trust. Understand?"

The girls nod in agreement and understanding.

"Now, I will write the Oath of Allegiance on the blackboard. Please copy this in your notebooks and memorize it. You will say this during your induction ceremony on our Führer's birthday." Fräulein Schmidt writes the oath and then turns back to face the classroom. "Everyone will now stand, turn to our Führer in salute, and repeat after me."

---

[12] John W. Santrock, p. 295

The girls stand from their chairs, raise their right arm, and in unison repeat the doctrine.

"I promise to be faithful to my Führer, Adolf Hitler. I promise obedience and respect to him and to the leaders he shall appoint over me."[13]

With their hands raised high, Fräulein Schmidt wants to solidify the girls' loyalty by capitalizing on their feelings. In order to do this, she must connect their feeling with faith and action, faith in the youth movement, and action by participation. Only when the two virtues merge will she have complete loyalty from her girls. The leader continues.

"Our Führer wants you to have the inner strength and courage to absorb all that is expected of you, for you. Our Führer wants all German people to be peace loving and courageous. You must be peaceful and courageous at all times. When nothing remains of us, your children must hold fast. We will not be torn from the flag. Heil Hitler!"

The children respond "Heil Hitler!"

"Everyone may now sit down."

The goal for all children in the Third Reich is to become the new Aryan race whose sole purpose is to, without question or hesitation, accept the ideology of National Socialism. The needs of the Reich take precedence over any needs they have to be ten-year old children. The National Socialistic indoctrination will lead these young girls into unquestioning service for their country.

Fräulein Schmidt continues to instruct them in their new doctrine.

"As you know, service in the Young Girls' League is a mandatory duty that demands devotion and dedication. After your formal induction on April 20th, our social evening meetings will be held every Wednesday after school in this room. Make sure you eat before attending your meetings because we do not want you to be distracted with hunger. In addition to learning about our Führer, I will teach you arts and crafts. We will also learn new songs and play music and games! Every Saturday, we will meet in the sports field for our afternoon sports training. This is of course, providing that the weather is good. In the event of foul weather, we will meet inside the school gym instead.

"At times, I will appoint you to specific duties. Sometimes, I will appoint you the task of setting up the meeting room, or I may send you as a courier during school hours. I may even assign you the prominent position of being the bearer of the flag during our marches, just as I did today when I appointed Trudel to be the flag bearer."

Upon hearing her name, Trudel sits taller in her chair, happily being recognized again for holding such a prominent position. The girls look at Trudel and some give her a jealous smirk.

"You must always arrive on time to your meetings. You must always do your best to set an example for the other girls. Your comrades will depend upon you

---

[13] The Hitler Jugend

when you are assigned your special positions. Such special requests from me will be your reward for doing such an excellent job in your group. Now, time is running short and there is much for us to cover. Let's talk about our music classes.

The girls like the sound of that.

"I know you will enjoy music class. We will spend hours singing and playing your own instruments and I will even teach you how to play the flute. We will learn ten new songs every month from our songbook "We Girls Sing." You will be required to practice and sing every day because this summer—" Fräulein Schmidt pauses, "we will be giving many local performances!"

The girls are delighted.

"If you already play an instrument and know at least one tradition folk song, please raise your hand."

Three of the girls raise their hands and tell the leader about their instruments and repertoire. The teacher picks up her Accomplishment book from her desk and makes a special note next to the three girls' names.

"Next week, I will be giving everyone new music to learn and we will start practicing. Now, who would like to sing and accompany the musicians?"

All of the remaining girl's hands are raised in excitement. Their interest is marked in the book.

"Good, next week, we will continue learning new songs," she says as she places the Accomplishment Book down on her desk. "Aside from music, acting and playing games will be part of our agenda. Whether its Kasper theatre, shadow puppetry, or impromptu plays, you will learn to use your imagination and be inventive. You will write your own stories and make up your own songs.[14] As I said before, we will entertain the townspeople with our plays and music during the outdoor summer festivals. The people will be very proud to see how much you have learned."

The girls listen attentively. They are fascinated by all the fun activities—games, puppet shows, and plays—than by all the ideology and propaganda.

The organization promises the girls camaraderie, adventure, and excitement, something that is unavailable in the traditional working family. The Young Girls League will become their primary social structure, replacing the family structure. Everything they do and learn for the next four years will revolve around each other and solidify their core beliefs. How they learn to work and play together inside this group will be the basis for how they will live once they leave the BDM, start work, or raise a family of their own.

Outside the building, Mitzi is keeping a tight grip on the windowsill. She stands on her tiptoes on top of a crate, peering through the window watching, and trying to listen in on the meeting. She longs to be back with her friends and feels horrible that she has been shut out. However, Fräulein Schmidt is well aware that Mitzi has been looking in the window for some time. The leader continues with the meeting.

---

[14] Bund Deutscher Mädel

"Ladies, your service requirements are determined by the master program that was given to me by the Reich's Minister for Education. If for any reason you cannot attend the social evenings, sport afternoons, or hiking trips, you must inform me beforehand."

The instructor pauses in her instructions, walks behind her desk, and sits down. She places her elbows on the desk, clasps her hands together, leans slightly forward, and looks into the young girls' faces.

Slowly, she begins. "As you know, we are missing one young girl. Would you like Mitzi to come back into the group?" Fräulein Schmidt asks.

The girls turn around and look directly at the food thief peering through the window. Trudel and Gretchen nod vigorously at their leader, with hope in their hearts that their comrade can return. Other girls pout, but Fräulein Schmidt raises her hand to the window and waves, encouraging Mitzi to come inside and attend the meeting.

Mitzi leaps with relief off the crate. She runs around the school building and through the front entrance. Everyone can hear Mitzi's shoes tapping louder on the terrazzo floor as she runs down the hallway. Approaching the meeting room, her pace slows and then stops. Slowly, the door opens and she peaks in.

"Please come in, Mitzi," Fräulein Schmidt gestures.

Bashfully, the cookie-stealer steps in and the door swings shut behind her.

"Is there anything you would like to say to the class before you sit down?"

Mitzi shuffles her shoes on the floor, her head hung in shame.

"I am very sorry. I didn't mean to eat the cookies. I was terribly hungry, and I promise that I will never steal again." The apology is accepted and without further hesitation, she runs back to her seat and rejoins her group.[15]

The balance of rewards and punishments received at this young age are a crucial factor for a child's self-development. If children are made to feel that their actions and behavior are repeatedly disapproved this discourages their self-worth. In turn, they will develop a sense of guilt that will persist as they grow into adulthood. Whereas, when a child is exposed to thinking critically about how their actions impact those around them, they will grasp a deeper meaning of their behavior, and develop an open mind to contemplate their wrongful actions before they occur.[16] This awareness prevents them making poor choices that otherwise may seem tempting. They are learning to reflect upon how their actions have a direct impact on those around them.

"Now girls, if there is an unforeseen emergency, or an illness that does not allow you to attend your meeting, you must bring a written notice of explanation from your doctor to me as soon as possible. If for any reason you cannot perform your duties, you will need to see the doctor for a full medical examination. Only he can write a note excusing you from your participation. Otherwise, there

---

[15] Mitzi Rotheneder
[16] John W. Santrock, p. 279

are no unexcused absences from your service. Even if you have bad grades in school, you must always participate in your service.[17]

"Next, everyone is responsible for the cleanliness and the neatness of this meeting room. It must be organized, and at all times, everything must be put back in its original location. This room with all its new furnishings has been provided for us thanks to your membership dues and the recent contributions made by your parents. As you can see, we no longer have to put up with those terrible old bench desks. Since all this furniture is brand-new, you shall respect it and take good care of it. For the next four years, this will be our social meeting room. You should be very proud for having such a beautiful room, ladies! It may be simple, but we will be using it extensively. You will even be able to hang your nicest paintings and mottos on the walls. Always remember that the way we keep this room is a true representation of our group.[18] Now, since you have marched perfectly today, I have decided that next Sunday we will participate in a twelve mile hiking trip up the Reisalpe!"

The girls are ecstatic. Fräulein Schmidt allows the girls a moment to revel in their excitement. It is not always necessary for the girls to be rigid in their expressions. As much as bad behavior is censured, enthusiasm is encouraged.

"To make our hike an enjoyable one, we will need to be well prepared. Please take notes. First and foremost, you will need well-conditioned hiking boots and a thick pair of gray socks. Now, if your boots are too big for you or if you only have thin socks, we recommend that you double up and wear two pairs of socks. I will inspect your boots prior to leaving. If you recently purchased a pair of new boots, I recommend that you wear them during the coming week. This will make them supple. You want to make sure your boots are seasoned before taking any long hiking trips. If you know you will have problems with blister, I recommend that you tape that area of your foot. You must take care of your feet at all times.

"Secondly, we must think about water and food. Since we will be hiking over twelve miles, each of you must bring your thermos filled with water, and one loaf of bread in your haversack. Please remember to conserve your water because water is precious!" Fräulein Schmidt smiles for she knows exactly where the fresh spring water supplies are on the route. She wants the girls to learn how to conserve their rations in case of emergencies.

"After our first hour of hiking, we will rest for fifteen-minutes. Now, the third point I want to make is that you drink plenty of water the day before the hike so that you will not become dehydrated."

Irma raises her hand.

"Yes, Irma, you have a question?"

"What does de—hy—drated mean?"

"Great question Irma, excellent! I am glad you are paying attention."

Irma feels proud that she had thought of such an important question.

---

[17] Bund Deutscher Mädel - "Jungmädelbund"
[18] Ibid

"When you are dehydrated it means there is not enough water inside your body. You become lightheaded, flush in the face, and weak. You might faint and when that happens, you will be rushed to the nearest medical center for emergency treatment. You never want to become dehydrated on your hiking trips because medical centers are very far away and we have no means of immediate communication with anyone to bring you to the nearest medical facility. Therefore, I must stress the importance of dinking plenty of water the day before. By ensuring you have food, water, and wear comfortable shoes, you are not only preparing for your trip, but you are also taking responsibility for your own well-being. Between now and next Sunday, talk among your comrades to make sure that they have taken the necessary precautions. Remember, it is honorable to watch over your fellow comrade. Are there any more questions? No? Okay then, let's continue down the list."

"The fourth item on the agenda is to make sure we do our warm-up and stretching exercises before we head out Sunday morning. From here on in, make sure you stretch every day for at least one-half hour. We stretch our muscles because we do not want anyone to incur any injuries. Stretching prevents our legs from cramping.

"Fifth on the list is our attire. You will need to dress very comfortably in loose clothing. You will need to wear your BDM uniform showing your district triangle. Also make sure that you wear comfortable panties."

The girls giggle.

"Class, please pay attention," Fräulein Schmidt says, clapping her hands sternly. "Thank you. We will leave the building on Sunday at exactly eight-thirty in the morning. We will march together to the top of the Reisalpe. During each leg of our hike, I will appoint a different girl to carry the banner. I will lead and Fräulein Brückner will bring up the rear. We want this to be a fun trip for everyone! We are hiking in service for our Führer. How we perform as a group will demonstrate to everyone how we behave as a unit. Therefore, you must at all times, stay in formation, be dutiful, and obedient.

"And lastly, if you should have any difficulties walking during our hike, you must immediately tell us. We are both trained for minor medical emergencies, so you do not have to worry if someone scrapes their knee, sprains an ankle, or feels faint. All right then, does everyone have any questions?" Fräulein Schmidt asks. "Now, let's start making our banners!"

The Meaning of the Flag

DEN LEADER FRÄULEIN SCHMIDT holds a piece of chalk in her hand, turns, and address her girls. "I am going to draw the shape of our pennant on the blackboard. I believe you have seen the BDM girls from the neighboring village carry their banners. Well, our banner is the same. We will have a diamond insignia on the front and a special rune symbol on the back."

On the blackboard, the leader sketches an isosceles triangle with the tip pointing to the right. "On the reverse side of our banner, a rune symbol will represent our group. I will go over the symbols with you in just a moment. In the meantime, I want you to draw this exact shape, as I have it up here on the board." Fräulein Schmidt watches the girls as they eagerly draw their banner. Helga raises her hand. "Yes, Helga, you have a question?"

Helga is a gifted and bright twelve-year-old girl who possesses unusual musical qualities that outshine her comrades. At the age of two, she started naturally learning to play easy childhood melodies on the zither. By the time she was eight years old, she was giving solo performances at the annual Kleinzell Cattle Parade Festival. She is quite mature for her age and requires minimal assistance when solving complicated problems. Helga's comrades admire her cheerful personality and look up to her for guidance outside the meeting room. Helga is a good role model and her friends try to emulate her. One day, she will no doubt make an excellent Young Girls' Leader.

"Why do we use a triangle and not a square shape for our flag?"

"Excellent question, Helga," Fräulein Schmidt acknowledges Helga as she is stalling to think of a profound answer to symbolically connect the girls to their banner. Since nothing is mentioned in the JM Leadership Pamphlet that indicates a specific meaning for their flag she needs to improvise. She decides to make up an allegory. What a better way to connect the children directly to their banner than with a story to interpret the hidden meaning behind the flag. She thinks her idea will bring a profound connection for she wants the girls to give their heart and soul to this organization.

"It is very important that you understand the exact and full meaning of our banner's design," she continues.

The girls' anxiously await with pencil in hand poised to write down the full significance of their pennant.

"Our pennant is specifically designed by the Reich's Ministry of Education. It is a representation of the command structure within our organization." The den leader speaks slowly for the girls to understand the meaning of their flag. This gives her time to embellish her story. "First of all, the color of the banner is black, which symbolizes pride and solidarity."

Eleven-year-old Erika raises her hand.

"Yes, Erika, you have a question?"

"What does solidarity mean?"

The den leader is delighted with the question.

"Solidarity means that we are one. Together, we share the common goals of our country. First, by pure German blood, secondly, by being citizens of the state, and third, that we are free of hereditary diseases."

Fräulein Schmidt writes the word "solidarity" on the board and underneath she writes the words "pure blood, citizens, and healthy."

Then, the den leader comes up with a brilliant idea so ingenious that she may even receive a special recognition for it when she mentions it to the director upon his visit. Confident in her reasoning, she picks up the pointing stick and taps the corners of the shape on the blackboard.

"Each corner of the triangle has a special meaning and the design is complete once the diamond insignia is placed on the inside of the banner. The insignia is the first and highest position because it represents our Führer who holds absolute command over his people."

Inside the pennant, Fräulein Schmidt draws an elongated diamond divided into four quarters. Inside the quarters, she draws the hooked cross. The girls copy the drawing into their notebooks.

"The top left corner of the banner represents, Baldur von Schirach, the Reich's Youth Leader. He is directly accountable to our Führer."

Fräulein Schmidt chalks a circle around the top corner of the banner and writes the initials HJ with the name 'Schirach.'

"The bottom left-hand corner represents Dr. Jutta Rüdiger, who is the head of the League of German Girls. She reports directly to Baldur von Schirach." Fräulein Schmidt places a circle around the bottom corner of the banner with the initials BDM and writes the name 'Rüdiger.'

"The very tip of the banner on the right represents Philipp Bouhler. He is our National Leader and Chief of the Chancellery. He is directly accountable to our Führer."[1] Fräulein Schmidt draws a circle on the tip of the triangle and writes the abbreviation NSDAP and the name 'Bouhler.'

Now, she needs to link the four point together! Surely, this explanation will impress the director and solidify her promotion. "Now watch very closely girls as I draw the lines from the circles to the diamond of command."

When finished, the den leader slowly turns around, rather impressed with her sensational work. She asks the class "Is anyone familiar with this diagram?"

Erika and Hanni raise their hands. The other girls are unable to answer this puzzling question. "I see somebody here attended church services, anyone else? Please, put your hands down now. It seems that only Erika and Hanni have an answer. I want you both to come up to the front of the class and whisper in my ear what you think this symbol means."

The girls obey.

---

[1] Philipp Bouhler

"Jawohl!" exclaims the leader. "Erika and Hanni will both receive a very special mark in the Accomplishment Book for their correct answer."

The two girls beam with pride and take their respective seats.

"This symbol is the Shield of the Trinity, which heralds the arms of our Führer and those directly under his command in the Hitler Youth. Our banner represents our connection with our Führer and the Youth Leaders, for we are all bearers of the banner!" Fräulein Schmidt feels completely satisfied with her brilliant symbology. "Now that we understand the meaning of our flag, our next step will be to settle on a rune symbol for the back, one that truly represents our group. Let me draw four symbols on the board for you to choose from, and then we will go over them one at a time.

"The first symbol I will draw is an arrow pointing upward. This is the Tiwaz rune. It is the symbol for the god Tyr who lost his hand in a battle with a wolf to save his kingdom. Tiwaz therefore, represents the sacrifice of the one for the well-being of all.

"The second symbol has a straight vertical line, with a triangle attached to the right side of it, like a thorn on a rose stem. This symbol represents Thor, the warrior. Before Thor was a warrior, he was very weak and childless. However, his father gave him a magic hammer that made him exceptionally strong. Therefore, he found a wife, and she in turn, bore him a son. One day, giants stormed into Thor's village to steal his son! Thor used the hammer to kill all the giants and save his son. Therefore, the symbol of Thor represents male courage as well as female fertility.

"The third symbol features a long line on the left and a shorter line on the right. These two vertical lines are connected at the top by a third horizontal line. The tall line represents a king named Ur. The shorter line represents his queen, Uz. The line on top represents their marriage. Thus, this symbol represents a couple joining as one forever.

"The fourth and final symbol I want to show you looks like a star. It is an X with a line straight down the middle. This symbol is called Hagal. It represents a mother who cares for and protects her children. She maintains the household and preserves her heritage. Hagal is a very wise woman.

"Now, I want you to decide among yourselves which of the four symbols we will put on the back of our banner. Remember, we also need something extra on the front to tell everyone who we are.

As the girls converse, Fräulein Schmidt walks to the cabinet and removes the black, red, and white pieces of material.

The girls quickly come to an agreement. Since Trudel is the smallest, the others had agreed to let her deliver their weighty decision. Trudel eagerly raises her hand. "We have chosen a symbol for our banner Fräulein Schmidt. We would like the symbol 'Tiwaz' to represent us."

"All right then, Tiwaz it will be. I will need someone to draw it out on a piece of paper so we can transfer it to the material. Did you think about the front of the banner? Have you decided what you would like to do there?"

"Yes, we would like our group number and den numbers on the front," Trudel replies.

"Excellent! I need you to all to come around the worktable here with your notebooks. For the remainder of our meeting, we are going to learn how to make our banners."

The young girls settle in around their large meeting table. Trudel and Maria go to the supply cabinet to procure the sewing box full of rulers, scissors, thread, and measuring tape. The den leader hands out the stainless steel clasps for each banner and the girls pass around the sewing supplies. Trudel stows the empty box in the cabinet as the den leader unfolds the black fabric across the table.

The banners are going to be twenty-two inches high by forty-one inches long. There is enough black fabric here to make ten pennants, one for each girl. The leader snips the fabric along the chalk lines as Helga and Erika assist in keeping the material taut.

The instructor hands each girl her black fabric panels and then shows them how to make the paper templates for the insignia and their group symbol. After the templates are cut, the girls use white chalk and outline their templates onto the material. Black will be used for the swastika, white for the diamond side quarters, the square panel, and the Tyr rune for the back panel. The red fabric will be used for the diamond quarters inside the insignia.

The den leader teaches the girls how to sew the pieces together. To assemble the insignia, the girls first sew the black swastika onto the white square panel using black thread and an even backstitch. The red and white quarter panels are stitched together, followed by the swastika panel being sewn in the middle of the diamond panel. Once completed, the finished insignia is sewn onto the banner. The buttonhole stitch is used throughout for the properties make it ideal to prevent the material from unraveling.

In the upper left hand corner of the pendant, the girls use chain stitching to sew their group number 11 over their troop number 527. Then, the girls stitch the white Tyr rune symbol on the back panel positioning it directly behind the HJ insignia on the front of their banner. The two panels are then sewn together using black thread and a buttonhole stitch, making sure to reinforce the tip. Lastly, the three metal clasps are sewn on the base using a cross-stitch. As they near the last hour of their first Young Girls' meeting, they finish the final touches on their banners and tidy up the room. Each girl shows off their masterpiece.

"Now ladies, it is now time for our music lesson! I will teach you a new song entitled 'Arise, You Young Wanderers'."[2] It is a traditional hiking song. I want everyone to open their music books to page 120.

The girls must learn this song before their first hike next weekend.

Before ending their social meeting, the registered photographer arrives. The individual photos taken will be placed in their service cards.

In conclusion, the young girls stand, raise their arms in salute, and sing the "Oath of Allegiance to Our Führer."

---

[2] Wir Mädel Singen, "Auf, du junger Wandersmann," p. 120 - 121

It is dark when the girls leave the HJ building and return to their homes. Trudel says good-bye to her friends and dashes down the road, anxious to tell her mother about her meeting and show off her new banner.

She arrives at the front gate of her house, swings open the latch, pushes the gate open, runs down the dirt pathway, and bounds up the stairs onto the front porch. She opens the door and runs breathlessly into the house yelling, "Mommy, Mommy!" only to discover Father Strobel, the priest from the parish church with Frau Bauer, the neighbor, sitting nervously in the living room. Frau Bauer is holding Franzel in her lap as he cuddles close to her chest.

Trudel has an uneasy feeling about this situation.

"Where's Mama?" Trudel questions hesitantly as she places her notebook and banner down on the table.

"She's not here right now, little one," Frau Bauer begins compassionately.

"What's Father Strobel doing here?" Trudel begins to tremble with apprehension as she approaches the woman.

"Father Strobel has something he needs to talk to you about, dear. Here, come and sit down so he may talk with you," Frau Bauer begs endearingly.

"Come here, my child," Father Strobel compassionately says to Trudel. He reaches his hand out to her in comfort. Reluctantly, Trudel walks up to the priest. She takes both his hands in hers and stands in front of him as he, with the utmost tenderness, breaks the bad news.

"It seems two men came by when you were at your meeting today and they took your mother away."

Trudel can feel her body go numb. The words Father Strobel speaks reverberate in her mind like a broken record. She cannot comprehend what she is hearing.

"We don't know where your mother went, Trudel, and we don't know when she will return," Father Strobel honestly admits looking deep into the little girl's eyes.

Trudel falls limp at his feet. The priest gently places his hand on Trudel's shoulder and continues. "Frau Bauer has promised me that she will keep an eye on the both of you. Right now, I need you to be a strong young woman and look after your little brother. You are now in charge of the home until your mother returns. Do you understand?" Father Strobel is genuinely concerned for the children's safety and welfare. "Will you do that for me, my child?"

Trudel is in shock. With her heart pounding, her eyes hunt around the room for clues. Finding none, she crumples in dismay. Her eyes drift up to the gold pectoral cross on the priest's chest. Trudel feels so helpless. She feels so alone. She feels abandoned and slips into a daze. Her field of consciousness narrows as if she is being sucked into a proverbial time warp. Her sense of space and time distorts. She feels detached from reality. The memory of her mother standing on the front porch waving good-bye repeats itself in her mind.

Frau Bauer stands and hands Franzel to the priest. She bends over to lift Trudel up off the floor. She seats Trudel on the chair opposite Father Strobel. Frau Bauer kneels down in front of Trudel and looks deeply into the girl's empty eyes. She cradles Trudel's hand in hers and softly strokes her hair, trying to sooth the frightened child. Frau Bauer rubs Trudel's cheek with the back of her hand trying to get her to snap out of her state of shock.

"Trudel ... Trudel, look at me," Frau Bauer says. "Your mother is fine. Your mother will be coming back home very soon."

Trudel blinks her eyes twice and looks directly at Frau Bauer.

"When?" Trudel inquires softly. "When is our mother coming back home, Frau Bauer? Why did they take our mother away from us? Who took her away?" Trudel questions as she begins to reawaken from her state of confusion.

"I don't know who took your mother away dear. I am so sorry, but we just don't know." Frau Bauer turns to Father Strobel for support, and then returns her gaze back to Trudel. "Now, you are going to need to become a very strong young girl, just as the Father asked you. You must take charge of this house and take care of your little brother. Do you think you can do that for me? Do you think you can do that for us, Trudel?

"Do you think you can do that for your mother?" the pastor asks.

"I think I can," Trudel slowly responds.

"Good, up my boy!" Father Strobel picks Franzel up and places him on his feet. As he stands, his loose black cassock flows with his body. The black fascia and silk tassels drop perfectly into place. His tone turns formal. "I will take my leave now, Frau Bauer. It seems that you have everything under control here."

Frau Bauer stands and sees Father Strobel out to the front door. Together, they whisper a few words and then he leaves. With both hand, Frau Bauer shuts the door behind him. She sighs and leans her head against the door for a long moment before returning to console the children.

"I must get back to the farm now my children. I am only a few houses away. I want you to know that I am here for you. I will stop by and check up on you until your mother returns. In the meantime, I want you both to get something to eat and—" Trudel cuts Frau Bauer short from finishing her sentence.

"I wanted to tell mother about my first Preparatory Service Meeting in the Young Girls' League today and she's not even here. When is she coming back?" Trudel asks as tears well up in her eyes.

"I am sorry dear. I don't know," commiserates the neighbor. Trudel leans her head in Frau Bauer's bosom and starts to cry. Frau Bauer wraps both her arms around the child, rocking her back and forth.

Franzel walks up to his sister and places his hand on her back.

"It's okay, sis. We'll manage." He wraps his arms around his sister. "Here, let me make you something to eat."

"I'll do it!" Trudel says as she snaps out from her despair. She walks into the kitchen and starts making scrambled eggs and ham for her little brother.

Frau Bauer feels tentative. "Are you going to be all right, children?"

Trudel turns toward Frau Bauer from the kitchen and snaps, "We'll be fine."

"Well, good, I will be on my way." Frau Bauer wraps her coat around her shoulders, opens the front door, and glances back at the children. "You know where to reach me if you need anything. Please, if you need anything, come over to the farm and I will help you," She walks out from the house and gently closes the door behind her. She opens the garden gate, turns and looks at the home. "God, please watch out over the little ones."

That evening, Franzel and Trudel jump into their mother's bed and hug each other. Trudel says a prayer for the safe return of their mother.

"Dear Lord, today, my brother Franzel and I turn to you to give you thanks for our mother. She has always taken care of us. She took the place of our father when he died. She has always been good to us, Lord. She reads to us before bedtime, cooks our meals, and mends our clothes. Did we do something wrong to make you take her away from us? Only our mother comforts us when we need her and we need her right now. We cannot live without her and we want her to return because she is our mother and we love her very much. We are so grateful for how she takes care of us. Please bless her Lord, wherever she is right now and comfort her. Tell her that we love her very, very much and we want her home right away. We will pray every day and night for her safe return. Please give her the strength to find her way home. Most of all, we forgive those who took her away. All we ask is that you bring our mother back home to us safely. We ask you this, in the name of Jesus, our Lord, and Savior, forever and ever." Together the children seal their prayer with the sign of the cross. "Amen."

Trudel and Franzel spend their first night alone in their mother's bed crying themselves to sleep.

The next morning the children continue their daily chores. They care for the farm animals, keep the house clean, and go to school. Franzel is responsible for bringing in the wood. He feeds the animals and makes sure their sheds are clean. Trudel takes charge of the cooking and house cleaning.

For breakfast, the children eat fried eggs from their chickens. For dinner, Trudel makes potato soup. This is the only dish Trudel knows how to prepare. After dinner, they complete their homework, wash their faces, brush their teeth, and then burrow into their mother's bed. They pray by candlelight.

By the second night, Trudel tosses in her sleep wracked with nightmares of grotesque faces mocking her. She hears the shadowy figures cry out to her. "Poor little children—they have no mother now." She wakes up in the middle of the nightmare crying, and sees Franzel is fast asleep besides her. By morning, she wakes up exhausted. She gathers her thoughts, prays before getting out of bed, and then starts her daily routine before going off to school.

Is there any hope? Perhaps, if she and Franzel are better children their mother would soon return home.

That Sunday, Trudel decides she and her brother will attend church at their small parish. They dress in their best clothes. They leave the house early and instead of walking on the main road, they walk the dirt path behind their house to the small parish on top of the hill. The path skirts along the edge of the Eben-wald Forest on the Reisalpe Mountain. Trudel does not want anyone in town to notice her or her little brother.

They stop at the foot of the stairs leading to the small, but stately fourteenth century parish perched on top of the hill. Trudel gives a longing look at the imposing bell tower staring down at her. She is hesitant, afraid of being ridiculed by the parishioners. However, she musters up her courage, takes her brother by the hand, and together they march up the fifty-six stairs leading to the parish built in honor of Mary's Assumption into heaven.

Before mass, parishioners gather outside by the narthex. Their emotionless faces stare down on the children as they pause from their conversations. Many town folk whisper about the disappearance of Frau Kerschner. The villagers take a step back and let the children pass. Portentous eyes follow their every step. The villagers fear an association with them would mark them next for abduction.

Trudel holds her little brother close and they file past the whispering crowd. They step through the open door and into the darkness of the vestibule. It takes a moment for Trudel's eyes to adjust before they walk down the nave, looking for an empty spot in a pew. Trudel finds a place on the right side of the church and quickly they sit. Trudel elbows her brother to kneel and say a prayer before mass starts. After finishing a short prayer, Trudel sits back on the pew and looks straight ahead at the wooden alter.

It had been created by the Linz sculptor Ludwig Linzinger in 1897 as part of the neo-gothic renovations. The relief depicts the Annunciation of the Blessed Virgin Mary and the announcement made by the Angel Gabriel saying that she would conceive and become the mother of Jesus, the Son of God. Trudel's eyes gaze upward toward the cross-ribbed vaulted ceilings. Twelve artistically carved wooden Stations of the Cross hang on the walls. The oldest bell in the district begins to toll announcing to the parishioners that mass is about to begin. The remaining few parishioners walk inside and take their seats.

Father Strobel enters with his procession. He walks down the nave, through the transept, and to the alter. On the refurbished chamber organ built in 1750 by Ignaz Gatto, considered "The Elder," the organist plays "Ave Maria."

The priest blesses the table, makes the sign of the cross, and waits for the canticle to finish before he begins his service.

"In the name of the Father, the Son, and the Holy Ghost, Amen. This mass is being said for the safe return of Frau Josefa Kerschner."

Some women gasp for they are unaware of the woman's sudden disappearance. Trudel blushes and lowers her head in embarrassment. For the next hour, she and Franzel try to listen to Father Strobel's service while fervently wishing for their mother's safe return.

When mass concludes, not one of the villagers console the two youngsters. Some children even tease the Kerschner children about the abduction. Several women speak in whispers. A disheveled man blocks Trudel in her tracks and growls, "Makes you wonder what Frau Kerschner could have done to be taken away like that." Trudel freezes in place. His young son contumely remarks, "Your mother is never coming home!" in Trudel's face. The mother hauls him backwards, and slaps him hard across the face. She turns to her husband and looks scornfully at him, pointing her finger in his face saying "Don't you dare say that to the children again. You hear me!"

Trudel and her brother scurry through the crowd, quite humiliated, struggling to ignore the comments. Trudel cannot believe the nasty remarks she has just heard. She grabs her brother's hand tighter and together, they run back home. She wants to escape. She wants her mother to return safely home and have it be just as it was before. When they return to their home, they change into the work clothes and begin their daily chores. Trudel desperately wants to hide from the world.

The next morning, Trudel solemnly finishes her household morning chores and with her brother, heads off to school. For Trudel, the day goes by very slowly. In class, she seems lethargic. After school, she does not care to participate with the other children. When she is asked to play, she tells her friends to leave her alone. She is very depressed. This stressful situation of shouldering her mother's responsibilities is making her feel overwhelmed. She does not have the emotional resources to cope with being an orphan. Neither does she have the full knowledge to care for herself, her brother, and a home. The world is closing in fast around her and she is all alone.

Trudel lags behind her brother as they walk home from school. He runs on ahead of her back to their house. She does not acknowledge him because she is deep in thought. She does not understand why her grandparents or any one of the neighbors do not come over and help or check up on them. Nobody stops by to say 'hello.' Frau Bauer promised she would come over, but she has not. Trudel is thinking about the past few days and what is going to happen if her mother never comes home, ever again. How will she be able to care for Franzel without any money? If her grandparents are not there for her, who will be there to take care of them?

Her thoughts race with imaginable nightmares of being taken away by the police, tossed into an orphanage, and forbidden to return home. What is going to happen to the house, to the chickens, to her cat? Trudel cannot stand to fail in her duty, yet the more she ponders her situation, the more depressed she becomes, trembling with terrifying thoughts.

Slowly, she realizes that she has been hesitating for a while in front of her own front yard. Beaten down by her thoughts, desolated, and disheartened, she walks past the daisies and the Provencal lavender that are beginning to blossom in the garden. She walks up the stairs onto the porch and realizes the front door is ajar!

"Franzel?" she calls out softly.

There is no answer.

Her breathing grows shallow. The muscles in her body tense and her palms begin to sweat. She begins to panic, thinking someone has taken her little brother away and forgot to close the door behind them. Maybe, someone else is waiting in the house to tell her that her little brother has been taken away. Maybe, criminals came to rob her home and kidnap her! Terror fills her mind as to what awaits behind the door. Trudel takes a deep breath and warily nudges the door all the way open. Trudel's heart skips a beat when she sees her mother in the kitchen preparing their evening meal! Franzel is sitting at the kitchen table waiting for his first real serving of food in four days!

"Mama!" Trudel screams in excitement. She throws down her notebook on the table and rushes to her mother standing by the stove. Josefa kneels down to embrace her daughter as if they would never let go of each other again.

"Mama, where were you? We missed you so much!" Trudel embraces her mother tightly in her arms.

"I missed you so very much, little one." Josefa's ordeal had ended. Now, she can focus on being with her family again.

Trudel's questions tumble out. "Where were you? Where did you go? What happened? Who took you away? When did you get back?" Trudel rushes through her questions hugging her mother tighter. She leans back to look at her mother's face and is in shock. Softly she asks, "How come you have a black eye, Mama?" Before Josefa can answer, Trudel carefully places her hand over her mother's right eye and removes it. She proclaims, "I will never let them take you away from us, Mother, never again!" Trudel hugs her mother even tighter.[3]

For the remainder of the afternoon Josefa tends to her children's needs. To restore a sense of normalcy, she decides it is time to teach her daughter how to cook an authentic Austrian beef goulash.

Trudel runs out into the garden and picks four yellow onions, six large tomatoes, two peppers, one parsnip, three large potatoes, four celery sticks, and a number of carrots. Sitting at the kitchen table, Trudel peels off the brown tunic skin from the onions, cuts off the basal plates and roots, and then chops the scale leaves into squares. She carves the potatoes into small chunks, then cleans, peels, and chops the rest of the vegetables.

Josefa hoists the heavy iron Dutch oven up onto the stove. She takes a tablespoon of lard and places it into the pot. She begins chopping the beef into one-inch cubes. "Trudel, place the onions in the pot and continue stirring them until they turn a golden yellow. I'll start adding the ingredients while you stir."

Trudel is more than happy to work in the kitchen, learning how to cook. She feels proud, for this is her first time being invited to make dinner with her mother. As they work together on the meal, Trudel fills Josefa in about everything that happened during the previous four days.

When the onions are just about to turn yellow, Josefa adds a tablespoon of paprika and a minced clove of garlic. She scrapes the meat cubes from the wooden cutting board and places them into the pot. The meat naturally lets out its own flavoring juices and the aroma from the simmering dish begins to engulf the room. The children's mouths water and their tummies grumble in hunger. Josefa takes one tablespoon of flour, some salt, and a quarter cup of water and slowly adds the ingredients as Trudel continues to stir.

Next, Josefa prepares the tomato sauce. As she waits for the stew to come to a boil, she walks into the pantry and grabs two jars of tomato paste that she

---

[3] Franz Kerschner

had canned the previous fall. She combines them in a large bowl with the diced tomatoes. When the meat is half cooked, Josefa adds the chopped vegetables and another cup of water.

Josefa's signature goulash is neither a soup nor a stew but it is somewhere in between. The viscosity of the flavored tomato sauce is her trademark. When the meat and vegetables are almost cooked, she allows Trudel to stir in the sauce.

For the spätzle dough, Josefa kneads together two cups of flour, two eggs, and a pinch of salt. She flattens the dough with her wooden roller on the chopping board. Then, she slices the dough into long, slender strips, then widthwise into smaller pieces. She rolls the pieces and then places the small egg noodles into boiling water where they cook until they rise to the surface. She skims them off the top and out of the pot then sets them aside to cool.

Since this is a special occasion, Trudel elegantly sets the table. She runs out into the garden and picks the daisies and lavender, runs back inside and places them in a clear glass bottle with water, crafting a colorful centerpiece. She sets the dinner plates in the center of the place setting, with the napkins and forks to the left, and faces the knives inward on the right, next to the spoons. The drinking glasses are positioned approximately one inch above the knives.

Josefa ladles out the goulash into bowls and her daughter distributes the servings around the table. Both children then sit down.

Trudel announces, "I want to say a prayer, Mommy."

Surprised, Josefa gives a slow nod. She removes her apron and joins her children. Franzel is so hungry and starts to whine.

"Be quiet!" Josefa warns. This is the first time she scolded him so coldly. Nevertheless, they each take the other's hand and bow their heads in prayer.

"Dear God," Trudel begins. "We thank you for returning our mother. We missed her very much and knew that if we were good children you would bring her back to us. Please don't ever take her away because we love her. We promise to be good children from now on. Amen."

Josefa was touched. "Thank you, Trudel. That was a very nice prayer."

The family eats a quiet dinner together. Josefa does not mind because she enjoys the silence and being near her children. She watches them devour the food and eat a second helping. After her dreadful ordeal, she begins to view her children differently. She intuitively notices a shift has taken place within her daughter. The ten-year-old is exhibiting signs of becoming autonomous. From this point forward, Josefa will continue to exercise general supervision and exert control while gradually allowing Trudel to engage in moment-to-moment self-regulation. Josefa will monitor and guide her daughters' decisions and actions, giving Trudel more freedom and independence. Her little girl is beginning to grow up.

After dinner, Trudel clears the dishes from the table, places them in the sink, sweeps the floor, and helps dry, and put the dishes away.

They retire into the living room and spend the evening singing traditional Austrian folk songs together, laughing, and playing. Trudel is proud to display her handmade banner. By nine o'clock, it is time for the children to go to bed.

They do not want to sleep alone. Therefore, they leap into Josefa's large, down-quilted bed.

"Tell us a bedtime story, Momma," requests Franzel.

"A story? I don't know. Let me see." Josefa pauses for a moment to think of a story her mother, Anna, told her when she was a little child.

"Once upon a time, in a very small house lived a boy named Peter and his mother. Peter was always in good spirits and very happy. He worked very hard on everything he could do for his mother. Nothing was too much for him to do. However, as many times as he worked so hard to make his mother happy, he would sit down utterly heartbroken. Do you know why?

"Why" Trudel asks.

"Well, that's because his mother was afflicted with painful arthritis through-out her entire body. The dear woman was in so much pain that she could not get out of bed to see the beautiful world outside. Not even in the summer, spring, fall, or winter. Her body was completely crippled. But Peter loved his mother so much that he…"

Josefa looks down and notices both her children are fast asleep.

She leans over, kisses the children on the forehead, and tucks them into bed. She walks to her wardrobe, opens the drawer, and pulls out a framed picture. She leaves the bedroom then walks into the living room and removes her crucifix from the wall. She hangs the portrait of her dictator and stares at the photo. She stares at the photo for a long, bitter moment. "You did this to me. You are *not* my Führer!" she fumes then spits on the photo.

Finally, she turns and retires to her bedroom, placing the crucifix on her nightstand. She blows out the candle and slips gently into bed with her children.

Josefa attempts to resume the family routine but is having difficulty with the children, especially at night. Although Franzel has no trouble sleeping in his mother's bed, Trudel keeps waking up in the middle of the night screaming from the horrible nightmares.

Josefa never explains why she was taken or what happened to her during the time she was abducted. She wants to forget about that terrible ordeal and put it behind her. However, when she finds herself alone, her prominent smile that once beamed is now replaced with a blank expression. She is lost now, deep in her thoughts. Her life has been invaded mentally, emotionally, physically, and spiritually. Her love for life has been extinguished. In front of her children, she resumes her normal duties with a false smile, but deep within her thoughts, she questions the invisible threats. The mother's perception of life is changing. A Great War, economic depression, poverty, and the death of her husband, have made her character strong. How many more hardships can she endure? Josefa had had the ability to view impediments being temporary, as opportunities to step up to the challenge of being alive. She has become a very resourceful, wise, and an independent woman, but being kidnapped had left her feeling vulnerable, and apprehensive.

Josefa knows that every reality check gives her inner strength. She makes the decision to take absolute control over her pain. From now on, she promises to herself that she will be especially careful not to discuss certain topics with anyone, since she no longer knows who she can trust.

And the early morning
This is our time,
When the winds
And the mountains sing.
The sun then makes
The valleys far
And the life, the life
That it will bring us.

~ Die Morgenfrühe ist Unsere Zeit ~
Hans Baumann

Hike on the Reisalpe

IT IS THE DAY BEFORE the girl's first hiking trip, Saturday, April 9, 1938. It has been a week since Josefa has returned to her home.

Trudel double-checks and makes sure she has the necessary equipment for the hike up the Reisalpe. She removes her uniform from the wardrobe and lays it neatly over the backside of the chair. She goes outside on the porch, polishes her hiking boots, making sure the bottoms are free from dirt, and then cleans her haversack. Throughout the day, Trudel remembers to stretch and drink plenty of water.

Early the next morning, the ten-year-old child jumps out of bed. She can hardly contain herself. The day has finally arrived! Wearing her white lace pajamas, she quickly jumps out of bed, and runs downstairs to wash, then dashes back upstairs to get dressed.

Her mother is in the kitchen humming to herself as she prepares breakfast for her children. Suddenly, she hears her daughter's heavy footsteps stomping from one side of her attic bedroom to the other.

The daughter races down the stairs, darts into the kitchen, grabs the loaf of bread, and puts it into her haversack. Trudel puts her thermos on the table, gives her mother a kiss, then runs outside to take care of her morning chores. After a few moments, Trudel sprints back into the kitchen. Out of breath, she sits down at the kitchen table next to her brother, Franzel.

"Are you forgetting something, Trudel?" the mother asks.

"Why can't Franzel set the table today?" Trudel angrily blurts out to her mother. "I have an extremely important day with my troop today!"

Josefa's mood instantly changes. She stops cooking, walks over to Trudel, and backhands her across her face. "Don't you *ever* give me that tone of voice again, young lady! When I tell you to do something, you do it. Now, move!" her mother commands.

Shocked and embarrassed, Trudel hides her reddening cheek with her hand. Slowly, she stands from her chair and shuffles over to the tableware hutch. She removes the plates and walks back to set the table. With her heart in a turmoil, she returns to the hutch for the cutlery.

She feels so guilty. She wrestles with her mother's sudden outburst, trying to understand her anger. This is the first time her mother ever hit her. She contemplates what had she done that was so wrong.

Trudel closes the drawer and finishes setting the table in silence.

Sitting down serenely again, Josefa serves the children their breakfasts. As the family eats, all is quiet except the scraping of the utensils on the plates. Franzel is oblivious to Trudel's hurt feelings and is more focused on eating. Trudel picks at her breakfast. She feels dismayed as she looks up and sees her mother's head bowed down toward the plate as she eats.

Josefa patiently waits for her daughter to speak. Josefa is wise and in this uncomfortable moment, she knows Trudel is silently assessing her previous behavior as so is she. Josefa feels very bad about hitting her daughter, but she wants obedience as well as respect from her children. She wants her daughter to be conscious of her actions. There is a strict code of conduct in Josefa's house and talking back is totally unacceptable.

Trudel just wants the awful feeling in the pit of her stomach to go away. She works up the courage to apologize. "Mother," Trudel begins softly. "I am very sorry. I didn't mean to shout." Not looking at the child, Josefa remains silent and continues eating. She is not ignoring the child but instead listening to every word her child is speaking.

"I am very sorry to have spoken back and have yelled at you Mother. I will never do that again."

This is what Josefa was waiting for her daughter's true apology. By taking responsibility for her actions, the awful feeling Trudel has inside her stomach is beginning to fade. She knows if she does not apologize now, she will regret this moment for the rest of the day and will have to face it once again when she returns from her hike. Josefa stops eating and places her fork on the table. She picks up the napkin, wipes her mouth, and looks directly into her daughter's eyes.

"Can you tell me why you spoke out in anger when I asked you to set the table?" Josefa asks addressing the child's behavior.

Trudel thinks for a moment not knowing how to answer.

"I know you are very excited about today's hike, but that does not mean that you can go around giving orders in this house. As a young girl in the league, you still have your duties and responsibilities in this house and I expect you to fulfill them. Understood?"

"Yes, ma'am," Trudel responds still thinking of what she can say to ease the turmoil she is feeling inside her stomach. "I'm truly sorry, Mother. I want to be a grown up too," Trudel says from her heart.

"Trudel, you are my beautiful little girl, and one day before you know it, you will become a beautiful strong woman with children of your own. Then you will realize what being a mother means. Do not rush the years along my little one. Enjoy this time now because one day you'll look back and wish you were this young again."

Josefa has a way to say the right words to ease the tension. She treasures her children and rears them with gentle affection and discipline.

Trudel gets up from the table, walks to her mother, and gives her a loving embrace. Josefa pulls her daughter close and whispers in her ear. "I love you Trudel."

"I love you mama." The tension is gone and the family resumes their breakfast.

After breakfast, Trudel helps her mother clean the table and wash the dishes. When she is finished, she gathers her banner, haversack, and thermos. By the front door, Josefa removes the climbing jacket from the hook, kneels down, and helps Trudel put it on.

"I want you to have fun with your friends today, okay? Learn as much as you can and listen to what Fräulein Schmidt has to tell you. Now go and have fun!" Josefa hugs her daughter and gives her a kiss on her forehead.

Trudel hugs her mother, takes a step back, and salutes. She turns and runs excitedly out of the house and down the road to the meeting room. Unlike her brother Franzel, she does not have to stay home and work on the farm. She is in compliance for her country and has a duty to perform today.

Fräulein Schmidt and Fräulein Brückner started planning for this hike a month earlier. At their previous social meeting, the leaders familiarized the girls with the overall plan, piquing their interest. The girls must know how to carry their banner, which route they will hike, and what songs they will sing. The purpose of this trip is for the girls to become acquainted with their surroundings. The educational goal for today's planned trip is for the girls to bond with nature. Most of all, they must conduct themselves accordingly for they are now representatives of the Third Reich.

The twelve and one-half mile route will start at the HJ building in Kleinzell, to the peak of the Reisalpe Mountain at the Reisalpenschutzhaus, and then back again. Along the way, the leaders will challenge the girl's courage, aptitude, and intelligence. The will learn about the local ecosystem, and everyone will meet Hanni, the charming old dairy maid who lives on the mountainside.

Depending on the terrain, the girls will march using either the single or the double-line formation. The single-line formation will be used for passing through small entrances, for walking along busy roadways, or for following the narrowest trails. Otherwise, they will be hiking in a double-line formation. On the first leg of their hike will be a march from their village up to their first resting stop, the Ebenwald meadows, but not without encountering their first challenge.

The young leader's bear total responsibility for the safety of their den. Their education comes from attending the National Leadership School in Boyden, Ostpreußen. Safety is one of their highest priorities and both leaders are fluent in first aid. Once they venture into the forest, the girls will be on their own, and they will have to depend upon each other for their own survival.

Hiking along the roadside or in the mountains can be dangerous. It is not easy to stop a loaded hay wagon or heavy tractor around a blind corner. Likewise, the mountainous terrain is challenging with rocky trails, steep inclines, and gorges. A month earlier, the leaders had thoroughly inspected the entire trail for water sources, shady resting places, and hazardous debris, such as fallen trees or broken fence lines.

Permission must be secured from the farmers before walking across their land. If any extreme obstacles had been found, the leaders would notify the appropriate farmers or forestry division.

Then, there is the issue of how to carry and care for their banner. As being carriers of these new socialistic values, reverence to the flag symbolizes their young, blooming unity as one. The black triangular pendant carries a red and white top to bottom-side quarter diamond with a central white square that contains the slanted black hooked cross. In the top left corner are the group and den numbers 11/527 sewn on in white lettering.

On the reverse side is a white arrow pointing upward to symbolize the strength of their unit, and their veneration to the heroic Norse mythological god Tyr, the son of Odin. For these young girls, their chosen upward pointing rune arrow represents both solidarity within their group and success in competition, characterized by selflessness. The spiritual undertone is supposed to awaken new levels of understanding, tested by suitable amounts of pressure. The Tyr-inspired child will learn to step up courageously by taking full responsibility for her actions. The girls feel it is a great honor to carry this symbol on their banner.

Overall, this first hike will teach these young maidens to become aware of both their actions within their surroundings and of their interactions with each other. Their bodies, minds, and souls belong to Germany and at all times, they must act dignified, obedient, and disciplined. On trips such as this, the leaders will teach the girls self-discipline through awareness.[1] In addition to carrying her own gear, each girl has her personal contribution not only through her food offering but also by song. She is required to have traditional German folk songs memorized and ready to suggest and sing when called upon.

Fräulein Schmidt is very pleased to see Trudel and her comrades arrive early at the school this Sunday morning. Once all the girls are present, they stand at attention, salute, and recite their Oath of Allegiance. Fräulein Schmidt takes roll call. Their attendance is marked in the book. They organize themselves outside in front of the building, stretch, and then fall in a two-line formation.

Since the length of their stride will determine the overall speed of the march, the two shortest girls, Trudel and Gretchen, will be appointed to lead their troop. Next in line are Maria and Gretel, followed by Irma and Margarita, Helga and Hanni, with the two tallest girls, Erika and Mitzi, in the rear. Fräulein Brückner will oversee the girls from the back of the column, as Fräulein Schmidt will walk along side. Little Trudel will carry the banner on the first leg of this trip.

The girls are horsing around until Fräulein Schmidt delivers the first militaristic commands of the day.

"Attention everyone, fall in! Line up! Company be quiet!"

Immediately the girls fall into their respective places in a double file. They stand in formation, upright with their chins up, chests out, and shoulders back. Arms are fixed at their sides. Their eyes are locked straight ahead and their unflinching gaze disguises their deep concentration in remembering all their commands. Heels are together, toes slightly apart. They do not talk. There is no facial or bodily movement. The girls stand erect, silent, and immobile.

Both leaders meticulously scrutinize the girls' uniforms. The leaders check to make sure each girl is carrying her membership and medical card, notepaper and a pencil. Each haversack and thermos is opened and examined. Lastly, their shoes are inspected for proper sizing and cleanliness.

---

[1] Jungmädel-Dienst im Monat Mai 1939, p. 12

Once the young girls' appearance is reviewed, the leaders step back and the command "left turn" is given. The girls simultaneously turnabout ninety-degrees and face left. The leader shouts, "in the same step march," and the column begins to march in place with their left foot striking the ground first at a pace of approximately 116 steps per minute to match the rhythm of their lively and bright, upbeat traditional Austrian hiking song, "From Grey Cities Walls."[2] Together, they count their steps to eight. Fräulein Schmidt commands "forward march!" With the banner raised high and their hearts filled with pride, they set forth on their first hiking trip up the Reisalpe!

The JM leader advances the girls from the HJ building. The den sings and marches through the village, heading towards the parish road at the center of town. Once again, both young and the old hear the familiar Austrian hiking song and come out of their stores and homes to line the streets. The entire community comes together to bid them farewell on their first big journey.

All the townsfolk are amazed by the precision of the children's column. The girls present themselves formerly, their fingers are outstretched, and their thumbs are pressed flat against their hands. Each time the girls' arm swings, the right hand is brought up to a point just below the navel.[3]

With a big smile and her right arm stretched out dutifully in front of her, Josefa watches the children file by. In dismay, she lowers her salute and continues to listen to their angelic voices until the girls round the corner at Mohr's Inn, out of sight, singing the phrase "we go out into the world."

Josefa's smile fades away as she steps inside the building and returns to her work. The worry, melancholy, and desperation that she is not allowed to show in public are kept well hidden behind her mask of implacability.

Trudel's impressionable budding sense of imagination is blossoming whether she is being instructed to make banners, learn new songs, or marching. These activities bond her to the national community spirit. Into her new, unfettered world, Trudel journeys enthusiastically in sisterhood and in song. She welcomes her newfound self-confidence. She feels an inner spark. She no longer perceives herself as a young girl but as a distinguished young girl in service. Her paradigm shifts from her childish "self" to her identity subsumed into "one unit." Her easily identifiable, black and white embroidered regional triangle on her left shoulder distinguishes her as serving in the South Lower Danube region. Everything about her, even her long black braids, now seems to have become an extension of her required attire. Trudel's coordinating uniform connects her to the millions of other young girls across Germany who serves in the League of German Girls.

Trudel's handmade banner represents her new ideals. Black signifies determination. Red represents hardiness, strength, and courage. White symbolizes her purity and allegiance. She carefully handles this symbol of her new principles. She will never allow her banner to drag on or even touch the ground. At all times,

---

[2] Aus Grauer Städte Mauern
[3] Franz Kerschner

it will be flown in an upright position at no more than a forty-five degree angle. Trudel is required to protect her flag at all costs. She will not permit her flag to be torn, soiled, or damaged in any way. She made this flag with her very own two hands and she silently vows to cherish it for the rest of her life.

Trudel slowly submits her will and character by surrendering some degree of control over her life in return for the thrill of adventure and a solid sense of self-worth. Her participation shows her transition from being a relatively carefree child frolicking through the countryside to taking responsibility for herself and her group.

Her new life is dictated by authoritarian rule. Challenges come from new directions and guidance is forthcoming, down through a chain of command by a single entity. Yet, Josefa knows her impressionable daughter remains oblivious to the totalitarian nature of the national bureaucracy that is steering her will.

The den leaders' straightforward instructions give these girls the practical common knowledge they can use at this time, focusing themselves on becoming self-actualized through the group's accomplishments and achievements. The two leaders are directly responsible for educating the girls to be vigilant about their own behavior and surroundings, to take good care of their uniforms, and to watch over the compatriots.[4]

This coming trek will test the young girls' courage, endurance, and strength. After all, the hike up the Reisalpe is not for the faint of heart. The obstacles ahead of them will measure their character, resilience, and leadership skills. The girls' enthusiasm for this day's adventure is high as they leave behind the familiarity of their own hometown.

By the end of their song, Fräulein Schmidt shouts the order to "Halt!" The girls freeze in their positions ending their step on their left foot. The leader shouts, "kick off" and the girls are free to fall out of line, chatter, and laugh. Their enthusiasm stands in stark contrast to their militaristic marching comportment. The leaders allow the girls to release their excitement before starting their difficult trek through the woods. Fräulein Schmidt calls the girls to attention by clapping her hands signaling to them to rejoin around her. Two adults and ten girls have just entered into the wilderness of the densely packed beech and spruce tree forest, which holds magical legends of hunters, alpine dwarfs, and caves.

The Gutenstein Alps span the Eastern Alp range in Central Europe, and are the northeastern most part of the Limestone Alps, reaching to heights of forty-five hundred feet.[5] Grazing on the diverse local flora, countless small animals roam free in their own natural environment, as do the carnivores that prey upon them. Wolves in the forest have even been known to attack the wayward, leaving half-eaten carcasses behind, while bears have been spotted standing guard near their cubs' mountain lairs.

The young group is now quite isolated in the wilderness and depend upon each other for their own survival.

---

[4] Gertrude Hödlmaier
[5] Gutenstein Alps

A green and double-white painted stripe marker on the aged larch tree signifies the path that leads from the road to the open meadows in Ebenwald. The tree-canopied entrance to the forest welcomes the girls.

After a few steps through a lush carpet of emerald grass, the trail turns into a damp, reddish brown dirt path with decaying leaves along the apex of this slender protuberance. On both sides of the esker, the ground angles sharply downward over one-hundred feet as the roots of the deciduous trees hold it in place. This long, winding ridge of stratified sand and gravel was formed over twenty thousand years ago within ice-walled tunnels by streams that flowed within and under the massive glaciers.

The path looks as if there is no end in sight becoming narrower as it winds deeper into the forest. A few thin beams of sunlight filter through the canopy, and illuminate the ground below. As the girls set forth into the forest, they are encouraged to use their imagination and compose new games or sing songs learned about nature.

Just then, Hanni spontaneously lifts both her arms like a ballerina and whirls around in the beams of the light that flows onto her body. The other girls follow suit, dancing and running around Hanni as she leads the pack. The leaders walk behind the young observing their spontaneous new game.

The path narrows further ahead as it ascends the slope, making it hard to navigate. The ground is wet and small rocks protrude from the soil. The girls lean forward and use the weight of their bodies to push themselves up the hill. To the left of the path a small, glistening stream trickles down the mountainside. Brown beech leaves blanket the forest floor. Nature's ornamental Terrestrial polypodium plants with its creeping hairy fronds are growing in the shade. Mother Earth provides calcareous soils nurturing clusters of her young wild ginger among the ferns. The girls reach the top of the hill and continue walking down the other side, through the forest until they come to a deep gully in the ground. During heavy rainstorms, floodwaters rage downhill between the two mountainsides and continually carve out the large trench. Standing on the bank, the girls can clearly see that this depression is deep and is impossible to jump.

The legend of the Schneider Ditch was born on the day when the local champion deer hunter, Herr Schneider, carrying his prize buck, had tried to come home during a deluge. He had to cross the bridge that once stood here. Suddenly, the skies closed and a lightning bolt crashed through the canopy. It was raining so hard that he could not see. As he crossed the span, an ill-fated flash flood blasted its way through the ditch, demolishing the bridge. Schneider's body was found a day later, floating in the Halbach River. A memorial featuring a hand-painted picture of Jesus on the cross marks the spot where he was killed.

The group gathers and settles on a strategy that will allow them to cross safely. Their plan is to collect fallen saplings and limbs, and then bind them together using heavy-duty twine. They are going to build a footbridge.

Both leaders were well aware of this obstacle and prepared for it by bringing enough twine in their backpacks.

Everyone except for Trudel fans out and scurry through the woods to collect their material. They return and begin to assemble a basic footbridge frame by laying down two long saplings. Then smaller branches are bound across with twine. On both sides of the bridge, the girls weave the twine over and under the branches, securing the crosspieces to the frame.

The next challenge is to position the bridge without breaking it or dropping it down into the trench. Fräulein Schmidt points to the large limb that hangs directly over the gully. She ties one end of her rope securely to a rock and throws it over the tree branch. The dangling rock swings back and forth, as she lowers it down over the trench. Fräulein Brückner then grabs hold of the rock with another stick and pulls it back towards her. She unties the rock and then secures the end of the rope onto the middle of the bridge.

Carefully, the girls pull on the other end of the rope, hoisting their makeshift bridge upward. Then, they swing it outward toward the rim of the trench. With some delicate maneuvering, the rope is let out and the bridge falls snuggly into position. The two banks are now connected and the girls congratulate each other with slapping 'high-fives.'

First, Fräulein Schmidt crosses making sure the bridge will hold the weight of the girls. She unties the rope and encourages the girls to cross. One by one, the girls follow each other over the bridge, carefully balancing themselves like tightrope walkers determined not to fall. As the girls hug each other victoriously, the leader finishes rolling the rope and places it into her backpack. The troop has just survived the crossing of the legendary Schneider Ditch![6]

The path continues diagonally along the leeward side of the mountain. They walk in single-file catching glimpses of their valley below through the forest openings as the markers lead their way.

The trail leads them to the left and becomes steep once again until the terrain plateaus off and becomes level. In the distance, they see through the trees a circular opening showing the emerald meadow and radiant blue sky. Eagerly, the girls run toward the great meadow of Ebenwald.

They sit on the grass and rest for fifteen minutes. The warm sun feels good. The girls take a moment to eat a slice of bread, drink some water, and chat amongst themselves of their challenging accomplishment. Trudel takes a moment to write about this part of her journey in her JM journal.

> "And the early morning is our time, when the winds and the mountains sing. The sun then makes the valleys far, and the life, and the life that it will bring us. How often have I been singing this song, but never before have I really seen with my very own eyes what it means to look at the dawn. The sun shines brightly today as we march down the road singing our hiking song. Our land, our forest, our meadows patiently call to us from afar. Nothing but blue sky is ahead of us as the clouds

---

[6] Schneidergraben

drift peacefully above. I am seeing my homeland in a brand new light of day with my comrades. Never before have I seen the small wonders that are magically appearing before my eyes. I wonder if my comrades can see what I see. As we approached the path, we were allowed to relax and enjoy our surroundings. I trotted along admiring the beautiful forest. As my troop neared the trench, we came together and figured out a way to cross the ditch. We made a big bridge and crossed. On top of the first hill, we saw the most beautiful view of the meadow and forest. This is where we made our first rest stop."

The girls sit on an old tree trunk that had fallen over. Fräulein Brückner takes this moment to teach the girls about the flora growing nearby. Next to the fallen tree, Fräulein Brückner points out the elderberry shrub. She walks to the small tree, picks off a white, star shape flower, and shows it around to the girls. She educates them about the benefits and side effects of this musk-scented plant. She points out the fine yellow, powdery pollen on top of the stamen emanating from the center nodule of the five pinnate bloom.[7] She explains how these flowers can be dipped into a light batter, deep-fried, and eaten. Left unpicked, the flowers turn to berries through a process called pollination.

The fertilized flowers turn into elderberries that are ready to eat by the last week in August, but not before then for they are highly poisonous. Berries can be cooked in a large kettle on low heat and the mixture turned into tasty jams and jellies. The entire plant can be used to make a hot medicinal tea to treat bronchitis, coughs, colds, and fevers, only if the brew was very strictly prepared.[8] Indeed, the elderberry plant has been used in Europe for hundreds of years to improve vision and boost one's immune system. It has also been used as a mild laxative to help reduce inflammation of the urinary tract and bladder.[9] Elderberry syrup is used in fruit pies and in wines.

With their rest period over, Trudel places her notebook and pencil back into her haversack. Heading for her place in formation, she spots a beautiful family of reindeer grazing along the edge of the meadow near the conifers. Inspired by the scene, she resumes her spot at the front of her group. Now, it is Gretchen's turn to carry the banner.

Heading in a southerly direction, the group continues their hike on the limestone granule road in song. Hiking in double formation, they pass the Grasser family cattle farm and enter once again into the Ebenwald Forest. Within a half an hour, they pass the trail to Hochstaff Mountain. At the clearing, the group makes a right turn onto the blue and double-white marked trail. After rounding the bend, they come to see the old Hinteralm log cabin ahead of them.

---

[7] Natural History Museum
[8] Gertrude Kerschner
[9] Sambucus nigra

Inside lives Hanni, the eighty-six-year old dairymaid who was at that very moment busy washing the dishes from her previous guests that had just left. When she hears the group of melodic young voices, she wipes her hands on her apron, turns and peers out the window. She sees the band of travelers walking in formation toward her humble abode, singing.

She walks to the front door, opens it, and steps out onto her little front porch. Standing just over four feet nine inches tall, the thick-boned, elderly woman stands holding onto the railing. She stretches forth her arm, palm facing upward in a welcoming gesture. Her blue skirt decorated with white flowers hangs to her knees. Her red and white, long-sleeved checkered shirt keeps her body warm, along with her brown ankle boots and gray wool stocking. Her yellow-and-white floral bandana partially obscures her grey hair and her large forehead. Her bushy, gray eyebrows float above her protruding nose and redden cheeks. Beyond her wrinkles though, her soft, green eyes radiates inner compassion and wisdom. She shares her gracious wide smile with these newcomers. She could be anybody's grandmother.

Holding onto the handrail, Hanni carefully steps down the wooden stairs and makes her way out onto the lush sub-alpine perennial grass. "Welcome girls! I am delighted to see that you have finally arrived!"

One by one, the girls walk up to Hanni, introduce themselves, and exchange pleasantries. Hanni points the girls toward the piped trough of refreshing, pure mountain water. "Please, refill your canteens, girls!" she chirps. "Let me go inside and prepare a little something for you to eat."

Although the den leaders graciously decline the offer, the dairymaid insists. Eventually, Fräulein Schmidt asks Irma and Margarita to help the woman with the food preparations.

The rest of the girls sit outside on the picnic benches and prepare for their next lesson. Gretchen carefully leans the banner against the fence before joining her seated comrades.

Across the road, the girls see over three hundred heads of grazing cattle spread out across the meadows. Some relax on the ground, enjoying the warm sun as calves frolic around them. Others stand and chew their cud, content in their peaceful surroundings. The continuous clanging of one cowbell marks the leader of this herd. A zigzag, split rail wooden fence around Hanni's log cabin is all that separates the girls from the livestock. Some girls have never been this close to so many large animals roaming free, so they are very pleased to have been invited to rest at Hanni's Hinteralm.

The girls are busy chatting among themselves until Fräulein Schmidt claps her hands drawing their attention. Quickly, they remove their notebooks and pencils from their haversacks and prepare to take notes.

"As you can see there are a number of different cattle grazing in the meadow. The white head cattle are called Fleckvieh and they were imported from Switzerland into Bavaria and Austria during the early 1800's. They are primarily raised for their milk production. Their hides either are usually a solid brown or have white-and-brown patches. The second set of cattle we see are called Murboden.

They are a dairy and meat breed cows that are often used as a draft animal. Their coats vary from yellowish to light red, with deeper red areas about the horns, eyes, and along the nose. The adult male is called a bull and he can weigh up to eleven-hundred pounds when fully grown. The female cow can have her first calf when she is twenty-four months old. When the baby calves are born, they weigh about eighty-eight pounds. These animals have a docile temperament and exhibit well-balanced behavior when they are part of a herd. However, it is not advisable to walk straight up and pet one of these cows because they may charge at any sudden movement. [10]

As Trudel takes notes, she catches a whiff of the bratwurst that is cooking inside the hut. Her stomach begins to grumble.

"Do you remember our Kleinzell cattle festival last fall?" Fräulein Brückner asks the girls. "These are the same cows from our annual parade. They are herded down from these alpine meadows through town to their winter stables in our valley."

As the JM leader continues with her lecture, Trudel daydreams about the first cattle parade she had attended with her family back in the fall of 1931. She was only four years old. Her father, Emmerich, had carried her on his shoulders so she could watch the decorated cows come down the road. What a joyous experience it had been! Over three hundred cattle were feted upon their return to Kleinzell after summering under Hanni's care, high up in the cool Alpine meadows of the Reisalpe. Trudel recalls how her father had told her that the sounds of the Oom-pah-pah band played in order to help the cows find their way home. She had watched Hanni's husband lead the head wreath cow and the rest of the herd down the hillside. She was so excited when she saw the cows walking down the road, and their bells ringing. The lead cow was decorated with elaborate wreaths and headdresses of greenery, Alpine flowers, and ribbons, while the others wore huge bells to ward off any evil demons the cattle might encounter on their way back down into the valley. This traditional way gives thanks for a good grazing season without any losses.

The jovial townsfolk had dressed in their traditional festive attire. They were gathered on the sides of the road to watch the cattle arrive home safely from their Alpine summer home. Trudel remembers the cow parade festival as it were only yesterday. She snaps from her fantasy world when the door to the hut opens. Out walks Hanni, Irma, and Margarita. Each carries a large wooden tray piled high with serving plates, forks and knives, napkins, bread, butter, and Hanni's delicious homemade bratwurst!

The elderly dairymaid is fit as a fiddle and is in high spirits when she hands out the serving of food. Trudel feels a pang of anguish in the pit of her stomach when she remembers her morning breakfast. Her memory quickly fades as soon as she is handed one piece of bread and a delicious bratwurst. Despite being hungry, the girls take a moment to set the table. Before eating, the girls hold hands and bow their heads together in prayer.

---

[10] Franz Kerschner

To the earth, that brings our food to us,
And to the sun who made it right,
The lovely sun, the lovely earth,
We will always remember you.

They excitedly discuss their hike thus far over a satisfying lunch. When they are through eating, they remove their notebooks from their haversacks and the den leader begins the next lesson about their village.

"Kleinzell is located in the Lower Danube region in Ostmark. Our Regional Leader is Roman Jäger, and he controls everything within this province. We must obey the laws that he executes!" the den leader orders in an authoritarian voice. "Now, I am going to give you a brief overview of the history of Kleinzell. You will be tested on this so make sure you take notes.

Our beautiful land is surrounded by a limestone Alpine mountain range called the Gutenstein Alps and within these mountains is a very large underground cave system. The primary industries in our hometown today are logging, agriculture, and tourism. For many years after the Great War, the people of this beautiful village went without work. With the help of our Führer, everything has become possible again.

"Our history starts over ten thousand years ago in the time when primitive people lived among these mountains. Since meat was crucial to their survival, the men of that time dedicated themselves to hunting and providing for their families. They understood the language of the animals. The women took care of the family and the homestead. They were appreciated because they were the bearers of life.

"During the reign of Emperor Hadrian in the first century AD, the Roman soldiers settled in Aelium Cetium, today known as St. Pölten. This began the era of the Holy Roman Empire, which lasted until 1806.[11] The Romans were the first ones to discover the healing mineral spring waters in Salzerbad.

"Even during the turmoil of the Black Plague or the Napoleonic period and the events of 1849, Kleinzell somehow remained unscathed.[12] By 1887, the construction of the Salzerbad Resort was complete, and by 1898, the Reisalpe Hostel too was opened to traveling hikers.

"The reign of the Habsburg dynasty which started in 1276, continued for more than six hundred years, until the breakup of the monarchy in 1918, at the end of the Great War. That's when Emperor Charles the First relinquished his power. The day after his departure, German Austria became a republic.[13] Within a year, the Republic of Austria formed."[14]

---

[11] Holy Roman Empire
[12] Maria Pannik
[13] German Austria
[14] Republic of Austria

"Our area, however, was not so fortunate to escape the Great War's destruction. Unbeknownst to many, a famous American major named Clarence M. Young was captured and was kept for five months in the detention camp of military officers in Salzerbad.[15] Salzerbad was famous for once being a prisoner of war camp where the American officers were treated very kindly. Today, it is open to the public as a beautiful spa resort."

Trudel finds this to be a very stimulating lesson. She loves learning about the history of her village.

Once the lesson is complete, the girls are grateful to finally put away their notebooks and begin a conversation with the dairymaid. It is an uplifting chat, for the other girls have no interest in the history of their tiny village. To them, Kleinzell is a just a sleepy little town nestled within the mountains. They were not bashful however, about telling the dairymaid what they are learning in the league. The girls love the attention and they enjoy listening to Hanni. She soon captivates their hearts by sharing her story. Fräulein Schmidt and Brückner watch the girls' enthusiasm when Hanni recounts her life story.

"When I was about your age, children, my father took my mother and me for a walk up this same forest road. We climbed to this very spot, to this beautiful, open pasture between the Hochstaff and the Reisalpe Mountains. My father said how much he loved this beautiful mountainside and how he wanted to move here one day and care for the cattle. Over the following year, he and his logging friends cut down a number of large pine trees near here. They later assembled them into this log cabin, and I've been living in it every summer since!"

"Do you take care of everything yourself?" Gretel asks.

"Not all the time. My sons live in the village below and they come up here and help. They're good boys."

"Are these all your cattle?" Trudel asks.

Hanni chuckles in delight at the question. "No girls, the cattle belong to the Bauer Family in the village. They hired my family and me to care for them. I am the dairymaid and my sons are the herders. My husband use to care for the cattle too, however, he passed away some time ago. However, every morning before sunrise, I drink my tea and eat my bread. Then, I grab my bucket of salt, let the chickens out of their coop, and go call for the cattle. You should see them come running when I call, '*Sae, Sae*'" the dairymaid says with a deep, jolly laugh. "Together the cows and I walk two miles along the alpine meadows where they graze all day. I throw the salt down on the rocks and they lick it off. Then, I walk back home to prepare for my wandering guests, such as you fine girls!" The dairymaid beams a big smile at the girls. "Walking keeps me fit."

"We've always heard the name Hinteralm but don't know what it means. Can you tell us?" Mitzi asks.

"Yes, I can tell you why we call this area of the mountain Hinteralm. My formal name is Johanna Hinterleitner, but all my friends call me Hanni. My father named this part of the mountain Hinteralm because it means 'an area of grasses

---

[15] Raymond Henle

and shrubs used for grazing.' Therefore, the family name will live on long after I am gone. When you make your home on such beautiful land, it's always right to name the place you live."

Erika gives the dairymaid a heart-filled hug. "I wish we can stay here with you forever. It is so beautiful here." Erika sighs deeply as she buries her head in the old woman's chest.

"Now, now, girls, do not be sad." Hanni cradles Erika in her arms. "You are starting a new life with new adventures and there is so much of the world to see. Look at me. I am a very old woman and you have your entire lives ahead of you," continues the dairymaid in her heavy Austrian spirited voice.

"But you're up here all alone. Who is going to take care of you?" Marie worryingly asks.

"All my life, I have lived in God's beautiful country. All my life, I have been a dairymaid. Every summer I come up here to care for God's creatures. In the winter, I return to my home in the village. God has always provided for me. I have never been sick. I breathe the fresh air and drink the pure mountain waters. That is God's plan for me. I am very blessed girls and I am quite happy. Please do not worry about me. I have no regrets and I miss and want for nothing at all. I am in very good health and I have all that I need. However, I want you to promise me something" the elderly woman asks of the girls. "Will you?"

They nod their heads anticipating the words from the wise old dairymaid.

"I want you to promise me that you will always be happy and that you will always live your life to its fullest potential. I want you to learn a little bit every day and be one with nature. Always be in the world because before you know it, time has come up behind you and one day you will ask yourself 'Where did the years go?'" Hanni mischievously giggles hoping that her statement will exercise the girls' ingenuity in answering or discovering for themselves its true meaning.

Trudel's eyes open wide when she hears this statement for her mother had just said the exact same thing over breakfast that morning!

"And, I want you to especially remember something…." Hanni pauses and makes direct eye contact with the girls. "Whatever difficult paths may come before you and whatever turmoil may come your way, know that you will always have the inner strength and wisdom to move through those turbulent times. God is always with and inside you. Just look around! God is everywhere! You are strong Kleinzell girls. Remember that for me, won't you?" she pleads.

Her caring, reverent attitude certainly impresses Trudel who asks, "Can we adopt you as our new grandmother?"

The other girls agree in approval at Trudel's suggestion.

"Why yes girls, you may," responds the dairymaid with a good-humored chuckle. "Now, that I am officially your Oma, let me show you around my humble home. Please come inside."

Everyone gets up from the picnic table and follows Hanni into her log cabin.

It is a simple, medium-size domicile with two large rooms in the front with a pantry and hay storage area in the rear. It is a first-generation home constructed of milled black pine wood siding, nailed horizontally over a pine wood frame construction sitting on top of a cement foundation. The doors and shutters are painted in a light shade of forest green, mirroring the natural surroundings, while the red painted frames provide a contrasting, decorative accent. The dark brown stained scalloped trim around the window frames complete the design. The cabin logs are stained with a dark shellac finish preventing wood-borne organisms from eating the wood. Fixed underneath each window are beautiful handmade flowerboxes overflowing with purple and white petunias. On the south side of the home, Hanni has already started her vegetable garden, and on the leeward side is her chicken coop.

The decision to build the home on this site was aimed at providing the inhabitants with the best central location for sunlight, spring water, and access to the livestock. The cabin is located directly on the main forest logging road making it easily accessible for wandering travelers to visit and rest. This way, Hanni can earn additional income by providing food and beverages for paying guests.

The dairymaid invites her visitors inside. To the left are her bedroom and a cozy sitting area with a small wooden table, two chairs, and a small couch. To the right is her kitchen. She heats the home using a white porcelain, wood-burning cooking stove. To the right of the stove is a handmade wooden chest with drawers that holds two large white porcelain pots for which Hanni washes her dirty dishes. Wooden serving plates sit on top of the cabinet. Glasses are covered with a dishtowel. On the opposite side of the kitchen, glasses line the shelves and on the floor sit a number of unopened beer bottles. The tongue and grooved pine wainscoting on the walls shine with a heavy coat of shellac. The walls are adorned with wooden plaques, dried herbs, decorative tinder fungus mushrooms, and framed letters from passing travelers. A large cowbell hangs to the right of her hand-carved commemoration plaque showing her smiling face. The mayor of Kleinzell has personally presented it to her the previous year honoring her thirty years of loyal service as the Dairymaid of the Hinteralm.

After the cabin tour, the girls stroll outside, leaving the JM leaders alone with Hanni. The girls huddle together by the watering trough and decided to make up a song they can sing together for their new honorary grandmother.

Fräulein Schmitt and Bruckner were all too happy to be entertained by the jolly old dairymaid's story for they knew it would be an insult to interrupt or walk away from her. Soon, they lost all track of time. The adults realized an odd silence had fallen outside, so they popped out of the cabin to investigate.

The woman step out onto the front porch and are surprised to discover the young girls standing in two neat rows. The impromptu choir was eagerly waiting to present a brand new song, their gift of appreciation to Hanni:

> Grandmother, Grandmother, we love you,
> You are the best in the whole wide world
> Grandmother, Grandmother, we thank you,
> We're proud to have a Grandmother like you!

Hanni feels most flattered. Tears come to her eyes. She wobbles down the stairs towards the girls and they all come running over to her for a warm group embrace. The dairymaid affectionately wraps her arms around them and kisses the girls on the forehead.

Not waiting to cut this precious moment short, Fräulein Schmidt allows the girls extra time. A part of her has a soft heart and she one day hopes to have a child of her own. After a moment, she organizes the girls. "Attention girls!"

The girls step back and give their formal salute to their new grandmother.

"Everyone line up!" Fräulein Schmidt orders. She turns and gives Hanni one last warm embrace thanking her for her kind hospitality. She turns back to her troop. "Gretel, it will be your turn to carry the banner!"

Tears fall from the dairymaid's eyes as she watches the little ones march away from her home singing,

> Arise, you young wanderers!
> Now comes the time, the time of wandering,
> It gives us joy, for we want to be gone on our journey,
> That is the best thing in life,
> And great waters, mountains, and valleys,
> Are everywhere[16]

Standing next to her split-rail fence with her saluting arm raised high, the dairymaid uses her handkerchief to wave good-bye. When the girls are out of view, she turns, wipes her nose, and slowly shuffles back to the picnic tables. She feels a twinge in her chest. She thinks she has probably exerted herself from all the excitement and love she feels for the young girls in the league. The dairymaid stops, glances around, and is amazed at how much brighter her world seems. The sky is a rich deep blue. She is acutely aware of the of the forest animals around her. She becomes very sensitive to the sweet fragrance of the wildflowers and fresh mountain air. She knows she is not alone. She feels a gaze upon her.

She stumbles alongside the picnic table, trying to keep herself upright and steady. Clutching her heart, she loses her balance and falls to the ground. With her last breath, she calls, "My God … it's beautiful," before closing her eyes forever.

---

[16] Wir Mädel Singen, "Auf, du junger Wandersmann," p. 120-121

The Myth of the Wild Flower

THE BAND OF HIKERS follows the logging road until they come to the hand-made signpost pointing them to the summit of the Reisalpe. Within a few hours, they will be arriving at the peak of the mountain. This shorter, meandering trail continues through the dense deciduous forest. The steep acclivity does not dampen the girls' spirit for they use makeshift walking sticks they found along the way to help them climb the steep, rocky slopes. This path leads to a small clearing. For a brief moment, the trees give way to shrubbery and perennial grasses before leading up into the conifer forest.

As they enter the dense woods, they notice the area is absent of under-growth. The delightful scent of pine fills the air. The lower branches are dead, partially broken and bare, free from the needle-like leaves. It is dark for little sunlight penetrates to the ground. Soft pine needles blanket the ground.

This area lies between the Alpine tundra of the north and the deciduous trees to the south. Black pine trees are the most common at this elevation having been survivors from the Ice Age. Living up to eight hundred years these trees produce a rich resin when they start to sweat.

Tree farmers know this forest well and visit it often. Not only are these ev-ergreens harvested for logging, the farmers use the pinesap to make resin. The sap is collected by removing a small piece of bark and scraping into the sapwood. Two wooden runners are hammered into the trunk, one on either side of the other. A third incision is made into the tree to hold the collection cup under-neath. When the tree begins to sweat, the buckets catch the sap droppings. At the end of the season, the runners and the cups are removed, leaving three scars on the tree. The trees then look as if they have a face with two eyes and a mouth.[1] The girls make up a new game to see how many faces they can find on the trees before reaching the end of the trail.

Their strenuous final climb through the switchback sub-alpine forest path is rewarded with a beautiful panoramic view from the gently sloping summit. Crowning the peak is a large wooden cross, three large boulders, and a Madonna. The majestic Gutenstein Alps and their jagged peaks soar in the distance. The mountains and its lush green forest seem to go on for hundreds of miles. It is a marvelous sight to behold.

Never before has Trudel seen such billowy white cumulus clouds floating so peacefully in such a captivating royal blue sky. Standing tiptoe on one of the boulders, she reaches out, and tries to touch the clouds. She silently vows one day to be free as a bird. She feels as if she is on the top of God's world! Trudel

---

[1] Franz Kerschner

senses that the divine is all around her. Then, she hears a faint voice whisper to her. "Learn as much as you can."

The den leaders relax at one of the picnic tables at the Reisalpen Hostel and allow the enthusiastic girls time to enjoy this moment before their next lesson.

The Reisalpenschutzhaus had been constructed on the peak of the Reisalpe so that hikers can relax and admire the stunning view.

Gretel runs over to the leaders' table. "Can I leave the banner with you while I go and play with the other girls?"

"No!" responds Fräulein Schmidt.

Gretel pouts and begins to carry on but Fräulein Schmidt scolds her. "You were happy to carry the banner on this leg of the hike. "Now it is your responsibility to guard it."

The flag-bearer learns to be mature by watching her friend play without her.

The girls discover an array of pretty purple and yellow flowers growing next to the rocks. They take care not to trample over these delicate perennials. Trudel jumps from the boulder then squats down and examines the plant closely. She picks one of the flowers, basks in its beauty, and places it in her pocket. She glances up when she hears the leader's call.

The girls' race each other toward the refuge hut. As they catch their breath, they settle in for their next lesson. Only then is Gretel allowed to rest the flagpole against the fence and join her comrades.

Fräulein Schmidt has a very strict curriculum to follow. The Reich's Ministry has provided the leaders in each districts a copy the "Young Girls League - March 1938" edition. This month's lesson is to teach conformity and obedience. Inner self-worth will be forged through bold new interactive experiences. Nature will be used as a means to ground their sense of national identity. They will come to appreciate the land that will align them with their new National Socialistic comprehensive worldview.[2] Fräulein Schmidt wants her girls to become familiar with their environment. She begins her discussion about the panorama.

"Today, we are sitting on the top of the Reisalpe Mountain. The Reisalpe is the highest mountain in the Gutenstein Alps and it stands 4,590 feet tall. It lies between Lilienfeld, Hohenberg, and Kleinzell. The Gutenstein Alps range is located in the northeastern most part of the Northern Limestone Alps range.

"Ten miles south-east is the village of Gutenstein." She points in the direction of the village. "You can barely see the village below, but it is there. Past the village is the mountain called Schneeberg. Schneeberg is in the easternmost part of the Northern Limestone Alps range and stands at a magnificent 6,811 feet tall. It is renowned for its distinctive limestone massif and steep slopes on three of its sides. It is often considered Vienna's personal little snow-capped mountain.[3] It is located in Puchberg am Schneeberg.

---

[2] Reinhold Sautter, p. 191
[3] Schneeberg

"Directly to our west is Ötscher. It is recognizable by its distinctive peak. It is the second highest mountain in the Northern Limestone Alps range, and it stands at 6,211 feet tall.[4]

The distracted girls are not paying quite enough attention to her lecture, so Fräulein Schmidt decides to switch her teaching approach. She calls out to the girl's, "Mitzi, Erika, and Helga! Let's play a little game of who can be the highest mountain in the area!"

The girls stand and approach their leader.

"You are among the highest mountains in the Northern Limestone Alps. Mitzi, you can stand here in front of the Schneeberg. Erika, you can stand here in front of the Ötscher, and Helga, you can stand right here for you represent the Reisalpe. Now, each one of you girls represents the tallest mountains in our area. Don't you feel as important as these mountains?"

The girls beam a smile and feel important for being specifically chosen by their leader.

"You may sit down now."

According to the monthly leadership pamphlet, playing games and storytelling is part of the curriculum. Up until now, the girls have expressed themselves by creating their own games. Now, to conceive a unity of 'one's thinking,' the leaders will interject storytelling into their lessons. Telling stories is viewed as an effective learning tool for teaching moral values for it engages the child's imagination by the use of language, mystical ideas, culture, and traditions.[5]

"Forty years ago, in October of 1898, the Reisalpe Hostel behind me was opened," Fräulein Schmidt explains. "It was a beautiful autumn day and over seven hundred people attended the elaborate opening ceremony. Black and gold flags fluttered in the wind symbolizing the pride of the Austrian-Hungarian Monarchy. Prior to the building's completion, the Austria-Hungarian Alpine club erected the new twelve-foot tall Christian summit cross. The carving in the crossbeam as it stands here today reads 'God's Beautiful Homeland.' Two hundred local villagers attended the festivity while five-hundred guests hiked here from far, far away.

"Everyone was dressed in their ceremonial Austrian and Bavarian clothing. They each displayed their spirit of unity. The women wore their dirndls as the men wore their lederhosen. All day long, a twelve-piece brass band with an accompanying accordionist played traditional Austrian polkas and folks songs. The event was spectacular! It opened with everyone singing 'The Day of Our Father.' All the voices echoed and rang out to the highest heavens.

"The organizer of the event was Julius Firetag von Hohenberg. He introduced the hostel's architect, Herr Hanz Kornberger, who stepped onto the platform and gave a speech. The architect said, 'I am deeply honored for being given the opportunity to design and oversee the construction of this alpine shelter. For three long years, my men and I have toiled under some severe weather conditions

---

[4] Ötscher
[5] Richard M. Dorson, p. 16

to build this hikers' refuge hut. On the other hand, sometimes the weather here was so gorgeous that it was obvious how God alone made our beautiful homeland. I would like to acknowledge the fine work of the stonemasons, carpenters, roofers, and local villagers who participated in the construction of this magnificent building.' He spoke about his closeness to the building, how his soul was living within every piece of wood, every nail, and in every block of stone.

"When the architect finished his speech, the organizer, Herr Kornberger, handed the keys to the Vice President and Director of the Austrian-Hungarian Alpine Club, Dr. Klozberge. He accepted the keys with great honor and declared to preserve the integrity of this shelter for future generations to come. But the festivities did not end there," Fräulein Schmidt says with a raised eyebrow.

"They didn't? What happened next?" Trudel wants to know.

"Herr Hohenberg introduced Frau Emily Steinböch, who read the Reisalpe poem. It goes like this.

> Great calm and deep peace is only with you
> When you are on this land
> What is the magic of the forest? Of the trees?
> Of the birds and the bees?
> Of God's great commands?
> The trunk of the great Black Pine still lives
> When it bleeds
> You are in the Alps so high
> Are you not dreaming of the Reis'alpine?
> Seek friendship with the ones you meet
> Learn to speak so they understand
> Anyone who brings the good towards you
> Will be your friend on this
> Mountain grassland.[6]

"The crowd gave a warm applause at the end of the poem. Herr Kornberger and Herr Klotzberge cut the ribbon and the refuge doors opened. Everyone gave a resounding cheer! Inside the new building, everyone noticed the fine woodwork and accent pieces scavenged from the surrounding forest by the Helenenthaler Alpine Club. Visitors to the hut would feel as if they had become one with the mountain. Everyone celebrated the occasion with Edelweiss beer along with Vienna sausage and bread!"[7]

Fräulein Schmidt is pleased to know that storytelling is part of her curriculum. She loves telling anecdotes to the children. "I have another story about the secret healing waters in Kleinzell. Would you like to hear it?"

She knows they will and she starts her next lesson.

---

[6] Reisalpe Poem
[7] Badener Zeitung

"The Reisalpe stands fourteen hundred feet tall and is the highest peak in this part of the Gutenstein Alps, which is why so many alpinists come from all over the country to hike in the Ebenwald forest, just as you girls are doing today. Well, not far from this very spot is a secret opening! It leads to a vast underground cave system.

The girls look at each other in awe. They didn't know there is an underground cave system inside this mountain.

"Kleinzell folklore tells us about a troll that lives deep inside the Reisalpe Mountain. He refuses to share the healing waters with anyone. He alone knows only of the healing springs until one day, many years ago, a mountaineer from the village discovered it." She pauses creating suspense.

Trudel loves hearing about the Kleinzeller Troll because her mother had told her this very same bedtime story many, many times before.

"The Kleinzeller Troll lives deep within the cave system. His job is to protect the sacred waters. Some villagers were quite ill but they were afraid to explore up the mountain to locate the source of the healing waters. They had heard scary stories about mountaineers never returning. However, that did not stop other wanderers from afar who still come in search of the famed source of the healing waters. They were unable to find the secret cave, but they would all claim to have seen small footprints in the mud alongside the babbling brook. Nobody knew what to make of these tiny footprints.

"So one day, a very old, arrogant man decided he would get to the bottom of the riddle. He followed the footprints from the brook all the way back to their origin. He thought that, if he could find the water source, he could bottle and sell it and retire a very wealthy man. Instead, the small footprints led him the long way around back to the center of Kleinzell!

"The old man was dumbfounded and confused. Since his first idea had not worked out so well, he thought that he would try something else. Therefore, he built a trap to capture the troll! He set up the wooden trap in the center of town. He waited all night behind a nearby tree, but he fell asleep. When he woke up the next morning, the trap was shut tight and it was empty!

"Then, the old man tried a new trick. He decided to tie a piece of meat to a long string, and tie the string to his toe. This time, the man brought along a net. That evening, he waited behind the tree. Alas once again, he fell asleep. Suddenly, he was awakened by the string tugging on his toe!

"When he opened his eyes, he could not believe what he saw! The troll was dancing around the small fountain in the center of town, holding up his prize piece of meat, and singing! Well, the old man seized his net, ran over, and captured the troll. It was at that time when the spring stopped flowing!

"The troll begged and pleaded with the old man to let him go. The old man refused. Instead, he took the troll home, locked him in a cage, and left with the key. The old selfish man with a very big nose strutted into town and lied to everyone announcing 'I saw the mountain troll today! He was carrying the healing waters with him back to his cave! The moment after he stepped into the cave, the opening closed by magic, and he disappeared!'

"Upon hearing this news, some desperate villagers headed straight up to the mountains in search for the cave opening. The old man just laughed and returned to his home to eat his prize piece of meat.

"One day, an alpinist who happened to be walking past the old man's hovel heard a beautiful baritone voice singing. From the street, the mountaineer peered through the windows, and was amazed at what he saw! He saw the troll and the troll saw him! The troll desperately begged and pleaded asking to be released from the cage. He told the mountaineer that the old man would not be back until nightfall.

"The mountaineer entered the hovel and sprung open the cage. Because of his kindness, the troll said he would reveal the secret location of the healing spring waters to him.

"Unexpectedly, the cocky old man came home early. He was very upset at what he found. He took his walking stick and he hit the hiker over the head and knocked him out! The next morning, when the mountaineer came to, he was still on the floor, with both hands tied behind his back. The troll was gone.

"You idiot, you went and released my magic troll! You will pay the price!' the old man threatened. "You will have to be my slave and do my bidding from now on!

"Outside however, the troll was hiding. He overheard the entire conversation. The troll waited patiently until the middle of the night when the old man was snoring. Then, he slipped back inside the hovel and released the mountaineer.

"When the old man woke up the next morning, the rope was bundled up on the floor and the mountaineer was gone. The old man stormed into the center of the village, but what he saw took him by surprise! The villagers were standing around in a circle. As the old man came closer, he saw the magic spring flowing up from the well again, just as it had before he had captured the troll! The villagers were drinking the healing waters, curing their ailments, and rejoicing.

"The villagers told the old man that some malicious fool had abducted the troll, but the noble mountaineer had rescued him. In turn, the troll had revealed the secret location of the healing spring waters. Now, only good people could drink the water, or else they would die. The old, conceited man refused to drink from the waters, and the very next day, he mysteriously died.

"Wanderers from foreign lands who have sipped from these waters have returned many times to our beautiful homeland for more. That is why there is a wooden statue of a mountaineer right next to the fountain at the center of town. It marks the very spot where the Kleinzeller Troll whispered the secret location of the spring to the mountaineer. Anyone who drinks from that fountain daily will live a long and happy life.[8]

"Now, I want you to take a moment and think about this story and what it means to you. Then, I want you to write down what you have learned. We will discuss it at our next social meeting," says Fräulein Schmidt.

---

[8] Franz Kerschner

Trudel ponders what the story means to her and what she has learned. She goes one-step further and symbolizes each of the characters in the story.

When everyone is ready, the girls gather their belongings and form their column. As one, they begin marching to the beat. It is now Irma's turn to carry the banner.

The hikers descend from the summit along the main logging road, following the blue and white markers back to the village. Conifer trees appear almost black against the deep blue of the late afternoon sky. The girls hike past the base of the Hochstaff Mountain and arrive at the fork in the logging road. Turning left will lead them back to Hanni and her Hinteralm while turning right will take them home to Kleinzell.

They turn right, continuing their descent on the side of the logging road. Cattle consume the dandelions that dot the fertile alpine meadows. Although the mountainside drops sharply away to their right, the grade of the wide forest road remains relatively level. This is definitely an easier and quicker way for the girls to hike back home.

Walking through the forest, they hear the birds chirping. A small green woodpecker darts overhead, calling kyü-kyü-kyück in search of his mate.[9] On a gentle guest of wind, a band of chickadees swoops overhead. The girl's banner flutters in the breeze as they merrily hike homeward, singing. They are happy to live in God's beautiful homeland, and even more than that, they love being in the Young Girls League.[10]

It will be another two hours before they reach the base of the mountain. Mother Nature provides special treats for the girls is the changing scenery of the alpine forest to pastures and back to the forest again. Their singing softens when they hear a vehicle come up the road. They jump safely to the side and allow the vehicles to race past them, blowing dust in their faces. The hikers do not mind because they are simply enjoying the novelty of the moment.

As they reach the clearing, they rest in the open meadow close to the edge of the forest. As the sun continues descending, the instructor takes a moment to discuss their alliance with their land.

"The spring gentian wild flower is the most beautiful color of the blue spectrum. This was the spectacular flower you girls saw growing around the rocks on the summit of the Reisalpe. Its purplish-blue, short stem supports the lanceolate leaves. It thrives in dry meadows with chalky limestone soils. It is becoming as rare as the Edelweiss because of its beauty. So many tourists pick this flower. However, it is considered bad luck to bring the flower into the house, because if you do, you will be struck by lightning. Folklore suggests that death would follow a loved one if this flower was ever picked."[11] Trudel shutters with fright for she has the spring gentian flower nestled inside her pocket! She tries to push the thought of death out of her mind by paying attention to her next lesson.

---

[9] European Green Woodpecker
[10] Gertrude Lippenberger
[11] Franz Kerschner

"The buttercup is a cousin to the marsh marigold, both of which we have seen growing on this mountain. The buttercup reflects a yellow color when placed underneath your chin. Although beautiful to look at, it is actually very poisonous to livestock. On the other hand, the marsh marigold is one of our surviving glacier plants. It thrives in moist, shady conditions. We will see the plant again during our descent into the woods past the junction.

"The dense forest canopy is formed by beech trees, which create a lot of shade. The beech is an excellent source of firewood for it can be easily split. It also burns for many hours with bright and calming flames. Most of the families use this wood to heat their homes. Your mother uses this same wood in her cooking stove."[12]

While Fräulein Schmidt continues with her discussion, Fräulein Brückner cannot help but overhear a strange rustling noise in the brushes behind her. Inconspicuously, she leaves the group and slowly makes her way towards the sound. She pulls back on a branch and notices a little boy hiding.

Fräulein Schmidt is curious as to why the young assistant leader has left the group. The young girls are attentive toward their leader and pay no attention as to what is happening behind them.

Fräulein Brückner kneels down and starts talking to the shrubbery.

"It's okay, you can come out now, little boy," she says with affection.

The boy stands up from behind the shrubs and looks at the woman standing before him. She reaches out, takes his hand, and escorts him out from the woods.

Hearing the rustling going on behind them, the girls cast a glance in their direction. Trudel's eyes open wide at the sight. The other girls let out a chuckle and look at one another in amusement.

Fräulein Schmidt stops her lecture. Trudel stands up and shouts, "What are you doing here?"

"Do you know this little boy?" Fräulein Brückner asks Trudel.

"That's my little brother, Franzel," she says.

"Ah." Fräulein Bruckner turns back to Franzel. "Does your mother know you are here?"

"Well, kind of ... I told her I was going into the woods to get some firewood and that's when I heard you coming down the trail singing," Franzel replies.

"And then, you got distracted. Can you tell me why you smell so bad?" the young assistant leader asks.

"I was playing with the ants. They were crawling on my arm and that when I started to smell," Franzel answers.

"What do you mean?" Fräulein Brückner asks.

"Here, I'll show you." Franzel excitedly runs into the woods, bends down for a few seconds, stands up, and then turns around. Hundreds of brown forest ants are crawling on his arm. Quickly, he blows on his arm and shakes off the crawling insects.

"Eeeewwww!" the girls respond in disgust.

---

[12] Franz Kerschner

"See, it doesn't hurt, it just smells bad." Franzel beams, feeling proud of his scientific find. The penetrating odor emanates into the air and the girls quickly get up and dash away from him.

Franzel loves the woods. The natural beauty of the forest and all living things within it captivate him, his soul, and his sprit. He is extremely inquisitive and has a natural bond with the land.

Fräulein Schmidt walks over to the brushes, pushes away the leaves revealing a large colony of forest ants. She smells her hand. "Phew-deivy! She cries. Quickly, she removes the thermos from her haversack and pours water over her hands trying to remove the awful smell.

At that moment, she recognizes Franzel's infatuation with nature and allows him to share his insatiable knowledge of the ants with her den, like how they work in a tight-knit community to break down organic materials thus aerating the soil. Supposedly, their bites relieve arthritis. As she listens to him speak, she gets the feeling that one day, Franzel is going to grow up to become an accomplished member of the Hitler Youth.

"Now, run along and go back home, Franzel. I don't think you want to be marching into town with the girls, do you?" Fräulein Schmidt chuckles.

"No way!" Franzel exclaims. He hurries a salute to the young leaders and quickly dashes away from the group, running down the road.[13]

The girls gather and line up to complete the last leg of their hike. Now, it is Margarita's turn to carry the banner. Surrounded by the firs, linden, and larch trees that characterize this dense forest level, the girls find their way back to the first road from which their excursion had begun.

The den leader orders the girls to compose themselves and line up in strict formation to complete their march back to their meetinghouse. At this time, Margarita passes the banner to Helga to carry.

Joyously, the girls sing adieu to the woods. In the distance, a few of the village folk hear the girls' returning. By honoring the girls in salute, they wait for them to march past.

The girls march back to the front of the HJ building. The den leader gives the order and the girls stop marching and stand at attention. The leader raises her right hand and gestures the salute. All the girls and Fräulein Brückner salute back, shouting their new German greeting. They lower their arms and stand in silence, waiting for the leader's summation.

"Today, we have climbed the great Reisalpe! Today, we are very happy. We are strong because our experience has brought us closer to our Fatherland. We end this hike with greetings to our Führer, Seig, Heil!"

The group echoes, "Seig, Heil!"

"Now go inside and take your seats."

The jaunty group returns to their meeting room. The girls love spending time together. The longer they can stay in their meetings, the happier they feel.

---

[13] Franz Kerschner

After all, they are spending time having fun instead of performing their rigorous home chores.[14]

Margarita places the banner against the wall and returns to her desk. The girls take their seats, anxiously talking among themselves. When the JM leaders enters the room, the girls spring to attention, standing beside their desks, and salute.

This day on the mountain has been a turning point in Trudel's life. She feels very proud to stand in allegiance with her comrades. She no longer views herself as a child, but instead as a young, mature girl. Her strenuous performance today hiking the Reisalpe has proven her worthiness not only to her but also to her country.

The girls sit down and open their notebooks. Fräulein Schmidt wishes to take advantage of the girls' high spirits by reviewing the upcoming indoctrination ceremony. She wants to stress the importance of their rite of passage for she will be teaching these young maidens to grow up and become obedient, service-minded, and dutiful, and live in comradeship within the community. Since their registration into the Young Girls League, these girls are learning to fulfill their duties to the nation and state. Their ideological training starts at the age of ten, and aside from their duties at home and in the school, service in the JM now also asks that they do their part voluntarily and joyfully.[15]

From their initiation into the JM, their training will comprise of learning an ideology that will set in motion their belief structure. It is a natural time in these young girls' lives to nurture their natural growth and conscious awakening.[16] For now, they are still young girls seeing their entire life unfold before them through innocent eyes. They will eventually come to learn to fulfill their duties for their nation and state. Nevertheless, they are only young girls, and they must learn from the beginning.[17] Not a vestige of the former child will remain. Her mind and life will be transformed forever.

"Now, we are going to discuss our ceremony. Can anyone tell me what the purpose of our ceremony is?" Fräulein Schmidt asks.

Erika raises her hand.

"Yes, Erika?"

"The purpose of our ceremony is to show our worth to our country and to be in service for our Volk."

"Very good, Erika. What does that mean to be in service for our people?"

Hanni raises her hand.

"Yes, Hanni?"

"It means we will no longer face hardship because we are now one with our country, working together to help everyone."

"Very good, Hanni, yes, very good. Gretchen?"

---

[14] Gertrude Hödlmaier
[15] Bund Deutscher Mädel – "You Too Belong to the Leader!"
[16] Building Camaraderie
[17] Idib

"That we are to be honest, tell the truth at all times and be loyal."

"Yes, Gretchen, that is correct too. We are in service for our Volk and for our State. But most of all, this ceremony is your first rite of passage and it will mark the transition in your lives from childhood to pre-adolescence."

"In approximately ten days, it will be our Führer's birthday. On this day, you will have your formal induction ceremony into the Young Girls' League. It is very important that you fully participate. You must understand why we perform this ceremony especially for you. You are the new generation of young girls. Between your parents, your school, and this movement, the adults are obligated to provide you with everything you need to know so that you can grow up into becoming mature young women. It is our responsibility as leaders to guide you appropriately so you may learn. You will inherit from us our learning. We will pass it on to you, and you will pass it on to your children. Just as the farmer takes care of his land and animals, we must prepare you for womanhood."

The girls giggle.

"Herr Auf!" The den leader scolds the girls. "This is not something to laugh at. There are severe consequences for your actions when you insult and laugh at the Führer! To take this ceremony seriously means you want to become a model German girl. Now, everyone pay attention!"

The girls snap to attention.

"This ceremony will mark a new beginning in your lives," Fräulein Schmidt continues.

Trudel envisions the ceremony in her head. She is fantasizing about how she will perform, what she will say, what she will do, and how she will act. The young leader calls her name. With her head held high, she rises from her chair with dignity and walks onto the stage. She stands in front of the entire village. All eyes are upon her. She stands alone, erect, and at attention. A mixed sensation comes over her. She feels intimidated and yet, she feels strong and worthy. All is quiet. The crowd eagerly waits for her to speak. They know her words are important, since they had come to listen to her. Her words will have meaning. When she speaks, the words flow easily as she accentuates her promise. She turns to her leader, salutes, shakes hands, and in turn, salutes the audience. The audience stands and salutes in return. They give her an overwhelming applause. She stands there admiring her followers for she has truly proven herself a leader.

Trudel drifts back to reality only to realize that she has missed the most important part of the den leader's instructions.

"We will practice the routine at our next meeting," are the next words Trudel hears. "Right now, we will learn our new line formation that we will use when marching onto the stage. The five shortest girls will be in the front row and the five tallest girls will be in the second row on stage. Now, when I call your name, I want you to come up in the front of the class and stand right here."

Fräulein Schmidt calls the names of the shortest girls' first. Trudel, Gretchen, Maria, Gretel, and Irma walk up to the front of the room and stand in a straight line. Margarita, Helga, Hanni, Erika, and Mitzi come up to the front of the room next and stand directly behind the shorter girls.

"Now, I want you all to remember this formation. This is how you will be onstage at the ceremony. When I give the command, you will face forward and march in formation. You will be in two columns when we approach the stage. The shortest girls will be on the left side of the column while the taller girls will be on the right side. The entire time, you will continue to march in place and in time with the music. Now, march forward!" The leader escorts the girls around the room twice and then orders them to practice as if they were walking on stage. "At our next meeting, we will practice this march at the auditorium. For now, just remember your positions and return to your seats."

Excitedly, the girls return to the chairs.

"Next, we are going to discuss today's hike on the Reisalpe. We had some difficult challenges on this first hike," as Fräulein Schmidt begins this portion of her discussion. "We had to learn to march together in perfect formation. We had the difficult challenge to build a bridge and cross over the Schneider Trench. Finally, we climbed the switchback alpine trail to the Reisalpe. We met Hanni and made her our new grandmother. In the forest, we had the pleasure of meeting Trudel's brother, Franzel, who shared with us his knowledge of the brown ants. I would like each of you to share your thoughts about this hike. What did you learn? What was the most exciting part of the hike for you? What would you do differently for next month's hiking trip? Trudel, you may start."

"Yes, Fräulein Schmidt," Trudel says as she opens her notebook. She starts reading from her journal entry about her experience. A few girls snicker at her.

"Be quiet!" the leader commands. "Please continue, Trudel. We are very much interested in what inspired you the most about our hike today."

Trudel reads her first entry from the time they marched in the woods until she came to rest in the meadows. The girls laugh at her and her face reddens in embarrassment. She is innocently revealing a vulnerable part of herself, and she is unprepared to be judged by her peers.

The leader takes notes and listens attentively to Trudel's beautiful prose describing her intimate feelings and thoughts. "What do you think it means to look at the dawn?" the den leader asks the class.

Erika raises her hand.

"Yes, Erika?"

"It means that we see our flag in the morning," the girl proudly announces with confidence.

"Na-uh," Trudel retorts. "It means that I am seeing how important my homeland is to us, because without our land, we have nothing."

"That is very good Trudel and Erika. You both have made astute answers to the same observation." The leader's approach validates both young girls.

"But, I don't understand," Trudel continues.

"What don't you understand?"

"When we were on top of the Reisalpe, I heard an angel whisper in my ear!" Trudel expresses her thoughts without reticence. Some of the girls start giggling.

"Be quiet everyone!" Fräulein Schmidt shouts. The girls immediately stop giggling. "What do you mean by that, Trudel?"

As I said, when we were on top of the mountain, I heard a beautiful voice say, 'Learn as much as you can,' and then the voice went away. I looked around and nobody was there. I didn't even know where the voice came from."

"Hmm, can you be more specific?"

"That's all I heard, just this beautiful voice of a lady," Trudel answers.

Just then, there is a knock on the meeting room door. Father Strobel bursts into the room. The girls immediately become still and quiet. The man apologizes brusquely for interrupting the session. He then approaches the instructor's desk and whispers into her ear.

The adults leave the room and stand in the hallway talking. The bewildered young girls cannot make out what they are saying.

"Maybe it is something very important," Margarita turns and says to Mitzi.

"Of course it is. They left the room, didn't they?" responds Irma in a sarcastic tone.

A few minutes later, the door reopens. Fräulein Schmidt is terribly upset. She faces away from the girls, trying to regain her composure. She walks over to her desk and sits down, avoiding all eyes staring at her. In a calm and restrained manner, she delivers the bad news.

"Hanni of the Hinteralm has just passed away."

Some of the girls gasp in disbelief.

"But, we just made her our grandmother!" Erika shouts. "She's not allowed to die!"

"Father Strobel has just informed me that Hanni died from a massive heart attack. The family has removed her body from her cabin. Her funeral will be in three days at the parish. She will be buried at her family grave in St. Viet an der Gölsen."

Some of the girls start crying and shake their heads in disbelief. Others sit in a silent state of shock. All are confused.

"But, but we were just there," Erika wails, her voice cracking.

"Yes, I know," Fräulein Schmidt, responds evenly. "These things happen."

Suddenly, Trudel remembered the legend of the spring gentian flower in her pocket. Had she caused Hanni's sudden demise by picking it? It is a dreadful thought!

The young leader wonders how to make sense for the children of this very unfortunate twist of events. "I don't know girls. Perhaps, her time has come. Remember what she said to us, that we must live our lives to the fullest and learn as much as we can!"

Just then, Fräulein Schmidt has an epiphany and looks Trudel straight in the eye, remembering the child's comment about the whispering angel's voice.

"I think we will need to end our session here. Everyone may return to your homes early. We will meet next Wednesday at 3:00 pm for our next meeting. On the twentieth, we will have our formal induction ceremony. Now, everyone leave except Trudel," the leader calmly orders.

The leader has a difficult time keeping her composure. She dismisses the girls without their formal closing salute. She is too upset to continue the meeting for Hanni was Fräulein Schmidt's grandmother.

The girls stand, grab their notebooks and haversacks, push in their chairs, and leave the room, all the while looking back at poor Trudel, wondering what she could have possibly done wrong.

Trudel remains frozen in her chair, watching the den leader with her head bowed down, hiding back the tears from her eyes as the girls leave the room. Trudel knows she is in terrible trouble. She knows she will be severely reprimanded for picking the spring gentian flower. She can feel the guilt buried deep in the pit of her stomach. She watches as the leader removes the handkerchief from her pocket, blows her nose, and then looks directly back at her. Trudel decides to take full responsibility for the death of Hanni. She walks towards the leader's desk and pulls the incriminating evidence from her pocket.

Outside, some of the girls are waiting for Trudel while others get on their bicycles and ride home. Irma, Maria, and Mitzi walk across the street and sit down on the bench. They wait for Trudel but she does not appear to be emerging anytime soon from the HJ building.

Irma is the type of girl who wants everything done right away. "This is taking too long," Irma complains. Irma's parents allow their daughter the freedom to make her own decisions by taking guidance and direction from them. Her father is in the SS and her mother is a homemaker. Her parents do not discuss politics with their children, but it is clear that they will never go against the wishes of the new dictatorship. Instead, they discuss the bureaucracy in whispers only, and behind closed bedroom doors.[18]

Irma annoyingly expresses her dissatisfaction with the situation. "Trudel must have done something terribly wrong to be ordered to stay behind." She gets up to leave. "I'm going. I will see you all at school tomorrow."

As dusk falls, Maria and Mitzi patiently wait for their friend. Mitzi finally walks across the street and peers into the window with Maria trailing behind her. All she could see is Trudel sitting at her desk, conversing with the leader.

"It looks like they are still talking. I cannot wait anymore. I'm going home," Mitzi says.

"Me too," says Maria. Together, the girls head off leaving their friend behind. They can only imagine what Trudel is going through.

An hour later, Trudel exits the HJ building and stands outside the main door looking up at the evening sky. All her friends are gone. She is alone, clutching her notebook in her hand, mulling over the conversation she had with her leader. She looks up and sees the vertically hung banner flags on either side of the main entrance fluttering somberly in the wind.

Trying to lift her sprits, Trudel sings the words to her new banner song. "Unsere fahne flattert uns voran." A few people walk by her. Slowly, she starts walking home thinking only about Hanni.

---

[18] Irmgard M. Nagengast-Rosich

Josefa is in the kitchen ironing the clothes when she hears the front door slam. She looks up and sees Trudel pouting. Her mother is a bit surprised when Trudel arrives home a little earlier than expected. The mother sets the iron down on the stove and walks over to Trudel.

"Hanni died today!" Trudel blurts out choking back the tears. "And I killed her!"

"Oh, my little love," Josefa says consoling her daughter affectionately within her sheltering arms.

Trudel wraps both arms around her mother's waist and bawls. "Mama, I am so sorry! We had just met Hanni on the way up to the mountain today. We stopped at the Hinteralm. When we left, she was fine. We sang her a song, she said good-bye to us, and then we climbed to the top of the Reisalpe. I picked this beautiful flower, but I didn't know it was cursed. Then, at our meeting, we found out that she had died! Father Strobel came in and told us," Trudel says through her tears. Trudel is heartbroken. She is experiencing grief for the very first time. In the short time she spent with Hanni, she felt a real grandmotherly bond forming. How could that bond have been shattered so quickly?

"Trudel, do not think for a moment you killed her," Josefa says consoling her precious daughter. "Hanni was a very old woman and today it was her time to leave us. Remember the moments you shared together. Cherish that moment for then she will live forever in your heart." Josefa cradles Trudel in her arms, rocking her back and forth to comfort her in her grief. "Now, why don't you let me take your haversack and you go and wash your face. I will make a nice hot cup of chamomile, and then you can tell me all about your first hiking trip."

Wiping the tears away, Trudel scurries to the washroom and freshens up. Josefa puts the haversack on the chair, moves the kettle onto the stove, and removes the dried chamomile flowers from a jar in the cupboard. Native to the Old World, the chamomile plant has a strong, soothing apple-like scent that emanates from its white-rayed flowers with yellow centers. Chamomile is the most used medicinal herb in Josefa's home.

Trudel returns somewhat refreshed and sits down. Her mother finishes brewing the tea as Trudel recounts her adventurous but sad day. Josefa lets her daughter talk.

Three days later, is Frau Hinterleitner's funeral. A large procession takes place at the parish. Father Strobel pays tribute to a woman who had dedicated her entire life to the mountains. His final farewell is moving.

"Johanna Hinterleitner led a purposeful life. Those who knew her were touched by her wisdom and by her love. She gave freely of herself, and she inspired others to value their own lives. Hanni found fulfillment in the beauty of nature, and especially the bond she had with animals. Her life demonstrates that high morals are achievable by any human being. She was always loving and compassionate toward everyone around her, and neither a World War nor poverty could restrict her joyful approach to life. She was faithful and subordinate. Hanni honored her husband and sons so that they could realize their potential as cattle herders on the slopes of the Reisalpe. She was an excellent dairymaid.

"Our meaning of life comes from within, the loving sacrifices we make for one another, especially for our family, friends, and neighbors. The most difficult circumstances in our lives often bless us with the most profound understandings of our true selves. Johanna Hinterleitner faced obstacles and fear with courage and in the process became a refined, dignified, and unselfish women. We are all very fortunate to have had her as part of our lives.

"Our difficult farewell to Frau Hinterleitner is in fact an opportunity for each and every one of us to learn. The tears we shed today are but the jewels of remembrance, for, it is not how many people will remember Hanni after she has passed, it is how many people's lives she touched while she was alive. That is was is most important to us. She now may rest eternally in peace. Amen."

When the sermon is over, a twelve-piece brass band plays "Nearer My God to Thee." Family pallbearers wheel the catafalque from the church. The quarter horses rear slightly when the coffin is placed inside the wagon. The intricate, ornate woodcarving on the side of the funeral carriage adds a dash of elegance to Frau Hinterleitner's final moments on earth. The coachman pulls tight on the reigns to control the horses. Once the pallbearers inform the driver that the rear carriage doors are closed the coachman slaps his reigns once and the carriage lurches forward.

The vehicle slowly descends the parish road. The somber villagers of Kleinzell bid a final adieu to the grand dairymaid. Out of reverence, the men hold their hats over their hearts. Women in their black funerary garments weep openly and watch their dear departed friend leave her home for the last time. The hearse will now travel eight miles to the cemetery at St. Viet an der Gölsen, where Hanni will be laid to rest next to her deceased husband and son.

Fräulein Schmidt watches Trudel, Franzel, and Josefa as they solemnly walk hand-in-hand back to their home. She still wonders how Trudel knew about her grandmother's death. She will have to keep a special eye on this young girl. She wants to know her secret.

Part Two

Becoming a Member of the Hitler Youth

"I promise to be faithful
To my Führer Adolf Hitler.
I promise obedience
And respect to him.
And to the leaders
He shall appoint over me."

~ Indoctrination Oath of the Hitler Youth ~

Induction Ceremony

TRUDEL ARRIVES AT HER next social meeting dressed in her uniform. Her long, thick black braided hair hangs in front of her shoulders. It is just a few hours after Hanni's funeral and her mother's consoling words has uplifted her spirits. She feels ready to resume her duties.

In this meeting, Trudel and her comrades will rehearse for their formal induction ceremony into the Hitler Youth that will take place in exactly one week. Even though the ceremony will be small, it does not preclude its significance. Hitler's educational regime focuses heavily on the youth for they have not been influenced by dissenting ideas that may contradict his doctrine. Trudel is learning the new paradigm of the larger, overarching system of the Third Reich. For a country to become powerful, all people must conform to these new laws.

The entire social evening is devoted to learning the ceremonial protocol.

"The induction ceremony is your right of passage from childhood into the Hitler Youth," Fräulein Schmidt begins. "Once inducted, you will become fine distinguished young maidens. Through your extensive training, you will become competent enough to contribute to your community. No one will ever put down a young girl and look at her as if she is merely a child! No! You will learn something new every day!"

There is no rest for these girls. Every minute will be saturated with National Socialist ideological training, intended to transform them totally in every aspect of their lives.[1]

It is up to the leaders and the parents of these young girls to comply with the new government regulations. The first requirement is the mandatory salute and song, which opens every meeting. Fräulein Schmidt begins the meeting.

"Now, what can you expect during the induction ceremony? Each one of you will be present and in uniform. Your uniform must be clean, ironed, and neat. Your shoes must be clean and highly polished. Your hair must be in braids. Your hands and nails must be clean and no one is allowed to wear makeup or jewelry. Is this understood?"

"Yes, Fräulein Schmidt," the girls answer.

"Please speak with your parents to help you prepare for this event. If they have any questions, ask them to come and speak with me personally. Now, let's go over the ceremony. When the music starts, I will lead you into the auditorium. You will carry your banners and march directly behind me. I will walk over to this side of the stage, and you will place your banners in the stands along the back side of the stage." The leader points to the floor where the flag stands will be lined up. "While you are facing your flags, you will salute your flag. When I give the command, you will lower your arms, turn around, and face the audience.

---

[1] Lisa Pine – Education in Nazi Germany, p. 18

When I shout the next command, you will take your seats in the front rows. Now, let's walk into the auditorium with our banners and practice what we have learned so far."

The girls grab their banners and walk out from the meeting room. The den leader escorts them down the main hall, and into the expansive and brightly lit auditorium. Fold-up chairs are in place indicating where the girls will be taking their seats. They practice marching into the room and up onto the stage. The girls secure their banners in the stands, salute, and on command, they turn and face the open room. They practice this routine until Fräulein Schmidt feels it is perfectly executed. Not until then, will the girls will take their respective seats off stage.

Standing on stage, the leader resumes her instructions. "When your name is called, you will walk onto the stage, salute, and give a short speech. You must regard that very moment as your first official public pledge to the Führer. Do you remember what we discussed in our last meeting about our personal speeches?" she den leader asks her troop.

Trudel feels a twinge of panic. She prays the leader will review this portion of the meeting she missed. She does not want to ask any of her comrades or appear ignorant.

"Your speech must be in your own words. Your words must be from the heart, so your parents cannot tell you what to say. You must not recite a poem either. Your words must be true, honest, and reflect your loyalty. I encourage you to practice your speech in front of your parents."

Trudel feels relieved that she reviewed this important step. The remainder of the evening is devoted to learning the four parts of the ceremony.

The next week is filled with excitement and camaraderie. Trudel and her companions discuss their speeches and practice their marches, turns, and salutes. This is no time to waste. Every spare moment is filled with rehearsing for this very important ceremony, the first of its kind in Kleinzell. The girls are looking forward to graduating into their new positions.[2]

A week later, on the forty-ninth birthday of the Führer, the high commanders at the Gothic revival castle of Marienburg attend a formal ceremony with their dictator. Millions of people around the country celebrate the ostentatious event through live radio broadcasts.

On this same day, the 20th of April 1938, Trudel is ready for her formal induction into the Young Girls' League of the Hitler Youth. She and her den had fulfilled all three preparatory requirements: the sports challenge, an evening social meeting, and an all-day hike on the Reisalpe. Today, Trudel will become a member of the Hitler Youth and her body and life will no longer belong to her. From now on, her she will belong to the state. From this point forward, she will be groomed to learn the principles of her new ideology.

---

[2] Gertrude Niederhuber

As Trudel leaves the school building with her peers, she observes the entire village preparing a glorious ceremony for her troop. The lengthening shadows of the late afternoon cast dark outlines onto the streets. The mood of the towns-folk subtly transforms and the locals become charged with expectations. Large and small ceremonial flags adorn the shops, homes, and public buildings. Everyone greets each other in a hearty salute. Shopkeepers meticulously wash their store windows and scrub the sidewalks. Men sweep the streets. Women place fresh flowers at the entrances of every building. Flags fly admirably high on the poles in front the HJ building and a fresh aroma emits from the bakery shops. Everyone is in a jovial mood.

As she runs home, Trudel senses the excitement in her tiny village. Everyone in Kleinzell is preparing to celebrate the birthday of the dictator voted into power only thirty-nine days earlier to assume control of the country, Austria.

Josefa was not yet at home from her minimum wage post office job that barely supports her family. Franzel is nowhere to be found either. Trudel flutters around the house preparing for this tremendous event. She wants her mother to be proud of her when she returns home and finds her house clean and spotless. Trudel only has a short time to take care of all her daily chores. She runs upstairs and changes out of her school clothes and into her housedress, apron, and work boots. Around her head, she ties a bandana.

Outdoors, she fetches fresh water for chickens, sweeps out their coop, lays down a bed of fresh straw, throws down some chicken feed, and collects the eggs. She carries the eggs cupped inside her apron and places them gently in a wooden carton inside the pantry.

Next, she grabs the brush and polishing kit, picks up her shoes from the floor, and sits down on the back steps. As she starts to polish, she hears someone playing "Not a More Beautiful Land in This Time" on a stringed instrument.[3] She has never heard a more beautiful sound in her young life! She recognizes the three-quarter time of the stirring Austrian folk song. The tone of the strings resonates through her, uplifting her spirit. She twirls around the garden waltzing to the music and hums to the melody as she polishes the shoes. She brushes the dirt off the soles and sides, taking care to clean in between the seams. Then, she carefully inspects her work and leaves them outside in the sun to dry. In time with the music, she hops up the steps into the house and puts away the polishing kit. Trudel wants so much to return to waltzing in the garden. However, self-discipline precedes her spontaneity and she returns to her chores.

Trudel picks up the area rugs one by one and brings them outside to hang on the clothesline. She grabs the wicker carpet beater, pulls tight at the end of each rug, and whacks it hard. She holds her breath as tiny dust particles take flight, choking the air around her. An uncomfortable layer of grit clings to her.

She leans the carpet beater against the watering pump, spits to clear her mouth, and brushes the minute particles off her arms and clothing. When she is relatively dust free, she takes her beater inside and places it back in the kitchen.

---

[3] Kein schöner Land in dieser Zeit

Then, she grabs the broom and sweeps the floors, ending her task on the front porch and stone walkway. She stows the broom back in the pantry and looks around the living room for her next chore.

Trudel notices that dust has gathered on the furniture. She grabs a bucket, runs outside, and fetches clean water from the hand pump. She dashes back inside the house, making sure to wipe her feet. With the cloth practically wrung dry, she wipes down the furnishings, then goes into the kitchen, and wipes down the cupboards and countertops. Trudel tosses the dirty water out into the grass and goes back to the pump for another clean bucket of water. She runs inside and washes the windows along the front of the house. Then, she finishes by scrubbing the stone steps, making sure to rinse with clean water.

With the house chores complete, she energetically prepares dinner. Trudel scoops up the wicker basket from the pantry along with a pocketknife and goes outside to the vegetable garden. After inspecting the pole beans, she concludes that quite a few are ripe enough to harvest. She firmly grabs the bean with her right thumb and index finger near the top where it connects to the vine. Then, she uses her thumb to pinch the pod loose. She repeats this process and throws a handful into her basket. Once the basket is full, she places her bounty on the steps. She goes inside and grabs the white enamel washbasin from the shelf and returns to sit on the stairs.

Now she can relax and listen to the beautiful music emanating from the neighbor's house. Trudel imagines the notes dancing around her garden. On a tree branch overhead, a crested lark joins in with its melodious whistle. Trudel begins chatting with the bird.

"I wonder who is playing that lovely sound. Have you ever heard of a more beautiful instrument in the world, Mr. Lark? It sounds like it has a hundred strings. Does it have a hundred strings? I wonder. Why have I not heard it before? Maybe, I should go and see who is playing. Should I? No, probably not. I still have chores to do."

She grabs a handful of pole beans from the basket and places them in her apron. One by one, she tops and tails them into the white enamel container, throwing the cut ends to her chickens. She is almost finished when she hears her mother coming through the front door.

"I'm in the back," Trudel yells to her mother.

Josefa hangs her coat on the hall rack, dons on her apron, and emerges out onto the back porch. She gives her daughter a kiss on the top of the head and sits down next to her. There is no need to thank children for doing house chores for it is simply expected of them.

In the traditional Austrian family, the mother teaches the girls practical household skills such as cooking, cleaning, sewing, and knitting. The holidays are celebrated together making arts and crafts for the entire family to enjoy. The father educates the boys in farming, livestock care, hunting, fishing, and logging. This division of labor is the natural way of life in this tiny rural village. The main Austrian family rules are always respected and obeyed for it would be unheard of otherwise. Parents love their children. They instill the values of their heritage.

The father is the head of the household and is the highest authority in the family unit. The mother supports her husband's decision and cares for the family and home. The role of the children is to learn the family trade whether it be farming, baking, keeping shop, managing a guesthouse, millwork, or iron works. Outside the home, everyone in the village is interdependent and each family has a specific social role to fulfill. The families rely on each other for their livelihoods. Villagers appreciate woodcarving and musical skills as special aptitudes, gifts for families who treasure these special crafts.

Without a husband, Josefa has been forced to be both mother and father to her children. To the best of her abilities, the single mother of thirty-seven years must teach her children the necessary life survival skills and basic common sense she had learned in her own youth.

"How was your day today?" Josefa asks.

"It was great! Did you see all the people in town preparing for our ceremony this evening! I am so excited. I cannot wait. I wish the time was here already."

"Your hour will come soon enough, Trudel. Do not rush it. Be patient and enjoy this moment right now."

Her daughter continues to trim the beans.

"By the way, where's your brother?"

"I don't know," she nonchalantly replies.

"When was the last time you saw him?"

"In school...he was playing in the field, or should I say practicing his march with some other boys."

There was a long silence.

"I hear there is a lot planned for you tonight."

"I know. I will be marching in the front row because I am the most important girl. Everyone will see me first!" Trudel straightens herself and proudly raises her chin into the air.

"Your brother and I will be there to watch you too," Josefa, reminds her. "Now, why don't you go inside, start a fire in the stove for me, and get yourself ready. I'll finish up with the beans."

Trudel kisses her mother on her cheek, throws the uncut beans into the basket, jumps up, and runs inside to prepare for this evening's event.

After Trudel dashes inside, Josefa pulls the dreaded document from her apron pocket and reexamines the announcement. The Reich notice requests both of her daughters' presence at the Young Girls' League ceremony this evening. How can she say no? Josefa has no choice but to comply with the new government orders. For over a month, she silently ruminated over ways to prevent her daughters from joining the Hitler Youth movement. Yet, Trudel's fate had been sealed by someone else's hand and Josefa could do nothing to stop it now. It was mandatory for all children of the National Socialist country of Ostmark to be inducted.

Josefa carefully folds the document and slides it back into her pocket. She looks up to the lark who is holding fast to the tree branch singing. She has a broader understanding of the world and her face is masked by her underlying anguish. As she is slicing the beans, she hears "Our Thoughts Are Free," being played on the zither.[4] She knows that soon it will be against the law to play such a song. Meanwhile, she enjoys humming along to the familiar tune for it was dear to her and her husband's hearts.

When she finishes topping off the beans, she folds up the knife and drops it into the pocket of her apron. She brushes herself down, shoos the chickens away, and takes the vegetable basket inside. On the counter, she begins to assemble a simple, light meal of potato pancakes, string beans, and cucumber salad.

Josefa removes the cast iron frying pan from the lower cabinet, places it on the stove, and throws in a teaspoon of lard. She bends down and selects a small, cast iron pot that she fills halfway with water. She adds the beans and places it on the stove next to the pan.

For being a war widow, Josefa Kerschner had received one-thousand Reich marks from her new government. With that windfall, she purchased a bicycle for Franzel, new clothes for Trudel, a brand-new washing machine, livestock, and a new Blaupunkt radio that sits on her kitchen counter.

She tunes in the radio dial just in time to hear the three downward-moving bass notes ushering in the first principal waltz melody to "On the Beautiful Blue Danube." "I must remember to turn on the radio more often," she says to herself. "It's so nice to have music in the house! Every time I hear this song, I just feel like dancing. In fact, I think I will right now. Nobody can see me."

Josefa waltzes into the pantry, where she picks out three large potatoes. Her housedress flows open as she twirls back into the kitchen, perfectly in time to the three-quarter beat. She brushes the dirt off the spuds, pours water from the pitcher into the washbasin, and uses a wet brush to scrubs the potatoes clean. She peels off the skins and puts them aside in a bowl. She places her grater inside a second bowl and quickly rubs the potatoes over the small holes to form short shredded slices. She does not remove the water from the bowl but instead adds flour, eggs, half of an onion, and a pinch of salt, mixing the ingredients together.

She sprinkles droplets of water into the hot frying pan and the beads burst with a sharp *pop*. She lovingly scoops a dollop of the potato mix into the pan. As soon as it hits the hot grease, the edges start to sizzle. Steam rises from the pot of beans, and she removes it from the direct heat, not wanting the vegetables to overcook and become soft, losing their nutritional value.

Wielding her spatula, she peeks under the pancakes. The moment they are ready, she flips them over and gently flattens them down while swaying from side to side in time with the waltz. She thinks back to the wonderful day when she had met her husband, Emmerich. It was the first spring day in 1919, after the Great War. The entire town was celebrating. She had been standing on one side of the beer garden wearing a beautiful hand-made, blue-and-white dirndl. When Emmerich had approached her, he had chivalrously taken her hand and kissed it. She had been nineteen, and he, twenty. The passionate young man had pulled her to him, and they danced. It had been love at first sight.

---

[4] Unsere Gedanken sind frei

Trudel comes running downstairs, dressed impeccably in her BDM uniform, ready to help her mother set the table.

Josefa awakes from her romantic reverie. "Go outside and call for your brother. He should have been home by now."

On the rear porch, Trudel yells at the top of her lungs, "Franzel! Franzel! Time to eat!"

The girl finishes setting the table. She and her mother are about to begin dinner without him when the back door opens and closes with a loud *bang!* Josefa's eight-year-old son runs into the kitchen and settles himself at the table. He appears disheveled and he has dirt all over his face.

"What on earth happened to you?" his mother asks.

"The other boys were showing me how to fight like a real soldier, Mama."

"Remove your clothes this instance and wash up right now! You are not allowed to eat until you are clean! Now go! Move you!" Josefa commands.

Franzel runs into the pantry, strips down, and leaves a heaping pile of dirty clothes on the floor.

"Mom," Trudel bawls. "I just clean in there and he had to go mess it up on me again!"

"You'll deal with it. Just please, eat your dinner now Trudel," Josefa sighs as she picks up her fork again. She refuses to allow her children's petty brawls ruin her precious memories of Emmerich.

Franzel washes his face and runs half-naked into his bedroom. He puts on his black shorts and white-collar shirt, and quickly returns barefoot to the kitchen, and sits down at the table.

"I don't want any trouble from you tonight, Franzel, okay?" Josefa warns. "It is your sister's big evening. When you are finished eating dinner, you will dress properly for Trudel's ceremony. I want you to wear your long breeches, white shirt, a sweater, and your good church shoes. Please make me happy."

"Yes, Mama," Franzel says staring at his steaming plate. "May I eat now?"

"Yes, you may."

Trudel sticks her tongue out at him and he snarls back.

Josefa tries to emanate thoughts of peace and harmony during the ensuing silence. Finally, she asks her daughter, "Did you hear that beautiful music outside earlier today, Trudel?"

"Oh yes, Mama, I did. Wasn't it magnificent? What kind of an instrument was that that I heard? It sounded so — graceful."

"It's called a zither."

"What's a zither?"

"It looks like a cross between a small harp and a guitar. You play it by strumming or plucking the strings. Usually, it sits on a table but some people play it on their lap. The box has a lot of strings that cover the entire top. You play it using both hands."

"That sounds complicated, but amazing."

"It is a beautiful sound, isn't it?"

Trudel thinks for a moment and comes up with an ingenious idea. "Do you think you can buy me a zither?"

Josefa chokes back on her food. "I don't know dear!" she coughs. "Let's see how things go over the next couple of months. You are starting in the League and I'm sure they will keep you very busy playing other musical instruments. You may not have time to practice a zither."

"But, we're supposed to learn how to play an instrument. Fräulein Schmidt asked if any of us knew now to play, and I raised my hand and told her I knew how to play an instrument."

"Oh, you did, did you?" And what instrument did you tell her you knew how to play?"

"Well, I didn't tell her exactly. I just told her that I knew how to play one."

"You did? Well, let's see what happens. Maybe if you are really, really helpful around here, the Good Fairy will bring you a zither."

"Aw Mama, there's no such thing as the Good Fairy," Franzel protests through a mouthful of bread.

"Yes, there is! I know, because I heard one in the garden today," Trudel says in response to Franzel's acquisition.

"What? You're lying," he retorts.

"Children, children! Stop arguing and finish eating. We can't be late this evening for Trudel's ceremony."

After dinner, Franzel forgets his dirty dinner plate on the table and dashes back to his room to change. As Josefa gets dressed, Trudel clears the table and washes the dishes. When everyone is ready, the family leaves and walks to the HJ building now located at the school.

Hand in hand, they walk down the road and hear the rhythmic ostinato sound of the Oom-pah-pah band playing in the outside beer garden at Rupert Scheicl's Gasthaus. The village is in a delightful mood, enjoying the festivities of their new leader's birthday.

As the Kerschner family walks up to the HJ building, they find the mayor is busy greeting everyone. He is an overweight man for his height. He has come dressed in his dapper three-piece, pinstriped, brown suit with his wing-tipped, brown, and white leather, laced up shoes. He wears his NS party member lapel pin on the left side of his chest. He has always had an eye on Josefa since her husband passed away. She despises him.

"And how is the lovely Frau Kerschner this evening?" the mayor asks.

"I am very well, thank you Herr Bürgermeister."

The mayor raises little Franzel's chin, forcing the boy to make eye contact. Franzel quickly extracts himself. "Looks like you have a mighty fine boy here, Frau Kerschner. Within two short years, it will be his time to join. I hear he was practicing his fighting with the other boys today."

"Yes, Herr Bürgermeister, he has" Josefa submissively responds. During these formidable years, women such as Josefa are expected to be docile towards men. It would have been seen as disrespectful if she had given him an earful about what she really thought of Franzel's fighting, especially in public, and here at her daughter's first major ceremony.

"Well, keep up the good work, my son!" The mayor pats Franzel on the head. "We are going to need strong men like you to protect us when we go to war." The Mayor pulls out his gold pocket watch and checks the time.

Trudel pouts at her brother upset that he is the one receiving all the attention on her big evening and not her.

"Yes, Herr Bürgermeister," Josefa says terminating the conversation quickly. Anger wells up inside of her. With all disregard for her welfare, she turns around, looks directly at him, and whispers in his ear. "It might take another two years for my youngest son to join, but in the meantime, you have both my daughters and my other two sons who will be proudly serving their country. How many more children do you need to fight your battles?" She takes Franzel's hand and snatches the handbill from the BDM girl standing next to her. Hiding her distress Josefa turns and walks inside with Trudel trailing behind.

The corridor is filled with people for whom Josefa does not recognize. Mothers articulate the importance of learning as fathers encourage enthusiastic boys to become men. This evening marks the very first induction into the Hitler Youth for all Ostmark children from ten to seventeen years of age. The ten year olds will be inducted first into their respective youth groups. The boys will be sworn into the German Youth and the girls into the Young Girl's League. The fourteen-year-old boys will then be enlisted into the paramilitary organization of the Hitler Youth Proper, while the fourteen-year-old girls will be inducted into the League of German Girls Proper; all groups headed under the Hitler Youth. The boy's upbringing will reinforce masculinity, vitality, and militarism, while the girls will learn their place through femininity, domestic training, and preparing them for their role in society.

Trudel tugs on her mother's arm, eager to check out the auditorium. Josefa allows Trudel to go peek, but only for a minute. Trudel walks over to the auditorium, slowly opens the door, and peeks inside. A few young BDM girls are making the final preparations and do not see Trudel peering inside the room. What she sees is absolutely beholding! Her heart skips a beat as she closes the door and sprints back to her mother who is speaking with Frau Bauer.

Trudel is in shock when she sees her own sister dressed in her JM uniform! Without a hint of discipline, Trudel runs to her long-absent sister yelling, "Anita, Anita!"

Anita turns around and sees her little sister running toward her. She opens her arms wide and accepts the embrace of her baby sister. "Trudel! I can't believe it's really you! I miss you so much!"

Trudel is so relieved to see her sister again. Anita has been staying with her grandparents for over two years working on their farm.

"I miss you too, Trudel. I've been meaning to ride my bicycle over, really, but I've been so busy lately that I haven't had the chance. How are Mother and Franzel?"

Before Trudel could answer, Fräulein Schmidt claps loudly enough to gain everyone's attention. The crowd in the hall settles down to a dead quiet.

"We'll talk more after the ceremony is over, okay?" whispers Anita as she gives her little sister a loving hug.

"Attention, everyone!" Fräulein Schmidt waits a moment for everyone to become silent. "We will shortly being the ceremony. All girls must come and follow me. The parents may take their seats inside the auditorium now."

Trudel feels a twinge in her gut for not saying a proper good-bye to her mother. She had thoroughly rehearsed it in her mind what she would say and do when this time came. Now, she feels a strange sense of loss. This is the last time her mother will see her as a small child. She wanted to give her a hug and salute her before joining her group. Now, that will not happen. The thought quickly fades from her mind, as she feels exuberant for bumping into her sister at the ceremony.

Josefa looks around and sees her two daughters together, walking toward their respective BDM groups. Even though she does not approve of her children joining the Hitler Youth, she is happy her daughters have reconnected once again. Maybe they will be spending more time together, she thinks.

The crowd meanders into the illustrious, transformed auditorium as the young girls walk with their leader into the adjacent room. The parents gasp in awe when they witness the display of colors and pageantry! Never before have they seen such a theatrical display of fanfare.

Josefa sits with Franzel in the front row behind the officials. Next to her are Frau Bauer and her husband. Frau Bauer's daughter, Margarita, is ninth in line in the new Niederdonau JM troop # 527. The parents talk among themselves about the appearance of the room. They wonder where the money came from to put on such a lavish display and how they were able to execute this ceremony in such a short amount of time. Patiently, they wait for the ceremony to begin.

Forty wooden seats for the inductees are arranged ten across and two rows deep on either side in the front of the stage. The girls will be seated on the right and the boys on the left. As the new inductees wait in the other room, the audience continues to fill with villagers until there are no more seats. Everyone is dressed in his or her best attire.

When the auditorium is nearly full, the mayor and his wife take their reserved seats at the front of the audience. Next to them are the chief of police, the city council members, the local doctor, the local vet, community organizers, and their wives.

In the adjacent room, the girls are gathering on one side while the boys filed in along the opposite wall. The leaders stand with their troops and review the final preparations, answering any last-minute questions. The children hold their banners over their shoulders, waiting for the signal from the German Youth Den Leader, Herr Adler, who will be leading the contingent of ten-year-olds. Herr Adler is only sixteen.

The distinguished HJ Squad Leader, Herr Wulf, is seventeen. He leads the HJ Proper. The red-and-white lanyard worn from his left shoulder to his left breast pocket characterizes him as the Major Junior Leader.[5] The girls quietly admire his youthful masculinity, though they giggle at the very mention of his name. Herr Wulf stands tall and handsome in his regalia, his blond hair, and blue eyes revealing him as a true member of the Aryan race. His black neckerchief, shorts, belt, and cross-strap, complement his uniform. His highly polished black shoes and his rigid-red-piped peaked cap featuring the rhombus badge and the party cap eagle together with his woven shoulder boards on his kaki shirt clearly announce his authority. His uniform is decorated with the yellow HJ regional insignia and with a red-white-red Swastika armband. The uniform for the younger boys is similar, although they wear brown ankle books, no lanyards, or armbands.

Foremost stands Herr Adler, followed by the DJ flag bearers, drummers, trumpeters, and his troop. In succession follows Herr Wulf and his HJ troop, followed by the young JM den leader Fräulein Schmidt and her troop. The newly appointed BDM Leader, Fräulein Brückner, leads Anita's group.

Trudel anxiously waits for the ceremony to start. Finally, the den leader shouts "Line up and stand at attention!" The girls stand silent and immobile, ready for their marching orders. Trudel feels her tense heart beating louder with every second that passes.

Herr Adler announces, "Troops! Fall in line! Company, standstill."

With a quick slap of the stick on the red-and-white flaming pageantry drums, the cadence begins. The crisp articulation of the drumbeats radiate throughout the building.

In the auditorium, the parents hear the beginning of the ceremony and turn toward the rear. The solemn horns fanfare from the hallway grows louder as the parade of youths near.

Two Hitler Youth cadets simultaneously open the doors and the procession enters the auditorium. The entire audience stands.

Josefa can see only the tops of the flagpoles from the various troops. First, she sees the double black and white Sigrune, followed by the DJ troop flag, and the JM/BDM banners. The troops march into the room singing,

> Our banner flutters before us!
> In the future, we take man for man
> We march for Hitler, by night and by necessity
> With the flag of the youth, for freedom and bread
> Our banner flutters before us!
> Our banner represents the new era
> And the flag will lead us into eternity
> Yes, our banner means more to us than death![6]

---

[5] David Littlejohn, p. 67
[6] Vorwärts! Vorwärts!

Josefa is appalled! Angrily, she thinks to herself, "What do they mean the flag means more to them than death? Who wrote this song? Why do they have to sing this song? They barely understand what's really going on. They are adopting those words unthinkingly! Ostmark is not at war. Are we going to war again? With whom do I need to speak? If I complain, will they take me away again?" She feels a sense of hopelessness.

The band marches to the side of the room as the group finishes singing their official banner song. The HJ leaders move to the side of the stage as the children place their banners into their respective stands.

It is an unbelievable site to behold. The massive red party flag looms high above center stage. Directly in front of the flag, propped up on the table in a large wooden frame is a portrait of their commander and chief. Along either side of the table cement blocks act as plinths to hold the flower vases, symbolizing the rebuilding of a nation and its flourishing economic recovery. In the front of the table are assortments of small shrubbery to conceal the empty space beneath. A second swastika flag drapes over the front edge of the stage amid a beautiful arrangements of flowers. Two small Austrian black pine trees in wooden planters accent the front center aisle between the two sets of chairs.[7]

DJ leader Adler shouts "About-face!" In one synchronized motion, the children turn to face the front of the room, and salute. Trumpets blare and the drums accent the filler beats to the introduction of the National Socialist German Workers' Party song. Everyone in the room salutes as the children sing.

> The flag is high!
> The ranks are firmly closed
> The SA march with quiet, steady step
> Comrades shot by the Red front and reactionaries
> March in spirit within our ranks. [8]

At the end of the anthem, each leader gives their order for their inductees to walk off stage. As Trudel descends the steps, she locates her mother in the audience. She beams and Josefa responds in kind.

The JM and BDM leaders file off stage and take their respective seats. It would be some time before the young girls' names are called.

Herr Adler opens the ceremony. "We gather here this evening to induct our boys and girls into the Hitler Youth! This is a turning point in their lives. We are be proud of their accomplishments and for their service to our great country.[9] I introduce you to Mayor Kunze."

---

[7] Professor Randall Bytwerk – Youth Ceremonies
[8] Horst Wessel Song
[9] Professor Randall Bytwerk – Youth Ceremonies

The audience applauds as the rotund mayor rises from his seat. He bows to the villagers and walks on stage. The DJ leader salutes the politician and withdraws himself to the left side of the stage.

"In a deep voice, the mayor begins. "I want to take this opportunity to thank everyone for attending this glorious evening. Our young leaders have worked very hard to train their youth. We want our youth to be strong, dependable, and obedient. They are the new bearers who are loyal to their country and to our Führer! What the Hitler Youth show you today is a result of their hard work. We should be very proud of them for their accomplishments. This is who we are and never again will we hold our heads down in shame. We can be proud to call ourselves Germans. There is no shame in being a German!"

The mayor then leads the audience in their national hymn.

> Germany, our holy word, eternal.
> Be you forever blessed.
> Holy are your lakes, holy your forests
> Holy your silent heights
> Down to the green sea.[10]

Herr Wulf, steps forward. He salutes Mayor Kunze. The mayor returns the salute then takes his seat. In a commanding voice, Herr Wulf addresses the adults, "Young people stand here today on the threshold of their lives!"[11]

The drummers slap a quick three-pace press roll that sharply ends with a tap stroke on the drumheads, echoing throughout the hall.

"We enter joyfully through the open door. We face our fate courageously. For a while, fate defeats the cowardly. God helps the brave!"[12]

In unison the drums roll.

"We the youth are the bridge from ancestors to grandchildren. With faith and self-confidence, our high spirits will lead the way. This is the new beginning of our lives! Our young people are not grown up yet. However, we will be the ones to instruct them in how to build character and become self-efficient. Today, these children are mature youths. You can see it in their performance. They show their loyalty by their obedience and discipline. They show their duty as they follow the law of the world!"[13] Herr Wulf's voice echoes throughout the hall.

Herr Wulf then addresses the young boys and girls league. "Until now you have been a child. If you misbehaved, you did not have to bear the responsibility. Your father or mother made good on the damage, and they forgave you. Now you will increasingly encounter people who will not forgive your bad behavior as your mother and father did. They will hold you responsible. If you have been well behaved and did whatever your father and mother told you to do, you must

---

[10] Eberhard Wolfgang Möller - "Germany Holy Word"
[11] Professor Randall Bytwerk – Youth Ceremonies
[12] Ibid
[13] Ibid

117

realize that you will increasingly encounter situations in which your father and mother will no longer be able to help you. You will have to make your own decisions. If you leave school, you will begin an apprenticeship, or if you continue school, you will have a future occupation in mind. You will move from the German Youth to the Hitler Youth or from the Young Girls to the League of German Girls. You will leave the circle in which you had become the oldest, and join a new one in which you will again be the youngest. You face something new in every direction. Whether in your apprenticeship or in further schooling, that is in your professional training, or in your personal lives, greater demands will be placed on you young men and women. How well you meet these demands will determine the remainder of your life. If you obey the laws of life you will succeed, and you will become useful men and diligent women. If you fail to meet life's demands, you will face a shipwreck. That is the meaning of this ceremony, of your transition. You must decide here between the good and the bad. Life is uncertain. Hard fate may strike some of you perhaps even destroy you. We are defenseless against such blows of fate, but they are rare. In most cases where life does not go well, it is a matter of personal failure. Each person has his good and bad aspects. Our will determines whether the good or the bad wins. That is the meaning of this ceremony. Here, before yourselves and us all, before your people and your Führer, and before God Almighty, you will pledge that the good will win in you, and that you want to become decent German people.[14]

Herr Wulf now addresses his passionate rhetoric to the young adolescents in the Hitler Youth Proper. "Hitler Youth and League of German Girls! If you have such teachers, leaders and comrades in the future, and use all your strength as well, the Führer's hopes for you will be fulfilled. You will become a hard, loyal, industrious, and successful generation. We will not need to be ashamed of you before the past or the future generations of our people. This is our proud hope and certainty we can give you in this solemn hour. The affirmation you will now give is not only spoken, but also realized[15]

"Today, you live in the free and strong country of Ostmark which is now part of Germany! Today, you will grow up in peace and have a very secure and structured future. You must hold this dear to you and never give it away.

"You must never lose sight of the promise our Führer has given to us, one people, one empire, one leader!"

"Within a few short years after becoming our leader, our Führer has rebuilt Germany! Beforehand, over seven million citizens were unemployed, and twenty-one million people were depended upon public assistance.[16] Industry has been reawakened, unions are disbanded, and the autobahn is built! In less than two years after taking office, our Führer reduced imported goods coming into the country, grew our economy, our military forces, and completely liquidated unemployment by putting over twenty-two million people back to work.

---

[14] Professor Randall Bytwerk – "Youth Ceremonies"

[15] Ibid

[16] Professor Randall Bytwerk, "We Owe it to the Führer"

"Before our Führer, our parents and their parents before them were divided into classes and groups, and Germany was defeated. Back then, someone who got his hands dirty by working honestly and industriously for his people was held in contempt by those who earned their money in other ways. German boys and girls, you must never again let Germany be divided into classes and groups, into parties and religious denominations. The community you had as Pimpfe or Young Girls you must also have as members of the Hitler Youth or the League of German Girls, and further on when you put on the uniform.[17]

"Even when the day comes that the Führer is no longer with us, you must be comrades for your entire life, and must respect every citizen who works, or who as a soldier is ready to give his life for Germany, and you must strive to become such a worker or soldier. The life before you is not a matter of good or bad behavior, or parental punishment, or cowardly behavior to avoid parental punishment, but rather it is a matter of proving yourself as a man or a woman. You will not have this strength if you do not have a living faith in God during your entire life. However, it must be a faith that leads you to serve God through deeds, not words. It must be a faith that makes you consider yourself God's tool, called through your work, your struggle, your creation of new life, to serve the eternal maintenance of order, justice, and life itself in this world. You must never feel yourself a servant or slave of God, but rather a fighter for God. One gives a comrade the greatest joy when one gives him a weapon in the certainty that he will never use it against us, but rather uses it to defend that, which is holy to us all. One does not give a weapon to a fool! God gave us weapons. The creative strength in our hands with which we work, the creative strength in our minds, with which we learn to seek and research, the strength in our hearts and souls, with which we believe, the strengths with which we create new life, these are the weapons God has given humanity. We would be fools if we did not use these weapons to work, fight, create order, and maintain life, but rather served life ill because we were lazy, cowardly, disloyal, and immoral. We would then be truly pitiable creatures before God![18]

"We must here give parents, teachers and the leaders of these boys and girls our thanks. When these children were born, they carried in their blood the ability to become German boys and girls, and eventually German men and woman. However, when they were born, they could neither speak nor think, nor did they believe anything. We thank the mothers, fathers, teachers, and the leaders of the German Youth and Young Girls that they raise these children such that they are now mature enough to stand here before the flags of their people and make an affirmation to Germany. The methods of education and leadership they will experience in the coming years will be different from those of their childhood. You know that you have a great responsibility, also, in the coming years to educate

---

[17] Professor Randall Bytwerk, "Youth Ceremonies"
[18] Ibid

and lead these young people. Fulfill that responsibility as well as you have ful-filled those in the past.[19]

"When you become a leader in the Hitler Youth, you will possess the deci-siveness in which to lead. In the hours that you are sitting there, in the stillness all alone, do you have the answers to the questions? Can you then overcome the challenges that are in front of you? That is how your parents brought you up and how you thank your comrades. Therefore, look into the future and ask which one it shall be!

"In this hour, we give to our parents, our teachers, our Führer, to the youths, the boys, and the girls. We stand by them and with them. We acknowledged you youths when you came into this world. You have the same blood as your parents. This is the proof that your parents raised you in their strong beliefs. Now, you stand here, in front of the flag, in front of the people, and in front of your leaders. You now have the knowledge of Germany!

"Therefore, German mothers and fathers, young people, boys and girls, you are thankful for the method of your parents' upbringing. Now the youth will lead the youth. In the coming years, we have a responsibility to lead our young people, to give them the responsibility to know their self-worth by learning from the Führer's labor. They have the ambition, the determination, and the inner strength! No matter where you go, this is the way it will always be!

"However, we must also give this warning: If you do not stand together, but become disunited, if you are not loyal, but disloyal, if you do not work and are cowardly, you will fall into terrible chaos and Germany will collapse. God will have no home in Germany any longer."[20]

The powerful words resonate moving the souls of the villagers. Together, the HJ youth stand and sing, "Where We Stand stands our Loyalty."

> Where we stand, stands our loyalty,
> Our step is the order,
> We march after the flag,
> Therefore, we can never go wrong,
> When we sing, we are loyal,
> It is bigger than our song,
> Very quietly, she carries our flag,
> She stands strong.[21]

From the audience, Franzel watches in envy as Herr Wulf calls the roster of names. The young boys walk onto the stage, recite his speech, salute, and then receive his official Hitler Youth membership certificate. The boy shakes the hand of their leader, salutes, walks to their banner, turns, and stands in front of it.

---

[19] Professor Randall Bytwerk, "Youth Ceremonies"
[20] Ibid
[21] Wir Mädel Singen, "Wo Wir Stehen, Steht die Treue," p. 80

Once all the young DJ's names have been called, it is time to honor the young girls. Trudel sits on the edge of her chair, waiting for her name to be called.

"Gertrude Kerschner!" the young girls' den leader shouts over the crowd.

Trudel proudly marches up the stairs and onto the platform. She salutes her troop leader, turns, and faces the audience prepared to recite her speech. Instantly, however, she freezes at the sight of the enormous crowd staring back at her. She had *no* idea so many people would come to hear her speak!

The room falls silent. Josefa holds her breath waiting for her daughter to begin. Someone coughs. Trudel stands rooted to her spot, unable to breathe. She can feel her heart beating heavily inside her chest. Her legs begin to weaken. She is petrified to move.

Fortunately, she spots her mother. Josefa's soft eyes are encouraging. Trudel glances over at her sister, Anita, who is sitting with her comrades. Still feeling apprehensive, the ten year old softly begins, "I, Gertrude, forth born in the Kerschner family in Kleinzell, will be loyal and faithful to my Fatherland and to my Führer. Before our new country was born, we were very poor with no home. Then, things changed." Trudel's tempo in her speech beings to speed up. "Now, we have a new home, I got a brand-new white shirt, and mother got a real job. We all have food on our table. My comrades and I learned how to make our banners. We climbed on the Reisalpe together and met our new honorary grandmother, Hanni, who died last week. That was a very sad time for all of us. We practiced very hard for this day. I hope we can continue to move forward in our new lives. I ask myself what it will be like when I am older. Our Führer has made a better world for us. If he can do this in such a short amount of time, imagine what else he can do for us and what we can do for him! All I know now is that I can keep my father's promise and for his wish to be fulfilled."

Everyone in the room is silent.

Silence after her speech was not what she imagined. She pictured a roaring applause. With nothing more to say, Trudel spontaneously spouts out "Did I do well, Mom? Are you going to buy me my zither now?"

The audience breaks out in laughter and applauds. Blushing, Trudel salutes her leader, accepts her membership certificate, salutes again, and walks to stand in front of her banner.

"That's my daughter," Josefa whispers to Frau Bauer while nodding her head. The mother wonders what promise Trudel has made to her father before he died.

After the young girls are initiated into the League of German Girls, they briefly remain on the stage for a group photograph before returning to their seats. The HJ and the BDM Proper are then inducted. When their conscription is completed, the photographer snaps their picture, and they return to their seats.

Herr Wulf then takes the stage. In a resonating voice, he requests the Hitler Youth in the room to stand. As one, the newly inducted youths stand. Josefa is startled. The auditorium floor shakes like an earthquake! The youths raise their arms in salute for their ultimate pledge.

"I promise in the Hitler Youth, to always do my duty,
In love and faithfulness, to the leader and to our flag,
So help me God."[22]

Herr Wulf concludes the ceremony. "All young boys and girls have now celebrated their change of life. We acknowledge our German people. They are of the will of God. They are in this world now. Where they fight for the people and when they die for the people, they will do it under the will of God. Their deeds are to us their holy obligation. [23] The boys and girls have reached a new pivotal point in their lives and we believe in them. We acknowledge that God gave them their strength. Therefore, the life of our people will always be and they will forever protect our country. We can succeed in our fight or if we die; only God can make that decision."

The Hitler Youth resound together 'We acknowledge this pledge."

"We want you to be clean and self-respectful. We want you to fight for our empire. The German land is our homeland. From this day forward, we will never forget that we are Germans."[24]

The Hitler Youth respond, "We acknowledge this pledge."

"We start a new year for our people! Wherever we fight, work, and grow, we are one! We are very blessed in our strong feelings of this experience! We are very proud of our new youths! We do everything for our people's community! This ceremony has now concluded. Be with God and be with our Führer. We end this first celebration with acknowledgement and greetings to our Führer, Adolf Hitler. Seig Heil!"

Everyone stands and salutes with "Seig Heil"[25]

The band plays the "Horst Wessel Song" as the newly inducted troops file back on stage to remove their banners. The marching band leads the troops on ahead, as the leaders usher the youths from the auditorium into the reception hall.

Anita and Trudel find each other in the hallway and embrace. Breathlessly, they reminisce about the ceremony. Josefa comes over and embraces her daughters. Franzel is standing next to them too, but he is busy observing the other villagers as they congratulate their sons and daughters.

"Here, Mama, look at my certificate." Trudel proudly unrolls her JM membership certificate. The strength of the country represents itself on the parchment by the right-facing open-winged eagle clutching in its claws a sword and a hammer. The symbol embossed on the document symbolizes patriotism, loyalty, and sacrifice. The text reads, "I promise to always do my duty with love and

---

[22] Reinhold Sautter, p. 30
[23] Professor Randall Bytwerk – "Youth Ceremonies"
[24] Ibid
[25] Ibid

loyalty to our Führer and our flag. Commitment into the Hitler Youth—20 April 1938—Gertrude Kerschner, was on this day committed by the Führer."

"Here, Mama, look at mine." Anita proudly hands her document to her mother.

"I am very proud of both of you girls, very proud." Josefa pulls the two girls close to her bosom and her daughters return the affectionate embrace. "This evening is special, and it is only for you. Now, run along with your comrades and finish with your ceremonial bonfire. Franzel and I will watch your parade from the street. I'll take these certificates home for safe keeping." Josefa hugs her daughter's hard one more time.

The leaders call their troops outside to regroup.

Josefa does not want to let go of her little girls.

The children fall into line with their comrades and walk outside to the rear of the building. As the girls fall into line and then disappear around the rear of the building, Josefa feels weary and wishes they were safe already at home in bed.

The beginning of the night procession is signaled by the lighting of the torches. The first torch is ignited at the front of the column. The blazing head of each torch then touches the one behind, and so on, until the fire has been passed through the entire column. Trudel lines up in her column and holds tightly to her torch.

On command, the flagpoles raises onto the shoulders of the youths. The drums beat, the trumpets blare, and the next song begins.

In step, forty children and their leaders march from the rear of the HJ building out onto Kleinzell Street. It is a grand exhibition. As in a military procession, they march past the waiting crowds towards the open field. The smoke from their fiery torches evokes a sense of safety and camaraderie. The townspeople marvel at the powerful procession. Sealing the girls' induction into service, the fire ritual will sear into their memory marking their intention to make the HJ their permanent home.

In anguish, Josefa watches her two daughters file past on the way to destiny. She sighs and turns away. Taking young Franzel's hand in hers she plods home, remembering happier days.

"Our will and our belief
Are together in unity.
We have eternal happiness
For the creation of life,
For we are in complete
Synchronicity."

~ Annemarie Leppien ~
Country Service Year Camp Leader
Schleswig - Holstein

Duties of the BDM Girls

THE INDUCTION CEREMONY marks the youth's rites of passage into a totalitarian movement where the state recognizes no limits to its authority. It strives to regulate every aspect of the family's private and public life wherever feasible. As is in the case with Trudel and Anita, they hold their torches high when they enter the open field behind the HJ building. A tremendous bonfire welcomes all new participants. The youths circle the massive bonfire and begin singing their patriotic anthem.

> Wake up, wake up Germany!
> You've slept long enough,
> Consider what God has appealed to you,
> Which He created for you,
> Consider what God has given to you,
> And you trust his highest pledge
> So you must wake up well!![1]

Herr Wulf steps up to address the youths. His articulation is clear and strong. "Tonight, Austria has come home! Tonight, you have been formally inducted into the Hitler Youth! Tonight, you are committed to give your will, your strength, and your lives to the Führer! Tonight, our hearts burn like these flames! From now on, we will carry the torch inside of us, and carry out our duties with obedience and confidence!"

Trudel's innocent identity is merging with the authoritarian movement. She is now, an integral part of the new German nation and its eight million young people strong. She now belongs to the State.

"Youths!" Herr Wulf continues. "You are the future soldiers and mothers of the Fatherland! Youths! From now on, you will always perform your deeds with loyalty, dedication, and commitment! To the heavens this fire burns. The earth creates what is new and burns away the old. Tonight, we stand on sacred ground! This is your true path! Youth! You will walk with purpose and face the morning sun. We are a holy spring in this new German countryside. Our beliefs create the new and wipe out the old! Never shall our words grow cold in us. We are born again. Out of this darkness, our pennants announce that Germany is awake! We will always keep moving forward. We will always keep our blood pure. We will always stay young, for that is our birthright. We are the new leaders who vow to our Führer absolute loyalty to our graves!"

---

[1] Wir Mädel Singen, "Wach auf, du deutsches Reich," p. 20

Such egalitarian spirit and camaraderie are the cornerstones of the new Ostmark Hitler Youth as its members blindly step boldly into their new future.

After the ceremony, Trudel and Anita walk home arm-in-arm, chatting. Anita feels elated that she will be able to spend the night at her sister's house before having to leave the next day and resume her duties with her own troop.

All is peaceful at the Kerschner home. The house is dark and when the girls enter, they can hear their mother snoring. Not daring to wake her, the girls tiptoe upstairs into Trudel's bedroom. They sit on the bed and share their experiences of the past few years. Anita voices her discontent when Uncle Karl chopped up her skis and used them for firewood.

Trudel talks about her amazing hike on the Reisalpe. She grabs her JM journal from the table and shows it to Anita. Anita is impressed with her writings.

There is a deep, heart-filled love between the two. Tonight, their sisterly bond has reawakened and they vow never to break it again.

Anita's stomach starts grumbling. "Hey! Is there anything to eat?"

"Sure! Mama bought some fresh bread from the bakery this morning and it tastes so good! How about slicing up a few pieces for us?"

"All right," Anita agrees. "I'll go downstairs and get us a few pieces."

"And make sure you put lots of butter on mine with just a little bit of salt and pepper, okay?"

"Okay."

While Anita pops downstairs, Trudel quickly jots down her memories.

"Today I became a young girl in the Hitler Youth. It was one of the most exciting days in my life! The ceremony was overwhelming. My sister and I, and our comrades stood in a large hall that was decorated beautifully with banners and flowers. All the parents came out to watch. Our leaders gave speeches and then they called our names. I gave a speech too! Everyone loved my speech and they clapped afterwards. That gave me a thrilling feeling inside my tummy. I proudly received my membership certificate and my sister got hers too. The drummers played, the trumpets blared, and everyone sang our national anthem! For the first time, I held a burning torch, and we all marched onto the field. We circled an enormous bonfire where Herr Wulf gave a speech. We all sang songs. Now, I am part of the Hitler Youth, along with my sister. I hope she and I can spend more time together because I miss her very much.

Anita scurries upstairs with a plate full of bread and butter. Trudel and her sister will stay up close to dawn, talking, laughing, and remembering old times.

The next morning is very difficult for the two sisters. Trudel is at a loss when her grandparents, Johann and Anna Kandlhofer, arrive in their horse-drawn wagon to take Anita back to their village in Halbach. Trudel cries as she runs down the road, waving her white handkerchief until Anita is out of sight. Each girl will be heading on her own path to serve her country. They will not see each other again for another four years.[2]

Trudel has little time to feel sad. Each day is filled with household chores, school, and the Young Girls' League activities. Monday through Friday, she is at school from eight o'clock in the morning until four o'clock in the afternoons. Wednesday afternoon is reserved for the Young Girls' social meeting, as Saturdays are reserved for their four-hour sports training. On Sundays, Trudel helps her mother with the chores on the family farm.

Every night, Josefa reviews her children's school homework. Her signature at the bottom of each page proves to the teachers that she is being a responsible parent by overviewing the children's homework. By nine o'clock the children are safe, tucked away in their beds, and fast asleep.

With the extra money Josefa received from the Reichsbank, she purchased her first washing machine and a second-hand zither for Trudel. She bought a brand new bicycle for Franzel. For herself, she bought two baby Cornwall black pigs, four white domestic geese, four white Peking ducks, two European rabbits, and two Angora rabbits. She is even able to start construction on her new home![3]

Trudel loves the new additions to the family and plays with them often. She grows attached to the animals by bestowing them with names. She calls the two geese Hansel and Gretel and her two pigs Thick and Skinny. She is unaware that her mother is breeding the livestock as barter and will use the meat, fur, feathers, and eggs to trade for straw, milk, flour, and music lessons.

Every day Josefa makes it a special point to spend time with her children. Monday is family day and the three walk together through the countryside or stay in and read books during inclement weather.

Tuesday is music day. In lieu of payments to the music teacher, Josefa barters a dozen fresh eggs per one-hour lesson. Trudel loves learning how to play her zither and zealously practices every night for at least one hour before bed.

On Wednesdays, Trudel looks forward to participating in her JM social meetings. The curriculum changes every month to synchronize with the ideological training and traditional holiday events such as Easter, the Führer's birthday, Walpurgis Night, May Day, Mother's Day, Summer Solstice, Harvest Thanksgiving Day, Advent, Winter Solstice, Christmas, and the New Year. Otherwise, Trudel's course of study remains consistent with the JM teachings including learning about home economics, personal hygiene, arts and crafts, serving within the community, learning ten new songs every month, hiking, playing games, and sports, all the while working towards her JM Proficiency Badge.

On Thursdays, Josefa teaches her daughter how to cook. Then, on Friday, Trudel learns how to bake.

Four hours are reserved every Saturday afternoon to participate in the Young Girls' sports afternoons, while Sunday morning is reserved for church services before returning home and helping her mother by working on the farm.

---

[2] Anita Leugner
[3] Franz Kerschner

Since Sunday's religious services compete for youth day, the HJ try to lure the children away into alternative Sunday activities. For Trudel, however, it is not mandatory to attend the Sunday HJ events due to the large amount of work she needs to do around the home.

Twice a month Trudel is responsible for washing the laundry. Household chores coincide with the JM home economics training. She will also voluntarily assist other mothers within the community and help with the household chores, care for the children, collect for the winter relief, even help the farmer with their harvest, or collect medicinal herbs in the fields.[4]

As Trudel helps with the laundry, Josefa has the chance to prepare a meal large enough to last the family a few days. If Trudel has all her chores and home-work completed, and if there are no youth activities, Trudel can then diligently spend more time practicing her zither. Nevertheless, today is laundry day.

It is no small feat to wash the clothes. Before Josefa purchased her new outdoor washing machine, the family arduously washed the clothes in the heated washtub outside or in the stream at the end of town. Now, washing the laundry has become much easier!

This new all-metal machine stands three feet tall on four legs. Inside the diffuser box, a drum rotates whenever the handle is turned. The drum features a latched door that opens, allowing the user to drop the clothes inside the cylin-drical container. Underneath the unit is a firebox. Once finished, the water drains onto the ground via an orifice at the bottom of the washbasin.

Trudel collects water from the hand pump and places it in the diffuser box. She stuffs newspaper, kindling, and a few pieces of coal into the firebox, then ignites the lot. Once the water warms, she adds ash lye soap and sets to turning the drum's wooden handle. This allows the powdery substance to mix evenly with the warm water.

Trudel darts inside, grabs the wicker laundry basket, and places it on the table next to the wringer. Using a washboard and a coarse haired bristle brush, she removes the heavily laden stains from the fabric before cooking the laundry inside the machine. She always makes sure to add the least soiled clothes first. After latching the lid, she starts turning the handle. The entire family takes turns, agitating the clothes in the rotating drum.

After some time has passed, Trudel uses a long wooden tong to remove the steaming clothes. It takes all her strength to lift the heavily weighed down clothes and place them into the cool water basin. She continually stirs the clothes in the washtub until they cool down. Then, she and Franzel play the wringing game. They remove the material from the basin and twist the fabric as tight as they can in opposite directions thereby releasing excess water. Finally, they help each other roll the laundry through the hand wringer before hanging it up on the clothesline to dry.

Trudel's mother brings the palliasse outside and removes the straw, leaving the sack for washing. She turns it inside out to make sure there are no straw

---

[4] Bund Deutscher Mädel – "The Years 1932 until 1945"

fibers clinging to the material. Josefa slowly lowers the sack into the simmering water. Due to its size, only one mattress sack can be washed at a time. When the water becomes too hot, Trudel carefully pours fresh cold water into the drum. With her mother's assistance, she removes the large sack, rinses it out, and then squeezes it through the wringer. Trudel then helps her mother hang the rest of the clothes on the line to dry. Before evening sets in, her last chores are to iron all the clothes and stuff the bed sack with straw.[5]

Involving children in daily household tasks has a positive impact on them later on in life. Not only do these activities release a child's pent-up energy, but daily chores builds their self-esteem, teaches them to stay focused, and prepares them for adulthood. Trudel feels she is an important contributing member of her family for she is taking on the responsibilities of a mature, young woman.

Without her knowing it at this time, Trudel's participation in the Young Girl's League is preparing her for an eight-month long elite rural educational program in the countryside called Country Service Camp (Landjahr Lager). This camp is meant to educate specially chosen girls to become responsible young woman who are physically fit and mentally ready to serve their people in any place where they may be needed. Conscription for Country Service is an honor.[6] Over the next three years, Trudel proves to her leaders that she is a dependable and hardworking Jungmädel.

One way to prove her merit is by earning the JM Proficiency Badge. It is minted in the shape of the letters JM on a plain, red-ribbon background within a sterling silver frame. In order to receive the clasp, Trudel will have to pass various tests within the span of one year starting after her twelfth birthday.[7] These tests include first aid, nursing, political knowledge, and most importantly, physical training that includes sports, calisthenics, and athletics. It is the pride of every young girl to achieve this merit badge through her dutiful performance.[8]

The exciting new world that lies before Trudel is opening into new vistas of opportunities and experiences that will feed her sense of adventure. For Trudel, these activities look like a lot of fun and she wants to participate. On the other hand, through careful guidance, the Reich Youth Leadership will dictate and shape the minds of the young in the four iron pillars of National Socialism until the time they complete their membership the Young Girls League (BDM).[9] The four iron pillars include race, military training, leadership, and religion.

The girls in the JM are being encourage to be brave, devoted, comradely, obedient, and honorable.[10] In and so much as comradeship is rooted in the sense of collective action to advance to a higher aim, the leaders view building esprit de corps as the key to building morale. Trudel shares this collective identity with

---

[5] Franz Kerschner

[6] Bund Deutscher Mädel – Country Service Year Pamphlet

[7] Ibid – The Jungmädel Proficiency Badge

[8] Gretel Reisinger

[9] Reinhold Sautter, p.166

[10] Sommerlage und Heimabendmaterial für die Schulungs

her group. For as her education progresses, she gains the valuable practical common sense knowledge. She takes pride in her training and does not view her membership as a burden, nor does she defy authority figures. She listens well and willingly performs her duties as is required of her. Above all, she understands how she can contribute and become a productive member of society. Trudel extrapolates from the National Socialist ideology that which interests her and disregards the rest.

The most important vehicle for socialization in the JM is the weekly social meeting for which their ideological education and training in the National Socialist Worldview takes place.[11] Afternoon social meetings are filled with stories about loyalty, honor, courage, and obedience.

During her first year in the JM, Trudel learns about the Führer, German sagas, Grimm's' fairytales, Germanic gods and heroes, the Saga of Niebelung and Gudrun. During her second year, Trudel learns about the great figures of German history. During her third year, she learns about the men and women battling for Germany. When Trudel is thirteen and in her final year of the JM, lessons are focused on Adolf Hitler, his Comrades, Germany's great poets, including authors, and classical music composers.[12]

All this intellectual stimulation awakens her lifelong thirst for knowledge and her passion for learning. In addition to her schooling, the emphasis is being placed on physical training, motherhood, health, first aid, hygiene, and home economics, with the alternative to sexual education being fresh, clean air.

Every month, the girls learn ten new songs from their "We Girls Sing" songbook. They learn new dances, give musical and theatrical performances, tell stories, make arts and crafts, and learn how to knit, sew, crochet, and play games like charades.

Charades sharpens the girls thinking, allows them to move their bodies, and promotes their creative expression.[13]

Another form of creative expression is making paper-mâché puppets. The puppet play is the last and most serious type of young-girl playing. It combines the free, spoken word and the use of their imagination by placing themselves within the story. The fun begins when the girls create a plot, develop their characters, set the theme, create the form, and write their own script using audacity and wit, with self-confidence and straightforwardness.[14] Once the characters and script are in place, the girls design and make their own puppets and theatrical sets. They design the characters and sets on paper in color before actually constructing anything. When finished, they don on their work aprons, cover the tables with newspapers and begin!

The paste they use to mold and shape their characters consist of equal parts of flour and water. It is a messy process! To make the head, Trudel crumples the

---

[11] Lisa Pine – "Education in Nazi Germany," p. 127
[12] Randall Bytwerk - "Worldview Education for Winter 1938/39"
[13] Reinhold Sautter, p. 173
[14] Ibid, p. 174

paper into a ball around her index and middle finger, thus creating an opening underneath. Then, she tears the newspaper into inch-wide strips, dips it into the paste, and smooths out the shape of the head. As the head takes shape, she adds the lips, nose, and ears.

As the girls play, they sing their song "All the While Be Cheerful."[15] The puppet heads are placed on short dowels to dry. Then, the girls paint the faces yellow or tan, the eyes blue or brown, and the lips with a deep rich shade of red. Strands of grey wool become locks of hair and braids are tied at the end with yellow ribbons.

Since there are so many characters in this play, the puppet's clothing is made from old dirndls, taffeta or cotton fabric. By gluing their garments to the bottom of the head, the material drapes over the hand thereby hiding the wooden handle. To bring the characters to life the girls use felt, wool, feathers, button, or any other material they can find.

Once their puppets are complete, they rehearse their script. By the following month, their invited guests come and see their performance. This is a very proud moment for all the girls because it is their chance to demonstrate to the towns-people what they have learned over the past three years in the JM.

Together, there are eleven characters in the chosen play of "Kasperle." Kasper is the hero, who is returning from his quest. His two best friends are Gretel and Seppel. His grandmother, Oma, is wise and is an expert of mannerism and cooking. The wicked witch constantly plays tricks on the hero, turning his friend, Seppel into a chicken, and distracting him on his journey. The robber is a fat and lazy man who steels from his neighbors. The police officer represents social law and puts the robber into jail. The old wizard has magical properties and helps Kasper in his times of need. The crocodile represents gluttony and eats everything in its path. The king cares for his subjects and rewards Kasper upon saving his daughter, the princess. In the end, they marry and live happily ever after.

This traditional play gives the girls a safe space to write their own storyline and bring forth their hidden feelings, fears, and concerns. They are encouraged to compose their own version using their personal life experiences. The goal of performing this time-honored puppet play is to teach the girls personal values and the conflict between good and evil. The performance displays challenges and even treachery. It teaches the importance of friendship, camaraderie, will power, patience, loyalty, appreciation, honesty, integrity, and love.

As the adults watch, the parents glimpse into their daughters' insight and gain a new perspective as to how they are making sense of their new enchanted world.

As the girls mature and move beyond her childish ways, they pursue more activities to challenge and sharpen their minds. When the girls are mentally fit and healthy, they will express plenty of ideas through their crafts that will help them build their self-esteem.

---

[15] Alleweil Fröhlich Sein

The fuel for creating these handicrafts, starts with strong work ethics. Work ethic is a set of values based on concentration and the steadfast application of assiduousness. Handicraft work awakens the creative forces that are present in every girl. When they work, they must perform their duties under the healthiest conditions, with self-confidence and diligence. Working with their hands will bring them genuine satisfaction that will teach them to appreciate their cultural heritage. Among some of the other items made besides puppets, the JM leaders allow the girls to make their own dolls, handbags, books, blanket, clothes, and wreaths. They can use all the natural materials they find within their surroundings, including, birch, hazelnut, bamboo, reeds, grasses, hay, evergreens, and even straw. [16] For instance, when they learn how to color eggs for Easter, they can use their imagination to create any design on any other number of items they make. They are taught how to make dough figurines by using flour and water. When May Day, Harvest Fest, Advent, or Christmas holidays come around, they make wreaths using greenery, ribbons, and flowers. Whatever they create in the League, they can bring home, show their parents, and use. When they travel or stay overnight on a camping trip, they can spend countless hours sharing their knowledge and skills with the other girls in camp.[17]

The production of goods for personal use at home, in the League, or at camp, is just the start. Gradually, their work becomes more challenging, requiring new materials, and techniques, all in accordance with the child's skill level. Arts and crafts build confidence and develop dexterity skills, which are extremely useful when sewing, embroidering, knitting, or crocheting.[18] Through crafts such as paper silhouettes, drawing, and painting, the girls discover they have a strong will to learn. Once they master the technique, they can do anything they put their minds to doing. What they are learning today eventually will be applied to their chosen vocation or they can teach to their children.

Right from the beginning, the JM leaders are responsible for teaching their girls to have the determination to perform all tasks set before them. In order to have a strong will, the girls must learn to naturally discipline themselves and conform easily to the rules.

Building one's self image is strongly rooted in the principles of education. Self-discipline is a conscious decision and children need guidance from authority figures. However, the moral thrust of the girls' training, despite the limited variety of general apprenticeship, is self-education.

Self-responsibility means the girls learn to hold themselves accountable for their everyday actions and decisions.[19] They learn how their actions or inactions directly affect those around them in their troop, their family, and in their community. When the children say they are going to do something, they keep their

---

[16] Reinhold Sautter, p. 180

[17] Ibid, p. 178

[18] Ibid, p. 177

[19] Ibid, p. 204

word. Integrity is the highest moral principle for that is the way of life for the Hitler Youth.[20]

In addition, the importance of physical health means participation in afternoon sports.[21] While the girls learn to strengthen their minds and their work ethics during the social meetings, the mandatory sports afternoon held every Saturday, requires courage and coordination.

Their sports afternoon prepares them for the beginning of gymnastics in the League of German Girls (BDM). After the BDM, they will have the opportunity to serve in the Faith and Beauty Society. Here, they will become fluent in artistic rhythmic gymnastics. The most gifted will go on to participate in the Olympics.

Dr. Jutta Rüdiger, the German psychologist and head of the NSDAP female youth organizations proclaims:

> "The task of our Girls' League is to raise our girls as torch bearers of the national-socialist world. We need girls who are at harmony between their bodies, souls, and spirits. And, we need girls who, through healthy bodies and balanced minds, embody the beauty of divine creation. We want to raise girls who believe in Germany, our leader, and who will pass these beliefs on to their future children."[22]

Physical fitness plays a very important role in the League of German Girls and it is an integral part of being in service. Whether it be in track and field, archery, volleyball, horseback riding, walking, hiking, marching, skiing, dancing, singing, bicycle riding, impromptu games, swimming, roller skating, gardening, jumping rope, relay races, soccer, lacrosse, badminton, long jumps, javelin, summersaulting, walking a tightrope, even helping with the harvest or collecting medicinal herbs in the field, these girls are always on the move.

Activities are conducted based on what is locally available. Overall, the girls are expected to be of healthy minds and bodies, and participation in the sports afternoon is just as mandatory as participating in regular group meetings.[23]

Gymnastics focuses on muscle strength, agility, and mental capacity with emphasis on the joy of movement.[24] Watching the gymnastic artistry of thousands of young women from the Belief and Beauty Society as they join in a eurhythmic collaboration is a remarkable sight. Their agility and coordination are beholding even when they are only rehearsing in their individual groups.

Physical exercise nurtures the young girls' self-esteem and builds confidence in her own abilities. By training and strengthening her body, she also trains and strengthening her character and mind. Through exercise, her body will become naturally tone and attractive. The desire to have a beautiful body image starts

---

[20] Reinhold Sautter p. 204
[21] Helga Brachmann
[22] Bund Deutscher Mädel – "The Belief and Beauty Society"
[23] Ibid – "Sports Uniform"
[24] Ibid

when they are very young. At every moment, the young girls must say to herself, "I believe in what I can do and it can never be taken for granted."[25]

To keep the body healthy and vibrant demands not just a beneficial sports routine but also proper nutrition. It is important for the young girls to establish good eating practices early by including at least seven times more fruits and vegetables in their daily diet rather than large quantities of meats, fats, and starches. An optimal amount of calories will ensure a healthy disposition. When the girls feel sick, are tired, and cannot perform, the Reich considers them under-nourished. Their solution is to eat green, leafy vegetables, go into the country to breath in fresh air, and drink the pure mountain water.

The girls also learn the art of gardening. Gardening involves more than just planting a seed in the ground and hoping it will bear fruit. The girls need to know how to prepare the soil, which plants complement each other to reduce insects and diseases, the various types of fertilizers that can be used to produce a bountiful crop, how to care for, and then harvest the plants. A vegetable garden planted in the spring will provide a rich return for the family up until the first frost. This is how a family becomes self-reliant, for what the girls learn about gardening during their social meetings, they can share with their family. In turn, the families will benefit because teaching self-reliance starts with the youngest. Even storytelling plays a vital role in the creative imagination of the young girls and connects them with their natural surroundings.[26]

One story Fräulein Schmidt reads to the girls comes from Reinhold Sautter's book entitled "Hitler Youth –The Experience of a Great Camaraderie."

"When you are standing in the valley and look up to the Alps, you see a magnificent mountain range, and hear the ringing of the cattle bells. You see the wide-open alpine meadows, the trees, and when you breathe in, you can smell the freshness of the outdoor air.

"When our Creator made the world, he made a model. This is why the landscape is so diverse. From the mountains with their rocky gorges, to the alpine meadows and pastures, from the golden wheat fields to the friendly valleys and their babbling brooks.

"The farmer works from sun up to sun down. Every day, he wrestles arduously with the stony soil to produce the grain to make our flour and bread. He plows his fields, plants his seeds, and waters his crop. As the plants begin to grow, he meticulously inspects his crops for insects and destroys those plants that contain a virus or disease. On some days, it can be so still and quiet that he sits and thinks about life in the valley below.

"The girls from the Young Girls' League, Country Service Camp, or from the League of German Girls, voluntarily help on Harvest Day and bless the farmer through her labor. At the end of the day, when the work is completed, everyone can sit down with a glass of wine, sing, and think about how well the wheat turned out to make the fresh bread. With glowing faces, the girls will say,

---

[25] Reinhold Sautter, p. 181
[26] Ibid, p. 197

'Goodnight—see you tomorrow,' and they will return the next day to help the farmer once again.

"The next morning, the girls are back in their place with happiness and joy in their hearts. Is it any wonder the girls want to hike to the farmer's land and help as much as they can? Whose farm it is, nobody knows, but she loves serving in the Young Girls' League and feeling important by contributing to her *Volk*. When her task is completed, she returns with her comrades, home to the low-land. It is there that we can hear them sing about Germany's fertile land and the wealth of the harvest."[27]

"By the times these young Bund Deutscher Mädel women turn seventeen, they will have indispensable practical knowledge and skills that will prepare them for their future responsibility as viable members of society. Over one-hundred thousand girls a year will freely volunteer their time, enter into the work force for three hours a day, and work wherever they are needed— in kindergartens, schools, train stations, large family homes, office buildings, private shops, or hospitals, to name a few. At the end of the working day, she may feel fatigued, but she is full of pride.

"When the BDM girl has completed her education, she can voluntarily join the Faith and Beauty Society that links fitness and rural crafts with racial purity and the sanctity of the soil. Here, the woman will continue her studies in fashion design and home economics until the age of twenty-one, when she will have the opportunity to become a part of the self-sufficiency program in the National Socialist Women's League. [28]

At the end of Reinhold Sautter's story, the leader asks her now mature JM girls "when you think back over a few short years, did you even think this could be possible? Is this not an inspiration for all of us to be more active than before and live a life of prosperity and happiness?[29]

With stories such as Herr Sautter's, the young Mädel learns strong work eth-ics, enabling her to perform her duties within the community. She knows what it means when she receives her full qualifications and begins to work. By the time she has completed her world training, she will possess diverse qualifications that will prepare her for her vocation, or for marriage and motherhood. Germany needs girls who are healthy and strong, and who are mentally and physically ca-pable, to accomplish the National Socialistic worldview. Germany does not want weak and lazy people depended upon the state for assistance.

In four short years, when the young girl fulfills her required duties, receives her badges, awards, and certificates, she will move on into the League of German Girls. Here, she will study for another four years.

---

[27] Reinhold Sautter, p. 194-196
[28] Ibid, p. 196
[29] Ibid, p. 206

(Note: Trudel will never complete her third year in the BDM and learn about the racial policies of the Third Reich and their blood inheritance for the battle-front will be on her doorstep, and the German empire will be collapsing all around her.)

During their training, those JM girls who show exemplary skills will receive a special letter from the Reich's Ministry of Science, Education, and Culture. They will be specifically chosen for the eight-month elite rural educational program called Country Service Year Camp.

After the girls learn to become a valuable part of the community, they will be given the opportunity to follow their individual talents and interests, or to further their educations accordingly, and to grow into their own unique personalities. Then, they will make their talents truly available to the community.[30]

Through her years of training, Trudel has proven herself as an obedient and disciplined young girl in the League of Young Girls. She has accomplished all her required tasks and has received her JM Proficiency Badge.

An official letter arrives addressed to Josefa from the Reich's Ministry. It states that her daughter has shown exemplary skills and has been specifically chosen to participate in the Country Service Year program. Trudel will soon leave her mother behind and travel over four-hundred and fifty miles from Kleinzell, to her new home in Seidorf, Niederschlesien, Germany.

---

[30] Bund Deutscher Mädel – "The Belief and Beauty Society"

Josepha and Emmerich Kerschner
1924 – Mariazell, Austria

Gertrude Kerschner – First row, sixth in from right
Class of 1936 - 1937

Josepha Kerschner – Postal carrier in Kleinzell, Austria

Josepha's baby pig

Hans, Emmerich, Gertrude, Franz, Anna Kerschner

Kerschner Family Farm house in Kleinzell, Austria

Josepha's brand new washing machine

First Row: Local Kleinzell Band Members
2ⁿᵈ Row from right: Johann Kandlhofer, Anna Kandlhofer, Carl Onkel, Minnel
3ʳᵈ Row from right: Gertrude Kerschner, Anita Kerschner, Josefa Kerschner, Aloisa Franz,
Johann Franz, Trossep, Anna Hoffer, Hilda Franz, Elfriede Lechner.

Country Service Camp – Seidorf

Left -Troop Leader - Fräulein Dieter
Middle –Economic Assistant Leader - Fräulein Grüber
Right – Camp Leader – Fräulein Albrecht

Morning Flag Greeting Ceremony

Landjahr Lager Seidorf Girls – Trudel is standing on 2nd step left

Landjahr Lager Girls – standing at attention – Trudel 1st row right

Balcony View

Seidorf Lake

Sports Afternoon – Maria Mikolasz-Dubiel standing 3rd from right
Courtesy of Peter Dubiel

Sports Afternoon — Ellie, Nelly, Steffi, and Maria

Airplane Game

Festive Day

Children's Afternoon – Trudel left with head turned

Children's Afternoon

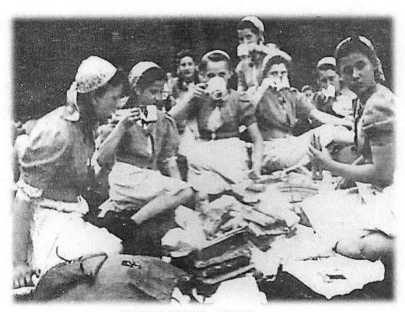

Afternoon Break – Big Trip

Landjahr Lager girls bathing on rocks – Big Trip

Bags at Train Station – Big Trip

Break after walking down mountain to Ruhberg – Big Trip

Landjahr Lager Seidorf girls eating lunch at Ruhberg Lager

Last day of Big Trip

Vang Stave Church (Wang Church) in Karpacz, Poland

Pig Baptism Parade

Trudel holding back pig with girls before being baptized

Pig "Thick" running out of Lager

Trudel and Helli – Pig Baptism

Local villagers invited to BBQ

Landjahr Lager Seidorf girls going to
Farmer Torge's house in Oberseidorf

From left to right: Fiancé to Fräulein Dieter, Maria Mikolasz-Dubiel, Steffi Pucks, Lager Fräulein Dieter, Albrecht, Grüber, Hans Mikolasz (Maria's brother). Courtesy of Peter Dubiel.

Marie Mikolasz, Steffi Pucks, Trudel Kerschner

Trudel in Zither Class – 1941 – 1st row 4th in from left

1942 – Trudel with Paula
Health Service Girls
(Gesundheitsdienst Mädel)

Trudel with her cousin
Elfriede Lechner

PFC Robert Sandor
87th Infantry Division
345th Infantry Regiment
Headquarters Co.
1st Battalion
United States Army Reserve (USAR)
Camp McCauley – Linz, Austria

Robert & Gertrude marry May 8, 1948 — Linz, Austria

Coming over on the S.S. United States - 1957

Home in Greenwich, Ct

Robert & Gertrude celebrating 35th wedding anniversary
Rainbow Room – Rockefeller Center, NYC – May 8, 1983

PART THREE

Country Service Year Camp

"We are the proud castle
Up on the mountain
And down in the valley
Stands our village
The blue sky smiles at you
And the sun always shines
For we are the Seidorfer girls!"

~ Landjahr Lager Seidorf ~
Camp Song

Traveling to Our New Camp

IT IS A COOL SPRING MORNING in April 1941. Trudel, dressed in her official BDM uniform, and Josefa, dressed in her best Sunday attire, are waiting outside the Rainfeld train station. The small timber frame, weatherboard-clad railway building stands roughly twenty feet at the peak of the cupola, fifteen feet wide by twenty-five feet long. Timber braces support the skillion roof that projects over the front of the building to form an awning. A high-back wooden passenger bench under each of the single-hung windows complements the structure and lends a warm appeal to this rural railway station. Separate bathrooms for men and women are located at the west end of the building, while at the east end of the building, there is a small porter's office, which doubles as the parcel and storage room. In the middle of the station, a wooden three-quarter glass entry door opens into the general waiting room.

As Trudel and her mother step inside the rustic building, Josefa and another mother exchange a cordial holy greeting, "Grüß Gott!"

The Kerschners walk to the back of the waiting room. Trudel places her luggage and precious zither next to the high-back bench and sits down. Made from sturdy hardwood, the curve slates in this piece of furniture provide comfortable seating for the two women.

Trudel takes a moment to glance around the room. Mothers are sitting with their daughters who are quietly talking among themselves. The girls are about the same age and they all have a suitcase next to them. Trudel sits there for a moment fidgeting, then stands, and walks around the room.

Clasping her hands behind her back, she strolls around the room and notices a glass-enclosed wooden case that holds the train schedule and other pertinent information regarding the Deutsche Reichsbahn railway line and its service. She double-checks the time on her ticket with the train schedule. She pulls her ticket out from the breast pocket of her climbing jacket and matches it against the time mentioned in the case. Her train is scheduled to arrive at 8:09 am. She refolds the ticket, places it back inside her pocket, and securely fastens the button. Through the office window, she notices a small wooden desk and a chair. A black Bakelite rotary telephone sits silent among the white cloth mailbags in the corner marked with the word "Post" in black lettering.

She turns away and confidently approaches one of the other girls.

"Hi. My name is Gertrude, but you can call me Trudel. Are you going to St. Pölten?"

"Why, yes, I am what about you? Where are you going?" the young girl responds.

"I am going to St. Pölten to meet my new camp leader, Fräulein Albrecht," Trudel replies.

"I'm meeting with my camp leader too, but I forgot her name. I'm heading to Landjahr Lager Seidorf."

"That's exactly where I'm going!" Trudel exclaims. "What's your name?"

"My name is Ingrid." The girls shake hands. "It's a pleasure meeting you."

"It is a pleasure meeting you too. We'll talk on the train later, okay?"

"Okay" Ingrid happily responds glad to have met a new comrade.

Trudel returns to update her mother. "Mama, that girl is going to the same camp as I am, isn't that great!"

"I think that's wonderful. You'll probably become very good friends during your time at Seidorf."

For a moment, both mother and daughter sit in silence.

"Mama," Trudel starts trying to fill the uncomfortable silence. "Can we go outside and wait for the train?"

"Certainly, my little one, we can do that," nods Josefa.

Trudel gathers her belongings and together the women relocate to one of the outside benches.

The cordial atmosphere lacks any flurry of activity considering the quest these girls will undertake. In contrast, Trudel's stomach is fluttering with excitement. Her expression remains composed and calm for that of a thirteen-year old girl who is about to leave her family for eight long months. Trudel places her hands over her jacket as she begins to feel a gut-wrenching pain in the pit of her stomach.

Trudel is dressed comfortably for her two-day journey. She wears her stylish fawn-color, waist-length climbing jacket, which is the most distinguishable piece of attire for this young BDM girl. The design is similar to the military uniforms of this time. This stylish tunic is shorter in the back than in the front to create a slimming silhouette. Light brown rayon lines the inside of this garment. The front of the jacket has four small, pleat patch pockets with Bakelite BDM/JM embossed buttons, which decorate the front and cuffs. The backside of the jacket has two small take-up tabs with a small metal buckle. The cloth lozenge shaped red and white diamond insignia bearing the swastika, as well as the black and white Süd Niederdonau regional triangle patch are sewn on the left sleeve. Affixed on the front left breast pocket is a smaller red and white diamond badge made from enamel. Underneath, she wears her mother's handmade, short-sleeve, white cotton blouse tucked into her casual, mid-calf blue wool skirt. Her grey stockings and brown lace-up shoes complete her uniform.[1]

---

[1] Bund Deutscher Mädel – "Winter Uniform"

"Stand up and let me see how you look, dear." As Josefa examines her daughter's ensemble, she begins to feel a twinge in her stomach at the thought of her daughter leaving home. She is nonetheless happy that Trudel is being given such a wonderful opportunity.

"I think I look fine, Mama. What do you think?" Trudel models her attire for her admiring mother.

"You look absolutely beautiful. Now, do you have everything you need for your trip?"

"Yes, Mama," Trudel confidently replies.

"And how about extra socks and underwear—did you remember to pack enough?"

"Mama, please." Trudel looks at the floor. "The other girls can hear you."

"And did you remember to pack your toothbrush and toothpaste?" Josefa asks going over the material list in her head.

"Yes, I did."

"Okay, I think you are ready then. Did you remember to bring your hiking boots? You're going to need them."

"They are right here," Trudel says, pointing to the vintage leather-and-tweed suitcase, she had borrowed from her grandmother, Anna. The valise holds all the requested necessities for her eight-month long stay in Landjahr Lager.

Trudel pulls her handwritten list from her pocket and reads it to her mother one more time. "I've got my hiking boots in the suitcase, along with my long stockings, undershirts, pajama, dresses, aprons, and hangers. I also have three pairs of socks and undergarments. I packed my sports shoes, bathing suit and cap, a pair of gloves, and plenty of handkerchiefs, which I tucked inside my boots. I also brought my sewing, washing, and cleaning kits. As the leaders requested, I am not bringing my purse or toiletry articles, and I am not wearing any jewelry."

Once Trudel arrives at camp, all other necessary, clothing will be provided for her. She will become responsible in camp for cleaning her own linens and clothes as well as repairing all her own garments.

"Did you remember to pack your hairbrush and bobby pins?"

"Yes, Mother. I think I remembered everything. I am a Landjahr girl now!"

"And, do you have your railway pass, membership papers, and writing kit? You will remember to write home, won't you?"

"Yes, I will, Mother. I promise I will write as often as I can."

"I love you, and I am very proud of you, Trudel," Josefa says as she gently cups Trudel's face in her hands. She gives the girl a quick kiss on the lips and begins to choke up. With her left hand on her daughter's shoulder, Josefa gazes into Trudel's eyes and with her hand, strokes the girl's thick black hair. "I want you to do your absolute best. Listen to your camp leaders, and pay close attention to everything they say." Josefa gives Trudel a loving hug and whispers, "You have a wonderful opportunity here, because the Reich is paying for everything." Josefa leans back, gripping Trudel's upper arms. "This will be your very first big assignment. The entire world is opening up to you. You are young and you can do anything you put your mind to doing. So, it's up to you to learn as much as you can while you are there, okay?"

"Yes, I will," Trudel lovingly responds, looking directly into her mother's hazel eyes.

Josefa believes she has dispensed enough motherly advice to her daughter and now, she is quite at a loss for words. The twinge in Trudel's stomach flares up again. Her dry throat tightens and with a scratchy voice, Trudel leans into her mother's ear and whispers, "I love you too Mama." They hold each other in a long heartwarming embrace.

Given Trudel's pure Austrian heritage which dates back to the seventeenth century, her dependable, obedient, service-minded and dutiful character, along with her accomplishments in the Young Girls' League, the Reich's Ministry knows she possess the right qualities and physical ability to withstand the rigors of camp life.[2] Country Service Year Camps are places of strict physical, intellectual, and moral education. They are not rest homes for the frail or only limited to suitable youths. Therefore, only those girls who have proven themselves are specifically chosen to attend.[3]

Though the Second World War began in September 1939, it has not reached the tiny villages of Kleinzell nor Seidorf. German troops are heading southeast into the Kingdom of Yugoslavia, and Trudel is traveling northeast.

Josefa and Trudel engage in small talk when they hear the remote chugging of a locomotive rumbling down the tracks. She sees the white smoke billowing over the deciduous treetops and hears the haunting sound of the whistle as it resonates throughout the valley, loudly announcing the arrival of the massive seventy-four ton German Empire DRB Class 50-3696-7 steam locomotive.[4] During this time, all the rail lines within Germany, Austria, Bohemia, Moravia, Sudetenland, and the Czech Silesia are under the control of the Deutsche Reichsbahn (DRB). To announce this takeover, all locomotives and railcars show the emblems of the NSDAP Eagle, and the letters DR on the cab.

"Look, Mama! The train is coming!" Trudel's apprehension flips back to excitement. All around her, the small station bursts into a flurry of activity.

The rhythmic chuffing sound ceases when the engineer pulls back on the lever, releasing the piston from pushing steam into this giant locomotive's boiler. He applies the brakes and brings this massive behemoth to a gentle stop.

The conductor jumps off the Donnerbüchse, and walks inside the station house. The other girls bid fond farewells to their respective mothers, board, and take their seats inside the coach.

Trudel and her mother now stand alone on the platform.

"I will miss you very much, my dear. Write as often as you can. I want to hear all about your adventures. I want to hear about where you go, what you do, and most of all, I want to hear that they are feeding you."

---

[2] Annemarie Leppien, p. 50
[3] Bund Deutscher Mädel – Country Service Year
[4] DRB Class 50

"I will miss you very much, Mama." Tears begin streaming down Trudel's cheeks. She affectionately hugs her mother and does not want to let her go.

"Oh, don't cry my little one." Josefa compassionately holds onto her dear daughter. Look at this as one great big adventure! You are going to spend lots of time with your new friends and have a lot of fun. Before you know it, you will forget all about me! Now, go, run along. The train is waiting for you." The two release from their embrace.

Trudel picks up her suitcase and zither and slowly walks to the carriage steps.

Emerging from the stationhouse, the conductor tosses the postal bags into the luggage compartment. "Do you need some assistance, Fräulein?" he questions.

"Why yes, thank you sir."

The conductor winks, picks up Trudel's suitcase, and places it on the platform steps of the steel green 1-Type Bi Donnerbüchse railway car.[5]

Trudel grabs the handrail and pulls herself up. She maneuvers into the carriage with her luggage and finds the first available seat next to the window. She places her luggage and zither in the overhead leather luggage rack. She sits down on the high back, wooden-slat bench, looks out the window and waves to her mother. The angst in her stomach is wrenching her apart. She feels anxious and excited at the same time. She stands and presses her nose up against the glass window. Tears stream down her cheeks. She opens the window, sticks her head out, and blows kisses to her mother.

"All aboard!" the conductor yells. The engineer tugs twice on the whistle's pull chord warning passengers that the train is about to depart.

Josefa holds a strong presence and she does not want her daughter to see her true feelings buried deep inside of her.

The engineer opens the cocks to dispel excess condensed water from the cylinders. From the undercarriage, the massive iron horse bellows a breath of steam. The brakes are released and the engine quickly jerks forward, pulling the cars behind.

Josefa and the other girl's mothers wave good-bye to their daughters. Trudel continues waving back until her mother is no longer in sight.

Feeling melancholy, Josefa shuffles back to her car. Sitting in the driver's seat, she begins to cry.

Trudel sits back in her seat, staring out the window when she hears a friendly voice.

"Hi Trudel, can I sit down next to you?"

"Hi Ingrid!" Trudel says as she wipes the tears from her eyes. For the next hour, the girls talk, get to know each other, and exchange stories before arriving at the St. Pölten train station.

As they travel west on the Leobersdorfer Bahn railway line, the train takes them along the meandering Gölsen River and through the Triesting Valley. Following the last of the foothills of the Gutenstein Alps, the train makes its first

---

[5] Donnerbüchse

stop at the market town of Trainsen. Then, it heads north to Wilhelmsburg, where they cross over the river and enter the outskirts of St. Pölten.

When they arrive at the terminal, Ingrid and Trudel disembark and look for their Landjahr flag and camp leader. It is an imposing station to the young girls. They are easily captivated by the number of people who transverse through the main terminal. Up ahead, Trudel and Ingrid see other young girls assemble by the green and white Odal rune pennant that marks the gathering area for twenty girls. The young leader is holding the flag as she greets them at the station.

"Hello, girls, I am Fräulein Albrecht, your Country Service Year camp leader," she begins. She passes the banner to another girl standing next to her, arbitrarily assigning her to the prominent position of flag bearer.

"When I call your name, I want you to come forward to receive your railway pass to Vienna. Then, I want you to take your luggage and line up in double file, starting here at our Odal rune pennant."

In alphabetical order, Fräulein Albrecht calls the girls' names. They receive their passes and line up. Ingrid and Trudel separate but make a mental note of where the other is standing. Once everyone has received their pass, the leader explains to the girls the procedure of their long two-day trip.

"When our train to Vienna arrives, you must wait for it to come to a complete stop. When I give the command, you will follow me to board. This will be an overnight trip. It will take us two days to arrive at our final destination in Giersdorf (Podgórzyn, Poland). Everyone has her assigned seat and at all times, we will be together in one car, understand?"

"Our first stop is the main railway terminal in Vienna. This is where we will be disembarking. It is a very large terminal and it is imperative that everyone stay close together in formation and keep their eyes on our flag. In Vienna, we will change trains and board a sleeper car that will take us to Prague. We will arrive in Prague tomorrow morning at 8:00 am. In Prague, we will disembark and then board a different train that will take us to Tetschen Bodenbach. From there, we will go on to Dresden. From Dresden, we will disembark and change trains to Görlitz. From Görlitz, we will ride on the outskirts of the beautiful Sudetes mountain range. By the afternoon, we will arrive in Hirschberg. From Hirschberg, we will board a trolley for Giersdorf. From Giersdorf, we will march to our new home in Seidorf. Our estimated time of arrival at the camp should be between three and four o'clock tomorrow afternoon. Country Service Year Camp Seidorf will be your home for the next eight months."

Some of the girls grin with excitement while others begin to feel homesick. One city girl pouts for she is not looking forward to this protracted journey, nor living on a farm taking care of dirty animals.

When the command is given, the girls march in file to the platform and wait for the train to arrive. Fräulein Albrecht commands the girls to stand at attention until the train comes to a complete stop. As the conductor hops off the passenger car, Fräulein Albrecht shows him the train ticket and asks which carriage is theirs. He points to the second passenger car. The camp leader turns back to her troop and gives the command. In one unified movement, the girls pick up their luggage and follow their leader aboard.

The girls flutter about the aisle as they help each other heave their luggage into the overhead racks. They settle down in their seats, sitting in groups of four, two on each side, facing each other.

Fräulein Albrecht walks up and down the aisle, counting the girls in their individual berths. Then, each girl calls out her name so that the leader can check it off her list. To ensure the safety of the girls Fräulein Albrecht then notifies the conductor that all the young maidens are present and accounted.

The conductor leans over the railing of the passenger car platform and waives to the engineer, signaling that they are ready to depart. The whistle blows twice. The girls grow giddy with excitement as the locomotive slowly chugs away from the St. Pölten railway station.

The highly diverse natural landscape thrills and inspires the imagination for anyone who rides on the Empress Elisabeth Railway Line between St. Pölten and Vienna.[6]

Once they leave the urbanized area behind, Trudel looks out the window and recognizes the Scarlet Cornelia cherry trees that flourish in the picturesque Pielach Valley of St. Polten.[7] The train passes through vast open fields of arable land where the farmers are preparing their next batch of crops. The gently rolling, fertile land of the foothills to the north and the romantic Alpine mountain range to the south is a peaceful contrast riding through this emerald paradise. Small villages and large farm homesteads dot the landscape. Imposing cloisters and churches look down on the towns and provide a spiritual refuge for their parishioners.

The mild climate in the Traisen Valley around Mostviertel and the dense Dunkelsteiner Forest, protect the vineyards from the cool westerly winds. Dry, chalky, and gravely soils produce the distinctive Grüner Veltliner wine.

As they approach the bend around the city of Eichgraben, the train begins its journey into the beautiful Vienna Woods. This Alpine area is rich in minerals, including lime and sandstone. The Brown Coal Mine holds their most precious mineral, gold.[8]

Located at the northeastern tip of the Northern Limestone Alps, the Vienna Woods form a wide arc around the north and southwestern sides of the city. The fairytale-like scenery with broad hillocks and beech wood trees are nestled among the black pines and castle ruins that are the foundation of mythical dwarfs and magical characters in every child's imagination.

As the train pulls into the Vienna station, the girls gather their belongings. They wait for the train to come to a complete stop before disembarking. In a single file, Fräulein Albrecht leads the girls from the platform to the main terminal. The leader excuses herself to inquire at the ticket counter for the location of

---

[6] Empress Elisabeth Railway
[7] Mostviertel
[8] Eichgraben

their next connection. While waiting, the girls pass the time and sing a traditional Austrian folk song. They stand tall, perfectly aligned, as their harmonic voices echo throughout the terminal. Some passengers stop to listen, while others busily hurry by.

When the young leader returns, the girls finish their song, form a double line, and together file down the stairs. They pass underneath the railway line, then up the stairs to Track #4. Here, they wait for the overnight train to Prague.

Soon, the locomotive arrives and the girls board their coach and place their belongings into their assigned compartments. Each berth serves as ordinary seating arrangements during the day and at night converts into sleeper bunkers. To the girls, this berth is the most luxurious accommodation they have ever seen! They feel as if they are traveling in first-class. The padded bunks come with four small pillows, linens, and blankets. Even though the fixed ladder over the window prevents a full view of the landscape, it allows the girls to climb up to the highest bunk. A full ledge swings down allowing them to enter and locks in the upright position preventing them from accidentally rolling out during the middle of the night. At the end of the corridor, are the washroom and toilets. The dining car is one car over.

The Emperor Ferdinand Northern Railway line takes the girls out in a north-westerly direction from the waltz capital of the world towards Prague. They cross over the Danube River, and into the beautiful countryside of the Protectorate of Bohemia and Moravia.[9] Since Country Service Year girls are in service to the Reich, they are permitted to travel through the newly acquired territories into Niederschlesien.

Trudel is forming new bonds in friendship. She shares her stories, talks about her adventures in the Young Girl's League, and her family back home.

The steam locomotive chugs through the Danube Valley passing the sedimentary mounted hillsides of the fertile wine-growing area in Wagram. The train gently rolls down the tracks passing the city of pillars in Gänserndorf, following the Morava River until it comes to a stop at the market town of Lundenburg. Trudel and her friends look out the window and see beautiful willow trees line the walkway in the park.

A new girl pokes her head into Trudel's berth and invites her companions to a sing-a-long before dinner. They leave the compartment unsecured and meet up with the rest of their troop in the dining car. The girls regale the other patrons with song, taking a short break for dinner, before resuming their spontaneous evening musical performance.

After the girls retire to bed, the train chugs on through the night, passing tiny villages, castle ruins on the hillside, fortified cities, and massive cathedrals with their spirals reaching out to the heavens.

The next morning as the train rounds the mountainside, the girls awaken to a beautiful rainbow sunrise. They fold the blankets and sheets, return the bunks

---

[9] Protectorate of Bohemia and Moravia

to their upright positions, eat breakfast, and then prepare to disembark in the ancient city of Prague.

As before, Fräulein Albrecht leads the girls' off the train. They transfer to the Imperial Royal State Railway line and soon they are on their way. Heading towards Tetschen-Bodenbach on the western side of the Sudetes mountain range, Fräulein Albrecht calls for the girls to look out the window as they round the bend of the Tetschen Cliffside. The troop is in awe of the massive stonewalls whose flowing geranium gardens overhang. However, their trip is far from over for Seidorf lays on the other side of the Giant Mountains.

Their journey continues northward along the Elbe River all the way into Dresden where they board the Emperor Ferdinand Northern Railway Line east to Görlitz.[10] From Görlitz, they switch to an innovative green local railway line that opened to the city of Hirschberg back in 1865. The Silesian Mountain Railway DRG Class E 91 locomotive does not operate at high speeds but slowly follows the Sudetes mountain range through the Hirschberg Valley toward the spa city of Bad Warmbrunn (Cieplice, Poland) near Hirschberg (Jelenia Góra, Poland). This three-axle superstructure has two driver cabs, one at either side of the locomotive, and powers with a 2200 kW engine. The center suspends within an articulated appendage as bellows protect the gangways between the individual sections of the engine rooms.[11] This clean-running locomotive symbolizes the strength of the Reich, for its innovative technology does not rely on coal for fuel, but electricity.

Right on schedule, the locomotive pulls the Donnerbüchse Thunder Box passenger coaches behind, almost silently whisking the girls through the valley to their next destination in Hirschberg.[12]

The gently rolling foothills of the Hirschberg Valley remind Trudel of her home. With the exception of the magnificent palaces, private manor estates, and parks that dot the landscape, she has never seen such wealth in all her life!

Trudel stands from her seat, slides the window down, and sticks her head outside. She closes her eyes and inhales a deep breath of fresh mountain air. She smells the freshly cut grass from the surrounding meadows mixed with cow manure and feels right at home. The cool air blows against her face and whisks her black braids behind her head. In gratitude, she beams a smile. Trudel opens her eyes and sees the Giant Mountains with the magnificent twelfth-century, castle ruin Kynastburg (Chojnik Castle) proudly looking down on the lowlands below.

Trudel hears Fräulein Albrecht give the order to get ready to disembark. Trudel pulls her head inside the coach, locks the window closed, and double checks around her seat to make sure she has her suitcase and zither.

When the train stops at the Hirschberg Central Station, the camp leader, Trudel, Ingrid, and the eighteen girls disembark, march down the stairs under the tracks, through the darkened tunnel, and walk up the stairs into the central

---

[10] Riesengebirge
[11] DRG Class E91
[12] Donnerbüchse

terminal. The mid-nineteenth century Romanesque Revival building features a clerestory of nine simple arches with rectangular windows. On either side of the main wooden entrance are two large, segmental, arched windows, divided by a single vertical mullion into eight lit compartments. Hirschberg Station is an old and impressive edifice. The lack of passengers gives the building a deserted feeling, while the diffused lighting makes the station feel dark.

The girls follow their leader, marching across the black-and-white checkerboard tile flooring out to the front of the building. They wait less than ten minutes for the Hirschberger Talbahn electric streetcar to arrive.[13]

Two electric doors on either side of the tram slide open, allowing the rapid exchange of passengers. Fräulein Albrecht stands by the side of the tram as the girls grab onto the handrail and step up into the little green electric trolley. Some passengers hold onto the leather teardrop handles while elderly passengers, mostly women, sit looking out the windows. Even though it has been a very long traveling day, most of the Country Service girls are eager to reach their final destination in Seidorf.

The trolley conductor rings the bell twice and the doors automatically close. He pushes the lever forward and the little tram quietly rolls down the tracks to its next destination.

The steel vehicle stands a little less than fifteen feet tall at the top of the roof's pantograph, thirty-three feet long by ten feet wide. Two trams connect to each other, allowing a total number of seventy-eight passengers to board both trolleys. There are twelve wooden-slat, back-to-back seats on either side of the cab, allowing passengers to look at the view from the six large rectangular windows. In the rear of the tram, a large wooden bench faces forward. In the front tram is the engineer's booth.

Silently, the tram leaves the main station in Hirschberg and quietly glides through the town center of Bad Warmbrunn passing the Schaffgotsch family palace. Periodically, it stops for passengers to board or get off.

At Hermsdorf am Kynast (Sobiezów, Poland) the trolley takes the right branch out of the city. Into the lowland countryside valleys, the tracks meander past fresh-water fishing lakes as it gently glides into the village of Giersdorf (Podgórzyn, Poland).

Standing at the front of the trolley, Fräulein Albrecht briskly claps her hands three times to get the girls' attention. "Okay girls, everyone listen up! In a few moments, we will be arriving at our destination. I want you all to look around your seats and make sure you have everything. When the trolley stops, we will exit to the left, and then line up in front of the terminal."

Excitement builds among the girls as they gather their belongings. As the tram rounds the last corner, the rural tram station of Giersdorf comes into view. The tram circles the small wooden structure and stops along side of the station. This is the end of the line for it will head back to Hirschberg.

---

[13] Hirschberger Talbahn

The girls disembark and are amazed at their first sight. They see a single, massive, vertical rock wall protruding out from the forest.

With their leader in front and their heavy luggage in hand, they set out marching in song towards camp.

Enthusiastically, the girls and their melody hike on the road two and a half miles through a coniferous forest of indigenous hardwood.

Through the clearing, they catch a glimpse of Lake Seidorf.

Continuing on their hike through the village of Seidorf, they pass rural farmhouses, churches, the city hall, the post office, a little theatre, a guesthouse, and the cemetery. The troop traverses the main roadway that leads west into Hirschberg and east into Arnsdorf. Passing more farmsteads on the bottom of the hill, the girls turn left onto a lone dirt road.

Walking the acclivity does not dampen their spirts. They feel relieved to have made the long trip and are excited to have finally reached their final destination.

Trudel feels proud when she walks under the wooden arbor entrance decorated by the locals with wildflowers and wreaths. A carved sign overhead reads "Landjahr Lager." Trudel and her troop pass by the courtyard where the national flag flutters a warm welcome. The house finally comes into full view!

The façade faces west and is composed of three floors with a gambrel roof, one large dormer, and a terraced parlor with a cement staircase entryway. The red gambrel roof slopes symmetrically from either side of the center ridge of the roofline and fans out on both sides into a pair of lower, steeper slopes. The proportionate dormer faces forward with adjoining windows alongside the two large casement windows over-looking the balcony. The main staircase leads into the parlor which projects beyond the home's exterior, creating a second-floor terrace. The parapet around the edge of the balcony holds empty wooden window boxes. The contrasting smooth stucco clad over the three-story block and timber frame building gives the home a humble appearance while the ground floor with its stone façade reinforces its dominance on the hill. With their last few steps, the girls end their hike at the base of the Dutch Colonial style home.

"Never forget that,
The holiest rite in this world,
Is the rite to land,
Which one wishes
To cultivate oneself,
And the holiest sacrifice is the
blood which one pours forth
for his land."

~ Adolf Hitler ~

Arriving at Camp Seidorf

FRÄULEIN DIETER the troop leader, and Fräulein Grüber the economic and assistant leader, walk out from the entrance of the manor home and down the steps to greet the girls in the gravel driveway. Fräulein Dieter calls out warmly to the girls' as they line up in formation with their luggage. "Welcome to Country Service Year girls! I am your troop leader Fräulein Dieter. This is Fräulein Grüber, your economic and assistant leader. I believe you already know Fräulein Albrecht, your camp leader. We sincerely welcome you to Camp Seidorf!

Fräulein Dieter continues. "I will call each girl's name, and when I do, I want you to proceed up these stairs and into the dining room with your luggage where Fräulein Grüber will assist you. At the table, she will give you your registration forms. Once you are finished filling them out, hand them back to Fräulein Grüber who will then assign you to your rooms. There, you will have one hour to unpack, settle in, change into your work clothes, and return to the main dining room for orientation and dinner. When you are finished unpacking, place your luggage outside of the room in the hall. This way, we may collect them and store them in the attic.

The girls perk up when they hear the word "dinner." They have traveled far and had little to eat. They would rather fill up their bellies than fill out registration forms.

"Barbara Achen, Hermine Azlsdorfer, Gabriele Burgermeister, Ingrid Eberhart, Elfie Fasser, Erika Hödlmaier, Sabine Jungmeier, Trudel Kerschner, Lotte Kirsch, Eleanor Mohler,…"

As soon Trudel hears her name, she follows Fräulein Grüber and the girls up the stairs and into the dining room. Trudel places her suitcase and zither behind her on the floor. She removes her coat, places it on the back of the chair, and sits down at the large table with her comrades, waiting.

Fräulein Grüber's responsibility is to oversee the administration and record keeping for every girl at camp. She is the head housekeeper and chef and she must teach the girls all aspects of home economics. Her weekly budget reports are sent to the Reich's Ministry. She hands each girl a pencil and the form.

Trudel begins filling out her form with her name, address, hometown, day, month, and year of her birth, her position as being the fourth child born into the Kerschner family, her parents' name, and their birthplaces. Trudel continues to list the skills she had acquired during her time in the Young Girls' League. These valuable skills include homemaking, cooking, setting the table, washing the dishes, washing and hanging the laundry, weaving, sewing, embroidery, art and crafts, gardening, raising livestock, hiking, marching, singing, and playing the zither. She proudly adds her first aid skills including how to handle abrasions, tending to bee stings, blisters, or burns, preventing cramps, dehydration, stopping nosebleeds, wrapping sprained joints, and setting broken bones with splints. She knows how to make a tourniquet by using her neckerchief and a stretcher by using her BDM jacket. She lists her favorite sports including hiking, bicycle riding, swimming, skiing, and sleigh riding. She notes her religious affiliation as Roman Catholic, and she attends regular church services every Sunday. Lastly, she wants to be sure to mention her JM Proficiency Award she earned for her knowledge in nursing, first aid, politics, and sports.

Trudel hands in her registration form feeling confident about herself. She gladly accepts the green-and-white triangle Landjahr patch. Then, Fräulein Grüber assigns her to room number eight. Quickly, she gathers her coat, zither, and suitcase, climbs the terrazzo staircase to the first floor and heads down the hall. The darkly stained pine doors are labeled with highly polished brass room numbers. At the end of the hall, she finds her room is located on the left. Slowly, she turns the brass door handles and then steps into her brightly lit dormitory room. She is amazed!

Three wooden bunk beds and three spacious blonde pine wardrobes line the walls. Above her bed is a carved wooden plaque with her last name, Kerschner. For the first time in her life, Trudel will be sleeping on a real mattress instead of a paillasse. She also has an authentic goose down pillow instead of a straw one!

Small tables and stools flank the cots. The bedroom is twelve feet high and one single light fixture dangles from the center of the ceiling. A three-quarter lite door faces west and opens onto the balcony that overlooks both the village and the lovely Lake Seidorf. Two double-casement awning windows with its blue and white checkered curtains face west and north.

Trudel feels very grateful for her new spacious accommodations. She thinks this is the most beautiful room in the entire Lager! She walks up to her bottom bunk bed and sets down her zither and suitcase next to her valise. She touches the wooden bed frame and caresses the soft flax linen sheets. She picks up the pillow, hugs it lovingly, and fluffs up it feathers.

Trudel steps toward the patio door, turns the brass handle, and walks outside to take a deep breath of fresh air. She takes a moment to familiarize herself with her surroundings. Her balcony overlooks the beautiful Giant Mountains. In the mid-distance to her left are the roofs of neighboring farms. She can see in the center of Seidorf and the church steeple she had passed by earlier. To the right, a million sparkles dance across Lake Seidorf like multifaceted diamonds radiating a shimmering hue of rainbow colors. Her gaze sweeps across the dense forest. Deciduous trees are bearing new buds. It is springtime at last, and the trees are awakening from their long winter's sleep. Small birds are dashing around the bare branches to and from their nests. Squirrels are chasing each other around the trees and leaping from limb to limb.

She also sees stone steps leading from the driveway down to a large open field. To the right is a long wooden building. Trudel jumps for joy when she notices a large pond in the distance with two springboards! She is feeling very blessed to be living in such a scenic area and in a beautiful manor home with her new comrades. She has always loved being up in the mountains and she relishes the location and view.

Trudel looks around her new landscape, taking in the sun as it sits above the Giant Mountains.[1] She steps back into the room naturally leaving the door opened, allowing the fresh air in. Pushing the curtains aside, she cranks open the north casement window for more ventilation. She looks down and notices her room is right above a second long storage building with a flat red roof. It has four doors and no windows. At the far right-end, a wooden shed is annexed to another building with doors, windows, and a large chimney. There are even chickens strutting around!

Trudel goes back and resumes her duties for she does not want to be late for orientation. She places her suitcase on the stool, unlatches the locks, and removes her clothes. She situates them neatly in her wardrobe then changes into her work clothes.

Other girls are settling into their rooms across and down the hall. As Trudel arranges her area, the door opens, and in walks Ingrid! The two embrace, very pleased to know that they are sharing a room together.

When Trudel shows Ingrid their beautiful outdoor seating arrangement, two more girls enter. Both walk back inside and welcome the newest roommates.

"Hi! I'm Trudel and this is my friend, Ingrid. What's your name?"

"Hi! My name is Steffi, Steffi Pucks."

"Hi! I'm Eleanor Mohler, but all my friends call me Nelly."

As the girls introduce themselves, they shake hands, and two more girls enter the room.

"Hello. My name is Maria Mikolasz, and this is Elli Musial."[2]

"Come on in!" Trudel says, taking charge. "You name plaques are over your beds. That's where you will be sleeping." Standing short of five feet two-inches, delegating assignments comes rather naturally to her.

The entire manor house is buzzing with activity. The girls bustle about and become better acquainted with each other, unpack their belongings, and change into their work clothes. Before they know it, a loud whistle blows announcing that it is time for orientation. The girls run from their rooms, downstairs, and compose themselves properly before entering into the dining room.

The main space is divided into three sections that take up half of the first floor. In the back of the dining room is a small sewing area with two treadle sewing machines. The main dining area features two large tables with fifty high-back chairs. To the side is another room that gives them access to the dumb-waiter. Post beams run the length of the entire ten-foot high ceiling and stained glass light fixtures provide illumination above the dining tables. Whitewashed plaster walls make the space feel bright, in contrast to the dark, highly polished, solid-oak flooring. Two sides of the dining room are ventilated by large rectan-

---

[1] Riesengebirge
[2] Peter Dubiel

gular casement windows with sheer white floral lace curtains. On the most prominent wall, hangs a portrait of their Führer encased within a gold wooden frame. His deep brown eyes seem as if he is watching their every movement.

In the corner, Fräulein Albrecht stands erect, next to the black board fully prepared with her whistle between her lips.

Once the girls take their seats, Fräulein Dieter begins the orientation. "We hope you find your accommodations suitable. Everything provided to you comes from the Reich's Ministry. The local villagers have also donated a few items for your use. You must always respect these gifts, because it is an honor to serve in Country Service Year Camp. We are here to serve in the people's community.[3] You must never take what we give you for granted. Only the most knowledgeable, courageous, and disciplined girls have been specifically chosen for Landjahr.[4] We have reviewed all of your personal records. Based upon your excellent qualifications, background, knowledge, and skills, each one of you are assigned to certain daily tasks. These assignments are on a two-week rotation period. First, we will tell you what you will be doing, and then we will show you what you will be doing. We expect you to learn and fulfill your duties throughout your eight-month stay in Landjahr. Next to my office in the main hallway is the bulletin board. That is where all the assignments and notices will be posted. Make sure you become familiar with the location for this is an important board.

"First, we will be performing our evening flag ceremony. The following girls will be the morning and evening flag bearers for the next two weeks. When I call your name, I want you to raise your hand. Eleanor Mohler and Elli Musial, you will be responsible for raising our morning flag. Steffi Pucks and Maria Mikolasz, you girls will be responsible for our evening flag ceremony. We keep the flags in the parlor. Make sure you become familiar with the location of the parlor. Now, we will perform our evening flag ceremony. Everyone line up!"

The girls quickly organize themselves. The flag bearers stand in the front of the line. When they have found their appropriate positions, the girls turn their heads to the right and space themselves one arm's length apart.

"Fräulein Dieter commands, "Eyes straight ahead!"

The girls turn their heads and face forward.

"Rechts um!" the troop leader commands next.

The girls pivot on their right heel ninety degrees to the right.

"Together, march!" Fräulein Dieter orders.

The girls' thumbs firmly press against their hands as their arms begin to swing back and forth in counterpoint to their legs. Singing their banner song, they march in single file, across the parlor and out the main entryway, down the steps, and straight across the gravel driveway into the courtyard.

They form a square in the field around the flagpole and finish singing their banner song. Standing at the head of the troop, Fräulein Dieter shouts, "Halt!"

---

[3] Volksgemeinschaft
[4] Maria Mikolasz

Steffi and Maria alone march toward the flag, do an about face, and stand at attention.

Raising their right arms in salute, the girls pledge their oath to their country and their Führer. Once their lower their arms, Fräulein Albrecht, the camp leader, addresses her new arrivals.

"Even though it is a difficult time for our people, we girls stand united as one with our Führer and our country under one flag. He is the one who has restored to the people their honor and freedom. He is the one who has shown us how to unite as one country. We always look to our Führer for guidance and direction. Without him, everything will fall apart and the Fatherland will be lost!

"When we unite as one, we are showing our Führer that we are willing to obey his commands. Only then can we call ourselves true Country Service girls. At all times, we must be loyal, dutiful, and obedient. We are in service to our country and to our neighboring farmers. We are here to support them. That is our mission. In turn, they will be supporting us by sharing their bounty. Without the support of each other, we are nothing. Remember, your leaders are here to teach you. We are here to educate you to become strong, hard-working women! Each one of you has the mind, the knowledge, and the discipline, but you must also have the 'will' to do the work that calls you into the Fatherland. If you do not have the will, then you are not German, and you cannot proclaim to come from true German soil!

"Our aim is to teach you to have a clear mind and to become conscious of your responsibilities. You are the future of Germany, and where we are now, you will be. You are the future of Germany. It will be and it must be! This thinking will grow into you as a natural expression of yourselves. Country Service Year Camp Seidorf will educate you in the truth, and our truth cannot be broken! We pledge ourselves to our Führer, to our Fatherland, and to our people. Let us sing:

> Germany, holy word, be you forever blessed
> Survive these times, you are blessed thee!
> Holy are thy lakes, holy are your forests
> From the crown, of your silent heights
> To the green of your sea![5]

At the end of the freedom song, the girls recite their Oath of Allegiance. Maria and Steffi meticulously untie the halyards from the flagpole cleat and then simultaneously lower the flag. They unclip their symbol of power from the snap hooks, and with the highest respect, fold the flag, and then turn to reattach the line to the cleat.

"This ceremony has concluded! Everyone, fall out!"

The sun turns ochre as it sets over the top of the Giant Mountain range. It will be completely dark in another hour. The girls relax their regimental stances and return to being girls who have traveled from afar.

---

[5] Wir Mädel Singen, 'Deutschland Heiliges Wort,' p.143

Compassionately, Fräulein Albrecht guides them on a tour around their exciting new surrounds. "I will now acquaint you with the camp. You are expected to remember the location and purpose of each room, especially the one where we hold our gymnastics!"

The camp leader leads the girls around the small estate. They walk from the courtyard across the driveway and down the granite steps to the large field at the bottom of the hill, into their sports field. This is where they will be spending most of their afternoons. The field is equipped with a pit filled with finely ground sand, a volleyball net, and two vertical posts with a crossbar on adjustable pegs.

To their right is a pair of tall, long buildings that house the workshop, music room, and indoor gymnasium. The camp leader shows the girls inside the first timber frame building. They walk through a small entry room and step down into the main space. To the left, large open casement windows overlook the sports field. To the right, three large worktables face the windows. Behind them, shelves and cabinets hold all manner of woodworking tools including saws, hammers, nails, and other materials. To the other side of the room houses their music stands. Chairs stacked on top of one another line the wall.

Fräulein Albrecht escorts the girls into the second, high-vaulted, open-frame building. As they step inside, they gasp! Their new gymnasium looks perfect with its high vaulted ceiling, brand-new balance beam, uneven bars, and vault! The girls hurry over to the equipment, ready to explore and eager to start gymnastic classes.

The tour however, is not over. The group leaves the sports building and walks up the granite stairs along the left side of the main house. Fraulein Albrecht shows the girls the Lager's storage buildings. She shows them the location of the supply room. This is where the housekeeping tools and equipment are stored. There are twenty aluminum-washing tubs and brooms, four washboards, a number of scrubbing brushes of various sizes, and a large metal trough next to the metal wringer. The garden room contains all their tools.

Next, the camp leader shows the girls the hay room that holds the straw bedding for the animals. After rounding the back of the hay barn, the girls cluster eagerly around the various animal stalls next to the tack room. There is a coop for the chickens and geese, and a larger stall for the two piglets. Trudel is so delighted to learn they have farm animals! In the distance, she sees the cattle grazing in the fields. She loves taking care of the animals.

Fräulein Albrecht ushers the girls across the driveway, down the stairs into the basement, through a turquoise-tiled washroom, and into the kitchen. The sizeable laundry area contains two large porcelain sinks and three showers. Aprons hang on hooks and the matching bandanas are in the pockets. In the center of the tile floor is a drain.

The girls head into the kitchen where Fräulein Dieter and Grüber are preparing the evening meal. Normally, the leaders would not be working in the kitchen. However, since the girls have just arrived from such a long trip, the women thought it would be a nice idea to participate in this evening's meal preparation—this time only, however.

The turquoise tiles and whitewashed walls of the commercially sized kitchen give it a bright and pleasant atmosphere. Large windows above the triple stainless steel sink look across the rear driveway toward the animal stalls. On either side of the sink are individual stainless steel work stations used for washing and preparing the food. In the center of the room stands a very large stainless steel table. Opposite the sink is an industrial size commercial stove and oven. The white tile keeps the heat in while six burners alongside of the flat top grill give it enough working space to cook for an army!

Next to the kitchen is a large pantry room. Three very large cold-storage rooms with heavy insulated metal doors double as bomb shelters. Across the room are steel shelves containing tableware and linen.

The girls walk up the terrazzo stairs and into the main hallway. The camp leader points out the location of the leader's office, the sick room, and a smaller music room. Next to the office door is the official camp bulletin board.

The group continues upstairs to the bedrooms. They are instructed to take their luggage to the attic on the third floor. Afterwards, they return to the dining room for the last part of their orientation. They take their seats and listen carefully to Fräulein Albrecht's lecture.

"Landjahr Lager is located on 7 Golden View. We are in region number four, district number twenty-one, and our troop number is one-hundred and fifty-four.[6]

"Now, forty girls will be divided into group."

Eleanor raised her hand.

"Yes?" the leader asks.

"Eleanor Mohler, Fräulein Albrecht, but all my friends call me Nelly."

"Yes, Nelly, you have a question?"

"You mentioned forty girls, but there are only twenty girls here."

"That is a very good observation, Nelly. Tomorrow, while you are performing your chores, we will be expecting another twenty girls to arrive from Upper Silesia."[7]

The girls look excitedly at each other. More girls' means more fun!

"Now, as I was saying, you will rotate your responsibilities every two weeks for the next eight months. Everyone will participate in home economics, farming, and gardening. We will have fun times too because in between our chores, we will display our talents to the local community by participating in various festivals and events. Starting tomorrow, we will help our farmers to plant their potato crop. At the end of April, we will hold Walpurgis Night, which is then followed by the raising of the May Pole. We will also celebrate Mother's Day with the farmer's wives. In June, we will celebrate the summer solstice and in August, we will take our big trip. In September, we will participate in the annual sports competition, which is being held in the city of Hirschberg. We expect you to do well. During the month of October, we will work very hard helping the

---

[6] The Hitler Jugend
[7] Peter Dubiel

farmers harvest their crops. By November, we will hold our pig baptism and afterwards, we will bid farewell to the villagers before returning home.

The girls smile at each other with anticipation.

"Every morning you will awake at six o'clock, dress appropriately for your assignment, and then wash. At six-thirty, we will march outside for our flag raising ceremony. In inclement weather, we will hold our flag ceremony in the parlor. At six-forty-five, we will eat breakfast. By seven-thirty, we will prepare for work, which will begin at eight o'clock. A whistle will blow at noon and that is when we will stop for lunch. From two to four o'clock, we will practice our sports in the lower field, or if the weather is bad, in the gymnasium. After sport practice, we will wash and change, take our coffee break, and read our mail. We will have another two hours to finish our evening chores. At six o'clock, we will perform our evening flag ceremony. At six-fifteen, we will eat a light dinner in the dining room. At seven o'clock, we will start our evening lessons. Sometimes we will tell stories, or perhaps sing and play music, or hold a political discussion. At nine o'clock, we will promptly retire to bed. All lights must be off and everyone must be in their beds at that time. Sunday will be your free day. At no time will you be allowed to leave the grounds without prior approval.

"Next, I will read off from my list your assignments for the next two weeks. This list will be posted on the bulletin board in the main hallway next to my office. There will be absolutely no complaining or whining! Everyone is here to work together, because our Führer demands this from all of us. Remember, we are in service to him and he is depending upon us to help the farmers because, their potatoes will be going to our soldiers on the front lines.

The girls anxiously wait to hear their assignments.

"When I call your names, I want you to raise your hands, Barbara, Herminie, Gabriele, Ingrid, Elfie, Ericka, and Sabine! You girls are assigned to the home economics group. You will be responsible for meal preparations, house cleaning, and laundry. Fräulein Grüber will be your instructor. She is waiting for you downstairs in the kitchen.

In an orderly fashion, the summoned girls walk downstairs to help the camp and assistant leaders, who are preparing this evening's meal.

"Nelly, Lotte, Elli, Anna, Kristin, Liesel, Renate, and Trudel are assigned to farming and livestock. At eight o'clock tomorrow morning, your group will start working on Herr Torge's farm, in Ober-Seidorf. You will do exactly as they say. You will return here after lunch and no later than one-thirty in order to participate in your afternoon sports activities. In addition to working with the farmers, you will be responsible for the care of our own camp livestock. Fräulein Dieter will be your instructor. However, since she is currently helping in the kitchen to prepare dinner, I will be instructing you in your work this evening. Your aprons and scarves are hanging up in the washroom downstairs. Please wear them at all times while you are working.

Trudel is ecstatic to hear that she will be going to Ober-Seidorf, helping the farmers, and caring for the livestock!

"Now, please go outside and gather the livestock behind our home and bring them inside to their stalls except for the cattle. They will remain outside. Make sure the animals have enough water and that the stalls are thoroughly cleaned. Before you leave them for the night, make sure all the doors and gates are securely fastened and locked. And above all, never give names to any of the livestock."

Trudel is the first to bolt from her seat, run downstairs into the washroom, and pick up her apron and scarf.

Fräulein Albrecht appoints Charlotte, Helli, Katarina, Aloise, Maria, and Steffi to the vegetable garden. "Now, while I go into my office and get some paper, I want you girls to discuss our garden. After I return, we will go outside and map the plot that we will use to grow our crop."

The girls know what to do. They discuss the vegetable and herb options as the camp leader leaves the room. They will plot a garden plan to scale, noting various environmental factors including shade, sun, excess run-off water, and wind. The diagram will be complete by indicating the positions of the various vegetables and herbs. Then, all the girls will help to till and cultivate the soil before planting. When she returns, the camp leader escorts her girls outside. They agree on the garden's location, the crop selection, and soil preparation.

Once the plan is in place, the camp leader walks to the back of the home and checks on the farm group.

A systematic procedure maximizes efficiency throughout the household, minimizing confusion. However, the first few weeks will no doubt be the most challenging period for both the girls and their leaders. The recruits must come to learn their places in the new household via their daily duties. Many challenges lay ahead for the leaders, too, who are required to calibrate an efficient work schedule.

Tonight, there is going to be a feast in the Lager! Deep down in the belly of the house, the girls move quickly. Fräulein Grüber already has this evening's dinner partially completed. For every meal, it will be her girls' responsibility to cook, set the table, serve the food, clear the table, wash the dishes, and put away the tableware. The girls grab their aprons and scarfs. Ingrid, Elfie, Ericka, and Sabine are assigned to kitchen duties.

Barbara, Herminie, and Gabriele are in charge of tableware. The girls count off twenty-three dishes, glasses, knives, forks, spoons, napkins, and one large tablecloth. They fill the dumbwaiter. Barbara closes the frosted glass casement doors decorated with yellow flowers and then pulls on the rope. She finds there is too much weight inside the elevator. She removes a few items then repacks the dumbwaiter. Barbara then hoists up the tablecloth, napkins, silverware, and glasses to the first-floor dining room. Herminie and Gabriele go upstairs to the pantry, open the dumbwaiter, and remove all the tableware within onto a serving table. Herminie returns the dumbwaiter to Barbara then helps Gabriele set the table. When Barbara finishes loading the items, she goes upstairs to help set the table. This three-girl table setting method seems to be working quite smoothly for them for the entire table is set in less than twenty minutes.

While Ingrid and Elfie assist Fräulein Dieter in preparing the roast meat, Erika and Sabine work with Fräulein Grüber in preparing the vegetables. Their stomach starts to grumble when Fräulein Dieter pulls the large roast out of the wood burning oven and places it on the oak countertop. The distinctive and enticing aroma whiffs through the house and the girls upstairs smell the enticing redolence of the juicy meat.

Wearing an oven mitt, Ingrid carefully tips the roasting pan just enough so she can scoop up the bubbling juices with a large silver spoon. She begins to baste the meat. Elfie goes into the pantry, finds the plates and casserole dishes, and places them on the prep table in the center of the room. Erika and Sabine remove the mash potatoes, carrots, and spinach from the cast iron pots and place them in separate covered dishes. Ingrid and Elfie move the roast into the serving tray and garnish it with onions, carrots, and potatoes. Fräulein Dieter then covers the plate and slides it into the dumbwaiter. Barbara hoists it up to the waiting girls upstairs. Next to go upstairs are the condiments as well as the vegetables, bread, and butter. As the girls finish their work in the kitchen, the farm group is outside tending to their livestock.

Trudel cannot believe her eyes when she hurries outside and sees all the farm animals roaming behind the building! Peking ducks and Norwegian white geese are relaxing by the small hand-dug pond. Chickens roam freely around the property. Two domesticated piglets watch Trudel from their fenced-in barnyard adjacent to their stalls.

Trudel knows exactly what to do. She darts into the coop and looks for fresh eggs. Carefully, Trudel picks up the eggs and places them inside the folds of her apron. She ferries an armful into the waiting egg cartons then returns to help with the livestock.

Lotte and Elli walk inside the tool room and grab their brooms and shovels. In the coop, they sweep the floor and collect the droppings. Dropping are an excellent source of fertilizer for the garden and for now will be placed in a special bucket marked with a red "X."

Anna and Kirstin check the food and water supply as Liesel and Renate muck out the stalls. The girls' team up and gather fresh bedding for the livestock. The chickens notice the activity and come running towards the coop. Anna throws corn on the ground, luring them closer with her universal chicken call. These farm girls require no assistance.

From a distance, Fräulein Albrecht watches and she is extremely pleased to see how well they are all working together. They are adept at their skills, having plenty of prior experience.

The girls lock the animals into the stalls for the night, making sure all the gates and doors and securely fastened. They return to the washroom, thoroughly washing their hands, and taking care to scrub under their fingernails. Before they return inside, Fräulein Albrecht inspects the girls' fingernails, clothes, and shoes. They remove their work shoes and put on their house slippers.

Up at the dining room table, the girls complement Herminie and Gabriele for the elegant table setting. A beautiful arrangement of wildflowers completes the room's focal point.

Fräulein Dieter rises from her chair to leads the girls in gratitude. "Let us stand and hold hands." All the girls rise from their chairs and take the other's hand. "Before we eat, let us take a moment to go around the room and give thanks to those who have provided for us."

Each girl expresses her appreciation for the marvelous feast they are about to eat this evening. When the last girl has finished saying her prayer, they all sit, and receive their supper portions. This is the best meal they have eaten in months!

During dinner, the girls hardly speak to one another. They are all devouring their food. The long trip has taken a toll on the girls' bodies too, for they are starting to become tired.

With their tummies full, the girls clear their dishes and bring them over to the pantry table next to the dumbwaiter. The home economics group clears the remaining items, sweeps the floor, wipes down the table, and neatly folds the tablecloth. The kitchen aids place everything in the dumbwaiter and lower it into the basement. Together, they go downstairs to complete their chores while the other girls retire to the parlor.

"Whether you are at the school desk
Or in a workplace
Doing your duty in the HJ and BDM
Or at home with your mothers,
You have tasks everywhere
That you must fulfill
If you want to be able to say
That you are one of Adolf Hitler's
Proper German boys and girls."

~ Rudolf Hess ~

Political Evening

BY SEVEN O'CLOCK, everyone assembles in the main parlor for an evening of political education. The leaders believe the girls have done an exceptional job for their first few hours in Camp Seidorf. Even though the girls are exhausted, Fräulein Albrecht praises and compliments them on a job well done.

"This is our second year of Country Service Year Camp Seidorf" begins Fräulein Albrecht. "Last year, we had sixty girls with us. They did a beautiful job when they decorated the camp with all their fine crafts and artwork."

"When do we get to start working on our crafts?" Steffi asks.

"Very soon, Steffi. However, there are practical guidelines you must become fluent in before we start our work. First, you must understand that we hold the future of Germany within our hands. Each of us has a duty and responsibility to our Lager, to our villagers, our State, and to our Führer. When we work, we not only work for ourselves, we work together and raise Germany higher as one people for the Fatherland. Our goal in Country Service Year is to educate you in becoming responsible young German girls who are physically and mentally ready and willing to serve. Conscription in Country Service is a great honor.[1]

"Now, think about it for just a moment. Think about how everything is structured for you within the League. When you were in the Young Girls' League, you learned the basic skills needed to prepare you for today. Back when you were ten years old, we gave you the work ethics to help your mothers. You are now adolescent girls who possess the knowledge to serve in this elite rural education camp. Country Service Year Camp will educate and prepare you for the BDM Proper and life itself. It is my duty and responsibility, along with your troop leader, Fräulein Dieter, and your assistant and economics leader, Fräulein Grüber, to teach you the practical skills you will need for your chosen vocations. We must all come together and accomplish the work for our people, the Fatherland, and our Führer." She pauses for a moment before continuing.

"Before our Führer, life was very difficult. It all began in June of 1914 when Archduke Franz Ferdinand of Austria, the Royal Prince to Hungary and Bohemia, along with his wife, Her Serene Highness and Princess of Hohenberg, Sophie, were assassinated in Sarajevo. Germany and Austria-Hungary declared war on Serbia thereby triggering the Great War.[2]

"Why did they kill the royal prince and princess?" Nelly asks.

---

[1] Bund Deutscher Mädel – "Country Service Year Pamphlet"
[2] Archduke Franz Ferdinand

"Well, there was one very angry man that did not like what was happening. He imagined that he could make things better by killing the royal heirs to the Austrian-Hungarian throne. It is a lesson we need to learn for it only takes one man to destroy a country, but it takes an entire nation to build it back up again. This is why you girls hold the future of Germany in your hands, just as our Führer holds our great nation in his hands."

Fräulein Grüber's picks up the conversation. "The Great War continued for four years. Over two million German soldiers were killed. On November 11th, 1918, an agreement was declared for the fighting to stop. Heavy and dark was the path of the German people for she had lost the Great War. Right afterwards, the German Revolution started.

"By June of 1919, the Treaty of Versailles was signed and it blamed Germany for starting the Great War. Germany was unfairly forced to disarm. She was stripped of all her weapons, had to make substantial territorial concessions, and pay 132 billion Marks, (equivalent to $442 billion in 2015) in reparations to France, Belgium, and England.[3]

"By August 1919, the German Revolution was over. The Weimar Republic was established and it replaced the German Empire. Friedrich Ebert became the first president of the German Reich.

"In 1921, the consequences of the Armistice were so great that the Weimar Republic could not pay its debt and its currency was fast becoming worthless. The less the currency is worth, more of it is needed to purchase one's daily goods. Our people grew exhausted and extremely discouraged. This sparked great fear among the working-class people. Those with no money started fighting and many people died. All around the country, entire industries began shutting down and many workers lost their jobs.

"By November of 1923, inflation in the Weimar Republic was insanely out of control.[4] The people were terribly disillusioned under these conditions and many prayed hard for a new era. When the German people woke up they finally realized that their money was rapidly losing value. It was at this point that they tried to spend it very quickly.

"Back then, our Führer was the party leader of the National Socialist Democratic Worker's Party (NSDAP). Only a few of the faithful wore in their hearts the desire for resistance against destruction. Instead of living in disgrace and being slaves to the different economic and social classes, our leader, not yet the Führer started planting a new way of thinking into the minds of the people. We will no longer be living in forcible bondage with dishonor.[5]

"On November 8th, 1923, our young leader decided to tackle this economic catastrophe by taking matters into his own hands. With the help of his associates, the Battle-League leaders, and six-hundred Storm Detachments (S.A.), he stormed into the Bürgerbräukelle in Munich and declared a revolution against

---

[3] Treaty of Versailles
[4] Weimar Constitution
[5] Mädel im Dienst, p. 7

the Weimar Republic. He declared a new form of government under the control of General Ludendorff.[6] After he spoke, the crowd of three-thousand roared in approval and together they finished triumphantly.[7] The next day, our Führer led a march that was two-thousand strong. Unfortunately, the marchers were met with gunfire, and many men were killed. Two days later, our leader was arrested for high treason and placed into jail for eight months.[8] During this time, he wrote *"Mein Kampf,"* which he describes his political ideology and vision for Germany's great future.

"By 1925, Paul von Hindenburg was elected as the second president of the German Reich. Over the next four years, the economy greatly improved. The people of Germany were very happy again, until one day in October 1929 when America's stock market crashed. A massive economic shock wave hit Germany so hard that it kicked the Weimar Republic back into another deep depression. Within a year, the country was suffering from massive unemployment. To try and stabilize the economy, the government slashed spending and tried to cut welfare benefits to its citizens. This did not work. Once again, the people revolted against austerity policies and turned against their government. They began to realize that our Führer was right all along. They began supporting the National Socialistic Democratic Worker's Party. Now, they had a choice! They could vote for National Socialism or they could vote for Communism and become one with Russia. The German people chose National Socialism.

"In January 1933, Hindenburg chose Hitler and his NSDAP party as the very last hope to save Germany from political, social, and economic destruction. This is when Hitler became Chancellor of Germany.

"By February, von Hindenburg issued the Reichstag Fire Decree, which put a halt to civil liberties. In March, von Hindenburg signed the Enabling Act and this gave Hitler's administration complete legislative powers.

"In 1934, Hitler carried out "The Night of the Long Knives," for which he received the personal thanks from Hindenburg.[9] This was a great turning point for the German government, because Hitler asked the cabinet to pass the "Law Concerning the Highest State Office of the Reich," which stipulated that upon Hindenburg's death, the offices of president and chancellor would merge under the title of Leader and Chancellor.[10] On August 2nd, Hindenburg died. He then declared the President's Office vacant and made himself Head of State.[11]

"Hitler held a referendum the 19th of August asking the German people if they would approve merging the two offices together. Ninety percent of the people voted yes. He single-handedly transformed the Weimar Republic into the Third Reich. After fourteen years of struggling through the very worst time

---

[6] Beer Hall Putsch
[7] Kershaw, p. 128
[8] Ibid, p. 129
[9] William L. Shirer
[10] Richard Overy
[11] Paul von Hindenburg

in our history, our great Führer took possession at the helm of Germany.[12] His goal was to restore total economic order and he did! Even though he was born in Austria, he had become a citizen of Germany and had made Germany his home. Within three short years, our Führer took a bleak landscape and turned it into one of the greatest and strongest nations on earth. He kept the promises he made. Within the first two years, over twenty-two million people were removed from welfare and returned to work. Thousands of factories re-opened their doors to welcome back the workers! In addition, only the strongest men built the autobahn with their very own hands! Our Führer ordered the manufacturing of the affordable and dependable Volkswagen so that the people could drive with pride on these new highways. German industry reawakened! Germans started buying goods from their own country instead of buying cheap foreign imports.

"On March 12, 1938, Austria became part of Germany. Over ninety-nine percent of the Austrians voted to unify with Germany. In Vienna, they welcomed their new Führer with open arms, and when the Führer—"[13]

"…And when the Führer came into Austria," Trudel excitedly interrupts Fräulein Grüber, "my mother received a lot of money! She bought my brother a brand-new bicycle, and we had more food on the table, and new clothes to wear. Mama even got herself a brand-new car and a washing machine!"

"That is impressive, Trudel," Fräulein Grüber says validating Trudel's comment. "As I was saying, all of Germany became prosperous once again. Without our Führer, our country would have descended into complete chaos. Even the National Socialist People's Welfare organization established an aid program called "Mother and Child," which today, has no equal anywhere in the world! This program employs thousands of trusted young girls like yourselves, as nurses and daycare workers to babysit children while their mothers' are off at work. It also ensures well-earned rest for mothers. By the end of 1937, some 252,000 mothers had received free vacations paid for by the State.[14] Moreover, in 1938, America recognized the miraculous work our Fuhrer did that their famous magazine 'Time' proclaimed him Man of the Year! We owe our lives to the Führer!

The girls nod their heads in agreement.

Fräulein Dieter, the troop leader, now speaks. "We cannot forget our young people and how they are serving our country with loyalty, dedication, and honor. Now, thinking back on where Germany was only twenty-seven short years ago versus where we are now, do you not think you should give your total obedience to our Führer?

The girls nod their heads in agreement.

"Our Führer watches over his people. He knows that you are the best from the Young Girl's League and that is why you have been chosen for Landjahr. It is our duty to work with the farmers in this area because their potato crop will

---

[12] Randall L. Bytwerk, "We Owe It to the Führer"
[13] Das Mecklenburgische Landmädel in BDM, p. 3
[14] Randall L. Bytwerk, "We Owe It to the Führer"

be sent to our soldiers on the front line. Our District Leader, Fräulein Elli Hubbe, has made all necessary arrangements. Our farmers know that you have arrived, so tomorrow, you will be starting on the Torge Farm." Fräulein Dieter turns to address the other leaders. "Is there anything else we need to cover?"

"I think we have covered enough this evening," Fräulein Albrecht replies.

"If anyone needs me then, I shall be in my office." Fräulein Grüber rises from her chair, clicking her black heels, and salutes the troop leader. She pivots on her right foot and then leaves the room.

Fräulein Albrecht resumes the conversation. "Our strength is in our farmers, so you young maidens will need to work very hard. Our farmers are depending on us. Starting tomorrow, you will be helping plant the potatoes. Make sure that all of you who are assigned to the farming duties are dressed in your work clothes. You will report to Fräulein Dieter outside by the foot of the stairs where she will escort you to the Torge Farm. All assigned girls to home economics will meet Fräulein Grüber after the flag ceremony in the kitchen to prepare breakfast. All the girls on garden duty will remain in the dining room after breakfast. Now, it is getting late. I believe it is time for us to head to bed. We all want a good night's sleep, so we can perform efficiently tomorrow, don't we?"

At eight-thirty, the camp leader sends the exhausted girls off to their rooms. They wash up, brush their teeth, and change into their pajamas. Before retiring for the evening, Fräulein Albrecht scrutinizes every detail of their rooms. Room inspections will become a morning and evening ritual.

The camp leader retires to her office where she meets with the troop and economic leaders. For the next hour, they drink chamomile tea, review the girl's performance, and make notes and comments in the girl's respective folders. By ten o'clock, they retire to their individual rooms. Tomorrow will be a hectic day.

"The east wind raises the flag
Because the east wind looks good
When they direct a signal to depart,
Our blood will hear the call"

~In den Ostwind hebt die Fahnen~

First Day at Camp

STANDING IN THE HALLWAY, the camp leader blows the whistle sharply. "Time to get up!" she yells.

"Why are we getting up so early? What just happened? I just went to bed," Trudel mumbles as she tries to shrug off her grogginess. For a split second, she is confused by the dark and unfamiliar surroundings that she forget where she is. This is not her attic bedroom nor is that her mother's voice she hears.

Just then, she remembers she is in Country Service! She throws her legs over the side of the bed and sits up, rubbing her eyes, then she donned on her slippers. In their pajamas, she and her five roommates rush to the washroom, passing Fräulein Albrecht on the stairs. Trudel hurries to wash her face and brush her teeth. The cold water quickly wakes her up. She dries off and runs back to her bedroom to quickly dress. She is looking forward to working on the Torge Farm today. She is so excited!

She slips on her work attire and makes her bed, ensuring that the fold in her sheets are tight in the corners and tucked snugly under the mattress. She fluffs up her pillow, smoothing the remaining wrinkles out of her sheets, then neatly folds her blanket and places it on the foot of her mattress. Her roommates follow suite. While she is folding her pajamas and sliding them under her pillow, Fräulein Albrecht suddenly enters the room without knocking.

"Attention!" the camp leader shouts. This is the military command she uses as a means for getting the girl's attention, disciplinary actions, or getting the girls into their formations.

Instantly, the girls stand erect at the side of their bed. Arms are down and slightly flexed. Fingers curl into the palm and thumbs are pointed down and placed against the seam of their dress. Feet face forward, heels together. Elli, Nelly, Steffi, Maria, Trudel, and Ingrid stand frozen in place, daring not to blink.

Fräulein Albrecht slowly enters the room with her heavy gait. Whenever the horseshoe-shaped metal plates on the bottom of her heels strike the floor, they make the appropriate rhythmic step sound for a military leader.[1] Hands behind her back, she walks slowly past the girls, looking directly into their eyes. Wearing her green lanyard and dressed in her official BDM uniform, she commands the highest respect with her authoritative presence.

Steffi's head follows her as she walks by, but quickly, she realizes her error and turns to face forward. The girls eye the woman as she inspects the room. Everything has to be precise.

The camp leader removes a Reich pfennig from her pocket and with a quick snap, flips the coin into the air. "This bed has passed the test," she announces.

---

[1] Bund Deutscher Mädel - "Shoes and Accessories"

She tests each mattress. If the coin does not bounce, she will rip the sheets off and order the bed to be remade.

The camp leader notices one of the pillows is not straight. Maria does not have enough time to put on her socks and is standing in her bare feet. Nelly threw her socks under her bed and Trudel is hiding her handkerchief in her sweater. The camp leader has her nose everywhere—under the beds, under the pillows, and even behind the closets! Fräulein Albrecht walks toward the girls then stops. She pivots on her left heel, turns, and walks toward the wardrobe. When she opens the cabinet, the clothes fall out onto her feet!

"What is this!" she shouts.

Immediately, panic sets in the girls stomachs.

"Come on girls!" she yells. "Get this room into shape now, move! I will return!" She marches across the room leaving the door opened behind her.

"Attention!" she yells as she enters the next room across the hall.

With lightning speed, Trudel and her roommates dash about their room and finish getting dressed.

In less than five minutes, Fräulein Albrecht returns. The girls' quickly line themselves up again at front of their bunks.

"Now, this is *much* better girls. This is exactly how I want the room to look every morning before you begin your duties. Now, go and wait outside the house," she orders. The girls race down the stairs and out the side door, onto the gravel driveway.

"What just happened?" Trudel wonders.

"I don't know," Steffi replies. "One minute I was sound asleep, and the next thing I know is that I am racing downstairs to wash up."

"That was a close one," Nelly comments. "I wonder if we have to do this every morning."

"I don't know," declares Maria. "But if we do, we had better make sure our room is totally organized before she walks in because I don't want to go through that again."

"Neither do I!" agrees Trudel. An idea strikes her. "Hey, let's make a pact that every morning our rooms will be in order *before* Fräulein Albrecht walks in, okay?" The girls concur and slap each other high fives to seal their promise.

Just then, four more girls dash out of the side of the building.

"What on earth just happened?" giggles Lotte.

"We were just talking about that," Trudel responds with a wry smile.

The girls engage in small talk as they wait for the other girls to arrive. Shortly, they will begin their morning flag ceremony.

Fräulein Albrecht continues to inspect every bedroom. The girls on the third floor hear the commotion going on downstairs and have advance warning. They race to make their rooms perfect.

When inspection is over, the entire troop assembles outside. The three leaders emerge from the side entrance. The girls hustle to get into formation, and in one synchronized motion, they stand at attention. Nelly and Elli are ready with the flag. Everyone lines up according to her height. Fräulein Dieter orders the girls to march from the Lager over to the courtyard flagpole. Their morning ritual begins.

"Hoist the flag!" Fräulein Dieter commands.

With their banner clutched securely in their hands, the bearers walk to the base of the pole. The girls ceremoniously unravel the Swastika flag. They clip it onto the brass swivel snaps and briskly hoist it over their domain. They secure the halyard onto the cleat, raise their right arms in salute, and sing "The East Wind Lifts Our Flag."[2]

> The east wind raises the flag
> Because the east wind looks good
> When they direct a signal to depart,
> Our blood will hear the call
> Then the land gives us the answer
> And it carries a German face
> For that, many have bled,
> That is why the earth is not silent

After the four-stanza song, they lower their arms. The girls stand at attention to hear Fräulein Albrecht's morning speech. The troop and assistant leaders stand on either side of her. Her elocution is flawless.

"Today is your first official day in Country Service Year," she begins. "We are very proud of your efforts. We can see from your behavior last night and this morning that you are true country service girls. As proud as our flag waves in the east wind on this beautiful morning, so should you be proud of yourselves standing here in service to your country. Today marks the official beginning of Camp Seidorf, 1941! Let us greet our Führer on this glorious morning!"

Everyone raises their right arm in salute and recites the Oath of Allegiance.

"I promise always to do my duty in Landjahr Lager, in love and loyalty to our leader and our flag."

They lower their arms and are ready to hear the leader's morning greeting. "For the next eight months, we will work together in camaraderie, in fellowship, and in community. We will work with our land, our Volk, and our Führer. Our culture and language is going to spread far because our language is the happiest in the world. We have the power, and we will always honor that which we work very hard for, not just for us, but also for our people." Now, let us conclude our morning flag ceremony with the singing of our National Anthem.[3]

> Germany, Germany above all things,
> Above everything in the world,
> When, for protection and defense,
> it always stands brotherly together.

---

[2] Wir Mädel Singen - "In den Ostwind hebt die Fahnen" p. 175
[3] Annemarie Leppien, p. 72

From the Meuse to the Memel,
From the Adige to the Belt,
Germany, Germany above all things,
Above everything in the world!

The girls follow their BDM leaders obediently inside their new manor home. The home economics group hurries to prepare breakfast. Gabriele quickly runs outside and picks fresh flowers for the table centerpiece. When the food finally arrives, all the girls stand around the dining room table, hold hands, and say a prayer. After grace, they sit and dig into their breakfast. Each girl receives a thick slice of home-baked, hard-crust sourdough bread with a slice of butter, a ladle spoonful of fresh scrambled eggs, a slice of ham, a cup of coffee made with fresh goat milk, and an apple. The girls devour their food and still have a half an hour left to complete their morning chores.

The farming group hastens outside and tends to the animals while Fräulein Dieter completes her paperwork in the office. At eight o'clock sharp, the girls remove their Landjahr banner from the parlor room, and with their troop leader, they hike eagerly towards the Torge farm, a half an hour down the road in Lower Seidorf. As they hike, the girls ask themselves many questions, which go unanswered. They cannot even sing right, they are all choked up.

Landjahr is not an original concept. An earlier program began during the Weimar Republic as a labor market policy for all young people, under the term 'State Aid.' In March 1934, participation became mandatory for all boys throughout Germany. In addition to working on the farms, the program incorporated the disciplinary measures of national political training. These Country Service Year camps replace the ninth-year academic curriculum altogether. Its leaders shielded these young men from parental interference and religious requirements. Since WWII started September 1, 1939, all fit young men had to leave these farms. Only since then, a select group of strong adolescent girls is chosen to replace them.[4]

The goal of Country Service Year is not only to serve the farmers, it is a national work program, designed to reduce youth unemployment. Camp Seidorf will educate and prepare them for possible careers in agriculture, horticulture, hospitality, home economics, and motherhood. Their daily salary for working on the farms is two cents each per day. The money will be handed over to their camp leader for safekeeping.

Originally, Seidorf was once a pagan forest village with its roots dating back to the early fourteenth century. It was founded after a great storm destroyed the Polish village of Broniów, far to the east. When the village peasants heard that the lands to the west were fertile, they picked up their remaining possessions and traveled over three-hundred miles toward the Giant Mountains. They settled in the tiny area of Seidorf. These new villagers logged the surrounding area to construct their new homes. They cleared the land for crops and livestock. Shortly

---

[4] Gertrude Hödlmaier

after arriving in Seidorf, the Hussite's attacked and destroyed the village, including St. Anna's Chapel, and the medieval temple. The peasants somehow managed to recuperate. To show their gratitude, they erected a Christian church to Saint Martin on the site of the old temple.[5]

Over the centuries, Seidorf continued to be plagued by famines, epidemics, hostilities of invading armies, reformations, and the overthrow of European rulers. It was not until the manufacturing of Damask table linen handcrafted by Seidorf weavers during the seventeenth century that economic growth finally began in earnest. The demand for fine linen made Seidorf one of the major crossing points between the Polish-Lithuanian Commonwealth and Bohemia. Aristocratic Silesian nobles such as Henckel von Donnersmarcks, Johann von Ballestrem, Phillip Gotthard von Schaffgotsch, Hans Heinrich X the Count of Hochberg, and Victor I, the Prince of Hohenlohe-Schillingsfürst, recognized the hidden wealth in this area. They set out to individually develop the surrounding land. One built a paper mill along the river in Arnsdorf. Another started mining for coal and lead. Others inherited massive tracts of lands on which to expand their vast farming estates. At the turn of the nineteenth century, the natural, healing, geothermal waters in the nearby city of Bad Warmbrunn became renowned, and tourism flourished.[6]

The main road through the village of Seidorf is Rübezahl Road and it is lined with farming homesteads. The majestic Baroque Church of Our Lady of Ostra Brama marks the center of town. Across the street stands the village theatre and guesthouse. The local school and post offices are just a few buildings away. On the outskirts of the village is the Torge farm and that is precisely where the girls are heading.

The landholder of the Torge Farm is Friedrich, the youngest of the aristocratic Schaffgotsch family. Together with this farm, he owns over sixty-six thousand acres in the surrounding Hirschberg Valley area, which includes Kynastburg Castle high up on the Giant Mountains. The villagers know this rural farming estate by its name, "Always Free."

However, the girls would come to know it as the "Torge Farm," since the Torge family has been overseeing the management of the property for generations. Their farm is required to supply potatoes to the German Army who are fighting on the front battle lines, and it is imperative that the girls start working immediately.

The middle-aged Frau Torge hears the girls singing as they march up the street and into her courtyard. Frau Torge is a slightly large woman and robust in her features from years of working on the farmstead. She is in extremely good health for her age. Wiping her hands on her apron, she slips out the back door. "Fräulein Dieter!" she says as she bustles over to shake the hands of the troop leader. "I can't begin to thank you enough for bringing us help! We are eternally grateful that you are here with us!"

---

[5] Malgorzata Jackiewicz
[6] Ibid

While the two women discuss the agenda for the day's work, the girls await their orders, and look around at their surroundings.

The sixteen-century, Upper Lusatian, two-story farm home is set back from the road. Its architectural vernacular complements the smaller Tyrolean style homes of the village. The foundational stones and square oak beams of the wattle-and-daub façade face east onto the main road. A separate timber-frame barn blocks the wind from the north while the rear of the homestead faces west, overlooking the fields. The open-ended rectangular farmhouse encloses a courtyard that is accessible through the sides and rear of the home. Only the front part of the extensive building contains the living quarters. The wings house the stables, a storeroom, and a workshop. A large workroom and bake-house are located toward the rear. On the far side of the courtyard, away from the main home, are smaller stalls for the pigs, and a large coop for the poultry. All the hay bales, tools, and farming equipment are stored in the barn, next to the livestock stalls. In front of the home, a beautiful flower garden is laid out. The patchwork patterns in the fields behind the home reflect the variety of crops and grains that are beginning to sprout. To the side of the house is the vegetable garden.

The girls will be working in the potato field under the direct supervision of Farmer Torge, and their troop leader, Fräulein Dieter. Nelly has been appointed to stay inside and help Frau Torge with the house chores, while Lotte, Elli, Anna, Kristin, Liesel, Renate, and Trudel will be outside planting the potatoes.

Fräulein Dieter escorts the girls to the barn to meet Herr Torge. He is a kind, late middle-aged man. He has distinguishing features and a strong muscular build from years of working the soil. His daily attire consists of a long-sleeve shirt, leather overalls, and ankle work boots. Since his sons had been drafted two years earlier to fight in the war, the man has been left alone to tend his crops. He found himself beholden to his government when the Ministry sent these girls to help.

His young helpers formally introduce themselves and reassure him that they are willing and capable of handling the heavy workload. With confident strides, the girls follow Herr Torge into the barn, where he begins his instructions.

"As you know, potato plants are grown from these little spuds that were gathered from last year's crop. Do you see the eyes on all these dried quartered potatoes here?" Herr Torge pulls a sample out from the burlap sack. "These here are the eyes that make the plant grow." He points to the tubes growing out from the spud. "We are going to need to take these spuds and plant them four inches deep, in rows three feet apart. Each spud will be twelve inches from the next. In total, we will be planting five acres."

The girls nod. They had planted potatoes in their own family's gardens many times, so they understand the procedure. None of them, however, had planted such a large crop before.

"Okay, now if you can grab these sacks and bring them outside we can start working." Herr Torge respects the girls enough to help them haul the fifteen-pound sacks out into the field. He gives each girl a hand spade and her own row.

The previous autumn he had prepared this field for the coming crop. Using a neighbor's oxen and plough, and with the help of last year's camp girls, he had harvested his crops, and then overturned the soil. More recently, he had been harrowing the field by smoothing out the rough ground left by his plough. Two days ago, he cut the spuds in quarters, and let them dry.

The team plants the spuds in the middle of the mound while Herr Torge supervises. Planting potatoes is backbreaking work. Kneeling on the ground by a sack of spuds, each girl digs a hole with her spade, plants a spud, and covers it with soil. Then, she moves the bag up one foot and repeats the process, hour after hour. Yet, they all work willingly and with much enthusiasm.

The girls pass the time with song. They chat gaily about their hometowns and their families, and they wonder what the year will bring. They are enjoying the camaraderie of work. It is a pleasant day to be outside in the fresh air under the sun. Fräulein Dieter encourages them to have fun while remaining mindful of their tasks. They perform their tasks right the first time for mistakes are discouraged and dampen productivity.

Fräulein Dieter leaves the girls working in the field and walks back to the farmhouse to speak with Frau Torge in private. The two adults are soon sitting at the picnic table under the oak tree while Nelly remains inside preparing lunch.

"How is Nelly working out for you, Frau Torge?" the troop leader asks.

"She is doing an exceptional job. Thank you for asking. Your new girls this year are working quite hard in the field. You must be very pleased with them."

"Yes, we are. The other leaders and I feel that these girls are better prepared for farming duties than last year's group. Maybe it has something to do with the war. I do not know. All we can do is observe and train them to be the very best they can be. We reviewed their paperwork last night, so the girls we selected to work on your farm were all raised in the country. You will find they are well versed in farming skills. We are very excited to have them this year."

"I am very happy to hear that, Fräulein Dieter. This is your second year commanding the Lager, yes?" Frau Torge asked.

"Why, yes it is. Thank you for remembering."

"I remember when we first met last year. That was right after my sons joined the war effort. I was excited to hear that our Führer was going to provide my husband and me with extra help on the farm. Otherwise, we would have had to give it up and do something else."

"I understand, Frau Torge. I believe that—"

The leader's sentence is cut short when she sees Liesel running towards her, screaming.

"Fräulein Dieter! Fräulein Dieter! Come quickly! Something has happened to Herr Torge!"

Quickly, the two women run toward the field and find Trudel and Renate kneeling down next to the farmer. He is unconscious. Trudel holds her damp bandana on his forehead. Renate strokes his hand, hoping he will wake up.

Frau Torge gasps then quickly claps both her hands over her mouth, preventing her from speaking aloud her fear that her dear husband is dead.

The troop leader rushes over to his side and kneels down. She knows exactly what to do. "Herr Torge," she calls as she pats his cheeks until she rouses him.

Slowly, he opens his eyes and regains full consciousness. "What happened? Why am I on the ground?" he says, placing his right hand on his forehead. "I was walking back over to check on the girls when I—I must have fallen."

"It's all right now, Herr Torge. You just had a little spell, that's all," explains Fräulein Dieter. "Sit up slowly. Trudel, go and fetch a glass of water."

"Bernhard?" His wife asks as she kneels down beside him. "How are you feeling?" she gently says.

"I am much better now, darling. It is by the grace of God that these young women are here. I don't know what I would have done without them," the farmer confesses.

"Now, don't say anything. We'll get you right into bed," his wife pleads.

"No! There is too much work to be done old woman! I can't be late on my crops. Don't worry, I'll be all right." The girls help him to his feet. "I'm all right, ladies!" he announces. "Just a bit of a spell, that's all. Just need to catch my breath, nothing more."

"I don't think you need to be out here working in this heat. Why don't you come inside and rest for a while?" his wife asks.

He relents. "Very well, Mama, as you wish."

Trudel returns with a glass of cold water from the well, hands it to Herr Torge, and he takes a few sips. As his wife helps him back to the house, the girls resume their duties.

"That was close!" Kristin said. "I am glad we are here to help."

Trudel glances across the field. "Let's hurry to plant these spuds so he can be proud of us. We only have a few hours left before lunchtime." Trudel begins supervising. "That's not quite deep enough, Kristin. These spuds love to be in deep holes. Here, let me show you." Kristin appreciates Trudel's assistance.

The warm morning is going by surprisingly fast. The girls already planted a quarter of the field when the lunchtime whistle blows. The girls haul their sacks of potatoes back to the barn, wash their spades, brush the dirt from their clothes, and stow their tools neatly away.

Out of appreciation, they go one-step further. The girls slip into the barn, carefully pick up any eggs that have just been laid, and bring them to Frau Torge. A couple of the girls stay behind to clean and muck out the stalls.

Nelly and Frau Torge soon bring out two large wooden platters filled with delectable open-face sandwiches for the hungry girls. They set it on the table beneath the grandfather oak. Surrounded by the flowers in the garden, the girls discuss their morning adventure with the farmer's wife over boiled ham with freshly grated horseradish, boiled eggs, cheese, fresh tomatoes, and thick slices of pumpernickel and rye bread. The cucumber potato salad has been dressed with oil and vinegar, salt and pepper, and a hint of sugar. The canapés are topped with Hungarian salami, cream cheese tinted orange with a sprinkling of paprika, and a sprig of parsley.

After lunch, they help wash and put away the dishes. They promise to return early in the morning as they jovially wave good-bye. Singing, they march up the road and back to their camp on the hill.

Everyone is excited about her first working day. Upon returning, the girls quickly wash and change into their sport outfits. Even though the well water is cold, they feel invigorated and refreshed, ready to perform their afternoon sports. Dressed in their regulated sports attire, they run down to the lower field and join the other girls.

Every afternoon from two o'clock until four o'clock, the girls perform their exercise routines. They use a variety of cardiovascular workouts, including rhythmic and acrobatic gymnastics as well as track and field. The daily exercises strengthen and tone their bodies, for with a strong body comes a strong mind. This is their consciousness.[7]

Training is not just limited to just the afternoons. Additional physical exercises come in the form of backpacking, hiking, rock climbing, swimming, dancing, bicycle riding, volleyball, running, and marching. The overall goals are to burn calories and lose fat, to strengthen the connective tissues, create higher bone density, and to challenge the cardiovascular system, thereby reducing the chances of high blood pressure.

During their time in the Young Girls' League, these girls learned not only that personal hygiene is vital to keeping a body healthy, but also that one needs to be educated in the proper intake of various food groups. Proper nutrition in combination with exercise is what sustains their vibrant health. They will learn all about the major classes of nutrients, including how carbohydrates, fats, minerals, proteins, vitamins, and water affect the mind and body.

These young girls are fast maturing into young women and their bodies need care. At a young age, they naturally learned to consume seven times more fruits and vegetables every day rather than depend on a diet high in starch, meats, or fat. Now, they will learn how to cook full course meals in order to serve up the desired nutrition within the framework of a balanced diet. Every evening, the home economic girls will learn how to prepare a different meal.

The Third Reich focuses on the healthiest, the strongest, and the most disciplined young girls for Landjahr. These girls will receive the very best education possible from the State. By 1941, there are one-hundred thousand girls serving in Landjahr, and Gertrude (Trudel) Kerschner is one of them.[8]

The world of this adolescent girl is beginning to open with infinite possibilities. Her inner fear is largely unfounded, for 'what if' does not cloud her judgment. Instead, she learns to think and ask herself 'how can I?' She is willing to learn. Trudel sets higher personal standards for herself and is committed to learning. She too wants her country to be strong and the very best in the world under the universal mindset of the "Volksgemeinschaft."

How can so few individuals control an entire nation of children into one mindset, that of serving their country unconditionally? If Trudel is not allowed to 'have her own mind,' how can she then be of "one mind together" with her country at such a young age?

---

[7] Mädel im Dienst, p. 10
[8] Bund Deutscher Mädel – "The Country Service Year"

Young subconscious minds only have one answer to all the commands it receives and this answer is "Yes."[9] Everything that Trudel learns from her leaders, her peers, and her parents is incorporated directly into her belief structure. At such an impressionable age, her subconscious mind has little ability to reject ideas unless she feels threatened or compromised. Trudel feels neither threatened nor compromised in the Hitler Youth. Instead, she feels valued as a 'girl in service' to her country. It has been instilled in her at a very young age that she is beautiful and that she "can do anything she puts her mind to doing." All the encouragement she receives from her mother and leaders gives Trudel both stamina and determination, which in turn give her courage, and the inner strength to succeed despite the odds. Thanks to her training, Trudel no longer feels trepidation. It does not even emerge into existence to dampen her spirit. Whenever she feels an inkling of nervousness, she deflects the energy by thinking about her situation, and figures out what corrective measures she can take. She squashes all false emotions. She continually strives to become a better person, to learn, and to do more. She is a natural achiever and has the highest personal standards for her life, based on values, principles, and an unyielding work ethic, all founded on an honest sense of integrity. Beginning at the age of five, she had learned from her mother some of the basics of helping around the home and in the garden, an experience that broadened later by the Young Girls' League. Now, Country Service Year camp will mold Trudel into a young woman and into an employable, productive member of German society.

The BDM has an activity-based approach to teaching. Instead of having the girls recite from memory what they have read in their textbooks, the leaders take pains to meld her convictions to her behavior. Participating in Country Service Year Camp accelerates Trudel's learning through her actions, deeds, and duties. She, along with thousands of her comrades, will disseminate from a young girl to a mature "Girl in Service."[10]

"Mädel im Dienst" (Girl in Service) is one of the many handbooks used by the Bund Deutscher Mädel. This required textbook instructs the girls about sports and gymnastics, self-defense, healthy living, exercising, and eating, as well as information and tips for organizing group meetings, day trips, and setting up cultural evenings. It also covers weeklong camping trips, first aid, self-defense techniques, reading maps and star charts, nature, and the like. This manual teaches them to preserve their honor for it awakens the joy of personal self-development.

These teachings do not force Trudel or her comrades to learn against their will. Landjahr Lager has an elite reputation and Trudel's mother willingly accepted the opportunity for her daughter to participate. From the onset, Country Service Year Camp symbolizes the positive image of youth with nature. Nature

---

[9] Bob Proctor
[10] Mädel im Dienst

is a vital component of the educational landscape, one that is helping to spread the "Volksgemeinschaft" ideology.[11]

"When the last day comes, you will show the Lord God your hands. Those who work and toil hard, rough hands may rest in heaven. And whoever has fine white hands but must first show his heart to God."[12] Such is the upbringing of the girls in Landjahr Lager.

The camp leaders also bear a colossal responsibility for the welfare and safety for all the girls.[13] Working together with the Reich's Ministry, the leaders' initial responsibilities includes finding a suitable home large enough to accommodate up to one hundred girls, arrange for the transportation to and from the camp, preparing daily work schedules and educational curricula, planning meals and the monthly budget reports, and overseeing the running of the household. They will teach the girls how to organize cultural festivities and events, and learn how to financially budget for an entire household.

These girls will come to understand the great honor that has been set upon their shoulders. They will come to believe in themselves and their abilities. They have sworn upon their lives to be the finest they can be for their country. The girls accept that their leaders are there to teach and in return, the youths have to be there as unconditional students. They are becoming stronger by using their body, mind, and spirit together. Their admiration for their Führer fuels their inner flaming desire to serve their nation, resulting in their spirits abloom with pride. The bonds and friendships they form in Country Service Year Camp will last a lifetime.

It will be no different among the leaders of Landjahr Lager. This elite group of women are the best and the brightest for they were specifically trained by the Reich's Ministry. When the Führer calls, everyone knows how to perform at their highest potential, for he expects nothing but the best.[14]

In fact, Trudel is learning new practical skills that will stay with her an entire lifetime. What she learns, she learns from her willing participation, for she knows she is here to serve her State, and in turn, her State will serve her. This is her cultural upbringing and this is her duty to her country. Trudel's instructors show her a new approach to becoming totally self-reliant and self-sufficient by working together in community.[15] Trudel and her young comrades are learning a new way to live. They are learning to be ready to handle life's adversities by standing together as one in the sisterhood of the League of German Girls.[16] Sports are another way to solidify their bond.

When the sweaty girls' finish their gymnastics, they run inside, bathe, change, and meet outside in the courtyard for their social coffee hour, taking a moment

---

[11] Volksgemeinschaft
[12] Annemarie Leppien, p. 53
[13] Mädel im Dienst, p. 8
[14] Ibid
[15] Mädel im Dienst, p. 199
[16] League of German Girls, History

to read their mail. Trudel feels a pang of discouragement when she does not receive a letter from her family.

She decides to make the best of this moment and play her zither. She begins with an easy traditional Austrian waltz, "When I Go to the Alm."[17] Some of the girls gather around her to sing.

Nobody understands why Steffi abruptly dashes out of the room. They are surprised when she returns with a dusty old accordion she had found earlier in the attic. For the next hour, the girls play, sing, and dance.

By six o'clock, they are somewhat reluctant to participate in their flag ceremony. Fräulein Albrecht claps her hands and orders the girls to line up. Struggling with the bounce in their step, the girls march to their flag. At six-thirty, they return to their Lager and enjoy a light diner. Then, the table grows quiet.

---

[17] Zither Melodies, "Wann Ich auf d'Alma Geh'"

New Girls Arrive at Camp

TRUDEL ASKS THE GIRLS sitting at the table, "Do you hear singing voices in the distance?" Everyone pauses for a moment to listen.

Sitting at the head of the table, Fräulein Albrecht responds, "I believe so. How about you girls go outside and see who it is."

Instantly, the girls look at one another, drop their forks on the plates, and race out from the Lager. Trudel pushes her way to the front of the line and witnesses a new group of girls coming up the driveway! The newcomers wrap up their hiking song at the front of the house.

"Welcome, girls!" Fräulein Albrecht proclaims from the top of the steps. The Landjahr girls flock to greet their new comrades. The camp leaders allow the girls to meet one another. After a few moments, she blows her whistle to get everyone's attention.

"Girls, go inside and finish eating your dinner and then tend to your final chores. I will tend to our new residents."

There is a buzz throughout the camp as the girls hurry to finish eating and complete their chores. They will have the opportunity to meet the latest recruits in the parlor during their social hour.

In the meantime, Fräulein Albrecht gives the new girls the orientation tour. In the dining room, she allocates assignments from the latest work schedule. Trudel is excited to hear that eight more girls will be planting spuds in the field with her group tomorrow.

When orientation is finished, the girls meet in the parlor to begin another evening of political discussion, which means being read to from the newspaper by Fräulein Dieter.

The troop leader shares what is going on in the world. Trudel does not understand how the German Defense Industry works or the meaning of how an autarchy government intensifies the agricultural sector for the development of replacement products to convert Germany into a self-sufficient country that converts raw materials into manufactured goods.

Instead of economics, Trudel's mind wanders to her family back home. She begins to feel homesick again, with that uneasy twinge in her belly.

"Fräulein Kerschner?"

Trudel's reverie was interrupted. Is she about to be reprimanded for daydreaming? Trudel hesitantly replies, "Yes, Fräulein Dieter?"

"Meet me in my office after this meeting," the troop leader commands.

Trudel's cheeks flush red with embarrassment as all eyes turn to stare at her. She feels socially humiliated because all her comrades had just witnessed her absentmindedness. She feels insignificant, stripped of her pride. Every girl in the room has instantly assumes the worst. Trudel formulates several excuses in her mind while the reading continues.

After Fräulein Dieter concludes the lesson, some the girls leave the parlor except for Trudel and her roommates.

"Wait here until you are called," the leader commands as she stands up from her chair and leaves the room.

One of the new city girls looks at Trudel and makes the 'shame on you gesture' with her index fingers. She too leaves. Trudel's roommates, Steffi, Nelly, Elli, Maria, and Ingrid linger briefly to console their friend, before retiring to their room.

The girls' day is winding down. The new members settle in, while others get acquainted with one another. A few gossip about Trudel and the price she will have to pay for not staying attentive. Why would the camp leader single the short girl out from all the rest?

At nine o'clock, the whistle blows! The camp falls quiet once again. Trudel's roommates turn in. For the second night, the camp leaders meet in their office. They review the paperwork of the new girls from Upper Silesia.[1] They make notes in their paperwork and discuss camp business.

Alone in the parlor, Trudel continues to wait patiently. She tries to predict what questions the leaders may ask, and she formulates responses in her imagination. She replays the daydreaming incident in her head and eventually concludes that she will just have to be honest and tell them the truth about feeling homesick. There is no reason for her to lie and cover up her actions. Whatever punishment she will receive, she will face it while vowing to pay better attention in the future.

Finally, Fräulein Albrecht enters the room. With raised eyebrows, she addresses the repentant girl. "Trudel, you may come with me now."

Her humble head bows and Trudel follows the leader into the office. She sits warily in the corner waiting for her punishment.

"There is a special reason why we have called you here this evening, Trudel." Fräulein Dieter starts. Slowly, Trudel raises her head, ready to accept her punishment. "The other two camp leaders and I believe that you possess exceptional leadership qualities. In fact, we think you should become a Leader Candidate! Therefore, for the next two days, you will prove your worthiness with the following assignments."

Trudel's sigh of relief turns into a resurgence of pride! She sits up, attentive, but still uncertain, quite unable to believe what she is hearing. She is going to be a leader candidate, overseeing the other girls for two entire days? She listens intently while they instruct her in her candidate duties.

"You must document everything you do in this book." Fräulein Dieter raises the notebook into view. "You must keep copious records, detailing all of your actions, orders, and tasks. You will inform us when each task is completed. Here

---

[1] Peter Dubiel, Oberschlesien

is the schedule of tasks you will complete over the next two days. Please become familiar with your list and execute the tasks in order. Understand?"

Trudel enthusiastically springs from her chair to receive the book from the troop leader. She tucks it under her arm and salutes. The woman then hands her an official whistle and an alarm clock.

"You may go now."

Imitating her leaders, Trudel pivots on her left foot, marches out of the room and down the hall. At the end of the staircase, she jumps with excitement! She grabs hold of the banister, races up the stairs, and bursts into her bedroom, waking up her roommates.

"Oh no, what happened now?" gasps Nelly.

"They just made me a leader candidate!" Trudel replies truthfully.

A puzzled pause ensues. "So, what exactly does that mean?" inquires Ingrid.

"That means I'm in charge of all the girls for the next two days! Isn't that exciting?" exclaims Trudel.

"What?" We have to take orders from you now?" Steffi pouts, throwing the sheets over her head, rolling over to face away. "Just great!" she mumbles underneath the bedsheets.

"Aw, it's only for two days, girls! It will be fun! Come on. Let's get some sleep. We have a busy day ahead of us tomorrow!"

"Trudel, as an assistant leader, oh God, what's next?" Maria exclaims as she pulls the covers up over her head too.

The other girls roll over and return to their dreams.

"The essence of leadership
Is not in command
But in service.
The statement of a great German said
'I am the first servant of my State'
Is also a fundamental principle
of
National Socialism"

~Baulder von Schirach ~

Becoming a Leader Candidate

IN THE LIGHT OF THE FULL MOON, Trudel sits on the balcony dreaming about her promotion. With clock in hand, she sets the alarm for five-thirty am. Quietly, she walks inside her bedroom being careful not to wake her friends. She changes into her pajamas and tries to fall asleep. The ticking clock does not help. The reality of her situation is sinking in. She thinks to herself, 'what if someone wakes up in the middle of the night', or 'what if there is an emergency?' All night long, she tosses and turns, afraid that she will miss the alarm. Exhausted, she finally falls asleep.

The wind-up device ticks down to five-thirty. The mainspring releases the drive gear and propels the small metal hammer back and forth between the two bells. Trudel jumps out of bed, quickly turns off the alarm, and quietly runs downstairs to wash. She slips back into her room and dresses into her official BDM uniform. *Fast, fast, fast,* is her mantra.

Stopping on the landing between the two floors, Trudel restrains herself. She does not intend to blow the whistle too early. Holding the clock in her hand, she watches it tick down to six. In a way, the young Führerinnen-Anwärterin looks forward to all the commotion, all on her command! She thinks this is going to be an easy day watching everyone else work as she supervises.

Precisely at six o'clock, the bells tolls signaling Trudel's first order of the day. Placing the metal whistle to her lips, she blows with all her might. The shrill radiates throughout the house and awakens everyone. On cue, the doors begin slamming and the girls dart past Trudel on their way down to the washroom. Trudel steps up to the third floor and blows the whistle again. "Everyone, get up!" she commands. A few more stragglers dash from their rooms and down the stairs.

Trudel retreats to the dining room and waits. She is to give the girls enough time to wash and straighten out their rooms before she begins the formal room inspection. She sits down and opens her brown leather book. On the first blank page, she writes:

> "It is 6:00 a.m. and I blew the whistle to awaken everyone. The girls are moving fast. They are rushing to get everything in order before I make the formal room inspections. Everything is moving like clockwork."

She waits until she hears the girls returning to their room. Slowly, she walks up to the second floor and begins her room inspections. With the book held close to her chest, she opens the first door and shouts, *"Attention, everyone!"*

The girls line up in front of their bunks.

Trudel walks up to each girl, examines her attire, and makes sure her nails are clean. She scrutinizes each room, inspecting under the bed, under the pillows, and inside the wardrobes. She flips a coin on the bed sheets just as she had seen how it was done by her leader. Then, she orders the girls to line up outside and wait for the morning flag ceremony to begin. With each room she inspects, she makes notations in her assistant leader's book, and then she returns to the office.

"All rooms inspected and the girls are waiting outside Fräulein Albrecht!" Trudel announces.

"Good, let's begin our flag greeting ceremony, shall we?"

Young Trudel proudly leads Fräulein Dieter, Albrecht, and Grüber outside. For the first time, Trudel's basic understanding of the military commands will be presented and scrutinized by the leaders. The military commands have two parts. First, comes the warning that a command is about to be given, and then the second command itself is given.

"Attention group! Fall in! Line up! Stand still!" Trudel orders as the leaders look on. "Now, count off—one!"

The girls count themselves off, up to forty.

Trudel pivots on her left foot, faces her leaders, salutes, and in her best commanding voice announces "Everyone accounted and present for!"

The troop leader nods her head in affirmation.

Trudel then pivots back towards the group. Standing in front of the column, she declares, "Face right! Now march!"

The girls instantly turn and start marching towards the courtyard. They form a square at the base of the flagpole, salute, raise their flag, and hold their morning flag greeting ceremony.

Fräulein Dieter recites the morning decree to her girls.

"You are the future of Germany. Where we are now, you will be. You are the future of Germany. It will be, and it must be!"

In the morning sun, Fräulein Dieter examines all the young girls who stand in formation. As troop leader, she will have to become quickly acquainted with their conduct, disposition, and aptitudes. Then, she gives her morning speech. "All the girls from Upper Silesia arrived safely last night, so we are all together now on this beautiful morning. After our morning duties, everyone will report inside after lunch where we will begin preparations for Walpurgis Night. This evening, we will be celebrating on top of our hill, and the entire village will come accompany us around a large bonfire. We will sing and ward off the evil spirits and welcome Ceres Erde. Tomorrow is our National Labor Day holiday. Instead of working, we will be celebrating with the farmers in town! We will march in a parade, and our village men will be erecting the Maypole in the center of town. We have been invited to participate in the festival and give a dance performance too!"

The girls are thrilled.

"So, instead of doing sports today, we will teach you the traditional circle and ribbon dances that you will perform tomorrow. Even if you do not already know the two dances, they are very easy. However, just to make sure, you will practice them in the field this afternoon after lunch. Before the festival begins, we will eat a hearty dinner. Then, we will walk up to the top of the great hill behind our camp and join with the villagers. Now, everyone, let's give our morning greeting to the Fuhrer!

The girls salute and recite their Oath of Allegiance before they head back to the Lager for breakfast and discuss the day's events. Trudel sits with her leaders and writes notes in her book. After breakfast, she first oversees the farm chores, and then gathers the girls outside. They form their column with Trudel leading them on, and with song in their hearts, they begin their hike down to the Torge farmstead for a morning of spud planting.

Trudel watches over the girls as they plant the spuds in the field. She inspects the housework and takes some time to chat with Frau Torge. Promptly at noon, Trudel blows the whistle and informs everyone that it is time for lunch. She feels a strong sense of pride when the girls report to her upon completing their tasks. Trudel notes in her book that everyone is happy to finish their work today. No one has any complaints and all the girls performed their duties without incident.

After lunch, the girls march back to camp, wash, change, and meet in the courtyard. At 1:39 pm, Trudel lines everyone up for inspection.

Fräulein Dieter arrives and begins showing the girls both variations of the Maypole dances they will be performing tomorrow.

As the girls are practicing, Trudel and Nelly walk into town to fetch the mail. The two girls gaily trot off down Golden View Road. They walk by the little farm houses and wave 'hello' to the farmers' wives.

The two cross the main Seidorf road with a skip in their step for they are enjoying the beautiful spring weather. They walk past the Tyrolean style houses and wave at the villagers. Total strangers wave back to them in a welcoming gesture. The girls feel welcomed in Seidorf.

As they round the corner, they come upon the Baroque church. They pause for a moment to admire the square tower of the Episcopalian church, crowned with a copper-plated onion dome that has long turned green. The semi-circular openings in each of the two large, red doors represent the morning sun and welcomes the parishioners.

Trudel turns the brass handle on the heavy oak door and the pair steps through the arched entryway into the cool of the vestibule. Nelly closes the door behind her. The girls walk in silence toward the altar and gasp at the beautiful sight before them. Above the triforium, sunlight penetrates the semi-circular windows of the clerestory, illuminating the nave and the altar below. The Baroque architecture centers on a dignified, well-crafted solid wood altar, which holds a distinction of wealth. Two pillars on either side of the altar support the weight of the balcony. Two pillars on either side of the balcony hold up the organ pipes above them, which is crowned by a burst of rays beaming from the blue wreath centerpiece. Above the alter is a large oil painting of Christ as he holds both hands open welcoming his followers.

Trudel lights a votive candle, makes the sign of the cross then sits in the pew and prayers for the soldiers, their families, her brothers, Hans and Emmerich, and her father. She vows to keep her father's promise. She misses him dearly and wishes he were alive. As she stands, she notices a dark figure dashing behind the pillar.

When they arrive at the post office, their friendly postmaster greets them and the three chat for a while. The girls walk out with their bundle of treasure. Trudel knows all the girls back at camp will be anticipating a letter.

Trudel flips through the pile, scanning the return addresses. She examines the pretty pictures of the postcards. She freezes when she discovers a card from her own family. It reads:

> Dear Trudel,
> We so much want to hear about your time in camp. Did you arrive safely? We love you. Please write as soon as you can. We miss you dearly. Love, Mother and Franzi.

Trudel is stunned that nothing more had been written on the card from home. Still, she vows to write back promptly since her family sounds anxious to hear from her.

By the time the two girls walk back to their new home, they have missed the first phase of the dance activities. Trudel quickly sorts the mail as Nelly joins her group. After Trudel finishes, she walks to the lower field and joins in on the dancing. Some girls beg to know if any mail had arrived for them, but Trudel does not breathe a word! That will remain her little secret.

She joins the girls for the next few hours, practicing the dances. At four o'clock, Trudel summons the girls for their afternoon coffee break. After handing out the letters, Trudel is worried about this evening's flag ceremony. She frets that the girls might not even show up on time. Soon, she cannot concentrate on anything else. She reports to the office where Fräulein Albrecht tells her not to worry about anything. All is going well and according to schedule.

What a relief. Trudel's heart leaps when Fräulein Dieter informs her that she is doing a splendid job. Everything is going to turn out just right.

Walpurgis Night

AFTER DINNER AND HEADING UP the evening's flag procession, the next task on Trudel's list will be to lead the girls up to the top of the hill. The girls will meet with the local villagers to celebrate Walpurgis Night. First, they need to learn the importance of the celebration. During the flag ceremony, Fräulein Albrecht explains the ritual.

"Today is St. Walpurgis Day and our ceremony will start with a great bonfire on top of Grodna Hill. Days beforehand, the villagers have been preparing by gathering dead wood. This wood symbolizes our offering to the pagan spirits and the bonfire purifies the air, thereby ensuring a bountiful summer harvest.

"This festival began by the people who lived in the highest mountains in Germany. For many centuries, they believed witches rode across the evening sky. St. Walpurgis was a female English missionary who was canonized on May 1 in 870 by Pope Adrian II. Because she wrote her brother's vita, she was deemed the first female author in Germany. She died in the year 777, and was canonized ninety-three years later. At Eichstätt, her bones were placed into a rocky niche and the rocks began to exude a miraculous therapeutic oil that drew pilgrims to her shrine.[1] The pilgrims collected the oil and placed drops of it on their crops. They were astounded by the rapid growth and copious harvest that ensued. To ensure future harvests, the peasants added the raising of the pole on the first day of May.

"In every home in the village this evening, the wife will lay down a broom across the entrance of her home. This prevents the demons from crossing over the threshold. The husband is responsible to walk around his land and crack his whip. This prevents the evil spirits from taking up residence on his farm or harming his crop or livestock. For extra protection, each homestead erects a small pine branch in the front yard. Then, the villagers continue the festivities around a great bonfire on the tallest hill in the surrounding area.

"Now, go out into the woods and collect as many sticks as you can carry and bring them with you. In addition, I want you to collect pinesap in the forest. Trudel and Steffi have been instructed in the procedure, so they will demonstrate it for you. They will be showing you the way through the woods tonight to the top of Grodna Hill. Everyone, fall out!"

The sap they start collecting will be used in the torches during their summer solstice ceremony. Tonight, their sacrificial offering will be bundles of twigs and sticks. Trudel gathers the girls together and lines them up. Night is falling, and

---

[1] Walpurgis Night

she orders everyone to stay close together. She feels responsible for their safety and wellbeing.

It will take the girls forty-five minutes to walk the path through the forest to the top of the great dome-shaped hill. In song, they leave camp and scamper playfully up the path. The yellow and double-white trail marker leads the way, avoiding the cliffs to the south. The trail meanders through a gently sloping terrain, crossing over a rivulet, and passing the dark grey angular granite outcrops born 320 million years ago. These massive boulders were compressed by glaciers and forced down on the side of the mountain where they have remained. Years of weathering have shaped these porphyritic rocks. Some claim to see silhouettes of hens, camels, and even a giant's head.

The final rays of the sun disappear behind Giant Mountain, leaving the woods in darkness. The girls reach the clearing atop of the hill, and the heady smell of the smoke filled air hits them. Smoke billows up over the massive castle ruins of Prince Henry and the flame from the fire can be seen for miles. Trudel and the girl stop to behold the magical sight.

Local villagers play lively folk music, dance, and converse with each other over food and drink. Some adults are dressed in their traditional lederhosen and dirndls. Others wear festive costumes depicting devils, giants, or witches. Cloaked in equally ghoulish attire, children run wild in and around the castle, chasing each other in play.

This is Walpurgis Night, when people herald the coming of spring by warding off the evil spirits of winter with fire! To frighten the evil spirits further, the village men occasionally ring their cowbells and crack their whips. The women carry lit torches topped with hemlock, rosemary, and juniper and throw them into the flames, symbolizing the burning of the witches. By warding off the evil winter demons of darkness, the people ward off agricultural disasters and starvation. Having survived the long winter nights, these witnesses are about to welcome the dawn of spring and the rebirth of life. [2]

Trudel looks around for her leaders but they are nowhere to be found.

Some village children come over to Trudel's group and ask them to play. A few delighted girls grab the toddlers' hands and go off while others stay behind. The gregarious ones slip away to mingle in the crowd and converse with their village neighbors.

Giant glowing flames cast eerie, flickering shadows against the ruined stone edifice. Little boys run back and forth towards the walls imagining that their shadows are giant monsters descending upon the castle! Witches, goblins, and vampires embody the magic of Walpurgis Night, a spirit underworld so deeply rooted in traditional pagan values. According to the legend, only a fearsome hunter, a stately prince, or a god, is mighty enough to engage in a fearsome battle with the evil spirits, to conquer and banish them once for all.

Out of the corner of her eye, Trudel notices three ugly, hunched-over witches using crooked walking sticks to make their way from behind the ruins

---

[2] Irma M. Nagengast-Rosich

212

up to the bonfire. The wretched witches reach into their satchels. They chant a special incantation, and then pull out a handful of magic herbs, each tossing them into the flames. Immediately, their crackling magic sends great sparks flying high into the air!

Once the witches step back from the flames, the villagers step up and throw their sacrificial bundles into the bonfire, thus empowering the great spirits to cast out the dark winter.

From beyond the flames, a red shadow figure soon materializes. He takes the form of the Devil. All the little children scream and run in terror. The three witches calmly hobble up to the creature. Hand-in-hand they break out in dance, circling around him, and chanting strange words.

Suddenly, out of the crowd bursts the hero with thick golden hair. He is a strong and powerful fellow wearing a red tunic, a gold belt, and leather sandals. He begins to wield his giant hammer. A battle rages, until with a huge bellow, the good warrior casts the evil adversaries out of the forest!

The play is over and the five adult role-players hold hands and bow for the applause.

At the stroke of midnight, a church bell tolls in the village below. The camp girls cast their bundles into the flames. They encircle the bonfire, and holding hands with the villagers sing a traditional song that pays tribute to the spring.

Under the waxing crescent moon, the troop leaves the festival and descends the hill. Back at headquarters, exhausted, the girls disperse to their respective bedrooms and immediately fall asleep.

Trudel walks through the entire house to make sure all the windows and doors are secured. She is in the basement kitchen checking on the back door when she hears the side door creak open upstairs. She tiptoes back to the foot of the staircase and looks up just in time to see dark figures sweeping into the hall. Cautiously, she creeps up the stairs and peeks around the corner. The shadow figure disappears into the office. Young Trudel follows, pushing the door open.

"So, *you* are the witches!" Trudel exclaims! "But, how did you make the fire crackle like that?"

Fräulein Grüber reaches into her sack and pulls out a handful of her 'magic herbs.' "You mean these? These are old pine needles. When you throw them into a fire, they crackle and spark, but don't tell anyone. Let it be our little secret."

With a knowing smile, Trudel acknowledges and quietly leaves the office. She feels a special bond with the women. Before she completely closes the door behind her, she pokes her head back inside the room. "Goodnight."

In unison, the leaders giggle before bidding Trudel a goodnight.

Tomorrow, Trudel will be performing her assistant leader duties all over again. With the last of her endurance, the leader candidate makes her way up the stairs and into her bedroom. She collapses on her mattress, drained, and falls asleep in her uniform. She did not even hear the ticking of her clock. She feels confident that all the evil spirts have taken flight from Seidorf and Grodna Hill.

Prince Henry's Castle Ruins
Grodna Hill – Sosnówka, Poland

Celebrating with the Farmers

THE CAMP COMMUNITY IDEOLOGY promotes collaboration between the girls and the villagers. This is in line with the Volksgemeinschaft, the working experience, and the girls' education. A special bond forms between them and deepens throughout their eight-month stay. Therefore, sustenance for Landjahr Lager Seidorf starts in April and ends in November, coinciding naturally with the planting and harvest seasons.

The camp's location in Seidorf is unique. The manor house is large and can accommodate up to sixty girls. It sits in close proximity to the village and the farms. Its dominance is projected by the Swastika flag flying high every day in the courtyard that can be seen from the village below.

Walpurgis Night has proved that the villagers are embracing the new girls wholeheartedly. Today, the festivities will continue with National Labor Day, the celebration honoring the efforts of all German workers.

The girls awake early and dress in their coordinating outfits that include a plain weave, white linen dress that stops just below the knee. Their dark green, full-frontal aprons tie in the back with crisscrossing shoulder straps. A white bandana covers their hair. Still in a festive mood, they are content to complete their morning tasks before accompanying their leaders to the May Day festival.

The annual raising of a tall oak maypole symbolizes the welcoming of spring in every village around the Germanic nation. It is a time-honored tradition that has its roots before the Iron Age, dating back to the Nordic legend of Thor. He is the god of lightning, storms, and oak trees, the god who protects humankind and lends his strength to farmers in particular. He venerates healing and fertility among women. "Thursday" bears his pagan name. Thor is a compassionate husband and father who bear many children. As the son of Odin, he personifies the soil of Ceres Erde (Mother Earth). He rides a chariot pulled by two goats. His home is considered his stronghold. His mountain-crushing hammer slaughters his enemies in his role as protector of the family, especially of revering his wife, Ceres. The oak tree is a symbol of Thor's strength and stands for the traditional values of integrity, longevity, loyalty, and most of all, fertility.[1]

With rakes and shovels in hand, the troop assembles at the backside of the manor home and march towards town, singing with zeal. Trudel and Nelly have the privilege of pulling the small wooden wagon that is overflowing with ribbons, flowers, and of course, the maypole crown.

---

[1] Thor

At the edge of the village, they come across the horse-drawn wagon. It is set to lead the parade and transport the thirty-two foot oak maypole. Mayor Werner Blasius of Hirschberg instructs the girls' troop to march behind the band.[2]

Trudel and Nelly lead their troop while their comrades line up three across behind them. The farmers follow behind the girls. The men wear their traditional Bavarian Tracht clothing and their wives proudly walk behind them wearing their Bavarian dirndls. At the end of the procession is the children's horse-drawn hay wagon, quaintly decorated with pine wreaths, flowers, and ribbons.

Trudel feels quite important to be standing near the front of the parade with Nelly, only steps behind the three camp leaders.

Mayor Blasius walks to the head of the procession and with a wave of his hand, signals the 12-piece brass marching Oom-pah-pah band to begin. The tuba player signals the introductory alternating downbeat root note, followed by the band who delivers the rhythmic accompaniment for the polka. The band starts marching in place waiting for the wagon ahead to start moving forward.

With a quick slap of the reins, the wagon master advances the four-harness team of horses and the parade begins!

Crowds of spectators line both sides of the street and watch the parade route. Young girls dressed in flowing white gowns with wreaths in their hair walk alongside the marching country service girls. Everyone beams a friendly smile and feels proud to be honoring the German workers.

This ancient Germanic celebration is in honor of the farmers and their wives. This day marks the beginning of planting season. The ideology has shifted and today, it focuses on the blood of the people and the soil of their land. Today, this traditional festival of labor amalgamates the farmer, his wife, and land under one common Germanic worldview.

As ancient Greek writers equate foreign divinities to members of their own mythological consideration, so did the German pagans in the tenth century who adopted these same practices.[3] At the end of the nineteenth century, the "Volksbewegung" (people's movement) was a populist movement with an underlying, romantic focus on pagan folklores.[4] German paganism connects mysticism with the historical culture based upon these ancient deities.[5]

Bestowed upon the farmer is the superior-like figure resembling Thor who has returned his rural values to the land. He embodies the preservation of his ethnic roots by his moral obligation to keep his land organic and pure. His strong work ethics helps him to cultivate the land and provide food for his family and country.

With her moral excellence in the management of the homestead and in the raising of her children, the farmer's wife exemplifies the Germanic spirits of virtuosity and virtue. The farmers' wives are revered as the most precious women

---

[2] Europeana
[3] Interpretatio graeca
[4] Völkisch movement
[5] Ariosophy

in all the land. The worth of a nation is shown in the preparedness of its women to become valuable mothers.[6] Each wife feels an innate sense of pride when she participates in this event, for she personifies the image of Ceres Erde the ancient Norse mythological goddess of the earth, agriculture, grain, crops, fertility, and motherhood. Holding a tuft of grain in her arm depicts her symbol. Her fertility symbol is the May tree that bears many fruits.[7] Her honorary celebration day is the first day of May. Ceres Erde bears two children, Móði and Magni, with her husband, Thor, the god of thunder. She is the provider of wheat and the protector who nourishes her young seeds. She bestows the gift of agriculture to humankind. She is the protector of women from girlhood into womanhood, from unmarried to married life, and into motherhood. At the end of life, she helps the deceased woman make her safe journey into the afterlife.[8]

As the farmer's wife manages the household and raises the children, the farmer manages the land and rears his livestock. The adults are conscious of their division of labor in the family, for their combined skills complement each other. Together, the farmer and his wife exemplify the core of German labor. It is their obligation and responsibility as adults to mentor the children of the land by implementing the highest work standards. The entire community works together to teach the children their path in life.

The procession walks through the town ending at the main square. Twenty men are on hand standing ready to heave the base of the pole off the wagon and into the hand-dug opening in the ground. With a great heave, the men lift and place the base near the hole, as others help roll a log under the tip of the pole. Men on either side maneuver the trunk into place.

Trudel and Nelly wheel their cart to the pole. With the help of Steffi, Elli, and Maria, they begin to decorate the tip. The local weavers had collaborated with the blacksmith to create a floral and ribbon metal crown. Garlands of local flowers adorn the metal piece.

Now comes the challenging part of raising the pole. Starting at the tip and working their way down to the base, then men use long sticks connected at the ends with a thick leather strap to push and position the pole upright. The drummers cavort various rolls, mirroring the suspense of the men as they gradually prod the tree from its horizontal starting position to its vertical standing point. One man orchestrates the movement of the men as two others guide the trunk into place. Once the pole slips into the opening, the men hurry to backfill the hole. The crowd rejoices and the band merrily plays.

Mayor Blasius walks up on stage to address his villagers. Dressed in his best attire he raises both arms toward the crowd. All eyes are upon him when he begins his annual May Day speech.

"Welcome, Seidorfers, on this beautiful day that honors all of our laborers. Today, the German soul awakens with a powerful yearning to plow our fields

---

[6] Lisa Pine, "Nazi Family Policy," p. 9
[7] G. Foderà Serio, p.20
[8] Ceres

and plant our crops! On our land, the soil lives. Woven into its very fabric of the soil is our internal strength. It is our longing, just as it was the longing of our ancestors, to plant the seeds and yield the crops."

The crowd applauds.

"Once again, the Führer has blessed us with many strong country service girls who have come to assist us this year. They will labor in the fields next to us and reap the harvest with us in the fall. We value their presence. From our hearts, we thank you."

The girls applaud one another, as does the crowd.

"Without you, we would not be able to start this year's crops. When the time comes to harvest the fields, we will rejoice! We will proclaim how dutiful the girls are in assisting us. Our farmers are the pillars of the community and our bread comes from hard work because our work ennobles us!

Everyone claps.

"We are eternally grateful and deeply indebted to these fine young women who have come from the far reaches of our country to help work on our farms. We all depend upon one another because we work hand-in-hand for the greater good of the German Reich. Therefore, we will never be without flour to make our bread, or sausage from our pigs. We will always drink fresh milk and have plenty of beer! Our own hands sow the food we need for our people. Everyone will eat the best foods because we work together as one!"

The crowd applauds and begins to feel hungry.

"Today, we acknowledge our farmers and their wives, the butchers and the blacksmith, our weavers, the camp leaders, and their girls. Know that we are here for you, just as you are here for us today! We joyously open our homes to you. Welcome to Seidorf!"

A chorus of villagers cheers in agreement.

"The people's strength lies in our willingness to work, which is driven by our beliefs. This maypole symbolizes the traditional belief of our ancestors, because they venerated the oak tree as sacred. In addition, we must strongly believe in our soldiers, who are even today are on the distant battlefields fighting for our country.

"Much of the potato crop we grow this year will be delivered straight to our boys at the front line. Therefore, let us protect and take care of our fields. For the sake of our Führer, our soldiers, our elders, our farmers, and our youths, we join with the country service girls, in the consecration on this first day in May. We dedicate it to our Führer and the Fatherland!"

The crowd applauses to the Mayor's declaration.

"And now, it gives me great pleasure to introduce Fräulein Dieter, the troop leader for Country Service Year Camp Seidorf."

The crowd welcomes her warmly onto the stage.

"My dear comrades!" she begins. "This is the second year of our camp. Only the finest girls from Upper Silesia and the Lower Danube regions have been specifically chosen by the Reich's Ministry to work here. They are eager to learn and to serve. Our goal is to help the farmers and to serve the people. You have the blessings of these strong and healthy girls, who possess the strongest will to work. We work together in strength, knowing that we belong here. Our focus is be on our community. We embrace our camp, our homes, our farms, and the land with the same principle—caring for our people. We hold true to our beliefs as stones are cemented together to hold the foundation of our homes. We stand before you on this day of new beginnings not as self-sacrifices, but as lovers of the land."

The crowd roars its approval.

Mayor Blasius and Fräulein Dieter turn to one another and shake hands. The local photographer snaps a quick photo for the newspaper.

As the troop leader walks off stage, the mayor heads over to the large wooden beer keg. He is handed a mallet and a spigot. Holding both high over the crowd, he shows everyone that the first keg of the year is about to be tapped. Positioning the spigot right over the cork, he drives it in with one solid blow. He hands off the mallet to his neighbor, who in turn, passes him a stein to fill. Since Mayor Blasius is the highest-ranking official in town, he is going to have the honor of drinking the first beer. Facing the crowd, he raises his foaming stein in tribute and proclaims "O' zapft ist! Let the festivities begin!"

As he downs a large mouthful of brew, the band plays on and the crowd cheers. The men whose muscles had helped raise the pole are the next in line to receive their beverage reward.

A jovial atmosphere spreads across the entire village green. The lighthearted, friendly feeling brings everyone together in a gesture of goodwill. Storytellers, poets, and hand-puppeteers, entertain the children, while the adults mingle, dance, eat, and drink. Before the maypole dances begin, the country service girls are free to frolic with the children, and participate in the activities.

The leaders mingle with the villagers, observe, and make a mental note how their girls interact within the community.

Trudel, Elli, Nelly, Steffi, Maria, Lotte, Anna, Elfie, Sabine, Renate, and Helli, accompany the children to watch the Kasperle puppet play. Trudel's new-found friend, Anna, enjoys sitting on her lap watching the performance. The child lacks not for conversational skills and continually questions the young adult about 'why the sky is blue,' or 'who that funny-looking puppet is.' Trudel bonds with the child easily. She admires the way Anna's eyes sparkle and how her face lights up every time she laughs. The child is so carefree and innocent. Together, the two laugh and tickle each other. When Kasperle uses the stick to beat the witch, Anna becomes scared and starts to cry. She buries her face into Trudel's chest. Trudel cradles her maternally, rocking her back and forth, whispering, "Do not worry, it is only a play."

When the performance is over Trudel and Anna, together with her comrades, walk to the front of the puppet theatre. Trudel knocks on the small theatre tabletop pretending to be a dignitary. "We request an audience with Kasperle."

As soon as he hears his name being called, Kasperle the puppet peeks out from behind the curtains. He bows formally and begins asking the children questions. At first, the youngsters are afraid to speak with the red-cheek, orange-face character wearing a floppy blue hat. Kasperle knows how to break the tension.

"Do you know where I can find the pickled nose of the witch?"

The children laugh and soon open their hearts and converse with the paper mâché figure. Their eyes sparkle and their cheeks redden from his banter. The children talk about everything with the puppet who listens and answers all their questions. Kasperle is a caring, compassionate fellow, who is always in a merry mood. The children shout, "We want to see the puppet play again!"

Anna squirms, trying to twist free from Trudel's arms. Once Trudel sets her down, the toddler runs off into the crowd. Trudel chases her into the field. That's when Barbara, Herminie, Gabriele, Ingrid, Nelly, Elli, Steffi, Maria, and Sabine, each with their own youngster, sees how much fun the two are having, and join in. The little ones spread their arms out wide, sway back and forth, purse their lips and blow, pretending they are airplanes flying through the sky.

Parents with their children sit on the ground watching the airplane game. Seeing all the fun the other kids are having, they wiggle free from their mother's arms. They are eager for a taste of autonomy, the freedom to leave their parental guidance and go play this new game.

Kristin, Liesel, Charlotte, Elfie, Katharina, and Aloise are in the animal pen petting the goats and pigs.

Marta, Magdalena, Helli, Sylvia and Dorota, meanwhile dubbed the 'city girls' from Upper Silesia, and are not interested in the farmers nor in their supposedly peasant lifestyle. They prefer to keep to themselves, looking down on all this boisterous behavior as immature tomfoolery.

At the designated time, the trumpeter announces the dance is about to begin. While some stay behind to finish cooking the great feast, most of the villagers gather around the pole to observe the ritual.

Long colored ribbons gracefully radiate out from the crown atop the pole. Participants seize the ends of the ribbons and step back into a wide circle. Once all the ribbons are taut, the dancers bow to one another. Facing forward, the children hold fast and wait for the music to begin. The first dance demonstrates a simple weaving pattern. The boys position themselves in between the girls. When the band begins to play "Tanz Rüber," the children begin to weave.[9]

The simplest Maypole dance is the Grand Chain. As the girls step clockwise, the boys step counterclockwise, both alternately ducking under the ribbons and lifting theirs over the next person.

In a variation called the Barber's Pole, the boys stand still while the girls move clockwise. Then, they switch and the boys move clockwise as the girls stand still.

Everyone is pleased with the performance.

---

[9] Wir Mädel Singen, p. 49

While watching, Trudel's girls are discussing the dance movements they learned yesterday during their sports afternoon lesson. As they walk into their position, they take hold of the ribbons, and wait. When the music begins, they demonstrate their complex choreography.

The jaded city girls find themselves staring with envy and a little competitive spirits begins to brew! The city girls put their heads together and decide upon their weave pattern. When it is their turn, they walk up to the pole and dance impeccably. The crowd laughs and applauds the girls for a job well done, knowing it was all in fun. Even the sporty rural girls approach the city girls and slap them with high fives.

Once the dance is finished, the ribbons remain weaved around the post.

Now, it is time for the boys to join with the men and show off their dancing skills. To impress the girls with their prowess, they perform the Austro-Bavarian 'Shoe Dance.' Always performed to the beat of a waltz, one boy stands in the middle while the other males, form a circle around him. When the music starts, they complete one full circle then drop to the ground, revealing the boy in the center. The center boy takes a few sharp dance steps. When he finishes the others take a step back and perform a series of jumps. They strike their thighs with the palms of the hands, cross one leg over in front of the other and then behind. They hit the heels and soles of their boots, rhythmically jump and stomp their feet, then turn and drop. The center boy follows suit. This pattern repeats for the duration of the dance.

On the side, the country girls giggle, pointing, and whispering about which is the cutest boy. As night creeps over the villagers, the men light torches and set the bonfire ablaze. Everyone gathers around the bonfire, holds hands, and sings.

The festivities continues when the women serve heaping plates of sausage and schnitzel, sauerkraut and red cabbage, dumplings, fruits, salads, apple strudel and plumb, pound and cheesecakes, flaky pastries, and cinnamon rolls. For the main course, the butcher brings out his prize-cooked swine. With the help of his workers, the beast is served on a large tray and placed on the main table for all to admire.

The sow is an appropriate sacrifice to Mother Earth. The pig is garnished with cooked apples, potatoes, carrots, and onions. Its skin is crispy with a deep, golden tan and the legs splay out in either direction. Hallow sockets remain once where the eyes were. Wielding a large carving knife, the butcher slices their feast into flanks. The tender meat easily falls off the bones, much to the delight of the hungry villagers.

After their festive dinner, the girls end their evening by participating in the "Mayrhofer Tanz," a fast-paced polka. Trudel bashfully watches from the side as everyone steps and hops behind one another in a large circle. She admires the way the adults dance so eloquently, twirling around in circles. "I wish I knew how to dance a polka," she says to Steffi.

Steffi hears the disappointment in Trudel's voice and takes her by the hand. "Here, I can show you! Come on!" They walk over to the dancers and face each other. Steffi places her arm around Trudel. "The basic dance steps are quick, quick, and then slow, quick, quick, and then slow."

Trudel holds Steffi's hand and wraps her other arm around Steffi's waist. Standing with both feet slightly apart, knees bent, Steffi slowly shows Trudel the polka steps. The two girls practice the movements, stepping on each other's feet and laughing in delight.

Two young handsome boys approach the girls, bow, and ask them to dance. The girls curtsey and take the hands of the boys ready to lead.

Trudel feels exhilarated. She is dancing with the very boy she had previously pointed out to her friends during the Shoe Dance. She cannot believe her good fortune, for this is the very first time she is dancing and she does not even know his name!

The two teenagers look into each other's eyes as they dance under the starlit evening sky. Trudel feels invigorated. The hairs rise on the back of her neck and she feels a pleasurable sensation fill her body. Adults look on, smiling.

A few minutes later, Trudel hears the leader's whistle blow. "I must go," she says, staring into his eyes.

"No, stay a little while longer with me, please," he pleads.

"I'm sorry, I really must go." Trudel curtseys and runs off toward the sound of the whistle. Glancing over her shoulder, she sees him standing there, pouting. She smiles and blows him a kiss. He snatches the kiss out of mid-air, twirls himself around, places both his hands upon his heart, and drops down on one knee. Trudel gasps at the romantic gesture and disappears from his view.

What a terrible time to leave all the fun! Dutifully, she grabs the wagon. The other girls gather their rakes and shovels, line up, and head back up the hill to camp. Fräulein Albrecht allows them to fall out from their strict positions and walk freely. On their way home, they sing songs, and take care when they cross the main road.

Half way up the hill, Trudel begins having trouble pulling the wagon. Erika and Sabine notice this and help. The group turns left past the little farm homes and continue up Golden View road towards their camp.

The leaders order the girls to return all the rakes, shovels, and wagon to their appropriate sheds behind the home before going to bed.

The girls use the very last bit of their strength to climb the stairs and collapse onto their bunks, all except for Trudel who feels as if she is still dancing on air.

A sharp whistle blows through the house. "Everyone, lights out!" yells the camp leader. Steffi jumps out of bed, turns off the light, and bounces back into bed. Everyone is exhausted and soon sound asleep, except for Trudel. In the stillness of the night, she stands alone outside on her balcony overlooking Lake Seidorf. In the distance, she can see the huge bonfire roar.

Cross of Honor of the German Mother

THERE IS NOT A MOMENT these girls are complacent, apathetic, or bored. Their entire day is perfectly organized and structured with the continuous monthly activities. The girls are having fun in camp. They work, learn, and play. They are healthy, strong, and disciplined. They form special bond of kinship between themselves, their villagers, and their Fatherland. They strengthen their way of life through sisterhood immersed totally in the well-being of their community and being one with nature. This is the meaning of Country Service Year Camp and the Odal rune pierced by the sword symbolizes a continuous strive toward the consecutiveness with the totality of life.[1]

In a grand celebration on May 8th, mothers across the nation will receive the "Cross of Honor of the German Mother." This civil order of merit is conferred by the Third Reich to honor the German mothers for their exceptional merit to the nation. The cross is in memory of the Führer's beloved mother, Klara Hitler. In a grand celebration, those mothers who have exhibited probity, exemplary motherhood, and who had conceived and reared at least four children are eligible for this state decoration. State officials will award the mothers who bore eight or more children a gold cross, with at least six children a silver cross, and those with four children a bronze cross.[2]

To express their love and admiration the Landjahr girls beautifully decorate the theater hall with flower arrangements, wreaths, and candles. A table overflows with freshly baked breads, pastries, and cakes. A gift basket for each honorary mother who receives the 'Cross of Honor' contains heartwarming handmade items made wholeheartedly by the girls. These include cards, embroidered napkins, handkerchiefs, doilies, tablemats, and hot plates. The village mothers are honored with gifts and a special performance in song. Each mother receives a special certificate with her name.

Frau Torge looks on admiring the other mothers who receive their honorary crosses.

---

[1] Odal Rune
[2] Cross of Honor

"We are all connected
Under our flag of solidarity
Since we found ourselves
As one people
No one is alone anymore"

~ Die Morgenfrühe ist Unsere Zeit ~
Hans Baumann

Our Workplace

HOURS TURN INTO DAYS and days turn into weeks. The true personalities of the Landjahr girls emerge, and Trudel, Elli, Nelly, Steffi, and Maria form a special bond of friendship. While working, they chat about how they are adjusting to their new camp lifestyle. The city girls begin to open up too, even those who are feeling homesick and are having a hard time acclimating to the paramilitary-like disciplinary measures being used to build their loyalty and self-esteem. It is not easy sleeping in a room with five other girls, or being together twenty-four hours a day, seven days a week. Some want their privacy back. Others cry, pout, or make a scene when they do not get their way.

Country Service Year keeps these girls working, learning, and physically fit. Their leaders place very high physical and psychological expectations on every girl.[1] Discipline extends far beyond the formal curriculum. The leaders are inculcating new virtues, building character, and solidifying the will to work so that the camp girls will mature into strong women, proud, and self-reliant. It is the duty of the troop leader, Fräulein Dieter, to inspire the girls willingly and to instill in them a higher code of ethics. It is the duty of the camp leader, Fräulein Albrecht, to instill in the girls the need to perform all their work with military-like rigor. It is the responsibility of the economic assistant leader, Fräulein Grüber, to teach the girls how to manage the home, including the finances. In a world of constant change, the girls' only stability now is to remain focused on their tasks. What they learn today will become the very foundation that will prepare them for adulthood.

The leaders notice friction building among adolescents and believe the cause is from the varying dialects the girls are using. To clear up the confusion, the leaders instruct all youths to speak in the formal High German language. Fräulein Albrecht thinks it will boost their flagging spirits if they write a letter back home to their families. When the girls turn in their letters for mailing, she notices a distinct improvement in morale, so she calls a group meeting outside to discuss ways to make their stay at Landjahr Lager more pleasant.

Underneath the large birch trees, the girls air their concerns as the camp leaders mediate the discussion. Fräulein Albrecht understands that this is a very important phase in the girls' development. The leaders are always available to discuss the girls' issues and suggest ways of resolving their differences. Issues need to be addressed and resolved, and good communication skills need to be learned in the process.

During the meeting, Fräulein Dieter asks Trudel to share her thoughts.

---

[1] Annemarie Leppien, p. 53

"It feels like I just arrived the other day. I am making new friend, learning new songs, and I love taking care of the animals. I remember something my mother said to me at the train station. She said that I must learn from my leaders and listen to them. She also said that I should be grateful for everything that is being provided for me by the government. I agree. We need to appreciate the comfortable beds, the food we eat, and for all the free education. I say take this opportunity to improve upon yourself! After all, what good is it when you don't know how to read or write, or work at all? That is not a life. Just think about it for a moment, what do you want out of your life? I remember where I come from, do you? My father died when I was very young. After his death, it was very difficult and my family lived in poverty, until the Anschluss, but after that, we had a better life. We had food on the table and my mother was able to find work so that she could finally buy us things. I want to share with you a promise I made with my father before he passed away. He told me that I should find a strong, caring man to marry and to take care of. He said I should have children and live in a beautiful large home on a lake. My father only wanted the best for me. Well, before that promise can be made, I have to learn how to work and become a good homemaker. I also promised my mother that I would work hard and learn as much as I can, because, I for one, am not about to take my time here at Landjahr Lager for granted!"

The leaders are very impressed with Trudel's response. She notices how she speaks like a leader, composers herself like a leader, and acts like a leader.

After a lengthy discussion, the girls agree to shelve their self-interests and focus on the services they can provide to their camp and to their community. They make an agreement to band together no matter what. They formalize their pact in their new Lager motto:

> Our will and our belief are together in unity.
> We have extreme happiness for the creation of life,
> For we are all in complete synchronicity.[2]

The rules are set. Everyone understands their roles and promises to be on their best behavior at all times. Given the opportunity to voice their concerns, they are gaining a deeper awareness and insight into their own purpose in life.

The leaders know exactly how and when to empower the girls. They understand the diversity between the rural and the urban cultures because each have different values. The rural girls who had arrived from St. Pölten are from the Lower Danube region and come from a lower standard of living, limited education, and fewer financial opportunities. The girls from the Upper Silesian region are accustomed to the extravagant, cosmopolitan lifestyle. The city girls must learn the 'Blood and Soil' ideology that extolls the virtues of rural living. By keeping them away from the sins of the city, these wealthier girls will adapt and learn to keep their minds and bodies pure.

---

[2] Annemarie Leppien, p. 39

It is the job of the leaders to align the girls with one universal worldview. This doctrine has to be reinforced with the objectives of serving and working together in harmony. This new ideological foundation supports the girls' own well-being and is designed to ensure the survival of the country.

During the outdoor discussion, Fräulein Albrecht needs to plant a universal thought that will inspire each girl to grow no matter what her individual talents are. She explains how the crops are in the ground and the fields that they've sown are producing their first shoots. Now, their focus will shift. She explains the value of having a strong work ethic.

When Trudel hears the words 'you can do anything you put your mind to doing,' it resonates so deep that she makes a note of it in her journal. This simple axiom becomes so ingrained in her that it changes her perception about life. She realizes that she is standing on the threshold of a new world! She feels alive and invigorated. Trudel has come to place a higher value on her own abilities and talents. She feels a boost in her self-confidence and she will demonstrate it in the tasks that are required of her. She wonders if anyone else in her troop feels the same way. As for the alternative, not doing one's fair share of work is intolerable.[3]

These discussions have several benefits; for it encourages better social skills, improves listening and communication skills, and bolsters the girls' desire to work as a team. Sometimes, negotiations and compromises are inevitable, true, but the close cooperation between the adults and the girls is making them feel valued.[4]

The girls do not view the backbreaking work beneath them. They know a country is only as strong as its people are. Their willingness to work confirms their previous lessons. Even at this young age, they are embracing their leaders whose encouragement lets them know that, by proudly working together, they are reducing the wartime hardships being felt by every working family. They are putting the collective's needs ahead of their selfish desires.

Since the spud planting is completed, the heavy farm work is over for the time being. The girls' curriculum turns towards developing their own creativity through arts and crafts.

The spacious workroom is located in the same building as the gym. Learning arts and crafts is crucial to the girls' psychological development. This will teach them to think laterally and learn the relationship between cause and effect. This creative work will test their temperaments, for arts and crafts demand patient persistence. One must concentrate when building a piece of furniture, making a flute holder, delicately embroidering a tablecloth, or sculpturing. The intense focus tends to disclose emotions hidden in the young heart and thought patterns buried deep inside the young minds. In the end, the finished product can be admired by all.[5]

---

[3] Annemarie Leppien, p. 11

[4] Jeanne Onuska

[5] Magdalena Shears

The crafting girls now dream up what to build and figure out how they are going to build it. They must show enough discipline to manifest their own work. Sometimes, the process may even uncovered a true natural talent!

The girls get to work with a variety of materials, textures, fabrics, tools, and equipment. Craftwork highlights each girls' individual talents and knowledge. With each new manual skill she learns, teaches her how to think, plan, develop, and embrace the law of dignified labor.[6]

During the evening, Trudel writes in her journal and describes her creative work in camp.

"Country Service Year Camp is wonderful! When you walk into our workshop, you would think you were in a furniture factory! At first, it seems like a lot of work, but after our leaders showed us what to do, and how to do it, everything runs very smoothly. We filled in the cracks in the wood furniture and started making toys for the children in the village. All the girls are busy hammering, sawing, grinding, and sanding. It was funny when Elfie hit her finger with the hammer and started cursing, saying it was the hammer's fault!

"On the other side of the room, my friends have been sewing by hand or sitting at their sewing machines learning how to make seams. Some of them knitted socks, sewed aprons, or repaired their clothes. We are learning how to make new dresses and blouses. We are having so much fun!

"Fräulein Albrecht is right. We can do anything we put our minds to doing. So far, I have made a leather pocketbook and two belts. I even learned how to weave a basket and learned how to make a mat using old material. Our leaders told us to make and bind a book that we will be writing in during our final exam. We also learned how to make our own little handbags for our feather ink pens and flutes. We work very hard every day and we learn a lot. It gives us a great deal of happiness. Because of the war, we must save our unused material. I really wish we had more. Everyone is making something she can take home and use.

"Tomorrow, I start my new assignment! I will be learning all about home economics and how to manage the household. We are learning so much here!"

---

[6] Reinhold Sautter, p. 177

Home Economics

THE SCHEDULE HAS ROTATED and now Trudel's group will learn about home economics. The goal is to teach them to become competent in homemaking, running an entire household, and managing the finances.

Since Trudel has always kept a clean home in Kleinzell, she believes that housekeeping takes little forethought. However, her home is small and the manor home is large with thirty rooms. She does not yet realize that a clean and well-run household requires far more work than just sweeping the floors and making the beds.

Trudel dons on her housedress, apron, and scarf. With her broom, dustpan, and aluminum bucket in hand, she sets out to work with Lotte, Elli, and Anna. First, her team walks from room to room, opening all the windows. They remove the area carpets and bring them outside, hanging them over the clotheslines. To free the dirt and fine dust particles, the girls use rattan carpet beaters and strike the carpets hard. Dust flies everywhere!

They return inside and sweep the floors. In the storage room, they grab coarse horsehair scrubbing brushes, and pour boiling water with Irmi cleaning solution into their pails. Starting in the third floor bedrooms, they work their way through the home. On their hands and knees, the girls scour the floors, hallways, and staircase, taking particular care to remove all the dirt from within the corners. On the first floor, they move on into the hallway, offices, sick room, dining room, and lastly, the parlor, before finishing outside scrubbing the entryways and outside steps. Next, they are responsible for waxing the floors until they 'sparkle and shine like glass.'

Kristin, Liesel, and Renate work together to polish the doors, mirrors, and wash the windows. Everything must be whistle clean. They remove the fingerprints from the door handles and trim. Linseed oil is used to polish the wood and a special brass polish makes the handles, door numbers, and hinges shine. Then, the team goes through the entire house and removes the curtains. They too are hung up outside on the clothesline to absorb the fresh air.

Sabine, Ingrid, and Steffi, polish the furniture, wash the interior and exterior of the windows, and thoroughly clean the washrooms, toilets, sinks, shelves, soap dishes, apron hooks, and toothbrush holders. The girls love working together in fellowship.

After a long day of hard work, Trudel approaches the housekeeper and lets her know all the work has been completed.

Fräulein Grüber lines the girls up at attention and orders them to wait until she completes the formal house inspection. Starting on the third floor the leaders inspects every room, corner, and niche. It will be obvious if the girls had not put their hearts and souls into cleaning. With her white glove, she makes sure that all the corners are clean, that no dust lingers on the chandeliers, and that no soap scum lines the shower stalls. If anything is missing, out of place, or dirty, the girls will be obligated to re-clean the entire area. Finally, Fräulein Grüber inspects the girls' cleaning tools, making sure they are not going to be put away dirty. Only when the entire house has met with the leader's approval, can the girls breathe a sigh of relief.

The following day is laundry day and much thought goes into organizing a systematic work schedule. Electric machines are unheard of at camp, which means mounds of laundry have to be washed by hand. Washing, wringing, drying, and ironing, the linens, towels, socks, tablecloths, shirts, underwear, dresses, skirts, aprons, and the sport uniforms for forty girls and three leaders is a gigantic task! It will take an entire day for this team of eight to complete.

After breakfast, the team sits in the dining room with their housekeeper, Fräulein Grüber, and divides the workload into manageable sections. Trudel, Lotte, Elli, and Anna will gather up all the linen and separate it according to how dirty the clothes are. Kristin and Liesel will build the fire and boil the water for the outside washing trough. Renate and Sabine will gather the appropriate tools and equipment and set up the assembly line outside connecting the large trough, the galvanized washtubs, the wringer, and tables. Ingrid and Steffi will remain inside and cook. Off they set to work!

Trudel, Lotte, Elli, and Anna venture into every room and collect the soiled linens. Starting on the top floor, they open all the windows allowing in the fresh air. They remove the bed sheets and pillowcases. Pillows are fluffed up and placed on the windowsills. The girls remove all the mattresses from their wooden bedframes and place them outside in direct sunlight. This will kill the dust mites.

Next, they collect the dirty clothes and separate them into three baskets. One basket is for colored clothes, one for whites, and one for the heavily stained clothes. Renate and Sabine collect the washboards and brushes. The girls use cold water from the hand pump to fill the pails.

Kristin gathers the kindling. She returns to start a fire underneath the large trough. She then adds Irmi laundry detergent to the mix as Liesel stirs with the large wooden paddle. The soapy water has to be near boiling in order to get the whites white.

Once the water in the tub begins to steam, the girls add the least dirty items first. As the home economic girls synchronize their tasks, their project begins to move like clockwork. Paddling agitates the clothes minimizing the risk of burning the material against the hot metal. Soap powder creates a layer of foam. The clothes become softer the longer they are 'cooked.' The girls monitor the clothes closely, periodically lifting the material out of the tub for inspection. If garments boil too long the fibers will break and the fabric may fall apart.

Using long wooden tongs, the girls fish the linens out of the steaming water and drop them into the scrubbing tubs. With coarse hairbrushes and washboards in hand, they scrub any remaining dirt and blood stains from the sheets all the while singing their laundry cleaning song. Kirstin feeds the laundry through the wooden cogs on the wringer as Liesel turns the large metal crank. Renate stands in position ready to grab the fabric as it squeezes out of the heavy, solid iron machine. Excess water drips down the legs of the wringer, creating streams of water that run downhill into the small drainage ditch.

The girls take turns hanging the linens on the clotheslines. Wooden pins hold the fabric in place. The laundry sways gently in the warm breeze, drying under the afternoon sun absorbing the clean fresh air.

All morning long, the girls work together washing, scrubbing, rinsing, wringing, and hanging. By lunchtime all the linens are clean and hanging out to dry. Trudel walks up to the drying linen on the line, grabs the material in her hand, and places it up against her nose. She inhales deeply. She loves how fresh and clean the laundry smells.

After lunch, the girls take down the bed sheets and pillowcases from the clothesline and begin ironing. The irons had been preheated on the kitchen stove. The girls work meticulously to make sure the linens are free from wrinkles and all corners are folded with crisp edges. If a girl discovers that any fabric is torn or ripped, she will need to stop and mend it by hand.

One group undertakes the task of making forty-three beds while the second group continues to iron the girl's clothes. Each item of clothing is easily identifiable by the individual girl's initials sewn into their garments.

The economic assistant leader, Fräulein Grüber, doubles as the steward of the camp. She checks the cleanliness of the entire Lager. She tours the building and makes sure all the tablecloths, towels, and napkins are properly folded and stowed away, the beds are neatly made, and the clean clothes are folded and put away in each of the wardrobes. Strick attention has to be paid to the details. Only after the girls have passed the laundry inspection are they permitted to put away all their cleaning tools. Once the water has cooled down, the girls push the heavy tub over, emptying out the dirty water. They meticulously clean their equipment, and wipe everything down.

Early the next morning, the girls meet again with Fräulein Grüber. Everything in the Lager is intended for the girls' well-being, but the requirements of daily living, including food, are the economic assistant leader's responsibility. Her food recordkeeping has to be impeccable, down to the very last details of what is consumed each day. At the end of the month, her reports are mailed to the Ministry of Education for their review.

The first part of this day's lesson is about nutrition. They will learn how to keep their bodies clean, healthy, and strong. The organic foods they grow provide the necessary sustenance for beautiful skin and hair, strong bones, nails and teeth. Organic foods help the girls remain free from disease. It keeps their bodies functioning properly and gives them a happy disposition. For a physically active lifestyle, the proper combination of carbohydrates, proteins, vitamins, and minerals are required. The girls know that excess carbohydrates turn into fat and the government does not allow these girls to become obese! Their daily fat requirement is low and comes mainly from the butter provided by the local famers. Protein for beautiful hair, fingernail, and smooth skin is also vital for building and repairing muscles, organs, and tissue. The girls glean the vitamins they need from beef livers, kidneys, hearts, and a variety of fresh vegetables. Sweets are limited to only very special occasions. Naturally, every day they consume seven times more fruits and vegetables than meats or pastries.

The largest meal of the day is consumed at noon whereas a light snack and coffee is served in the late afternoon. The girls do not lack for what they need to keep their athletic bodies physically fit. All meals are planned according to a special menu prepared two weeks in advance. Over the next two weeks, the girls will learn how to plan menus and prepare full course meals. Much planning goes into the daily meals so that they can be served hot and on time. When planning their meals, they sort out the type of utensils to be used for what meals will be served on that day. They keep track of the food inventory and the cost of their supplies in a special accounting book. All the food preparation has to be fast and punctual. They even create a little song.

> If every day would be Monday, pasta day,
> We would be happy and gay.
> If every day would be Tuesday, strudel day,
> We would be happy and gay.
> Wednesday is dumpling day,
> Thursday is meat day,
> Friday is fasting day,
> Saturday is (the number of days they have been at the lager) day
> Sunday is our resting day."[1]

For breakfast, each girl receives one large ladle of scrambles eggs, a slice of ham, sourdough bread, and one tall glass of unpasteurized milk. The eggs are gathered from their chickens, the bread comes from the flour purchased from the local wheat farmer, which they learn how to bake themselves, and the milk comes directly from their cows. Large plates of hard-boiled eggs, tomatoes, radishes, cucumbers, lettuce, spinach, cheese, and a variety of meat, are served to make open face breakfast sandwiches. Every morning before breakfast, the girls stand around the table, hold hands, and give thanks with their prayer:

> "Lord, let our acre and our food, be for our people as we
> bring it in, and hold us strong and at the right time, to wake us up
> in the morning sunshine."

The surrounding countryside offers an abundance of food resources. The fish farmer from Glausnitz (Głębock) barters for his fresh Crucian carp. Beef, pork, chicken, and ham are supplied by the meat farmers in Seidorf (Sosnówka),

---

[1] Lotte Landl, p. 25

and the orchards in Saalberg (Zachełmie) supply fresh fruits, including an abundance of apples, pears, and cherries.

From these ingredients, the girls learn to create a wide variety of main dishes including Kasespatzle, made from wheat flour and egg, served with cheese, Eintropf, a 'one pot stew' with vegetables and meat, Kartoffelpuffer, made from grated potatoes mixed with flour, eggs, onion and seasoning, Sauerbraten, grilled chicken, and Trudel's favorite Knödel. Side dishes include braised red cabbage, warm apple and cabbage slaw, cucumber and potato salad, and Erdäpfel salad. Soups are made from apples, chickens, potatoes, lentils, and zucchini. On special occasions, apple strudel and even cherry pies are made!

Every two weeks the plates, napkins, silverware, dishes, glasses, pots, pans, and food staples are counted for inventory purposes. The girls record in their register the costs of their food staples, and cost to feed each person. Such skills are in good preparation for work in the hospitality industry.

Trudel is very excited when she hears the news that the girls will participate in a cooking contest tomorrow. Trudel loves to cook. She enjoys mixing the ingredients and tasting the results. She is both nervous and excited for she will have to showcase for the leaders and their guests what she has learned so far. All day long, she thinks about what she is going to make. She discusses with the other girls what would be the easiest and best-tasting meal, cake, or pastry. She sets her mind on cooking potato dumplings.

The next day, the girls are standing in the kitchen, whispering about the finer points of cooking. The door opens and all three camp leaders walk in holding papers in their hands. Their smiles show a hidden agenda.

Fräulein Grüber explains the rules of the competition. The economic leader tells the group that they must make their selection unassisted, to use the recipes that were taught to them, and that they only have two hours to complete their chosen assignments. The girls must fully concentrate on their cooking and no one is allowed to speak or use a recipe. Each meal must be perfectly prepared because the women's committee from the village will come and personally taste their dishes and announce the results in their local newspaper!

Trudel is stunned! She was under the impression that she can choose to cook whatever she wanted. However, that was clearly not the case. Her heart had been set on potato dumplings, and now, she has no clue what she will be cooking! It could be anything!

One by one, each girl warily walks up to Fräulein Albrecht and reaches for a folded slip of paper. She holds it in her hand and then quickly unfolds it. Each girl is assigned one dish. One girl will be making noodle soup, while the others will be making pancakes, pork roast, dumplings, sauerkraut, a green tossed salad, or a plate of sandwiches. The lucky girl gets to bake a cake! Some of the girls jump up and down with excitement while others look disappointedly at their leaders. However, that will not help them now. It's too late. Everyone gets to work and the competition begins!

This will test the girl's memories to see whether or not they have been paying attention in Fräulein Grüber's cooking classes. She has been teaching them many recipes over the past two weeks. This is big challenge for the girls.

In her BDM leader's uniform, Fräulein Grüber paces back and forth with her hands held behind her back. She looks over the girls' shoulders and inspects their cooking techniques. Everyone is absorbed in the competition and focuses intently on their dishes. Trudel thinks to herself, 'Am I using the correct ingredients? Are the measurements correct? Is the temperature hot enough in the oven? How will my food taste when I am finished?' Trudel takes pride in her cooking and hopes she does a good job.

The girls pick up the pace when the leader gives the one-hour countdown mark, then the half-hour mark, and the last fifteen-minute mark. With every count down, the girls move faster, bumping into each other, dashing around the room, and dropping items on the floor. The kitchen becomes a mess.

When the leader blows her whistle all action stops. The competition is over. Only the taste test remains.

The dining room table is set eloquently. A center vase contains chrysanthemums and yellow globeflowers, which accent the violet marsh gentians and saxifrages, set in short glasses in front of each table setting. The formal place settings are precise and geometrically spaced with the utensils balanced on either side of the dinner plate, with the bread dish in the upper left hand corner opposite the glasses. The truth will reveal itself shortly. Did the girls pay attention or not?

The girls hoist the food up in the dumbwaiter to the dining room and serve it to the selected farmers' wives. These women are master cooks in their own household and are the very best in the village of Seidorf. As the wives settle in and start talking with the leaders, the servers stand at attention, not daring to speak or even move until called upon.

Trudel's heart jumps when the first woman cuts a small piece of her pork roast and guides it to her mouth. Trudel took extra special care to baste the meat with its own juices, making sure to cover the potatoes, carrots, and onions and slightly browning the tops. She made her dish just as her leader taught her. She watches the woman's face closely for any signs. She cannot tell whether the farmer's wife is enjoying the meal or not. Instead, the woman picks up the pencil, marks her paper, and then resumes eating.

Fräulein Albrecht orders the girls to resume their duties and to start cleaning the kitchen. Trudel continually looks over her shoulder as she walks down the hall watching the women eat. She and her comrades descend the stairs and what they find is chaos! The kitchen is a complete disaster! Pots and pans are piled up on the stove, the center table is covered with food scraps, and flour has been spilled on the floor. The top leading edge of the oven is covered with black residue from the smoke. Soon, the girls are helping each other clean, sweep, wash, and wipe everything down.

Kristin and Liesel decide to sneak upstairs and listen in on the women's conversation. At the bottom of the stairs, they look up just in time to see Fräulein

Dieter staring down at them. Quickly, they hasten back into the kitchen and resume their duties.

Only when the kitchen is spotless does Fräulein Dieter order the girls to come up into the dining room. They remove the dirty plates and utensils, and then re-set the table for dessert. It is not until the formal taste test has been completed and the committee has thoroughly discussed their comments with the chairwomen that the girls are allowed to eat any leftovers. The judges bid a fond farewell and compliment the girls on a job well done.

The home economics group resets the table for themselves. This is a positive and non-coercive atmosphere for the goal is to introduce new dishes and expand their food choices. Fräulein Grüber compliments them on a job well done. She reviews each dish without malice, and announces whether the cook had prepared the food properly. As the girls are sampling each other's cuisine, they discuss how the food tastes, what improvements they can made, and whether or not all the ingredients were used. This is a learning experience. It is meant to inspire and encourage the girls to learn new recipes, and to understand the nutritional value of each meal served.

Trudel listens intently to the comments. She is learning the art of cooking. There is no individual winner in this competition for everyone is a winner.

During the evening social hour, Trudel writes a long entry in her journal about her perceptions of Country Service Year Camp thus far.

"When you do not open your eyes by yourself, you will never be happy again. The morning fresh air is our time and we believe in our strengths. It comes to us from working hard. We always pay attention and learn, because eventually what is being taught will come naturally.

"We believe in one God and He brings us together. We are created to find ourselves, in our strengths, in our hopes, and in our dreams. Think about your friends, your land, your God, and your Führer.

"God created us to work together and that is the way it will be. In our people's mind, God is our Creator. As people, we must find ourselves, in our virtues, our strengths, and our unique gifts so that we can give and help one another, willingly. We are ready because we believe in ourselves. We work hard to show what we have learned. We perform our work dutiful and with pride. The people, the land, and our Führer give us what we need and it is from there that we find our inner strength.

"Our will and our belief are together as one. We have extreme happiness for our rebirth and for life for we are in complete synchronicity with each other.

"Therefore, when we go out, we sing our songs,—we have strength in our words, for our words have meaning.

"We are extremely happy in our beliefs. Our eyes watch as the sun rises naturally over the mountains. The sun can never look down on us as if God would not have created it. How could we think otherwise?

"The morning sun smiles down upon our hearts, our land, and our healthy German people who are happy in life and are connected with nature. We fulfill our work duties and everyone can look and praise us because of the efforts we put in to show them how much we have learned.

"When we rest in our free hours, we spend time with nature, smell the clean fresh air, and drink the pure mountain waters. We talk among ourselves and look back on all our accomplishments. We can honestly say, 'Look at what our creator has done for us.' Remember all the good things in life. Remember how pretty and happy it can be in your life. Enjoy!

"We are free to think. We are aware and when we look around and walk upon the land, we see His majesty in the Alps. Only God can create our inner strength just as He did when he created the granite in the highest mountains in Germany.

"We must never forget our responsibilities to our people, our country, and to our Führer. We must never lose our inner strength—that is expected from us. We must show that what we can accomplish glitters and shines, just as the sun shines. Our hands work and the sun is made from God's hands.

"In every field that surrounds us and in every piece of dirt, our food grows. We care for our food and we will work together to take care of it and harvest it when ready. Our food grows by our own hands and we are proud that we can produce our bountiful crops. The Almighty gave us the seeds to put into Ceres Erde and she will provide our people a mighty harvest of food. Germany is our holy land for eternity!

"Because of our hard work ethics, we will rest on God's day. We appreciate and look toward the morning sun and say, 'Germany has God's blessing all around us.' In the distance, we can see forever, the lakes, the forest, and the hills. God places His hands over this land to shine and lead us to the green oceans afar.

Newspaper Report

THE SUMMER DAYS ARE GETTING LONGER and warmer and the nights remain pleasantly cool. On this beautiful Sunday morning of June 22 1941, Trudel and her roommates, Ellie, Nelly, Steffi, and Maria, are outside tending to the farm animals. Behind them is the beautiful panorama of the Giant Mountains. The girls are discussing what they would like to do before this evening's summer solstice festivities when they hear an unexpected voice hollering from inside the home.

"Come quickly, everyone! Come quickly!" Fräulein Grüber shouts as she runs from her office into the dining room. "There is a special report from our high command in the newspaper!"

Hearing the commotion going on inside the house, Trudel and her comrades run inside. The announcement races through the camp like a bolt of lightning. Everyone runs into the dining room and gathers to hear the breaking news.

Fräulein Grüber reads from the newspaper. "Just before dawn this morning, our troops moved into their assault positions. Four million soldiers are pushing into the east along an eighteen-hundred mile front line from the Baltic Sea to the Carpathian Mountains."

Trudel is very interested in hearing any news about the war. Her two brothers, Emmerich and Hans, are fighting, however, she does not know of their whereabouts. In her heart, she prays that they are going to be all right. After all, they are her brothers and nothing will happen to them.

"It goes on to say that our enemy is trembling before us. Our great forces have come alive out of the darkness and from the forest. They are now penetrating the soils of our adversary. Projectiles blast from our tanks in a fiery explosions of great force. Plumes of smoke and fire billow on the other side of the border, signaling our triumphant invasion of the Soviet Union."

The girls listen attentively, trying to grasp the magnitude of the situation.

Fräulein Grüber continues reading. "At five o'clock this morning, our Reich's Minister, Joseph Goebbels, read the Proclamation of War on behalf of our Führer. He announces to the world that ..." Fräulein Grüber stops reading and places the newspaper down onto the table. She takes a deep breath just as Fräulein Albrecht and Dieter walk into the room.

"The Proclamation of War is published in today's paper," Fräulein Grüber sadly informs the other two young leaders. In disbelief, they sit down and listen. "It reads as follows, 'People of Germany! National Socialists! After long months when I was forced to keep silent, despite heavy concerns, the time has come when I can speak openly.

"When the German Reich received England's Declaration of War on the 3rd of September 1939, the British attempted once again to frustrate any attempt to begin a consolidation, and thus a strengthening of Europe by fighting the then strongest power on the continent. England formerly destroyed Spain through many wars. For the same reason it waged its war against Holland. With the help of all of Europe, it later fought France. In addition, around the turn of the century, it began to encircle the German Reich and it began the World War in 1914. Germany was defeated in 1918 only because of its inner disunity. The results were terrible.

"After first hypocritically declaring to be fighting only against the Kaiser and his regime, they began the systematic destruction of the German Reich after the German army had laid down its arms. As the prophecy of a French statesman, who had said that there are twenty million Germans too many, began to be fulfilled through starvation, disease, or emigration, the National Socialist movement began building the unity of the German people, thereby preparing the rebirth of the Reich.

"This new revival of our people from poverty, misery, and shameful contempt was a sign of a pure internal rebirth. England was not affected, much less threatened, by this. Nonetheless, it immediately renewed its hateful policy of encirclement against Germany. Both at home and abroad, we faced the plot we all know about between Jews and democrats, Bolshevists and reactionaries, all with the same goal, and that is to prevent the establishment of a new people's state, to plunge the Reich again into impotence and misery.

"The hatred of this international world conspiracy was directed not only against us, but also against those peoples who had been neglected by fortune, who could earn their daily bread only through the hardest struggle. Italy and Japan above all, alongside Germany, were almost forbidden to enjoy their share of the wealth of the world. The alliance between these nations was, therefore, only an act of self-defense against a threatening, egotistical world coalition of the wealth and power.

"As early as 1936, according to the testimony of the American General Wood to a committee of the American House of Representatives, Churchill had said that Germany was becoming too strong again, and that is therefore had to be destroyed.

"In the summer of 1939, England thought that the time had come to renew its attempts to destroy Germany by a policy of encirclement. Their method was to begin a campaign of lies. They declared that Germany threatened other peoples. They then provided an English guarantee of support and assistance next as in the World War, let them march against Germany.

"Thus between May and August 1939, England succeeded in spreading the claim throughout the world that Germany directly threatened Lithuania, Estonia, Latvia, Finland, Bessarabia, and even the Ukraine. Some of these nations allowed themselves to be misled, accepting the promises of support that were offered, and thereby joined the new attempt to encircle Germany.

Trudel looks at Steffi in total confusion. "What is she talking about?" Trudel whispers in her ear.

"I don't know," Steffi whispers back.

"The results of their efforts, in every nation, were only chaos, misery, and starvation. I on the other hand, have tried for two decades to build a new socialist order in Germany, with a minimum of interference and without harming our productive capacity. This has not only eliminated unemployment, but also the profits of labor have flowed increasingly to working people.

"The results of our policies are unique in the entire world. Our economic and our social reorganization have led to the systematic elimination of social and class barriers, with the goal of a true people's community.

"Therefore, it was difficult for me in August 1939 to send my minister to Moscow in an attempt to work against Britain's plan to encircle Germany. I did it only because of my sense of responsibility to the German people, above all in the hope of reaching a lasting understanding and perhaps avoiding the sacrifice that would otherwise be demanded of us.

The girls sit lost in the political ramifications with little grasp of the potential impact of this announcement on their own personal lives. Due to the severity of the situation, however, the girls are obligated to remain seated and listen through to the end of the article.

"German people! At this moment, an attack unprecedented in the history of the world in its extent and size has begun. With Finnish comrades, the victors of Narvik stand by the Arctic Sea. German divisions, under the command of the conqueror of Norway, together with the heroes of Finland's freedom and their marshal, defend Finnish soil. On the Eastern Front, German formations extend from East Prussia to the Carpathians. From the banks of the Pruth River, from the lower Danube to the Black Sea, German and Romanian soldiers are united under Rumanian Chief of State General Antonescu.

"The purpose of this front is no longer the protection of the individual nations, but rather the safety of Europe, and therefore the salvation of everyone.

"I have therefore decided today once again to put the fate of Germany and the future of the German Reich and our people in the hands of our soldiers. May God help us in this battle."[1]

Fräulein Grüber rises from her chair. The room is silent.

"What does that mean?" Steffi asks.

"Oh, it's nothing to worry about, girls," Fräulein Dieter says as she puts her arms around Trudel and Elli. "Now, let's turn our attention to the atlas. I will show you where our camp is located and explain where the soldiers are fighting."

In the largest military operation in the world, Germany invades the Soviet Union, the communist giant to the east.

Trudel listens to Fräulein Dieter elaborating on the mysteries of German foreign policy. "Why can't everyone be happy where they are living right now?" "Why does anyone have to fight or go to war?" she asks to herself. Trudel

---

[1] Professor Randall Bytwerk, - "The Führer to the German People"

watches the stick of the instructor as it points to one part of the map and then back to another. War does not seem real to her.

When the troop leader finishes her explanation, she orders Maria and Steffi to write a report about the Proclamation of War. It must be completed and on her desk by Tuesday morning.

With the unexpected lesson of the day behind them, Fräulein Dieter orders the girls to complete their morning tasks and to begin preparing for the summer solstice celebration this evening.

Freedom of the Flame

THE GIRLS GATHER PINE BRANCHES and saxifrage from the surrounding forest. They make wreaths and decorate their wagon wheel, which is standing against the flagpole. Sticks and branches that were collected earlier are piled up next to the fire pit.

In the middle of the field, the troop leader shows the girls how to lean pieces of tinder up against each other to create high flames once the bonfire is lit. A protective ring of rocks encircles the firewood. Paper and other kindling inside the small opening at the bottom of the tripod structure will ensure a quick start when lighting the fire.

An appropriate cleansing ritual for the summer solstice will be to spend the rest of the day swimming. Excitedly, the girls run up to their rooms and gather their suits, caps, and towels. Singing, they hike gingerly to the bottom of the hill. They cross the main street onto the narrow gravel path and head toward the pond. In the wooden bathhouse, they change into their suits and meet their leaders on the platform.

The pond is just the right size for the villagers to seek refuge in its cool, refreshing waters. Few are taking advantage of it on this day. One woman is lounging on the extended platform on the far side, sunning herself, and three other visitors sit in their lounge chairs at the beach side. A long stack of logs blocks the view of any passing onlookers. A rope with buoys marks the shallow end. At the deep end stand the three and nine foot high springboards.

The girls stand in two lines wearing their black bathing suits and white caps. Marta, Magdalena, Helli, Sylvia, and Dorota have only lived in the city and do not know how to swim. They are told to move to the shallow end and wait for further instructions. For the city girls, this will be their first day of learning how to swim!

Those who can swim take this opportunity to entertain themselves. The country girls run and jump off the deck into the water. They devise various games for themselves, like lining up in one long row, holding the hand of the other and in one fell swoop, they all jump into the water.

Steffi and Maria pretend they are drowning and show off their rescuing skills. They swim back to the dock, climb up the ladder, screaming with glee, and push each other off the platform and into the water, before popping back up to the surface with a mouth full of water.

The country girls know how to swim and start a little competition to see who can swim the fastest from the dock to the platform and back again, or who can hold their breath and swim the longest underwater.

At first, the city girls look on with envy, but soon, they are learning to paddle and the breaststroke. Those who catch on quickly are taught the freestyle form of swimming. Fräulein Dieter slowly guides the girls out into the deep water and back again, building their self-confidence. When she feels the city girls are capable enough, she encourages them to swim by themselves over into the deep side of the pond and back again. After a few hours, she demonstrates how to dive off the springboard.

The girls stand on the deck and observe their instructor dive off the three-foot high diving board. It does not seem too difficult. Marta, Magdalena, Helli, Silvia, and Dorota band together refusing to learn how to dive, believing that on their free day off they can make their own rules. They casually sit down on the dock and start talking among themselves, defying Fräulein Dieter.

Fräulein Albrecht will not tolerate such disobedience. Using her strongest disciplinary voice, she commands the girls to stand up and jump! Embarrassed by the public scolding, the city girls snap to attention, line up, and reluctantly jump into the water and swim.

The leaders observe the girls and rate their diving and swimming proficiency in their accomplishment book. It is important to know which girls possess champion swimming abilities because once the war is over, one of these girls may have the opportunity to represent their country in the next Olympics.

Fräulein Dieter announces a diving competition. This will be a test to see who can gracefully dive and create the least splash. Three points will be awarded for best takeoff, flight, and flexibility and one point will be given for the best entry into the water. All scores will be recorded in the BDM Proficiency Book. Those with scores above eight will move on to the high board and compete against one another. The girl with the most points will win the first-place ribbon, and if there is a tie, each will compete against the other.

For some, jumping off the springboard is easy. Those girls, who are finding it difficult to jump, are encouraged by their comrades to be more courageous. The sense of trust, openness, and security is growing within the group. The leaders pay close attention to the group dynamics. They realize that when the girls take small risks and are successful in their attempts the group gains an inner feeling of accomplishment thereby deepening their sense of fellowship.

One by one, the divers take turns jumping off the low board. Since the leaders are striving to bring balance between the city and rural cliques, they believe taking a day to swim and dives are neither complicated nor intimidating. Each girl will simply perform to the best of her abilities.

Silvia, one of the girls from the city, does not resurface right away. There is a strained silence on the platform. Everyone lines the edge and stares anxiously down at the water. Silvia gasps for air and flails when she surfaces. Then, Fräulein Dieter dives in and quickly swims to her aid. The leader places her arm under Silvia's chin and using the other, swims back to the platform. Nelly and Maria reach out, grab Silvia by the arms, and pull her up onto the platform. Silvia then collapses and rolls on her back, coughing up water. Fräulein Albrecht races to her side and performs first aid while the other girls cross their fingers. When Silvia regains her composure enough to stand up, the relieved girls give a cheer!

Since everyone has completed the first round, scores are tallied. Next, the names are called for the high dive off the nine-foot high board.

Trudel's heart starts pounding like a locomotive when hears her name being called. She did not know it but she had successfully passed the first round. With both hands holding on to the ladder and her right foot on the lowest rung, she freezes in fear. Breathing heavily, she says a short prayer to herself before climbing. Standing alone on the top of the board, Trudel looks down at her peers. Far below, many eyes are staring right back at her. In fun, they begin goading, "Jump, jump, jump!" The city girls, including Silvia, tease Trudel, and chant, "Come on Trudel chicken noodle, Tru-del, chick-en, noo-dle!" The troop leader commands the girls to be quiet.

From below, the board did not seem very high. Her perception has changed. Now, Trudel is staring down at the black waterway beneath her. She cannot even see the bottom, but she knows that she has to jump. Everyone is waiting. She imagines the dive in her mind. She remembers the techniques the other girls in front of her had used. She thinks back on her leader's words, "I can do anything I put my mind to doing." Fear turns into anger. "I'll show them that I can jump!" she thinks to herself.

The troop leader shouts, "On my mark! Ready? One, two, and three!" Without hesitation, the leader blows her whistle.

With her eyes straight ahead and her chin held high, Trudel takes four steps forward. Near the end, she springs up off the board then back down. To gain the most momentum, her arms circle down alongside her body and around. With knees bent, she pushes down hard on the board. She feels like she is moving in slow motion. Her arms swing around her side stretching her body forward as it rises into the air. Reaching the apex of her trajectory her body follows a parabolic curve as gravity naturally pulls her downward towards the abyss. It seems as if a lifetime has passed but within a split second, Trudel holds her body straight and with her arms in front of her, she plunges into the water below. She hears the muffling splash then everything goes quiet. The cool water feels smooth and is most refreshing alongside her body. She opens her eyes and can see the brown tint of the pond water. With both arms straight out she cups her hands and propels herself underwater, kicking with one solid stroke.

Trudel's head pops out of the water to the sound of cheers! The tremendous smile of her face reveals a feeling of accomplishment. She swims out of the way and to the side of the platform wanting to jump all over again!

After everyone has completed their high dives, Fräulein Albrecht tallies up the score in the proficiency book and announces the results of the dive competition. "Trudel Kerschner is the winner!"

Trudel's friends hug and congratulate her. She proudly walks up to the leader, salutes, and bows her head to receive the award. She turns around and looks at her comrades. She notices the city girls rolling their eyes in contempt.

With the competition over, the girls shower, change, and hike back to their camp in song. Their bodies feel energized. They bounce and skip along the road, singing. The sun is still high in the sky when they arrive back at camp, just in time for their afternoon social hour.

In the parlor, the girls anxiously wait as Fräulein Albrecht takes the mail and reads the names off of the envelopes and postcards. Everyone wants to receive a letter from home, but not everyone does. Trudel jumps to her feet when she hears her name. She salutes and proudly accepts her postcard. Back in her chair, she glances down. Nothing is more exciting than getting mail from home!

> 12 June 1941
> Our Dearest Trudel,
> We are so happy to receive your letter and to learn that you arrived in Seidorf safe and well. We are very happy to hear that everything is going very well and that you are making new friends. We are all very proud of you. Unfortunately, we have some bad news for you. We are very sad to inform you that your grandfather, Bernhard, has passed away. We will miss him very much. We visited Tante Aloise, Uncle Johann, and Hilda. They all love their new house in Rainfeld. It is not that far away and they said we could visit them anytime. We wish you all the best from our hearts. We miss you dearly and patiently wait for your safe return. Love and kisses, Mother, Franz, Opa, Oma, Hilda

Trudel holds the card dear to her heart. She feels a twinge inside her chest and wonders what her family is doing today. However, the strict daily schedule gives Trudel little time for reflection. For the remainder of the afternoon she will practice her singing and procure her torch with the other girls for this evening's summer solstice ceremony.

To enrich the solidarity of the group, more relaxed activities include learning a repertoire of songs survived by the Young Hikers (Wandervogel) movement are learned.[1] Some songs coincide with the annual Summer Solstice festival and recast the veneration for National Socialism and their Führer. The folklore of German heritage places a central importance in educating the Hitler Youth in National Socialism.[2] German folk songs focus strongly on community building and offer the means to awaken the social consciousness. Music improves group cohesion, builds character, and loyalty. Music is the glue that solidifies friendships. Most of the songs the girls learn are from the required songbook, "We Girls Sing." Trudel writes about singing in her journal.

> "Singing always makes me happy. We start each day with a half-hour of singing and playing our instruments. I'll tell you, nobody thinks about how tired we are even though it is the

---

[1] Landjahralbum
[2] Rachael Jane Anderson, p. 1

beginning of our day. When you hear the beautiful songs we sing and the music we play, everyone naturally comes around and wants to sing along.

"At first, it was difficult because we sang out of harmony. Once we practiced and learned the songs, we can sing them perfectly. It doesn't matter what part of the country you live in because everyone knows the same songs.

"We sing a lot of folk songs about nature, our mothers, and our Fatherland. During our three-hour weekly rehearsals, we learn new songs about the stars, the trees, our people, our countryside, and our flag. On the holidays, we sing about the farmers, and the workers. We have even learned to sing in three harmonies. Sometimes, the simplest song can turn our heads when we get it right. Sometimes, we make mistakes but with much practice, when we all come together in one voice, it sounds so beautiful! We are so proud of each other and we do not want to stop because we just want to sing.

"Before we learn a new song, Fräulein Dieter explains to us the meaning of it and where we can sing it. Then, she teaches us how to sing the song. Every day, we practice singing our songs. When we finally get it right the leader praises us for doing such a fine job. My heart stirs when I listen to the beautiful songs we sing. Tonight we will be singing many songs to our Führer, our flag, and for our Fatherland.

"I am also learning how to play the flute. We must pay special attention to how the notes sound. Not everyone plays the flute correctly, but we still love to learn. Fräulein Dieter tells us we must have patience, study, and learn.

"We also learn music theory. Some days our wish is to learn all about music because it brings so much happiness into our hearts. When we listen to Mozart or Beethoven, we ask ourselves 'How can they write such beautiful music?' We don't know where did they get all those notes from?' Sometimes I ask myself 'Did they hear the song in their head first or did they write it down and then hear the song?'

"Tonight, Herminie and Steffi will give a performance and recite a new poem at our summer solstice ceremony. Heidi and Helli will play their flutes. Oh my God! I have been listening to them practice and everything is coming out wrong! It's amazing how Fräulein Dieter has so much patience inside of her. I must continue to practice my zither too because I will be performing tonight!"

The value of song lay not only in its power to inspire divine thoughts but to influence the character of these impressionable young listeners. Their new beliefs

245

and ideology tap into folk values that forge within the listener a powerful sense of obligation, giving these innocent girls a sense of purposeful identity. Songs will play an important role in tonight's event.

The solstice ceremony will pair their femininity with the element of fire, which is directly associated with righteousness and high moral standards. All BDM girls are considered the 'future guardians of the home' and are expected to uphold these standards. The symbolic purpose of the ceremony is to release the old by burning away traces of the past and to re-awaken the girls' consciousness. The celebration of solstice cradles a nationwide gathering of all German youths, and the element of fire represents its community.

With a magnifying glass, Fräulein Albrecht demonstrates to the girls how to light the ceremonial urn. The belief is that the sun contains all life force for the earth and that it will be borrowed, as it will be used later on that evening.

The sun goddess is named Sunna and she is the sister to the moon. Sunna is personified in Norse mythology. It is foretold that she will be killed by a monstrous wolf, through beforehand; she will have given birth to a daughter who will continue her mother's course through the heavens.

After the ceremonial lighting, the girls leave and gather materials to finalize the completion of their individual torches.

Late in the afternoon, the girls return and with their leaders, they sit on the wall and help each other make their torches.

Pine pitch that has been collected throughout the year is simmering in a metal pot melting. While it liquefies, the girls carefully use their knives to cut cross-shaped slits into their green oak branches. They open up the tips of their torches by wedging short twigs into the slits. The twigs form the basis of a guard, thereby, opening up the branch and creating a receptacle in which to hold the pitch. The girls then interlace bast fibers from the flax plant around the guard and through the opening. Eventually a receptacle is created and ready for pine tar. Dried-up clumps of amber and rolled-up bast are stuffed down into the opening using a stick. Much care has to be taken when transferring the hot sap. The girls use an old wooden ladle to spoon the pitch into the receptacles. Once completed, the torches are set off to the side and allowed to cool.

By ten o'clock that evening, everyone is formally dressed in her uniform. Fräulein Albrecht leads the young maidens from the parlor to the rear of the house where Fräulein Grüber and Dieter are waiting to hand each one of them their symbolic flames. It is pitch black outside and the girls have a hard time seeing. Only the lit torches of the two leaders light the way. The girls line up in a double column. One by one, the torches are ignited and come alive.

The torch parade marches in unison down the gravel driveway to the steps and eventually into the sports field where the two-hour re-birthing ceremony will take place. This is Trudel's first time participating in this pagan ritual.

The girls circle the massive council fire. Wood crackles as flames shoot skyward. Sparks gracefully dance on the current of the wind.

Fräulein Albrecht begins the ceremony in a booming voice. "Tonight, we celebrate our heritage! Let us give praise to our Führer!"

Altogether, the girls recite their oath of allegiance as the conflagration roars under the starry sky.

"I promise to do my duty in Landjahr,
With love and loyalty,
To our Führer and to our flag,
So help me, God."

Fräulein Albrecht clears her throat. "Since ancient times our ancestors have honored the golden disk of the sun as the giver of life and warmth. She is like a wheel rolling across the sky. Her name is Sól and the wheel is her symbol because she moves in an arc over the earth. Each day of her course is predetermined. At six o'clock in the morning, she rises in the east. At the twelfth hour, she is high overhead. Come six o'clock, she is in the west. By midnight, she has set behind the mountains, only to rise again the next morning and complete her full circle. The ancestors mark the passage of the calendar year by visualizing the spokes on a wheel.

"Now the summer solstice is the longest day of the year, for the sun reaches its highest point in the sky. By contrast, the shortest day of the year is the winter solstice, when the maximum elevation of the sun is at its lowest point in the sky. Connecting these two points is a line that is roughly east to west. In our latitude, the starting point of the sun on Midsummer Day is in the northeast, and it ends in the southwest. That line crosses the first line, and the resulting X is part of the ancient six-spoke wheel of the Hagal rune.

"Our forefathers brought with them an incredible experience that became very important to their own future. Tonight, we re-discover their future in our heritage. We should always honor our heritage, for we believe in it, as opposed to ghosts or other superstitions that we do not believe in.

"In ancient times, our people celebrated the summer and winter solstices. In their minds, the light and dark connect with one another. Although the winters are dark and very hard, the people persevere.

"The bright summer light is still the master over the long winter's darkness. If we compare then to now, after the death of the Nordic people, what does it all mean? We can say that those are very sad memories. In the winter, the sun moves further and further away, creating the harsh cold, but when the sun comes closer it brings warmth back to the earth. After a summer rains, we see beautiful rainbows filling the sky with marvelous colors. When the sun sets over the horizon, the sea quickly swallows it. However, the next morning the sun reappears again behind the mountains. Once again, the rising sun is a beautiful sight to behold. In the mornings, the summer sun warms our soils and makes our harvests abundant. In the evening, it descends into the darkness of its grave. We must ask ourselves, 'Just as the sun lays itself down, can we possibly, as people, lay down our lives for our land?'

"In mid-winter, we watch the sun go down into its grave, but we see it the next morning, it is reborn like an infant. The sun becomes alive again and shows its power, just as we are born again. Therefore, we celebrate the rising of the sun as we rise up together as one."

Trudel feels an unstoppable power building within her soul as she listens to the inspiring proclamation. Now, it is Fräulein Grüber's turn to speak.

"Tonight, we give of ourselves in this celebration. At this very moment, in every corner of our great nation our young boys and girls are standing together around fires to release themselves from the bondage of their pasts. You are all free. You are all healthy. Tonight, you are awakening from your death, and we celebrate your resurrection. How long will we celebrate our sacred fires burning around our nation? How much longer will we celebrate the sun as it gives us our freedom? In our triumphant moment, we know we are the light and the life in this mid-summer night. Together we raise our hands in salute and say, "Heil Hitler!"

With an eerie echo, their call reverberates down into the valley below.

Before she continues, Fräulein Grüber pauses to savor the essence of the moment. "On some favorable nights, the lucky ones are blessed to witness a few short hours as the colored lights whisk through the sky. This solstice celebration is the marriage of the year to our people here on earth, for which we are eternally grateful. After tonight's celebration the sun will begin to lose its power and move further away, and the earth will once again descend into the darkness of the winter night. Then, a new cycle of life will begin. Our ancestors died but their life force is resurrected through the birth of their children. Such is the circle of life.

"Thousands of years ago, our ancestors were enlightened about the death and resurrection of the sun. They shared their truth through the same folklore we are celebrating this evening. We are very fortunate that we have these stories to share. We have collected thousands of years of German folklore and have written it all down. This is our legacy, this is our heritage, and this is the history of our nation!

"The young sun goddess, Sunna, daughter of the king Mundilfàri, was killed by the powerful wolf. The summer silver knight brought her back to life and she gave birth. Birth and death are at the core of our folklore. Birth and death are the same for they are the two sides of one door. To enter one room always means leaving another. It depends on which room or which life we are in as to whether we say, 'Entrance' or 'Exit,' life or death. For he who understands it, death holds no terrors.

"However, he who did not go his proper way in life and sinned will see his guilt in death. There is an after death. It is no place of torture, nor is it hell. To see one's guilt is the severest judgment and at the same time the greatest penalty. Judgment and punishment are within you. Neglected work can only be made up by double effort. It will once more be your choice, either to work toward the world plan, or to be its enemy. That is the only death that there is, to become a force for destruction rather than for creation, and this death is not physical. It is your free choice to decide which side you belong, on God's side or the Devil's side. What we call birth and death is only the door between two worlds. There is no birth and there is no death, only change, and we can go confidently through the door, for all the worlds were created by one hand. Therefore, be happy because the tears we shed for our loved ones are not for sorrow but instead for their happiness in everlasting life."

"As in death, the year ends and the sun start anew. It is a new year written for all living animals and all living plants in nature. Even in our lifetime, there are times set apart for us when we are very young, when we are in our middle years, and when it comes time that we get old, and we die. We are reborn again. Yes, our whole life is of coming and going! We die and we are resurrected again! And, it is our destiny to be born, to live, to die, and to be resurrected!"

Trudel shutters with fright. For a moment, she thinks about her brothers Hans and Emmerich. She wonders whether or not they know about this important ancient ceremony and know about the meaning of death and being reborn again.

"That is why the Nordic people were sure of themselves and in their resurrection. We can do nothing to change the inevitable. As we contemplate our own deaths, we must think about our destiny. This is the most profound seed we can plant in you girls this evening."

Fräulein Grüber steps aside to let Fräulein Albrecht continue the discourse.

"Our forefathers looked not only upward at the sun but around at the smallest creatures in the forest and at the trees that shelter us. Trees have deep, strong roots, as does our heritage, our legacy, and our folklore. The ash tree, which grows over two hundred feet tall, creates a gigantic canopy. This immense tree is central to our lives and is considered very holy.[3]

"Our gods visit the World Ash tree on this day to assemble Odin's house. Its branches extend far into the heavens as its roots extend into the depths of the earth. When Odin speaks the World Ash tree shivers. The old tree groans and the giant slips free.[4] Odin walked away with his enlightenment, including the knowledge of the rune stones, by sacrificing, in this case, his eye.[5]

"The symbol for Country Service Year is the Odal rune pierced by the sword. It represents the bond we hold between the land and our people.[6] The Odal rune symbolizes our life force, our spirituality, our home, and nurturing of the land. The Reich has vowed to protect its families and the farms they inherit. In each family, the land will pass from father to son. No one can ever take away that land! Our Führer recognizes this inherent law. He is sworn to protect our land, our soil, and our people. Only death and destruction can come to those who relinquish this right.

"Our thoughts must encompass the totality of life, this Nature into which we are born! This is by far the deepest meaning of becoming and the true essence of our way of thinking! We shall always return to the soil from which we have

---

[3] Fritz Weitzel, p. 9 - 12

[4] Yggdrasil

[5] Odin - Prose Edda

[6] Odal Rune

been born and in which we are united as one people!" Fräulein Albrecht trembles, no longer reciting from her well-prepared script. Her passionate words are flowing naturally from her heart and soul. "Our kinship, our family, and our coming together are deeply rooted as the roots of the ash tree. When you think back to your elders, to their laws, and to their comings and goings, look deeply back upon how they have built this new rhythm of life for you.[7]

"Since our celebration tonight is handed down to us from our Nordic ancestors, we must be grateful to them for bringing us their fire, their trees, and most of all, their sun wheel. These riches we are inheriting grown on the graves of our ancestors, and you are our newborns. You will be protected under this inheritance for your entire life![8] Now, let us lift up our hearts as we listen to our girls' recite our poem 'Dying and Becoming.'"

Herminie and Steffi step forward and recite the poem by Frederick Niche.

> Everything goes and everything comes back.
> Forever the wheel rolls around the sun signs.
> Everything dies and everything blossoms and comes back.
> But, the wheel of the sun is always there forever.
> Everything is bright and everything is new,
> And you will become used to it.
> Forever you will build your house
> Around the signs of the sun.
> Someday, the spokes will split and
> Come back together again
> Then, we will all greet each other, and
> We will become happy again.
> We are true to one another forever!
> The ring around the sun is new and is true forever.[9]

Herminie and Steffi walk back to their respective places in the circle. The only sound is the crackling of the massive bonfire.

Trudel's gaze follows the sparks upwards to the heavens. The third quarter moon and a billion stars look down upon her in the crisp summer night air.

'How many have died before me, to give me life?' she wonders.

"Together, let us sing 'Summer Solstice'," commands Fräulein Albrecht.

Trudel hands her torch to Ingrid and walks to a chair positioned at the head of the circle. Heidi and Helli accompany her on their flutes. Standing on either side, Trudel plucks a few strings to make sure her Zither is in tune and together, they unite in song.

---

[7] Fritz Weitzel, p. 12
[8] Ibid
[9] Ibid

People will be people, blood will be our blood
The flame will climb up to the heavens
This is our Holy Fire!
From stump to stump, from people to people,
A sacrifice of the assault, for we are all of one heart.
High on the German Cathedral, it must glow in God's sunshine
People to people, blood to blood
Go up into the heavens, the holy ambers of our flame
You will burn in the fires, from stump to stump[10]

Trudel, Heidi, and Helli return to the circle. Ingrid passes Trudel's torch back to her. Fräulein Albrecht cries out "Now! Let us pledge our will to the Führer!"

This has to be our reality and belief.
My belief is with me in this world.
The highest is in God, for he gave us this world,
And what he gave to the people.
In Him, I believe.
I will always do my very best.
In Him, I give my life.[11]

"Let us pledge to the summer solstice fire," the camp leader announces.

Now burns the fire of our ground, in wells and in ditches.
The fire burns from ancient and sacred laws,
And in us are ancient and sacred times.
We cannot begin our fest in happiness.
We celebrate only when the fight is over.
But, we have much hope and understanding
For the hardship and privation of this present time.
High is the sound up to the night sky, our flames
High beats our hearts, and our thinking is free
The way we stand here today in our circle forever,
So is our start from the beginning of our people.[12]

"Let us conclude our ceremony this evening with singing 'Our Flag on High.'"

By throwing their torches into the massive bonfire, the maidens strengthen their bonds between themselves, the divine, their leaders, their country, and their Führer. With their arms raised high in salute, they sing their national anthem, the "Horst Wessel Song."

---

[10] Fritz Weitzel, p. 55
[11] Ibid, p. 33
[12] Das Lied der Getreuen, p. 37

The flag on high! The ranks tightly closed!
The SA march with quiet, steady steps.
Comrades shot by the Red Front and reactionaries
March in spirit within our ranks!
Comrades shot by the Red Front and reactionaries
March in spirit within our ranks!

Clear the streets for the brown battalions,
Clear the streets for the storm division!
Millions are looking upon the swastika full of hope,
The day of freedom and of bread dawns!
Millions are looking upon the swastika full of hope,
The day of freedom and of bread dawns!

For the last time, the call to arms is sounded!
For the fight, we all stand prepared!
Already Hitler's banners fly over all streets.
The time of bondage will last but a little while now!
Already Hitler's banners fly over all streets.
The time of bondage will last but a little while now.[13]

"This evening has concluded. May we forever give thanks to our Nordic ancestors for giving us the strength to build the strong work ethic for our entire German Reich! There is no end to our life circle for our fire is the holy flame that will glow into the future of our descendants. This is the meaning of our flame for our flame brings us our freedom! Heil Hitler!

---

[13] Horst Wessel Lied

Theatre Performance

IT HAS TAKEN THE GIRLS months to prepare for this evening's theatrical performance. They had diligently worked in the shop constructing their set, writing and rehearsing the scripts, and sewing their costumes all the while handling their daily chores, participating in afternoon sports, and being schooled in home economics.

Two week before the performance, they inform the villagers of their play by posting a notice on the town's main bulletin board.

What started out as a simple impromptu game while in the Young Girl's League has now developed into a sophisticated performance based upon the culture and folklore within this region of Lower Silesia.[1] Theatrical performance is one of the most serious types of venues in which the young girls can express their creativity and knowledge. Writing the script, acting the parts, and creating the scenes combine the free, spoken word. The creative imagination awakens by designing each performance with a warm, never hurtful humor, with some audacity and wit. This evolutionary development from childhood to adolescence increases the girls' self-confidence and teaches them straightforward thinking. Singing and performances are an essential component in the development of the girls' ideological upbringing.[2]

There is much excitement throughout the camp today. Herr Torge leads the two-ox-drawn hay wagon up to the camp. Two men accompanying him and help the girls load it up with the sets and costumes. Some of the girls hop on board and ride it into town while the others follow on foot.

The men assist in unpacking the wagon and positioning the sets onstage. A second group of girls decorates the hall with bouquets of flowers, ribbons, and greenery. Fold up wooden chairs are lined up perfectly in front of the stage. A framed portrait of their Führer prominently hangs next to the entrance door while their large national flag crowns the center of the east wall. They want to make sure their guests feel at home.

Herminie and Heidi will be positioned outside by the table to collect the admission fee. In addition to the funds they have earned from the farm work, the money they are raising tonight will help cover their costs for the big hiking trip in August.

The girls' flutter about backstage making last-minute preparations, and rehearsing their harmonies. The troop leader, Fräulein Dieter will host the event

---

[1] Niederschlesien
[2] Reinhold Sautter, p. 172 - 174

while the economics assistant leader, Fräulein Grüber, will direct and cue the actors backstage. The camp leader, Fräulein Albrecht, will attend to the invited dignitaries.

Trudel peeks out from behind the curtain and watches the people mingle. Everyone is dressed in his or her finest attire. She excitedly runs back to the girls and announces they will have a full house this evening. The excitement builds backstage. Trudel flutters about then runs out to peek through the curtains once more. This time she notices there are no more chairs for the people to sit in! It is standing room only! She looks around the auditorium and notices her camp leader is speaking with some very high officials. She can tell by the way that they are dressed. A lump forms in her throat and she swallows hard. She becomes very nervous for she has never performed in front of such a large audience or in front of such important people. She must remain calm and compose her thoughts.

No one anticipated such a large turnout. The hosting girls quickly race next door to the brewery to seek out more chairs for their guests. Backstage the girls fidget and fumble with last-minute tweaks to their costumes.

"Okay, places, everyone!" Fräulein Grüber claps her hands together to elicit the girls' attention. The economic assistant leader gathers them one final time for a motivational talk before they line up behind the curtain.

Fräulein Dieter steps onto the stage and the applause from the audience engulfs the room. She bows her head in polite gratitude and waits for the crowd to settle down.

"With all of my heart, I welcome each and every one of you this evening to the Camp Seidorf Theatre Performance. It is with my greatest honor that I welcome our very prominent guests.

Sitting in the front row next to Fräulein Albrecht are the regional officials from the Hitler Youth, the League of German Girls, and Country Service. The highest-ranking member attending is the Governor, Karl Hanke.[3] The prominent leader wears his distinctive SS uniform. Joining him is the Regional Leader, Herbert Hirsch, and his Chief of Staff, Hans Bänsch."[4] Sitting next to the men, are the women who represent the League of German Girls. Fräulein Suse Ghent, the Lower District Leader sits next to the Chief of Staff.[5] Sitting next to her is Fräulein Ghent's replacement, Fräulein Rosel Herrmann, who will take over her position at the end of July. She will oversee the girls' big trip in August.[6] The crowd cordially welcomes the female dignitaries.

The dignitaries had arrived yesterday to inspect the administration and the management of the entire camp. In a private meeting, the leaders reviewed all the personal records of each girl, including the financial records for the camp.

---

[3] Karl Hanke
[4] The Hitler Jugend – Gebiet #4, Niederschlesien
[5] Horst Adler, Schweidnitz im Jahre 1937
[6] Horst Adler, Schweidnitz im Jahre - 1941

They also began arranging for the big hiking trip in August. Everything is under strict control by the regional administrators who directly report to their commanding officers at the national level.

Perfectly composed, Fräulein Dieter continues with her introduction. "What is our life without music or the arts? What would our heritage be without bringing forth our traditions? How can we pass on our legacy on if we do not teach our children?" Fräulein Dieter pauses. "Our promising young generation is our future. We must raise our children with a strong will and a desire to work. It is through a strong purpose in life that we form a unity with our nation. The goal in Country Service Year is to educate them in the necessary life skills they will need to become productive members in society. They must be ready at any time to serve their country. They come to us to work. Country Service Year builds the fundamental character of the girls through loyalty, discipline, and obedience. The girls' performance tonight echoes their love for their country and their joyful outlook on life, for it is their daily expression of being.[7] Please give them a warm welcome." The troop leader bows, the crowd applauses, and the performance begins!

Positioned high above center stage is the dominating portrait of their Führer, mounted in a golden frame and accented on either side by their national symbol. Bouquets of local flowers, greenery, and ribbons adorn the entire front length of the stage. Small potted pine trees accent each wing. Everyone is dressed formally in her uniform. The choir stands erect and tall. Their highly polished shoes reflect the house lights.

The musical accompaniments are positioned at house right. Trudel is poised in a chair with her zither in her lap. Steffi is holding the accordion she had found in the attic, which is now highly polished and glistens under the house lights. Nelly, Elli, and Maria are standing on either side with their flutes.

The girls open with a lively 4/4 meter tune. The town folk clap along and tap their shoes to the rhythm of the beat. For the next thirty minutes, the girls sing a repertoire of folk songs about camaraderie, nature, and their homeland.

They close their first set with a devotional love song to their country, "We Are All Connected."[8] In the key of E minor, the single note plucked on the zither begins the piece and the girls' spirit reaches out to the people.

> We are all connected,
> Under our flag of solidarity
> Since we found ourselves as one people
> No one is alone anymore,
> We are all obliged,
> God, our Leader, and our blood.
> Raised in our faith,

---

[7] Wir Mädel Singen, Foreword by Maria Reiners
[8] Pflichtleider Des Bundes Deutsher Mädel – Alle Stehen Wir Verbunden p. 9

Happy in our work that everyone does,
We all want to be as one
Germany, we are brightly standing by your side
We want this high alliance seen in all your glory

A harmonic two-note cadence at the end of each verse punctuates a pause, ending the piece in a strong feeling of repose.

In their perfectly pressed attire, the girls beam smiles at the waves of approval they receive from the audience. The curtain closes. As the girls are backstage changing into their costumes, Fräulein Dieter walks out onstage and introduces the next performance.

"For many months, our girls have labored on a play they wrote which captures the essence of their feelings about Seidorf and the legendary castle of Prince Henry. Our devoted young girls designed and built their own sets, sewed their own costumes, and wrote their own script. Every day, they diligently rehearsed their parts and …"

Behind the curtain is pandemonium. The girls race around changing into their costumes for the next act. The clothing room bustles with confusion and disorder. Clothes hang over the chairs and lie on the floor as the girls hasten along bumping into one another. In the burst of excited chaos, Trudel loses her shoes. Frantically, she pleads for help. Steffi and Nelly rush to her side when Fräulein Grüber calls and cues the girls to their positions onstage. Trudel has no choice. She hurries barefoot to her position. The curtain opens and part two of the performance begins.

In the painted backdrop scene of the Giant Mountains panorama is a family of deer that is peacefully eating grass. The mighty stag stands alert. Stage right shows a dilapidated hovel made from worn boards donated by the farmers. The roof is made from straw and a broken shutter hangs from the window. A dark blanket covers the shanty's doorway. Stage left shows the painted forest and the castle ruins on top of Grodna Hill with a massive rock waterfall cascading into the healing spring waters below.

Trudel narrate the play. She is wearing a plain white housedress with her white bandana and green apron. She is standing stage left and barefoot. A few people in the front rows notice she is not wearing shoes and begin to giggle. She feels so embarrassed but makes light of the situation and believes her character is supposed to be barefoot. With the written script in her hand, she begins to narrate the Tale of Prince Henry.

"It is now many, many centuries since a young noble named Henry was hunting in the valley that lies before the Spirit of the Mountains near the ancient village of Seidorf."

Kristin walks onto the stage. She is playing the part of the young, noble hunter, Henry. She is dressed in a blue long-sleeve shirt, lederhosen, grey wool socks, a hunting hat, and boots. Buckled around her waist are three rosettes. She is carrying a make-believe wooden rifle she carved from a tree limb she found in the woods. As Trudel narrates, Kristin acts out her part.

"In the heat of the pursuit, Henry follows the stag from the waterfall to the foot of the hillside on which are seated the ancient castle ruins."

Kristin prowls onstage making believe she is stalking the large buck.

"The heat of the midsummer day is taking a toll on Henry's strength. He looks away and within a blink of an eye, the deer runs deep into the forest and disappears from his view. In despair, the young noble is determined to get his prize buck. With the last bit of his strength, he climbs up the side of Grodna Hill and succeeds in reaching the summit. Tired and thirty he sits himself down, takes the last sip of water from his pouch, then falls fast asleep underneath the massive stone tower ruin. While he sleeps, Henry dreams of a beautiful maiden wearing a cascading white robe made from swan feathers."

Elfie emerges from between the sets. She is wearing a long, white sheet, and a garland of flowers crowns her head.

As Trudel narrates the play, the actors act out their parts.

"The maiden opens her robe and presents the young hunter with a golden chalice of cool, refreshing waters from her magic healing spring. Henry cannot believe his eyes and he is not dreaming at all! As he takes the vessel from her hand, he notices her flaxen hair and her radiant, sapphire eyes. Her complexion is as smooth as tulip petals. Her loving eyes penetrate deep within his soul. In a single draught, Henry drinks the contents from her golden goblet. The water courses through his masculine physique and soon his heart sears with love."

"From where do you come?" Henry asks.

"I am the Maiden of the Healing Waters. I am the protector of the magic spring, and I have heard your plea," Elfie replies.

"The maiden intuitively understands his desire and answered his calling. He extends the golden chalice back to the maiden. He moves in closer to touch her golden locks and smooth skin, but the passionate young pair are interrupted by a horrific voice in the distance."

Offstage, Helli imitates the crackling voice of an old wicked witch. The crowd laughs in delight. Trudel is pleased that the audience is enjoying the story.

"I must go now," the young maiden hurriedly says.

"The maiden removes the chalice from Henry's hand and places it inside her white feather robe. She turns around and spreads open her wings, then flies away."

Elfie briskly runs in a circle around Kristin, then darts between the sets, and runs offstage.

"Try as he might to embrace her Henry trips and falls as she flies off into the heavens and disappears." The crowd laughs. Trudel looks toward the crowd and feels happy that they are enjoying themselves.

"Henry gets up, brushes himself off, and rushes after her in anguish. Amidst his cries, she continues to fly away. Forcing his way through the forest, a giant eagle swoops down and blocks him directly in his path."

Barbara comes out from behind stage left wearing a dark brown blanket and a paper mâché eagle's head. The crowd applauds at the sight of the eagle knowing it is the symbol of their country. "You are forbidden to seek the princess!" the feather creature commands in her deepest voice.

"I must have her, Eagle, I must," Henry pleads.

"No! I am the Great Adler the Winged Spirit of the Giant Mountains and I order you to return to your home and never come back. I command you to leave this instant!"

"As he flies away, the giant eagle flaps his enormous wingspan and a gust of wind flings Henry down the hillside knocking him unconscious," narrates Trudel. "Henry awakes weary and heart-stricken, overwhelmed with much sadness. In the distance, he hears the melodic voice of a young woman singing. Thinking it might be his beloved maiden he hides behind the sculptured rocks and peeks around the corner."

Elfie enters stage left, kneels down on the stage, and pretends she is washing her hair.

Trudel continues. "It is his beautiful maiden and she is washing her long, golden hair in the healing spring waters singing a very sad song," That is Helli's cue to walk onstage.

Helli plays the part of the witch. She pushes aside the blanket and walks out from the hovel over to Elfie. "Suddenly, a horrible-looking witch walks over and pokes the beautiful maiden three times in her side with a stick."

"I hear you singing that dreadful song," the witch crackles. She is wearing a black robe, a crooked witch's hat, and has on a large nose made from paper mâché. She takes her staff and gently pokes Elfie on her side three times. "You will never leave me, you hear me! You will never find your prince because he does not exist! Do not even think for one moment that he will build you a castle. Now, hurry up and get my dinner ready," the witch orders.

"Reluctantly, the young woman stands, wraps the white feather robe around her, and walks into the old hovel to prepare the witches evening meal.

"So that is her secret!" Henry whispers to himself behind the rock. "In order to make her my bride, I must build her a castle!"

"To make sure she will not get away from him a second time, Henry sneaks into the hovel in the middle of the night and steals the magic robe. As the morning sun rises over the horizon, Henry is on top of the hill rebuilding the old castle ruins."

Henry places the robe on a hook and makes believe he is building his castle.

"Every day, Henry looks at the white feather robe and dreams of making the maiden his bride. When Henry finishes building the castle he returns to the hovel with the magic robe to confront the wicked witch."

Backstage, the girls release a rope and a painting of a complete castle drops down over the image of the ruins. The audience laughs.

"Old witch," Henry yells. "I am Prince Henry of Seidorf and I have built my maiden a castle on top of Grodna Hill. I have come to claim my bride!"

The old witch looks disgusted. "You are a fool!" she snickers. "When you took her robe, you took her life! The senseless girl cried and cried because you had stripper her of her magical powers! When her tears dropped into the spring water, she turned into a statue! Go see for yourself. She is standing by the healing spring in Bad Warmbrunn. You will never save her! My servant is gone forever!" The old witch stamps her stick down hard on the ground.

"In a complete state of shock, Prince Henry runs with the feather robe from the witch's hovel to the magic springs. He claws his way through the dense woods only to discover his beloved maiden standing there, frozen in time." Elfie stands poised with her right hand above her head and her left arm around her waist. She has a faraway look in her eyes.

"Tightly clutching the magic robe in his hands, Henry drops to his knees and cries out."

"Oh, what have I done to my beautiful maiden? Oh Great Adler, Winged Spirit of the Giant Mountains, please help me!" he pleads.

"Immediately, the great eagle swoops down from the sky and lands next to the young prince," the narrator speaks.

Barbara comes swooping out from behind the mountain set waving her arms. The audience chuckles at the sight.

"What on earth have you done?" the eagle inquires.

"I have killed her! I have killed my beautiful maiden. Oh, help me, Great Adler. What can I do to bring her back to life?" the prince questions.

"I have been watching over you Prince Henry. I see your love has given you the strength to build the Maiden of the Healing Waters a stone castle on top of Grodna Hill. You have proven yourself worthy!" the great bird benevolently speaks. "I warn you, there is only one way you can set her free. You must give something of yourself in order for her to come back to life."

"But what do I have? I have nothing," the prince responds.

"Yes, you have. You have fought courageously and without fear. You have won three great battles. Your father, the king of Lower Silesia, proudly decorated you with three rosettes. Do you remember what the king said to you about those medals?"

"He gave me the first metal and is for my strength. The second metal is for my courage and the third is for my love of the land."

"That is correct Prince Henry. You hold these three symbols dear to your heart. Now, you must give them away. Pin these three medals on the feather robe and wrap the robe around the maiden."

Barbara exits the stage flapping her brown blanket.

"Immediately, the prince pins his three rosettes on the maiden's robe then drapes the robe around the maiden's shoulders. Just as the eagle had predicted, the maiden magically comes back to life! Proudly, Prince Henry carries the maiden back to the castle where they are married and bear many children."

Elfie emerges from between the sets carrying a newborn child wrapped in a white blanket. She walks to her husband, Kristin, the Prince, and together they admire the newborn baby.

Trudel continues with her narration. "When Prince Henry's father, the king, dies, Henry becomes the new king. Together, they have many grandchildren. However, when King Henry dies, the Queen Maiden is very sad."

Elfie turns to Kristin. Together, they hold hands, turn, and walk out of sight. Elfie re-emerges by the waterfall.

"In her grief stricken state, the Queen Maiden wears her magic robe with the rosettes and returns to the healing waters to cry. She had completely forgotten what had happened to her the last time. When her tears drop into the water, she materializes back into the statue from where she once came. At that moment, there is a great earthquake and the stone castle tumbles to the ground and fall back into ruins." Backstage, the girls are rolling stones in a wheel barrel.

A stagehand pulls on the cord so that the painting of the castle on the hills was lifted out of sight, revealing once more the crumbled ruins behind it.

"Today, the Queen Maiden of the Healing Waters is memorialized forever as she stands as a bronze statue in Bad Warmbrunn. The magic of the spring waters freely flow at her feet. The end."

Trudel bows. As she walks toward the center of the stage she joins with Barbara, Kristin, Elfie, and Helli. All five girls bow together then dash behind the curtain as it was closing. Delighted at all the clapping, the girls hug each other. It is now time, to prepare for their final presentation.

While the troop leader addresses the crowd, the girls change into their new costumes. As Katarina and Dorota throw sticks around the stage floor, Aloise and Sylvia throw down the bales of hay by the hovel and mountainside. Marta and Magdalena quickly tie their donkey onto the hitching post inside the stall. The animal hides from the view of the audience by standing behind the dark brown blanket covering the entrance to the makeshift hovel. Once everything is in place, the curtain opens and the next short play begins. Once again, Trudel narrates.

"Found deep in the woods lives the mountain giant named Rübezahl."

The audience claps for they know this tale well.

Barbara pushes back the blanket of the hovel and walks onto the stage. She is tall and large boned for her age. Her disheveled appearance depicts that of a mountain man with long, brown hair, and a beard. Pillows stuffed under her clothing make her appear heavier. She wears a brown wool vest over a large, white dropped-shoulder shirt tucked inside a brown pair of corduroy pants. A simple rope tied to the side holds the vest closed. She walks with a large stick. Wrapped around both her calves are white linen held in place with brown leather belts. She borrowed a pair of mountain boots from Herr Torge. A haversack drapes over her chest and she holds a full cloth sack over her back.

"The villagers know of the legend of Rübezahl quiet well," Trudel says as she introduces the character. "He is the Lord of the Giant Mountains and he controls the weather. When he becomes angry, he will send lightning and rain-storms or cover the land with heavy fog or snow. When he is in good spirits, the sun shines, the sky is blue, and the weather is warm. He is generally a friendly giant and gifted in the healing properties of the local plants. Elder mothers seek his guidance and men fear his presence. Many bad men have been led astray while returning home on their paths. When people mock him he avenges hard by casting down foul weather and when people speak nicely of him, the waterfall flows in Giersdorf."

Dressed as peasant children, Marta, Magdalena, Katarina, Dorota, and Sylvia run out from behind the hovel and pretend to torment the giant by pulling on his clothes and kicking him in the shins. Marta snatches his walking stick right out of his hand! The giant pushes the girls aside and retrieves his stick.

"Since the year 999, he has never lived among the villagers. Embittered by the defiant children and greedy parents, he left the village vowing never to return. With a very large sack in hand, he took the precious jewels and hid them in his mountain cave. He vowed one day to return everything when the people learn to work harmoniously again."

The giant pushes the girls aside and they scurry behind the hovel. Barbara walks toward the cottage, pushes the drape to the side, and disappears inside. The giant reappears without his sack and walks around stage gathering the sticks.

"One day, Rübezahl was out gathering wood for his fire when he met with a small dwarf."

Little Liesel cheerfully prances out from behind the mountain set. She is wearing a little dwarf costume she made from scraps of green and red flax cloth and her red hat flops to the side.

"Oh, there you are Rübezahl!" Little Liesel says with a chuckle in her voice. "I've been looking all over the mountains for you."

"Why are you looking for me, dwarf?" Barbara replies in a cold-hearted tone. "I have no business with you or anyone else in the village." Barbara tries to sound forceful. "Now, go away and leave me alone!"

"Oh, yes you do giant! You *have* business with me today," Little Liesel snickers. "It has been many, many years since you have paid a visit to the village. I overheard the miller talking and he has been telling everyone that you do not exist anymore!"

Trudel explains to the audience, "Falsehood and injustice have spread among the people. Hearing this news, Rübezahl becomes very angry and starts breaking his sticks over his knees."

"They should respect and not defy me!" the giant yells. "I don't exist any-more? Well, I will show them!" he exclaims.

"Rübezahl storms into his hut and magically transforms himself into a ..."

Trudel pauses. She has given the cue but nothing happens. In the lengthen-ing silence, a member of the audience coughs, and others shift in their seats. There is a commotion backstage. Trudel anxiously decides that she had better repeat the cue. "Rübezahl storms into his hut and magically transforms himself into a ... into a ..." Trudel stands helplessly stranded on stage. Finally, she yells "Donkey!"

The reluctant creature was at last pushed onstage. The sympathetic crowd bursts out laughing and applauds. Little Liesel grabs hold of the animal's reins and smiles bashfully. "This is Rübezahl."

After the audience settles down, Barbara uses her deep voice and projects it into the crowd, pretending that it is coming from the donkey. "I command you to lead me into town, dwarf!"

Liesel leads the donkey around stage. Soon the villagers step out from behind the hut and start to mingle about.

"Little does the donkey know," narrates Trudel, "that the dwarf had plans for the giant. Yesterday, the old baker stole a ten Mark pieces from him and now this is a perfect way to get all his money back and then some more! The donkey and the dwarf arrive at the miller's house and knock on the door."

Sabine plays the part of the miller. Her pretend wife, Sylvia, is standing beside Sabine. She is dressed in a traditional housedress. Like Barbara, Sabine has a pillow stuffed under her oversized, long-sleeved white shirt and baggy pants. She wears a white baker's hat, a green apron, and a large paper mâché nose is tied behind her head. The front part of her clothes is covered in flower. She gives the impression that she had just finished arduously grinding the wheat, turning it into flour.

Trudel continues. "The baker and his wife live very well. They have much money and own a beautiful large home. Because they own the largest bakery in town their prosperity increases year after year."

"How can I help you dwarf?" the miller asks.

"Yesterday, you told me you were in need of more help," replies the canny dwarf. "I am here to sell you my donkey. He is a very hard worker and will grind your wheat and turn it into flour."

"And, how much do you want for this beast?" the miller asks.

"I will give you a fair price for this very hard-working animal. I only want twenty-five Marks."

"What! Are you crazy? That is too much money. I will only give you twenty, tops!"

The dwarf hesitates for a moment, strokes his chin thoughtfully before saying, "That will work just fine for me."

The miller pays the dwarf and grabs his new donkey's reins. The dwarf leaps excitedly into the air, clicks his heals together, and runs off into the woods."

"Goodness! I wonder what that was all about," says the miller's wife.

"The miller was very pleased to purchase such a strong, healthy looking, and cheap animal to do his bidding for him," Trudel narrates.

"At least I don't have to pay him to work," the miller nudges his wife in her side and laughs.

Trudel introduces the next character in the play. "The miller then summons his servant."

Ingrid plays the miller's servant. She appears in a plain white housedress wearing slippers. Her long black hair is braided perfectly behind her head.

Her master commands, "Take this donkey and give him some hay to eat! I want him to be strong as an ox for tomorrow's work. He is going to grind all the grain in the storage room."

Ingrid leads the animal away by its reins. Near the back of the stage, she picks up some hay from the floor and holds it close to the donkey's mouth. Abruptly, the girl squeals, lets go of the reins, and hastens back to the miller and his wife.

"Now, what do you want?" scolds the miller.

The servant is trembling with fright. "Lord! The donkey is bewitched! I gave him some hay—and he started speaking! I swear it! He told me he did not want to eat the hay! He would prefer a big roast and chocolate cake instead!"

The audience enjoys the joke.

"Don't be absurd! Donkeys can't speak!" the miller retorts.

Trudel narrates. "Well, the miller certainly did not want to believe the story but he went to the barn anyway to take a look for himself. With anger in his heart, the donkey stands still with fixed eyes on the miller. The miller takes a handful of hay, holds it out toward the donkey's mouth, and strokes the animal on the head. Just then, the donkey kicks the miller to the ground."

Sabine pretends to be kicked by the donkey and falls to the ground.

"I demand to be fed roast and a cake!" Barbara exclaims from behind stage, making pretend the donkey can speak.

"Startled, the miller gets up, takes a step back, and tries to escape. In horror, the miller watches as the donkey magically turns back into the giant Rübezahl!"

As Trudel narrates, the donkey is led off stage and Barbara appears from behind the shanty.

"Miller, you are stingy and greedy! You stole money from the dwarf yesterday, and I want it returned to him right now!"

The miller reaches into his pocket and offers the giant all his money. "Here, giant, take this money. This is all that I have. Please do not hurt me. I know now that you exist. Give all this money back to the dwarf and tell him I am sorry and that I will never do it again."

Rübezahl accepts the money. As fast as they can, the miller, his wife, and the servant run from the mountain giant and off stage.

Barbara circles around the stage. She meets little Liesel and hands her the sack of stolen money.

"From where did you get all this money?" the dwarf asks.

"I punished the covetous miller! He will never do you or anyone wrong again." Rübezahl replies.

Trudel narrates. "The giant and the dwarf shake hands. The dwarf helps the giant return all the precious jewels back to the villagers, who dance in thanks and promise never to do wrong again. The end."

The curtain closes and the audience applauds. The curtain opens and the actors' line up in a row and bow to the audience. The crowd cheers, the actors bow one more time, and the curtains close.

Fräulein Albrecht walks on stage in front of the curtain and waits for the applause to end. "Thank you, thank you, everyone." She gives a short speech, giving the girls time to change back into their BDM uniforms, and to remove the sets from the stage. Trudel tunes her zither.

"We would like to dedicate our closing number to our mayor, Mayor Blasius," Fräulein Albrecht proudly announces to the audience.

The curtain opens and Trudel plucks the introduction note to the traditional folk anthem of their region, "The Giant Mountain Song." [9] This original revanchist piece was written in 1914 with devotional lyrics about Lower Silesia. The revised lyrics speak of the mountains, the folklore, and nature.

> Blue Mountains, green valleys,
> In their midst a little cottage
> Splendid, this little piece of the earth
> And there I am at home.
> As I long ago first came to this land
> The mountains looked me over,
> In my childhood, in my youth,
> I myself didn't know what was happening in me
> O my dear Giant Mountains,
> Where the Elbe flows so homely
> Where Rübezahl with his dwarves
> Weaves still legends and fairytales
> Giant Mountains, German mountain range,
> You, my dear home!

The girl's harmonies blend so easily with the instruments that it touches the souls of the listeners. For a moment, they all forget about the war raging in the east. The girls link arms and the entire audience joins in a sing-a-long. Trudel's eyes sparkle happily for all her comrades, guests, and dignitaries. She feels one with her country. When the piece is over, the audience gives the girls a standing ovation. Arm-in-arm, the girls bow as men in the back of the hall shout "Bravo! Bravo!"

Mayor Blasius takes to the stage and gives a short commemoration speech, thanking the girls for the wonderful evening and superb performance. He reminds everyone in Seidorf to watch out for talking donkeys and Rübezahl.

After everyone says their good-byes and slowly file out from the hall, they walk down the roads and return to their homes. A few men stop at the local brewery next door. Backstage, farmer Torge and his wife praise the girls for their

---

[9] Das Riesengebirgslied

fine plays and musical performances. In the theatre, the dignitaries congratulate all three leaders for a well-thought-out performance. They promise to give the highest reports to their superiors.

The girls dismantle the sets and pack everything into Herr Torge's wagon. They walk alongside singing all the way back to their camp. After unloading the sets into the workshop, each girl gives Herr Torge, his wife, and the two assistants, a loving and grateful embrace. They put away their costumes, retire to their rooms, and collapse in their beds, exhausted.

The Maiden of the Healing Water
– Cieplice, Poland

"We love the long fields,
They open before our eyes
We feel the happiness
We feel the strength inside of us
Which is never ending."

~ Gertrude Kerschner ~

We Help with the Harvest

THE MORNING STARTS OUT WARM and beautiful. During breakfast, Fräulein Albrecht brings out a list and announces that she will choose twenty girls to work for the next week on Farmer Torge's farm. She asks who among them knows anything about cutting and raking the hay. Farmer Torge will instruct the girls how to cut, overturn, dry, and stack the hay. It is imperative that they follow his exact instructions. Fräulein Albrecht starts calling out the names and Trudel is wondering will she be called next? Then, her name is called. She jumps up and shouts "Hooray! I'm going to Upper Seidorf!" She runs from the dining room, grabs her scarf and apron, and runs outside to complete her morning gardening chores. Trudel, Aloise, Sabine, Heidi, Helli, and Erika have thirty minutes to finish weeding the garden before leaving to work on the Torge farm.

Twenty girls procure heavy wooden rakes from their storage shed. In a double column, they enthusiastically hike with Fräulein Dieter to Upper Seidorf, singing their Lager song.

> We are the proud castle up on the mountains,
> And down in the valley stands our village,
> The blue sky smiles at you and the sun always shines, for
> We are the Seidorfer girls, we are the Seidorfer girls.
> We march happily to our work singing our song,
> Country Service Year Camp Seidorf! Ahoy!
> Sometimes the sky is full of clouds and it starts to rain,
> But with the returning sun, everyone is happy again,
> The mountains put their arms around us,
> For He take care of us, we are in God's hands now
> And he will never let anything happen to us

They arrive and discover that most of the grass has been cut, and is lying in the field drying. Now, their work begins. Herr Torge has been adopted by the girls and now they address him as Uncle Bernhard. He shows Trudel how to use the sickle as Nelly's group is taught the art of raking and overturning the stalks carefully using their heavy wooden rakes. Trudel describes today's work in her journal.

> "How beautiful the grass smells when it is cut. Cutting the grass was a real problem for us. When Uncle Bernhard swung the sickle, his body turned with the swing. I tell you, it takes a very strong swing to cut the grass especially in the morning when it is wet with dew. The arch of the blade has to hit the hay just right. Then, you can hear the grass crackles

when you mow it down. Sometimes, my blade got stuck in the ground and the Uncle Bernhard just laughed at me and said, "You'll get it right!" All day long, I tried and it wasn't until the second day I swung better. When Uncle Bernhard saw me, he clapped his hands and said I have the swing and now, I can go out and cut grass all day long!"

For many hours, the girls work systematically to cut and overturn the stalks. It will take a few days for the summer sun to dry all the excess moisture from the hay. Turning the hay too often or too roughly can cause the drying leaf matter to fall off thereby reducing the nutrient value of the animal fodder. Indeed, the hay can spoil if not dried and bailed properly. If this happens, toxins will form in the feed causing the animals to become sick and die. The girls must learn how to dry and store the hay properly in the barn to prevent it from building up moisture.

Under the baking summer heat, Trudel and her country comrades do not gripe about the long hours, the laborious work, or their open blisters. Unlike the whiny city girls, the country girls understand their importance of a healthy farm crop as their personal contribution to the greater good for the German people. This generation is being raised with the law of dignified manual labor fused together with individual pride. The work expected of this generation will guide their lives, strengthen their abilities, and discipline their attitudes for each one of them has a responsibility to guide the others by their own examples.[1] Moreover, without the girls help, the animals would starve and die in the harsh upcoming winter.

Frau Torge, now adopted as Aunt Else, compassionately tends to the girls' lesions by applying her homemade healing ointment. She delicately bandages their fingers with pieces of cloth with the ends sewed together. Aunt Else appreciates all the girls toiling in the hot summer sun. To show her gratitude, she brings them each fresh buttermilk. Every day the farmwoman prepares a large lunch, always making sure that every girl is properly nourished. The girls must sustain their strength until sundown, when they return to camp. All week long, the country girls work to overturn the grass before raking it into long rows.

The fun begins at the end of the week when Uncle Bernhard allows the girls to ride out into the fields on his horse-drawn hay wagon. They stop at the first windrow. Everyone jumps out except Trudel who is responsible for laying and piling up the hay inside the large wagon. Elli, Nelly, Steffi, Maria, and Barbara, stand on one side of the wagon while Anna, Kristin, Charlotte, and Helli stand on the other side. As Uncle Bernhard steers the wagon along the rows, the rest of the girls pitch the hay up off the fields and into the wagon. They stay mindful of the sharp tips on their pitchfork tines. With each toss of hay, the stack grows higher until the wagon finally overflows! When their work is done, some of the girls jump on board and go for a ride.

---

[1] Reinhold Sautter, p. 187

"We're rolling out now, girls. I want everyone to hold on real tight before we start moving." They steady themselves when Uncle Bernhard takes the reins and with a *'cshlick-cshlick,'* the command is given for the horses to move forward. The impulsion is strong and controlled as the girls jolt slightly backwards. With their work finally completed and with song in their hearts they harmonically sing their working song.

We love the long fields,
They open before your eyes.
We feel the happiness,
And we feel the strength inside of us,
Which is never ending.

Trudel feels proud for having accomplished the heavy task. She loves being outside in the fresh air, working. She sits with Elli, Nelly, and Steffi on top of the wagon. Maria, Barbara, Anna, Kristin, Charlotte, and Helli walk alongside with the rest of the girls from camp holding in the rear. Uncle Bernhard steers into the courtyard of his farmstead and stops by the barn doors.

Starting in the rear of the wagon, each girl grabs a large bale of hay and carefully stores it in the barn. Uncle Bernhard is impressed with the girl's natural ability to stack the hay and praises them for a job well done. Their bonus comes when Fräulein Dieter receives their weekly wage of one dollar and eight cents per girl for their six-day workweek. This money will go towards the 'Big Trip' they will be taking the third week in August.

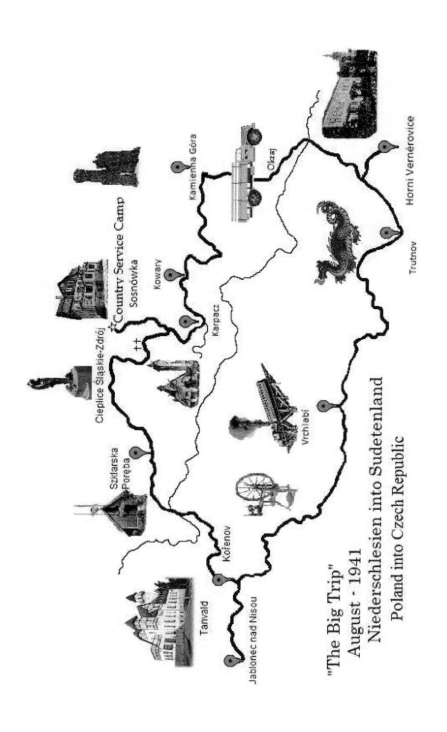

"The Big Trip"
August - 1941
Niederschlesien into Sudetenland
Poland into Czech Republic

The Big Trip

THE HIGHLIGHT IN CAMP comes in August when the girls head out and hike throughout their countryside from Niederschlesien into Sudetenland and back again. The girls must be in excellent physical condition. The girls will be examined by the local doctor to determine whether or not they are fit to participate in this highly anticipated event.

Fräulein Albrecht reviews the daily agenda, where they will hike, when they will rest, how they will march, what they will see, where they will stay, what they will sing, what they will wear, how they will pack, how much to pack, and how to comport oneself. At all times during the journey, the girls will be required to act dignified. This trip will test their obedience and discipline. Their leaders will scrutinize their endurance, disposition, and behavior. While they were in the Young Girls' League (JM), they participated in one-day trips. Therefore, they understand the procedure. However, this is their very first 'Big Trip' in the League of German Girls and they will be traveling for one week on foot.

Naturally, all forty girls are very excited. Starting at an altitude of 2,625 feet, they leave their camp behind and begin their trek through the Hirschberg (Jelenia Góra) Basin. Their matching attire distinguishes them as country service girls from Seidorf. They march concurrently side-by-side in rows of three with their fully loaded backpacks, gray blanket, and cooking ware. At the head of the column, Trudel carries the green and white group pennant. Their first overnight stop is in Schreiberhau, (Szklarska Poręba, Poland), twelve miles away.

They pass Lake Seidorf and the two ancient stone penitential crosses marking the entrance to the weaver's village of Märzdof (Marczyce, Poland). They continue marching through the hardwood-tree-lined streets of Giersdorf (Podgórzyn) singing. The landscape is dotted with freshwater ponds that supply the area with local carp and trout. The tree-line street canopies provide ample shade from the morning sun. They follow the outskirts of the city of Bad Warmbrunn (Cieplice) and along Kamienna (Stone River) where they stop and rest. These girls are not even tired for they are determined to reach their first night's destination. They are having fun too, laughing, and singing. Their pace quickens when they spot the imposing church tower designating their destination in Schreiberhau (Szklarska Poreba, Poland). Next to the church is the farmhouse where they will spend the night.

The farmers welcome the leaders and the forty girls with open arms. The wife shows them to their sleeping quarters in the barn where they drop their backpacks and make their individual hearths. They will be sleeping in the straw tonight.

The allure of the gently rolling Giant Mountain range to the south and the granite Jizera Mountains to the north make Schreiberhau a popular hiking destination. In the early part of the fourteenth century, German colonists settled on a plot of land owned by the Knights of Teplice in search for gold and other precious stones.[1]

The girls visit the Hall of the Fairytales (Sagenhalle), originally built in 1903 as an artist colony. The wooden structure depicts Nordic elements including snakes, dragons, and runic inscriptions. Inside, many exhibits display Germanic mythology and ancient pagan beliefs. A large hand carved image associated with the legend of the Mountain Spirit and paintings by local artists are on exhibition.[2] Two paintings that impress Trudel the most are 'Rübezahl' and 'Percival' by the renowned artists Hermann Hendrich.

Their next stop is the massive glass factory located in Ober Schreiberhau (Upper Szklarska Poreba, Poland). The girls walk along the Stone River to the 'Josephinenhütte,' and view the beautiful art-deco crystal and glass pieces. In 1617, Bohemian glassmaker Wolfgang Preußler originally built the small glass factory. Several generations later, Franz Pohl, the son-in-law of the last Preußler, Christian Benjamin Preußler, persuaded Count Leopold von Schaffgotsch to build a new, larger glass factory on the same site. By 1842, the massive stone factory was completed in honor of his wife, Josephine. It is the largest glass manufacture in Lower Silesia.[3]

Inside Trudel and her comrades stroll around admiring the exquisite handmade pieces. Trudel picks up one elegant glass vase and admires the simplicity of its design. Upon closer inspection, she is mesmerized by the rainbow colors refracting through the prismatic lead crystal.

Fräulein Dieter spots Trudel handling the merchandise and orders her and everyone else not to touch the displays. The leader promises the girls that if they hurry through they can go down to the river for a swim.

The troop returns to the farmhouse and changes into their black regulated bathing suits. To appear discrete, the girls wear their dresses over their suits. Carrying their blankets, they hike along the mountain path leading into the subalpine forest. They climb the slope to a low summit that provides them with a beautiful panoramic view of the mountains and valley below. Every direction they look holds a surprise for them for when they look down they see the waterfall and a giant watering hole!

Overjoyed, they rush down the dirt path to the stony riverbank. They kick off their socks and shoes, placing them neatly on the rocks next to their dresses and blankets. Then, they jump wholeheartedly into the cold mountain water.

A manmade rope swing challenges their courage. The river upstream attracts their curiosity as well. The current is strong and they hold each other's hands to

---

[1] Szklarska Poręba
[2] Sagenhalle
[3] Szklarska Poręba - History

keep their footing while crossing. They laugh, splash, and let the water flow from the falls and onto their backs, giving them a natural massage. It is an easy life.

In the evening, they go to the movie theatre and watch the film "Above All in the World."[4] This dramatic film chronicles the plight of the German people caught by the outbreak of war and the strength of the German nation to stand tall. It is a propaganda film portraying the British, French, Poles, and Jews as warmongers, profiteers, and cowards. In the end, all that is important is returning to the Fatherland. Trudel does not like seeing the movie and all the destruction.

Come evening, the girls settle down in the barn for the night. Laying in straw, Trudel pushes aside her doubts and sleeps soundly.

The girls rise early to help the farmer's wife. They help prepare breakfast, milk the cattle, clean out the chicken coop, feed the pigs, and weed the garden. It is another beautiful morning. The girls enjoy giving back to the humble farmers in appreciation for their hospitality.

They sit outside on the grass and eat their breakfast. A slice of bread with butter and a cup of coffee is all these girls need to get them started on this second day. They bid farewell to their gracious hosts, and set off on their fifteen-mile trek into the countryside. They head towards Tannwald in Sudetenland (Tanvald, Czech Republic).

Leaving Schreiberhau, they enthusiastically hike in song, southwest down the road that crosses over the Isergebirge (Jizera) mountain range. When they reach the border, the girls show their papers to the appreciative guards who warmly welcome the young ones into Sudetenland (Czechoslovakia).

In Harrachsdorf (Harrachov, Czech Republic), they rest for fifteen minutes before resuming their quest. As the band of hikers continues up the mountain they come across the picturesque Lausitzer (Lusatian) river. Lining the river are massive boulders knocked down from their high perch during the Ice Age. Twelve-thousand years of weathering have smoothed the rough edges of these giant boulders. Continuous water falls into swirling crystal pools surrounded by the dense sub-alpine forest. In the winter, boulders carpeted with a thick layer of snow lay silent along the gurgling sounds of the river, as the trees hang their limbs downward, patiently waiting for spring's arrival. In the summer, the deep, lush green coniferous forest comes alive with chirping birds and ground animals foraging for their next meal.

The troop crosses over a smaller branch of the river and enters the scenic mountain village of Bad Wurzelsdorf (Kořenov, Czech Republic). Frau Holle, the local weaver, is anxiously waiting for the girls' arrival for she has made fresh pastries and coffee to welcome them. Frau Holle introduces herself while the girls eat some needed snacks. She spends the entire afternoon teaching the girls how to make linen from the flax plant.

"Did you know that the clothes you are wearing are made from plants?" she starts. "Think about that as you are finishing up your snacks. Let's take a moment to walk outside and I will show you the fields." The girls' finish eating and follow

---

[4] "Uber Alles in der Welt"

the weaver outside into the backyard where they see the green five-foot fiber crop growing.

"This is my crop of flax plants. We will harvest these stalks and make clothes out of them," Frau Holle says as she proudly displays her flax plants.

"It looks like hay," Elli comments.

"Yes, flax plants are similar to hay but the stalks are much slender. Within these stalks are the flax fibers that we use to make linen."

"How can you make linen from a plant?" Trudel asks.

"Here, I will show you." Frau Holle escorts the girls out into her field and shows them the plants up close. "We harvest these plants in August. The plants are pulled up from the ground, roots, and all. We cut the roots off and lay the green stems out under the sun to dry. Once the plant dries, the flax seeds are removed and stored in separate containers. The stalks are tied in bundles and left to soak in water for ten days. This process called retting loosens the fibers inside the stalk turning it into straw. The straw is removed from the water and laid out to dry. Once the plant is dry the next step is to break away the flax fibers from inside the straw." Frau Holle demonstrates for the girls. She takes a handful of straw and places it on the tabletop between a set of blunt wooden blades. "By gently beating the straw with the upper jaw of the beating machine the outer layers of the plant break loose and fall to the ground. The flax is beaten until the woody stalks separate from the blonde fibers. This process is called breaking the flax." She pulls the flax from the machine and shows the girls the blonde fibers. "Then, we take this wooden scutching knife, hang the fibers on this rack, and then scrape off the remaining pieces of straw."

"Can I try it?" Maria asks.

Frau Holle hands the scutching knife to Maria and she practices the brushing technique. "It is just like brushing your hair only harder because of the tangles," Maria laughs.

"That's right. The next process is where we remove the tangles. Here, let me show you." Frau Holle takes a handful of flax and pulls the fibers through a bed of nails evenly driven and spaced in the wooden heckling comb. "This process is twofold for it removes any remaining straw and splits and polishes the fibers. However, we can also heckle the fibers using a heckle wheel."

"You can?" Sabine asks.

Frau Holle places the blonde fibers over the board and pushes down on the foot pedal. The paddle wheel spins, lining the individual fibers parallel with each other. With every stroke of the paddle, the fibers become shiny and soft. She allows the girls to feel the new texture of the hair-like strands. The hairs feel just like silk.

"This finer flax is called 'tow.' We card it like wool, and then I spin it into thread using a spinning wheel. Let me show you how I spin linen threads out of these fibers."

Frau Holle leads the girls inside her large workshop. Finished dresses hang on the racks next to the table clothes, napkins, and handbags. Most of the room is taken up with her spinning wheels, looms, baskets, materials, and large tables full of fabric.

Frau Holle walks to the spinning wheels and demonstrates how to spin the fibers. The spinner sits at the stool and pumps the foot pedal that turns the large wooden drive wheel via a crankshaft and a connecting rod. This leaves both her hands free to draft the fibers spinning it into strands of yarn.

The girls listen with amazement and soon are asking if they can take turns on the spinning wheel.

Frau Holle chats with the leaders before showing the girls the final process. "Girls, please follow me to the loom. This device is used to weave cloth," she says pointing to the complex machine. "These sets of lengthwise yarn are held taught by the frame, and they are called a warp. This stick here is called the yarn shuttle. I insert it crosswise and it goes over and under the warp threads, like this." She quickly draws a line of flax thread through and with ease demonstrates how the fabric is woven together thereby creating the linen. "Who wants to try?" Frau Holle asks.

The girls line up and are eager to learn and try their hands at each stage of the procedure. For the remainder of the day, the girls help Frau Holle in her shop.[5] The weaver is pleased to answer the girl's questions. She re-demonstrates any procedures necessary until the girls have a good understanding of the entire process.

At the end of their workday, Fräulein Albrecht catches the girls' attention. They quickly put all their tools and materials away, pick up their backpacks, and line up outside. With their banner flying high, they march in song from Frau Holle's house. She returns their waves, grateful for all their help. She knows that she will never see them again.

The column gaily hikes off the main roads, passing through small villages and fields into the forests. They ascend and descend the hills, until they reach the city of Tannwald (Tanvald, Czech Republic) where they arrive at their next destination.

The farmer's wife welcomes the travelers and shows them to the barn attic where they will spend the night. As the girls finish organizing their sleeping arrangements they help the farmer's wife begins their feast. She is so happy to host the Country Service Year girls that she makes a grand dinner for everyone. As the city girls work in the kitchen cooking and setting the table, Trudel and her country comrades help muck out the stalls, feed the livestock, fill the watering troughs, and weed the garden.

Free food and lodging does not come without the expectation of the girls to work at their hosts homestead. Bartering work in exchange for a place to eat and sleep comes naturally to these girls. They do not expect payment for their service for they feel proud to demonstrate their home economic and farming skills.

---

[5] Malgorzata Jackiewicz

After dinner, the girls perform and sing various songs for the farmer and his wife. They play games of charades and shadows. By nine o'clock, everyone settles into their respective places and beds down for the evening.

The next morning, they awake early to begin their two and one-half hour, eight-mile hike west to the city of Gablonz (Jablonec, Czech Republic). Their morning routine is the same. They wake up at sunrise, wash at the hand pump outside, salute their banner, and pack their backpacks. Then, they help prepare breakfast. After their morning meal, they help on the farm. Since their next destination is only a short hike, the girls spend the entire morning helping the farmer with his livestock and crops, and then help his wife by cleaning the inside the home, and caring for the children. Once their tasks are complete, they leave the farmers and march in formation holding their banner high. People come out of their homes to watch the patriotic girls march along the street. German soldiers stop conversing with their fellow officers and smile as the young girls file past.

After two hours of walking, they find a nice resting place in the park and nestle themselves down. Their backpacks are starting to weigh heavily on their backs.

After break, they hike another half an hour to the outskirts of the city of Gablonz. They hike up the hill to their next destination at guesthouse Nickelkoppe. Trudel thinks this is the most beautiful building she has ever seen! The girls are greeted by the keeper of the manor home with open arms. She is glad that her troop is being welcomed at each rest stop. After the day's hike, Trudel settles into her room and takes a moment to write in her journal.

"This is our third day of our big trip and we are staying overnight in a very prominent building overlooking Gablonz. We are very tired from so much walking and are glad to have that 'monkey' off our backs. Our building has many rooms, magnificent views, and even a large tower overlooking the Isergebirge Mountains. When I look out the window, it almost seems as if the mountains are saying 'hello' to me. There is a very large hall and we waited here for our instructions. The rooms are beautifully decorated and the owners are very friendly to us. They give us anything we want, lots of food to eat, and comfortable beds to sleep in. We spent the entire day learning about ways to fight against cancer by eating right, exercising, and staying clean by using the proper hygiene techniques. I already know how to do that but I did not know anything about the plants that fight off cancer. They told us eating flax seeds with cottage cheese helps, so does garlic, broccoli, carrots, the seeds inside the cherries and apricots, elderberry, mushrooms, raspberries, rosemary, and tomatoes. I did not like the pictures of the cancer patients I saw. They looked very old and frail. I feel very sorry for them. I wish I could do something to help them. Even little children had cancer. After the lecture, the mayor came in and told us a story about how this entire area was devastated during the Thirty-Year War. The city girls got bored and wanted to go into the city and look around but for some reason, our leaders prevented us from leaving. After the lecture, I walked around the grounds and climbed the stairs up to the top of the tower. There, I dreamed about being the princess and one day, my prince will come, sweep me off my feet, and take me away to a land far, far away land. I can always dream, because dreams do come true. I've always dreamed of traveling, and here I am, traveling the world!"

On day four, the girls arise before daybreak, wash dress and prepare for the next excursion. Trudel is in a bliss, thoroughly enjoying this trip through new lands in the company of her troop.

Leaving the lodge behind and with their flag raised high, the girls march in a three-line formation with their monkeys once again, on their backs. Down the hill, they march while singing all the way to the railway station in the city of Gablonz. The leaders show their tickets as the officials inspect the girl's backpacks. The troop boards the train for their two-hour ride to Hohenelbe (Vrchlabí, Czech Republic).

The slow cog transport meanders through the mountainous terrain, passing small villages and towns. Steam billows from the locomotive bearing the eagle emblem. The train chuffs its way through a three-thousand foot long tunnel. It passes over impressive stone viaducts, crossing streams and rivers, through dense forests, and rattles across open sub-alpine green meadows.

The girls, especially Trudel, are enjoying this relaxing time together. She, Steffi, Nelly, Ingrid, Elli, and Maria share all kinds of stories with each other. Trudel loves watching the impressive mountain views move pass her windows. Once again, she pulls down the window, sticks her head out, and breaths in deeply the fresh mountain air. She loves feeling the wind rushing past her long black braids. She thinks 'if only there is a way I could travel like this all the time.'

In the early afternoon, the troop disembarks in Hohenelbe (Vrchlabí, Czech Republic). Trudel notices that the town is very simple and plain just like the train station. The mayor meets with the leaders and introduces himself to the girls. They follow him into a large hall in town. He is very nice to the girls and takes care of them. He makes sure the girls have fresh whole milk, fresh butter for their bread, and drink real bean coffee. That afternoon, he lectures about the history of his fine city.

"Our city of Hohenelbe is known for its ironworks. Thanks to our proximity and easy access to the Elbe River, we became a major supplier of swords and firearms during the Thirty-Year War. Together with the processing of iron, the most important artisan sector became the textile flax industry. In addition to the traditional urban guilds, the weaver's guild rose very prominently, and weaving flax began to develop and take root. In fact, by the eighteenth century, the cloth gained notoriety and was exported all around the world! Our village prospered tremendously. This brought more artisans into the area and the city began to grow. Many highly skilled laborers, including bricklayers, tailors, traders, shoe-makers, weavers, drapers, dyers, furriers, seal engravers, wheelwrights, butchers, stocking-makers, belt-makers, soap-boilers, potters, shopkeepers, hatters, watch-makers, saddlers, gunsmiths, and rope-makers, made Hohenelbe their home. In 1865, Empress Maria Theresa was here with her son, Joseph II. He was consid-ered the People's Emperor and on several occasions he visited this city.[6] In 1938, Hohenelbe became part of Sudetenland and proudly joined the great German Empire."

After their discussion, the mayor invites the girls to swim in his town pool. He leaves with Fräulein Albrecht to secure their sleeping quarters for the night while Fräulein Grüber joins the girls in the pool.

On the fifth day of the trip, the girls hike back down to the train station and board for their two-hour ride through the mountains. They disembark in Trautenau (Trutnov, Czech Republic). When daily excursions exceed fifteen miles, transportation is provided for the girls. Otherwise, they hike.

The mayor of Trautenau meets the leaders and the band of travelers at the station. He is pleased that they have arrived on time and without incident. He spends the entire day with the girls, showing them through his city.

The girls enjoy walking along the city streets and learning about the renais-sance and baroque architecture. They pause at the massive fountain when the mayor begins his lecture.

"Legend has it that the name of Trautenau came about by a mighty knight named Trut, who fought bravely to slay the giant dragon that lived in a cave high up there," he says pointing to the mountains. The girls love hearing stories. "Over the centuries the city fought in many wars. We were attacked by the Huss-ite. We also fought in the Thirty-Year War. We won the very bloody Battle of Trautenau in 1866 during the Seven-Year War. Let me take you girls up to the top of the hill and show you the abandoned military fortifications."

The girls hike up the mountainside, enjoying the panorama. Once again, they are getting annoyed at being stuck with the heavy "monkeys" on their backs. At the summit, they were quite impressed by the ruins and underground corridors. They gratefully set their backpacks down and begin exploring the dark tunnels and surrounding areas. This former defensive military outpost was constructed to defend the city against the country's enemy.[7]

Back in the city again the troop joins the mayor at a showing of the movie "Without War." Afterwards, the mayor expresses his gratitude for their visit and bids them good day.

They hike thirteen miles through the forest of hornbeam trees with their smooth grey bark trunks. Hardwood trees flank on their right side of the road with the limestone mountain range on the left. They walk through the impres-sively attractive and less inhabited valley of Erlitz following the Upa River east

---

[6] Hohenelbe
[7] Trutnov

to Ober Wernersdorf (Horni Vernérovice, Czech Republic). The valley offers a good nesting grounds because the mountain range blocks the prevailing easterly winds. The moderate current of the river carves deep into the earth.

As they near their hosting camp, the valley opens to a large agricultural area with linen manufacturers and cotton-weaving mills. Smoke billows from the chimneys and the surrounding area is barren from trees. Carrying their banner high and marching in formation, they sing happily announcing their arrival at Country Service Year Camp in Ober Wernersdorf.

The hosting girls, originally from Prague, hear their guests singing and rush to meet them at the gate with open hearts.[8] After the young girls introduce themselves to each other, the guests are shown to the sleeping quarters in the barn. Once they are settled in, they perform their flag evening ceremony then help with the various chores around camp. Their evening comes alive when they change into their pajamas, line up in rows, and begin marching through the manor home singing.

The boys from Trautenau Camp No. 638 heard rumors about the female arrivals and decide to sneak on over and talk with them.[9] Some girls sneak outside to meet the boys and some tease them through the windows. When the camp leader hears the commotion, she puts an immediate end to the shenanigans. The boys run into the darkness and hide in the forest. Fräulein Albrecht reprimands the girls and orders everyone to bed. That evening, the boys' tiptoed back to camp to visit the girls sleeping in the barn. Discretely they attempt to get the girls' attention, but jump when Fräulein Albrecht opens the door instead! Startled, the boys run melting back into the woods never to be seen again. Trudel does not want to think about the disciplinary measures they will receive when they return to their camp.

Past midnight, the girls awake with a jolt as the first thunderbolt strike near their barn. The horrific storm keeps the girls up for most of the night. They huddle close to one another and some are very frightened. Fräulein Albrecht comforts the girls by telling them a story about how the angels are bowling in the clouds with God.

Early the next morning everyone wakes, hurries to wash, dress, and lines up outside for the morning flag greeting ceremony. One hundred girls march in a two-line rote formation into the courtyard and form a very large square around their flagpole. Afterwards, they march back to camp and eat breakfast outside. Trudel enjoys the wholesome poppy seed and cottage cheese strudel and the rich bean flavor of their replacement coffee. Everyone seems extremely happy to be singing songs of fellowship. The Seidorfer girls are sad to leave.

Thoughts of the boys are pushed from Trudel's mind by her focus on her footsteps and songs. She is looking forward to her next destination, though. At the Trautenau train station, the mayor meets up with the girls once again. He

---

[8] Ernst Birke
[9] Hitler Youth Basic Handbook, p. A76

informs Fräulein Albrecht that he has arranged for the girls' transportation northeast to the border between Sudetenland and Niederschlesien.

Excitedly, the girls hop into the back of the 1938 Opel Blitz A-Type cargo truck with its high-chassis and long box-like platform body made from wood.[10] Forty girls and two leaders make themselves comfortable in the back of the truck, sitting on the backpacks. The driver shuts the wooden tailgate, shakes hands with the mayor, and leaps up into the pressed steel cab. The mayor waves good-bye to his guests. The driver pushes in the clutch of the three-ton pickup truck and grinds the vehicle into first gear. The girls wave good-bye, riding away in song.

The wind blows in their hair as they ride through the hardwood forest on the Okraj Mountain Pass back into Niederschlesien. From earlier days, this was the smugglers' route. In 1937, the Germans built a tarmac road allowing them access into this picturesque part of the country. The predominant sub-alpine vegetation zone of spruce, pine, cloudberry, and lichen trees prevails along the side of the road. Near the apex of the mountain pass, the terrain gives way to a rocky desert covered in granite rubble. At the top of the ridge, 4,429 feet above sea level, the easterly winds pick up. They cross over the summit and stop at the guard post and shelter home, which marks the border between Sudetenland and Niederschlesien.

A guard orders the truck to stop and everyone out. The camp leaders present their BDM membership and health certificates. The guards inspect their backpacks. The girls wave good-bye to the driver as he turns around and returns to Ober Wernersdorf.

Now, the girls continue north on foot. They begin their two and one-half hour hike to Landeshut (Kamienna Gora, Poland). A second truck meets the girls at the Landeshut train station and drives them west to Schmiedeberg (Kowary, Poland). In the back of the truck, they happily sing, for they are nearing another girl's camp.

The Reich's Ministry of Education, Science, and Culture consider the girls' voices musical instruments and singing is viewed as physical exercise. Singing develops the vocal muscles and requires little strength. The air freely moves in and out of the body, thereby improving lung capacity and brain function. As more oxygen flows through the body it improves the girl's mood and reduces fatigue. Singing keeps the girls focused and brings them closer together in comradeship. [11]

The host camp hears their singing as the Seidorfer girls come around the corner. They run from their lager and greet them at the main entrance. More than sixty girls welcome the Seidorfer girls to Country Service Year Camp Rest Mountain in Kowary (Ciszyca Mansion).[12] Their three-story home and property

---

[10] Opel Blitz, 'Lastkraftwagen'
[11] Anita Leugner
[12] Landjahr Lager Ruhberg in Schmiedeberg

are much larger than Camp Seidorf. In the rear of the property is a sprawling old castle ruin.

The girls celebrate their evening at Camp Kowary with a flag ceremony. They feast on a delicious meal. During the evening social hour, the visitors sing with their hosts before retiring to the adjacent barn. It is the last night of the girls' big trip.

The next morning promptly at six-thirty, the forty Seidorfer girls and the sixty Rest Mountain girls, together with their leaders salute their flag. Standing among her comrades, Trudel feel exhilarated. Never has her life been filled with such excitement. Besides the deep bond of fellowship, she feels as if she is on top of the world!

The girls quickly eat breakfast, pack their backpacks, and help the hosting girls with their livestock, garden, and household chores. At eight o'clock, all one hundred girls line up in formation to begin their six-mile hike southwest to Krummehubel (Karpacz, Poland), to see the famous Norwegian-style church on the hilltop.

In their respective groups, the girls and their leaders hike across fields and open pastures. The Seidorfer girls wear their white dresses and green aprons, followed by the Rest Mountain girls in their light blue handmade dresses. Each camp must wear different colors to signify their designated camp.

The group breaks formation when they ascend the steep, rocky dirt path traveled by so many before them. Walking through the pine forest, Trudel uses a walking stick to traverse the steep terrain. She leans forward and the weight from her backpack helps her up the hill. As they near the remote village of Brückenberg (Karpacz Górny, Poland), the group walks through the forest openings and come upon the darkly stained, wooden, four-post single-nave stave church. Impressed with its appearance the girls walk around the grounds and explore the cemetery behind the church first.

Fräulein Grüber escorts the girls to the white-plate monument and begins her lecture. "Countess Friederike von Reden of Buchwald is considered the Mother of the Hirschberg Valley. During her lifetime, she worried about the poorest peasants and established a meal center for her commoners. She is best remembered for transporting and erecting the Stabkirche Wang (Vang Stave Church) on this site. She instrumentally approached Count Christian Leopold von Schaffgotsch of Bad Warmbrunn and recommended the relocation of the church from Norway right to this very spot. Without her, this building would not be here.

"Originally built in the twelfth century on Lake Wang, the ancestral Vikings found many of their beliefs bestowed upon this magnificent wooden structure. They built this church to resemble a Viking ship. The artisanship of the Vikings used their shipbuilding techniques to construct this from Norwegian pinewood. After many years of neglect, the church came into disarray. In 1842, the Prussian King Frederick William IV purchased the building and had it shipped in crates to Krummehubel (Karpacz, Poland). Many river barges and horse-drawn wagons transported it piece by piece through arduous conditions until the crates finally reached their destination on the side of this mountain. It took many skilled laborers a painstaking two years to clear the land and reconstruct the church.[13] The Runic inscriptions above the entryway are a true symbol of our Führer's beliefs. Now, let's take a moment to walk inside the building."

Trudel looks up and notices the long dragon necks staring down at her from above. She imagines what life may have been like over seven hundred years ago in Norway and wonders how they built this marvelous church by hand. Majestic lions stand upon the capitals facing outward implying that they are guarding the gates.

Trudel walks through the entrance and notice the columns are exquisitely decorated with tangled snakes and plants. Winged dragons, secret runic inscriptions, and faces with forked tongues greet her as she walks into the building. A cloister surrounds the church, protecting the interior walls from the severe winter weather and a tall granite tower protects the building from the north. The gallery was once used to hold weapons. It now serves as a place of penance. Trudel enters the vestibule, sits in the wooden pew, and admires the interior of the building with its decorative carvings. Over one-hundred and seventy-five glass windows admit light into the interior of the building. Four giant single hand-hued Nordic pine columns support the ceiling. Two large decorative iron chandeliers hold eight candles each. In the apse, Jesus hangs from the large wooden cross behind a simple altar.

Trudel kneels and says a prayer for those fighting in the war. She asks God to watch over her family, her brothers, and for a safe arrival home with her troop. She lights a candle in remembrance of her loved ones that have gone before her. Exiting via a corridor, she walks through the timber-frame structure that leads out to the church's massive stone tower.

On the foothills of the Giant Mountains, the country service girls bid each other a fond adieu. The Rest Mountain girls return to their camp, as the Seidorfer girls march the remaining six miles home.

Trudel is content to return to her camp. She drops her 'monkey' off onto her bed and pops downstairs to the bulletin board where her duties for the next two weeks are posted. It turns out that she will be tending to the garden. A special field day is planned for all the girls to learn about the medicinal plants from the gardener at Schloss Arnsdorf (Palace Miłków). It is only during her spare time, she will be allowed to play with the animals.

This past week-long trek will not be the last of her expeditions. Before she leaves Camp Seidorf, she will explore the surrounding countryside. She will walk through the city of Bad Warmbrunn and view the epitaphs and crypts at St. John the Baptist Catholic Church. She will visit the mountaintop ruins of Schaffgotsch castle in Kynast (Chojnik) and hike up the steep path to St. Anna Kapella. Moreover, under the waterfall of Giersdorf, she will be having fun climbing on the rocks and jumping into the pool of crystal clear waters. It is a wonderful life in Landjahr Lager Seidorf.

---

[13] Malgorzata Jackiewicz

We Practice for our RJA Badge

IN SEPTEMBER, HUNDREDS OF GIRLS from the surrounding districts participate in the annual sports competition, which is held in the field outside the city of Hirschberg. This mandatory event is a way to earn the National Youth Sports badge, comprised of an oak-leaf wreath with the "RJA" in stylized letters to its center with a swastika at the base. It gives them the opportunity to compete against the other BDM troops within the area.[1] Trudel forever remembers this competition in her journal.

"We better have our heads together because we have to show everyone what we have learned. Weeks before the competition, our leaders drill us outside in the field. There is no more dreaming because we are now competing for our RJA badge. Every girl is dreaming of being awarded this pin. Even when we first started in camp, we were always thinking 'Will I make it?' The high jump is the most difficult to make. I don't like to jump over it because it is made out of wood and not rubber. Everything is so hard and you can get hurt. Then, comes the long jump. We must jump at least eleven feet. Some of the girls can jump farther than that but we have some girls who can never do it, so they fail. However, if you are willing to show them that you will try they will give you credit for that too. Good Will is always there. We also need to run two-hundred and fifty feet. We must be in great shape. It is very hard and it is not as easy because we must run with our full foot down and not on our toes or on our heels as in walking. We train every day, running to the finish line, and do not stumble. Then, we had an iron ball to throw. It weights fifteen pounds. We never did that before. However, the sand is soft. We must concentrate and put our entire mind and body into the movements because we had to throw that ball at least sixteen feet and if not, we do not make it. We are very strong because we can throw that ball. It is true that we have big muscles. I noticed that one girl threw the ball twenty feet! Some girls even made it to twenty-seven feet! Even before getting our RJA pin, we must show that we can march fifteen miles in one day and we did that on our big trip, over the mountains, through the forest. In addition, we need to swim in the pool from one side to the other in our best time.

---

[1] Reichsjugendsportsabzeichen

"A happy heart and a strong Will,
That is our humble beginnings,
We don't stay too long laying down
For our Will is as high
As the Heavens.
With our hard work
We will not have any burdens
anymore."

~ Gertrude Kerschner ~

Harvesting the Potatoes

TRUDEL LOVES WORKING WITH THE FARMERS and she writes about her experience harvesting the potatoes it in her journal.

"On a dry day in October, the last potato harvest of the season begins. It was made very clear to us that harvesting the potatoes is very hard work and we should take care when bending over and lifting the large wooden baskets onto the wagon. We know we are going to be working from very early in the morning until nightfall. Luck is on our side because when we take the potatoes out of the ground and brush them off, someone is behind us to pick up the smaller potatoes. We have a lot of fun because we are behind the plough and only have to pick up the big potatoes. We started a competition to see who could fill up their baskets first with the most potatoes. All of a sudden, we heard them calling us in for lunch! Everything was set up beautifully outside on the picnic table and boy were we hungry! Fräulein Grüber and Dieter helped Tante Else prepare the lunch. As we ate the big farmer sandwich, everyone was sharing her stories. Our leaders told us to eat because after lunch we will go back into the fields to work.

"When we returned to the fields, we saw the big baskets sitting on the top of the wagon and our little collection baskets were empty and sitting off to the side. A lot of the farmers will tell you that they wanted their potatoes separated according to size but Uncle Bernhard did not mind because the potatoes were all cleaned and put into the same baskets. We sorted them out later on in three groups, the big ones, the medium size ones, and the little ones that would be used in salads. The smallest ones were for the chickens. Each farmer wants his potatoes harvested a little bit different. Some want them cleaned and sorted before putting them in the baskets and other wants the cleaning and sorting done back at the farm. Nevertheless, that is double the work. Our leaders tell us how the work must be performed. Elli, Nelly, Steffi, Maria, and Ingrid work in my group and each one must do her work right the first time.

Like me, we are very happy to help the farmers because we know we are helping our country and our soldiers on the front line. The afternoons go by so fast because there is so much work to do. We can talk to each other and we tell stories or sing our harvest and potato songs. We don't even have to think!

"We leave at 6:00 and hike back home to our camp. We need to be punctual because when we return we still have our evening chores to do before dinner.

"When we arrive back to camp, everyone is standing outside the doors and they clapped. They greeted us and told us what a good job we did because we are all young girls working in service for our country. Even Fräulein Albrecht complimented us on a job well done. We are all very happy when the field was emptied in two days!"

Pig Baptism

ON NOVEMBER 1, 1941, ALL SAINTS DAY, the girls are divided into two groups of twenty. They visit the local cemeteries in Seidorf to clean and garnish the graves with flowers, wreaths, and candles. When one grave is completed, they say a short prayer for the dead before moving on to the next grave. All day long, the girls meticulously pull the weeds, remove the dead plants, and wipe down the headstones.

The final celebration is held on the second Saturday in November. This is the day when the girls honor the two pigs they have been caring for over the past seven months. They are now fully grown.

Before Fräulein Dieter takes her vacation on the 2nd, she appoints Trudel to supervise the pig baptism. Delighted with the challenge Trudel announces that she will need the assistance of a few girls to help organize the event. The girls do not endear themselves to the personality of these farm animals by naming these three-hundred pound porkers, for all year long, the girls simply address them as "pig."

Steffi, Nelly, Elli, Maria, Helli, Ingrid, Sabine, Erika, Elfie, and Lotte, are all interested in helping Trudel plan and organize this lively event. This is a tremendous undertaking, and the girls are delighted to assist. During their meeting, they discuss the Christian baptism ceremony as it represents the rite of admission, consecrated by the anointment of oil and water. They know the baptism of the Jesus Christ, took place in the Jordan River when John the Baptist poured water over Jesus' head, proclaiming him the Son of God. The girls worry about how they are going to take two fully grown, three-hundred pound swine and dunk them in the river. Steffi jokes about baptizing them in the pond. Then, she suggests they seek the advice of the local priest.

Enthusiastically, the girls visit the local Evangelical Church in Seidorf and ask the minister, Hans Lobisch, for his assistance about how to plan a baptism.[1] As Trudel takes notes the minister explains the signs and symbols, and how the parents and the godparents need to be present, along with witnesses and invited guests. Most importantly, the baby needs to wear a white dress. The girls giggle and the priest gives them a perplexing look. Then, he remembers how the camp girls approached him last year for the same advice. He gives a brief overview of the four stages of the baptism ending with the last words of good will.

Pleased with their detective work, the girls hurry back to camp. With much enthusiasm, they sit and plan the celebration and the fest, discussing the details of the baptism and freely sharing their thoughts. Trudel listens intently and

---

[1] Werner Samjeske

makes notes of each member's ideas and concerns. The girls feel delighted when they decide upon the time and location of the event and whom they will need to play which roles. Together they will handle the decorations, send out the invitations, write a script, and even create a new pig song!

On the day of the ceremony, Sunday, November 9, 1941 everyone is in a festive mood. The guests arrive and are dressed in their best. They watch as the procession marches from the house, through the courtyard, ending at the pigs' stall. Wearing their formal BDM uniforms the 'witnesses' wrap themselves in their gray traveling blankets.

Leading the procession is Fräulein Albrecht who plays the part of the priest and officiates the sacred rites. Her imitation black robe resembles a priest's cope that opens in the front and fastens at the breast with a clasp. A white bib is fastened to the cape. Standing next to her is Fräulein Grüber who is playing the part of the godmother. She carries a bouquet of flowers and wears a simple housedress and apron. Next are Trudel and Helli, who are wearing white bed sheets over their shoulders and carry decoratively carved walking sticks. Steffi and Nelly are followed by the rest of the camp girls and the invited guests.

The girls did a beautiful job cleaning and decorating the pigsty with new straw, pine wreaths, ribbons, and flowers. Petals adorn the entrance to the stall, symbolizing this joyful event. In Germany, pigs are a sign of good luck and it is a great honor to care for them all year long.

Trudel opens the gate and enters the stall with Helli, Steffi, Nelly, and her two camp leaders. She closes the gate behind her and they begin the ceremony as everyone looks on. Trudel and Helli hand over their walking sticks and accept the ribbons from Steffi and Nelly. The girls struggle to place the ribbons over the pig's heads. Everyone laughs at the sight.

With everyone in place, Fräulein Albrecht begins the christening. "In the name of the Father, the Son, and the Holy Ghost. Amen."

Everyone makes the sign of the cross.

"Let us pray, Almighty God, on this day, and look graciously down upon our gentle creatures and upon those who witness this ceremony. Drive out the evil spirits and open the heart of these swine unto the house of the Lord. In loving kindness, the Country Service Year Girls of Seidorf have taken care of these revered animals since their arrival. Over the months, these animals have grown from small piglets into healthy large hogs. We thank you Lord for bringing our lucky pigs to us. Amen."

Everyone affirms with head bowed and together they say, "Amen."

Trudel and Helli hold the pigs as the priest walks up to them and places a little salt in their mouths.

"Receive this salt so you may become pure," intones Fräulein Albrecht.

The pigs squeal and try to get away from the girls.

"May you make your way joyfully from this life into God's hands and his everlasting life. Peace be with you, pigs."

The witnesses reply, "And also with you."

Fräulein Albrecht hands the salt vessel to Steffi and Nelly hands her the oil. Fräulein Albrecht turns back to the pigs and dabs a few drops of oil onto their foreheads. "I anoint you pig with your new name Thick" she says as she rubs the oil on the pig's forehead making the sign of the cross. Then she walks to the second pig. "I anoint you pig with your new name Skinny" she says, repeating her motions. "From now on you will be known as Thick and Skinny."

The priest takes a step back and makes the sign of the cross. "May you both be eternally blessed for the remainder of your lives. You have served with duty, with honor, and in loyalty. We thank you for living here with us on our farm and we are blessed to have taken care of you." Fräulein Albrecht hands the oil back to Nelly. Elli hands her a tin bucket half full with water. She turns back to the pig and continues the ritual.

"Will you be baptized?" Fräulein Albrecht asks the pig.

"Yes, I will," answers Fräulein Grüber on Thick's behalf.

Fräulein Albrecht scoops a handful of water and sprinkles droplets onto Thick's forehead.

"Will you be baptized?" the priest asks Skinny.

"Yes, I will," answers the godmother.

The priest sprinkles water on Skinny's forehead. "I baptize you both in the name of the Father, the Son, and the Holy Ghost. Amen."

The crowd replies in unison with "Amen."

"Now, go in peace, Thick and Skinny, and may the Lord be with you. You may do as you please for the remainder of the day."

Trudel and Helli release the swine, who run around the pen. Together in a joyful manner, the girls sing their new 'Pig Song.'

"This ceremony has concluded," the priest announces. "Let our pigs now roam free for the rest of their lives for tomorrow they will become our dinner!"

The gate opens and the pigs make a mad dash into the garden. Trudel and Helli race after the pigs and watch over their every move. The girls lead them out from the garden to the lawn where they relieve themselves. With a vivacious laugh, Trudel looks up and sees the photographer who snaps a picture forever solidifying her image on film.

The girls follow the swine toward the house. The pigs run up the stairs, through the parlor, and into the dining room. They push themselves under the tables, nudging the chairs out of the way. The guests and attendees have never seen such a sight! They line the front entryway staircase and watch. The pigs race down the hallway into the leader's offices, back out into the dining room, through the parlor, and down the front stairs. The guests applaud! As Thick trots out the door, the girls rain petals down upon her. Her ears bob up and down as her little hoofs carry her down the stairs. Skinny follows close behind.

Trudel and Helli charge out of the house in hot pursuit. Spontaneously, all the excited girls chase after the pigs. Trudel's white cape falls off as she struggle with Skinny, trying to hold her by the ears. Maria, Ingrid, Sabine, Erika, Steffi, Ellie, and Nelly assist Trudel in slowing the pig down. Elfie and Lotte grab a big bucket of water and pretend to throw it at the pig, mischievously dousing the girls instead! The girls laugh and release the pig from their grip.

The adults supervise the comical scene and take delight in the whole affair. For the remainder of the day the girls entertain themselves playing with the pigs and by giving musical performances for their guests who are drinking coffee and eating cake.

At the end of the day, the guests thank the leaders for a wonderful afternoon. They all look forward to returning for the feast! Trudel and Helli round up the pigs and return them to their sty. Trudel kisses both on their foreheads. She kneels down and takes Thick's head in her hands. "I love you Thick," she says as the swine wiggles away. She pets Skinny on the head and gives her a playful pat on her rump. "I love you Skinny." She says a short prayer for both of her dear pets and gives each one a final hug goodnight. The next day will be their last!

Pig Slaughter

In her journal, Trudel recounts the day of her pigs being slaughtered.

"We are all very nervous on the day of our slaughter fest because we are wondering if we will pass the inspection. Days before, we worked very hard to get everything ready. We were told to clean the washhouse from top to bottom for we were not allowed just to clean it. We had to scrub the floors and walls with very hot, soapy water because it had to be spotless.

"The butcher arrived with his helper and the inspector. They looked at everything. We were relieved to know that we passed the inspection. It was a nightmare listening to the screeching and hollering of the pigs as we stood outside the door. We were horrified because the pigs were led into the room by a cord and we did not know what they were going to do with them. "Then, we heard the first shot. A few girls put their hands over their ears and cried because there was no more squealing. We knew that was the end of Thick. We felt so sorry for her that we said a little prayer so that she can make her way up to heaven.

"The butcher called us into the room and told us to scrub Thick from top to bottom. That was our job. When we were finished, the butcher and his helper cut open the stomach, pulled it out, and cleaned the intestines. Some of the meat was cut and then grounded.

"We used a special machine to make the sausage. The butcher placed the intestines at the end of the machine and we mixed the ground meat using the ingredients he told us to use. With both ends tied, the sausage was placed in a big kettle to cook. When the sausage rose to the surface of the boiling water, it cooked for another ten minutes or so and then it was done. The butcher instructed us in making the blood sausage using different ingredients and the blood from the pig. The rest of the pig was hanging outside on a very strong rope. Then, the cutting began for the bacon and ham. The butcher cut off the different parts of the meat and we placed it into our big pot with salt, water, and spices. It is my responsibility to turn over the meat. After it's completely cooked, we took the meat out of the pot and brought it down to the smoke house so that it could smoke for at least a week. "We made a lot of salt pork, roast, cutlets, bacon, and ham. The butcher removed the brains, lungs, and kidneys. He taught us how to clean the membranes from the organs. Then, we soaked the brains overnight in lightly salted water. We took the lungs and kidneys and boiled them in big pots with potatoes and onions. When everything was cooked, the pieces were cut into slices, dipped into flour, and then fried. Yummy, everything tasted so good.

"You would not believe your eyes if you could have been there in our house and smelled the pork cooking and watching how we made the sausages. All of us were working together. Boy, were our mouths watering! By lunchtime, the first butchering was finished, but we needed to clean the entire room with very hot water one more time so we scrubbed, and scrubbed, and scrubbed. Then, it was Skinny's turn. I cried. She was my favorite pig. "Our invited guests would be arriving promptly at four o'clock for our last feast and everything had to be ready on time to serve, and it had to be hot too!

"After all the work was done, we drank coffee and ate cake. Then, we started playing because we had a few free hours of time. It was funny because we played a game called The Donkey was Hollering. Then, we sang a few songs followed by the main meal. We were so very hungry after working so hard that day and smelling the food cooking in the kitchen. There were so many things to eat and we did not know what to grab first or where to start. We had sausage, boiled meat, cooked meat, ribs, sauerkraut, mustard horseradish, bread, brains, kidneys, lungs, soup, salad, and potatoes. It was a real feast! We couldn't eat as much as we would have liked to eat but our guests liked it very much and that made us all feel wonderful!

"After dinner, we danced through the entire house. Our guests, our leaders, and all the girls danced the Polonaise polka. We were getting so hot and sweaty from all the dancing that we had to sit down. The evening went by so fast and by ten o'clock, we danced our last dance.

"Our last festive evening together had finally ended. We felt heavy in our hearts because we did not want the evening to end. I suggested we sing a few songs together and we did. Mayor Werner Blasius of Hirschberg and the BDM district leader, Fräulein Elli Hubbe, shook our hands and thanked us for a wonderful evening. All our invited guests thanked us for the beautiful hours we had together sharing this time as one big family. Quickly, we cleaned everything and went to bed. Within a few minutes, we were sound asleep.

Our Last Visit with the Farmers

"OUR TIME IN LANDJAHR LAGER SEIDORF is soon ending," Trudel writes. "For the last time, we will pack our bags and make our beds. Before we leave, I asked if we could visit with the farmers one last time. Fräulein Dieter said she would ask them. It was not until a few days later that we were given a choice. We could spend this coming Saturday evening visiting for a few short hours or spend the entire day on Sunday with them. We were thinking what they would have for us. We knew our leaders and the farmers had something up their sleeves. It was their deep secret.

"We got up early Sunday morning, and were so excited! We took our showers, dressed neatly, put on our clean shoes, made our beds, and made sure our rooms were in perfect order. Everyone wanted to be the first one ready but we had to wait until noon. When the time came, we waited outside dressed in our best clothes. Our leaders came out and looked us over. They inspected our clothing, our fingernails, and the bottom of our shoes. I could feel my heart beat inside my chest. Then, they told us to go ahead and have fun!

"Now, just picture it for a moment. We are sitting in the backyard of the farmhouse in our Sunday best dress, drinking coffee and eating cakes, and we were barefoot! We just could not dream that we were allowed to sit there in their beautiful garden wearing no boots. It was such a memorable experience because we just sat there listening to their stories. They told us about their home and land. I was interested in hearing how their ancestors migrated here hundreds of years ago. For many years, they toiled the soil for the noble Schaffgotsch family. They showed us pictures and explained many things to us that we did not understand. Of course, every girl was so excited and wanted to talk about where she came from, what her life was like living in the country or in the city, and what they plan on doing with the rest of their lives. When I was talking, I sounded like a real pro. Then, it started raining, and we brought everything inside.

"We brought something for us to do, like needlework, knitting, or sewing. When we sat in the living room, we could smell the fresh aroma from the brewed coffee and baked cakes. Everything tasted really good!

"Then, the big surprise came! Uncle Bernhard pulled out this very large box and placed it on the table. We were wondering what could possibly be inside. Tante Else took off the lid we all leaned over and peaked inside the box. There must have been a hundred envelopes inside that box. On each envelop was a girl's name and we were wondering what could possibly be inside those envelopes. We were not allowed to open them until we were told. Boy did we have a surprise! In each envelope was a set of pictures from our time at camp! We were very happy. We compared and exchanged pictures, laughed, and remembered our past times. It was wonderful to be able to have photos of our time in Country Service Year Camp Seidorf.

"When the sun came out, Tante Else said maybe the children would like to go outside and do a little walking. She asked us what we would like to do with the children and we immediately said we wanted to go outside and play with them in the grass. We ran around in the meadows and in the fields. It turned out to be a very nice, warm day. We walked along the stream and put our feet in the water. We were all very sad when it was our time to say good-bye. We gave our aunt and uncle a loving hug and before leaving, we recited a poem for them.

Our Volk need to have a Fatherland,
Fields, grace land, and a house,
Everybody will look for it.
Our Volk need to have a Fatherland,
Work, industry, and a house
In which everyone is happy.
Our Volk need to have a Fatherland.
Children and everything is ours,
And, some of them stay outside, to protect all this.
Our Volk need to have a Fatherland,
Everybody indivisible needs to have their own Fatherland.
The seeds will be there to put them anew in Mother Earth.

"We wished them well and we walked happily back to our camp with our pictures in our hands and songs in our hearts. When we came home, we talked about our experiences. We were so happy to be back in our beds with our happy faces smiling."

Our First Snow

TRUDEL'S DREAM OF SNOW has finally arrived. She wakes up early, rubs the frost from the window, and peeks outside to see the landscape has turned into a magical winter wonderland. Sharply, the whistle blows and the day begins with a cold shower.

There is no time to play in the snow today. Not only do their personal belongings have to be clean, organized, and packed, the camp has to be winterized and prepared for the arrival of the next set of Landjahr girls come spring. All provisions being left behind will be inventoried and stowed neatly away.

With the small farm animals gone and the vegetables canned or shared with the neighbors, the leaders inspect the lager for anything else that might need to be sewn, repaired, or replaced. The girls will need to make small presents to give to the local schoolchildren, their parents, and the farmers. In the meantime, their daily routine continues. Everyone still has her duties to perform.

Trudel and Steffi gaily run down to the post office to pick up the camp's mail. The two pass by a brand-new sleigh in the store window and wish they had the money to buy it. Their dream of playing in the snow is thwarted thus far by their work schedule. On their way back to camp, they take the opportunity to thrown snowballs at each other.

When they return, they find the camp is bustling in a flurry of activity. The leaders finally gave permission for the girls to go outside and play! Unbeknownst to the girls, the leaders knew of the skis and sleighs stowed all summer long in the back shed. They cannot run fast enough through the deep snow and up the hill behind their manor home. Trudel, Elli, Nelly, Steffi, and Maria are ahead of Marta, Magdalena, Helli, Dorota, and Sylvia. Nelly jumps up and pulls down on a tree branch causing a mass of snow to tumble down all over the city girls. The country girls laugh at the city girls who become very angry and start throwing snowballs. Everyone including the leaders are participating in the fun.

All day long, the girls take turns using the skis and sleighs, making snow angels, and racing downhill to see who can go the fastest and the farthest. When Fräulein Albrecht accidently slips, the girls pile on her and roll around in fun. The snow gets on their clothes, under their hats, and down their backs. By the end of the day, everyone is so tired and hungry that she cannot wait to fall into bed.

"When the last days come
You will show the Lord your hands.
Those who work and toil hard
Rough hands may rest in Heaven.
And whoever has fine white hands
But must first show his heart to
God."

~ Annemarie Leppien ~
Country Service Year Camp Leader
Schleswig - Holstein

Last Week at Camp Seidorf

THE TIME HAS COME for the girl's final exam. This test covers everything they have learned during their eight-month stay. The test covers nursing and first aid, and even political knowledge. There can be no mistakes. Whoever does not pass will not receive their BDM Proficiency Badge. All year long, the camp leaders accentuate the importance of learning. It is known that if the girls do not master the smaller hurdles in life like reading, writing, and acquiring practical common knowledge skills, they will be unprepared to face life's difficult challenges as adults. The camp leaders take full responsibility for the girls' educations for the final exam reflects on the leader's competencies as well.

In the final part of this test, Fräulein Albrecht asks the girls to review their time in camp and to write about it in the journals they made during art class. The photos they had been given earlier will help them remember.

"And there, you can see that it is recorded in black and white, what we did, and how we did it. This way we can take it home and have it forever," Trudel writes in her memoir.

Trudel passes her exam. During the formal ceremony, Trudel stands in front of her comrades and receives her proficiency badge. She feels quite dignified when Fräulein Dieter pins the solid silver, oblong, red-white-red ribbon BDM badge on her chest. Then Trudel salutes and recites the poem she wrote to the group.

> "A happy heart and a strong will,
> That is our humble beginning.
> We don't stay too long laying down,
> For our will is as high as the heavens.
> With our hard work,
> We will not have any burdens anymore."

The leaders hold a formal farewell gathering for the girls before they leave camp. All day long, it t seems as if the entire town comes to pay them a visit, to thank them and bid them good-bye. They watch as the girls take their flags down for the very last time. It saddens some of the girls to hand their goodbye presents to the farmers' wives, and to the children whom they have become so fond. However, Marta, Magdalena, Helli, Dorota, and Sylvia are extremely happy to be returning to the city. Country life does not suit their interests and they vow never to return!

Nelly, Ellie, Steffi, Maria, Ingrid, and Trudel, hold hands and vow to come back one day. The country girls share their pictures, show off their awards, chat about their memories, and express their plans for their futures. When Trudel gets to this part of her journal, in her Austrian accent, she tells her daughter:

> "When I arrived in Seidorf, I was just a simple thirteen year old girl. I had just graduated from the Young Girls' League. During my time in Landjahr, I felt like I was truly a "Mädel im Dienst." I learned so much during these eight months in camp that I was given a choice. I could continue my apprenticeship in Country Service Year and eventually become an assistant leader, or with the knowledge and skills I learned, I could chose a vocation like working in an office, a hotel, a restaurant, in a daycare center, become a mother's helper, or even a nurse. When I received my BDM Proficiency Badge, I held my head up very high. I was very proud of myself because I can say that I knew nothing when I arrived, and now look at what I have learned! My practical training not only prepared me for the workforce, it is the foundation on which I live. Country Service Year Camp was a life building experience for me." Then, Trudel pauses before interjecting "…and what I learned, I hopefully passed along to you."

The past eight months certainly made a deep impression on Trudel. She was grateful to have been given the opportunity to be a part of Landjahr Lager.

For one last time, the girls join in camaraderie and song. Trudel has been practicing her zither for months. As her final gift to everyone, she gives a solo performance and plays "Ava Maria."

Standing with packed bags on the tram platform in Giersdorf, Trudel feels heartbroken. She bids farewell to Fräulein Dieter, Fräulein Grüber, and her comrades. The girls cry and release their embrace when the electric tram pulls in around the station. The returning girls to Ostmark board and take their seats along with Fräulein Albrecht who will escort them back to St. Pölten. Even though it is very cold outside, Trudel opens the window and pokes her head out, waving goodbye to the sisters she leaves behind. Tears stream down her face as the tram gently pulls away.

When the train arrives in Vienna the next day, Trudel, Elli, Nelly, Steffi, and Maria are very sad to see each other go. They vow to remain in contact and visit each other as often as possible. They promise one day, they will return and visit Country Service Year Camp Seidorf, together. Trudel rides the train with Ingrid back to the Rohrbach station.

Trudel and Ingrid step off the train in Rohrbach. Once again carrying her suitcase and zither, Trudel feels the two-day return trek has gone by quicker this time. Her mother runs up and greets her, practically suffocating her with her Austrian bear hug. Trudel and Ingrid embrace and say their final farewells to each other. They vow to visit as often as they can.

Only after returning to the family home in Kleinzell, does Trudel hear about the fate of her older brothers. Josefa received a letter saying her sons Emmerich is missing in Kiev, Ukraine and Hans is missing in Stalingrad, Russia.

To cope with her sadness, Trudel studies to become a medical assistant and receives her health service papers and insignia, a red life rune on a white oval cloth with a red and white surround. Trudel will proudly wear her badge on the lower left sleeve of her BDM jacket.[1]

Six months later, Trudel's sister, Anita, writes to inform her that a server position has become available in the prestigious Black Eagle Hotel restaurant in Mariazell where she is working. Situated in the picturesque Salza Valley, Mariazell is the most important pilgrimage site in Austria. Trudel writes back and informs her that she will gladly accept the position and will be arriving shortly. For the next three years, Trudel and her sister work as servers in the restaurant, along with her new best friend, Hedwig (Hedi) Kraushofer.

---

[1] Bund Deutscher Mädel - Gesundheitsdienst-Mädel

Trudel in Salzburg with the Salzkammergut Mountains behind her

Remembering Your Mama

HEDI TAPED HER MEMOIRS for prosperity. Speaking in her heavy Austrian dialect, she fondly remembers Trudel. Just before Hedi passes away, she gives the tape to Trudel's daughter, Cynthia.

"I remember the first time I met your mama. It was in 1942 and we were both fifteen years old. We both came to Mariazell and worked in that big hotel. We were so scared when we first arrived because we did not know which way to go or what to do. Trudel had her sister there, Anita. She was already working there so that helped. We worked there for three years and we had a good time. We became the closest of friends. We roomed together, we worked together, and we were together on our day off. We worked very long hours, six days a week, and we worked very hard, from early in the morning until very late at night. Sometimes, we were so tired at night that our feet ached from working the whole day. Sometimes, we had over five-hundred people to serve. All the tourists came from all over the world.

"We usually had off on Tuesdays because we had to work all weekend. When we had our day off, we would usually have so much work to do. We had to wash our clothes, polish our shoes, clean our rooms, and stitch our clothing. Sometimes, we would go down to the lake, and we rented a boat, and me, and Trudel, we would just go out there, and we would sit in the boat all afternoon and talk. We just talked about all kinds of things, like how we were going to get married. I would have a daughter, she was going to have a son, and our children will get married. You know, just like how young girls talk," she chuckles.

"We worked there for three years, and the war was getting worse. Before they closed down that great big hotel, they brought in a whole bunch of college students from farther up in Austria. We had to just help work and serve them dinner. After they left, the German SS came in and took over our hotel. We were so scared.

"I remember one night, they were just trying to … nearly … they just wanted us to come into their rooms and we were just scared to death! So, Trudy and I decided that we were going to run away and we were going to leave the hotel that night. Anita stayed behind. She could not come with us because she was leaving for Bamberg and her new position as an Air Force Female Helper working in radio communications.[1]

"I remember that day very well. It was the night of April 13, 1945. Very early in the morning, about five o'clock, we packed our little bags and we walked up on the road and hitchhiked all the way back to my hometown, in Annaberg. By

---

[1] Luftwaffenhelferinnen

the time we got a ride on that big old army truck, a bunch of refugees was sitting in the back. They were leaving because the war was getting closer. We had to change rides twice and we got another ride on another big old army truck. Nevertheless, we made it to my house, and Mama...well, my mother... she didn't know what to think when all of a sudden here comes the both of us! She was just so happy to see us! Trudy stayed with me for three days and then she hitchhiked back to her hometown in Kleinzell.

"I tell you, by that time, the war was getting closer. The Russians were coming closer. We heard they made their way into Vienna. Every day, there was shooting and bombings. It was so bad.

"One day, I received a letter from Trudel and she said that she and her brother, Franzel, were going to come and see me. They walked the thirty miles from Kleinzell to Annaberg, where I lived. They were so hungry because they had no food. I still had a little garden, vegetables, and potatoes. Mama said to tell them to come in, fill up their little bag with food. They stayed for a few days.

"I decided I was going back with them to their house. I remember it so clearly. We started walking at six o'clock in the morning and we did not get to Kleinzell until seven o'clock that evening! It was such a terrible, long walk. Our feet had blisters and we could not even walk anymore. Trudy's mother was so happy to see us. Then, I got sick and had to stay in Kleinzell for about two weeks. Once I was better, they walked me halfway home and then I walked home the rest of the way by myself.

"I didn't hear anything from Trudy until six months later when I received a letter from her. She told me that she made her way into Linz with her mama but her brother, Franzel, who was in the Hitler Youth at that time had to stay behind and fight the Russians. She asked me if I wanted to come up there because she had a job waiting for me.

"I wrote her back and told her I would be there as soon as I got all my papers in order. A couple of weeks later, I was able to leave the Russian section and cross the border. I finally made it to Linz. The job she had for me was right down the street from where she worked in her restaurant. It was like old times again! We worked together, we roomed together, and I was so happy to be away from the Russian sector and in the American sector. It was 1946, and that was when Trudy met your daddy, Robert. I met his friend, Willis. The two of them were serving in the U.S. Army. We started going out on dates together."[2]

---

[2] Hedwig Kraushofer-McLeod

Baptism of Fire

After completing his training at Camp McCain in Grenada, Mississippi, Private First Class Robert Sandor of the 87th Infantry Division, nicknamed the "Golden Acorn," embarks on the troopship Queen Elizabeth bound for Europe. Piloted by Captain Bisset, the 11,891 men and 1,061 crew are crowded, but not uncomfortable, for there is no double loading.[1]

The ship is divided into three zones: red, white and blue. Each man is issued with a color label indicating the zone in which he will berth. He is required to wear it throughout the voyage and for him any other zones are strictly out of bounds.[2]

Pulling from the pier at 0630, October 17, 1944, the Queen sails from New York Harbor and points her bow towards the distant horizon. The sea is calm, the weather is clear, and the trip is uneventful. No one knows when the vessel alters her course to avoid a reported enemy submarine; however, many comment on the fact that the ship is unescorted.

Shortly after dawn on the fifth day, the cry "Land Ho!" is heard. All who can rush to a vantage point views what proves to be the southern tip of the Emerald Isle - Ireland. The day is bright and clear as the Queen plows northward through the Irish Sea. Field glasses do triple duty as the young soldiers try to catch a glimpse of a land of which they have heard much, but know little.

Early that evening the anchor drops in the Clyde River, midway between Gourock and Greenrock, Scotland. With the ship having already been blacked out, no sight-seeing is possible, but many a porthole opens quietly in darkened cabins to reveal lights flickering on the shoreline.

Dawn reveals a harbor jammed with fighting crafts of every description including aircraft carriers, sleek destroyers, submarines, freighters, battleships, and transports. Puffing lighters swarm about the Queen and the business of unloading almost twelve-thousand men and their equipment is soon underway.

Twenty-year old PFC Robert Sandor from Glenville, CT, is serving in the 345th Infantry Regiment, Headquarter Company, First Battalion. His division is attached to General George Patton's Third Army. He sets foot on foreign soil in Greenock, Scotland. With his fellow soldiers, they board the English trains. With coffee and doughnut in hand, given to him by a beautiful brunette from the omnipresent American Red Cross, he begins his foreign duties. It is a new and exciting experience for him.

---

[1] WWII Troop Ships
[2] Alan Chanter

Traveling by day, the men have the opportunity to view parts of Scotland and England. Their journey's end finds the Regiment scattered over a twenty square mile area in England's Midlands – the famous pottery area surrounding Stoke-on-Trent. Regimental Headquarters, Service Company, and the First Battalion set-up in the village of Biddulph. Equipment is unloaded, uncrated and checked.

From Oct 23rd until November 30th, Biddulph is their home away from home. New equipment is received and military activity is confined to combat preparations of weapons and physical conditioning. They march over the surrounding countryside, study German from their phrase book, familiarize themselves with the German weapons being used, and identify enemy aircraft. These are the primary tasks and subjects of the Golden Acorn.

The 345th patiently wait for their marching orders as the Special Services and the local Red Cross establishments provided dances, moving pictures, and concerts by the Regimental Dance Band. Some men tour the nearby points of interest. A Post Exchange is in operation within each Battalion, and the local shops are rushing out souvenirs. The local "Pubs" introduce the new American soldiers to warm beer and ale and a few fortunate men draw three day passes to London; while others visit Liverpool, Glasgow, and Edenborough.

With a holiday atmosphere prevailing, Thanksgiving dinner is served at midday, November 23, 1944, turkey with all the trimmings. When movement orders are received that evening, the Regiments' race into action and prepare to take its leave of England.

Entraining all during the night of the 25th and the following morning finds the 345th marching through the streets of Southampton, enroute to the docks. The welcoming Red Cross Club-mobile is on hand at the pier to serve hot coffee and doughnuts to the servicemen as they wait to board. The men board either of the two Landing Ships, the Empire Lance or the Invictus. Soon the vessels pull into the harbor and wait until dark before putting out across the English Channel. Late that evening the vessels arrive off LeHavre Harbor in France and anchor for the night. The next morning, the ships move inside the breakwater and the troops disembark onto the Landing Craft Infantry where they are ferried to shore.

Motor convoys await to carry the regiments to a bivouac area. PFC Sandor disembarks in his heavy combat gear and with his battalion proceeds directly to an apple orchard near Rouen in the Red Horse Assembly Area of the European Theatre of Operation Communications Zone. A fine rain starts falling and the soldiers are cold, tired, and hungry. Sandor takes the first watch for the night as his buddy's construct makeshift tents to protect them from the elements.

The following day, trucks arrive and transport the men to an apple orchard in St. Saens, France. Rain, cold temperatures, fog and mud combined to make Sandor's life miserable. Little could be done to relieve his monotony. When a dry spot can be found, he writes a letter to his mother. When the rain stops falling, he joins his buddies in song and old fashioned gab sessions around the camp fire. Conversations switch between pin-up girls to advice on how to clean their rifles.

PFC Sandor and his regiment are becoming impatient for action. They have trained hard at Camp McCain and waited a long time to reach the battle zone. They had demonstrated by their late training in the States that they are a well-organized, smooth functioning team. They are ready to translate "Invictus" their Regimental motto, into a reality by proving themselves to be unconquerable.

On December 4, 1944, movement orders arrive and Sandor's division board the 40 & 8 French railway cars towards Metz. Pulling in under the very eyes of the Germans on the surrounding hills, kitchens are set up, and plans are made to receive the balance of the Regiment the next day.

By December 6th, Companies A and B along with the 345th Infantry relieve Companies E and F of the Second Infantry and takes a defensive position surrounding Fort de Plappeville outside of Metz. Heavy fighting starts five miles south-west. Sandor watches lightening-like flashes silhouetting the hills around Ft. Driant, followed by the dull roars of artillery. There is no front line for the division has drawn up in a complete circle surrounding Metz. The heavy firing continues as the 87th Infantry Division fights onward to secure their location.

The first of the main enemy forts to capitulate is Ft. St. Quentin, followed by Ft. Plappeville on the 7th, and Ft. Driant on the 8th. The forth and most powerful, Ft. Jeanne D'Arc, remains under the control of the Axis. Fighting mostly at night, intermittent artillery barrages are answered only by German small arms fire. The 345th patrols the area looking for Germans seeking to escape rather than surrendering to the Americans. By 0300 the next morning, the infantry moves towards Ft. Jeanne D'Arc. Two Germans from the fort successfully pass through the Second Battalion's line, walk up to the guards at the Regimental Command Post and surrender unconditionally.

Incessant bombardment of the enemy at Ft. Jeanne D'Arc commences as the 334th Field Artillery Battalion, a part of the 345th Combat Team, moves into position near the Regiment's own Cannon Company. By December 10th, massive mortars of the battalion join in and the barrage continues until the 26th Division's 101 Infantry Regiment arrives to relieve the 345th on the 12th.

Such is the baptism of fire for the 345th Infantry Regiment, the first unit of the 87th Division to actively engage the enemy. Fort Jeanne D'Arc surrenders several days after the Regiment departs from Longeville lés Metz and the historic Battle of Metz becomes history.

Heavy fighting continues as the men dig in at Gross Rederching near the Saar-German border capturing Rimling, Obergailbach, and Guiderkirch. The 345th secures the first German community in Medelsheim, Germany, a village nestled in the valley just south of the front line. On December 23rd, orders are received that the 44th Infantry Division will relieve the 345th and that they will move, by motor to Cutting, France, some forty miles to the rear.

On Christmas Eve, barns and homes provide a degree of warmth and comfort for the men. Mail from home is distributed during the night and a fortunate few receive Christmas packages on time.

It is a bright, clear, and crisp day on Christmas. The aroma of a turkey dinner waffles in the air as the cooks and bakers work most of the night to make sure their feast will be ready by midday. The soldiers agree that there is a Santa for the cold dampness of the fox-holes are forgotten and the holiday atmosphere prevails. That is until the big Army cargo trucks begin arriving and move the Regiment once again. Still in high spirits, officers and men alike, fall to with a "will" to get on with the grim business of war, on the day commemorating "Peace on Earth – Good Will toward men."

PFC Sandor remembers his first war-time Christmas night for he and the entire division are on the road – their destination unknown. The temperature drops to new lows and everyone is concerned with how they are going to keep warm on their tortuous two-hundred mile move.

All night long, the convoy winds its way through the dark roads of France, avoiding all large towns, traveling on the back roads, avoiding the Autobahn.[3]

On December 16th, 1944, German Field Marshal Von Rundstedt launches his offensive in the Ardennes forest and the 87th in thrown into battle. Amid grueling sub-zero temperatures and weather conditions, the 87th throws back massive German attacks and fights on to link up with the U.S. First Army, lifting the siege in Bastogne, thereby playing a critical role in winning the Battle of the Bulge. The "Golden Acorn" of General Patton's Third Army seizes St. Hubert from enemy forces and preserves it intact for the benefit of the Belgian citizens. In a fluctuating battle, the 87th captures Moircy on December 30th, then Remagne on the 31st.

On January 2nd, the division takes Gérimont, by the 10th Tillet, and reach the Ourthe River on the 13th. By the 15th, they move into Luxembourg to relieve the 4th Infantry Division along the Sauer River, and by January 23, 1945, seize the town of Wasserbillig in Luxembourg. This area is now liberated.[4] By the 28th, the 87th races to the vicinity of St. Vith, Belgium. By the end of the month, they attacks and capture Schlierbach, Selz, and Hogden.

After the fall of Neuendorf, Germany on February 9th, the division goes on the defensive until the 26th when Ormont and Hallschlag are taken in a heavy night attack.

They cross the Kyll River in the Rhineland on March 6, take Dollendorf by the 8th and after a brief rest, return to combat on March 13th, crossing the Moselle by the 16th and clearing Koblenz by the 19th. Despite strong opposition, the division crosses the Rhine on the 26th, consolidates its bridgehead and secures Grossenlinden and Langgöns, Germany.

On April 7th, the division is still going strong as it jumps off in an attack that carries it though Thuringia into Saxony. Plauen falls on the 17th of April and the division takes up a defensive position on the 20th four miles away from the Czechoslovakia border.

---

[3] 87th Infantry Division pgs. 57 – 67
[4] Casey Camper

By May 6th, the 87th takes Falkenstein and maintains its position until Victory in Europe Day. [5]

From Metz to Plauen, across the German Saar border...Cracking the Siegfried Line...Spanning the Moselle River and on to Koblenz...Over the Rhine...Racing with savage fury through the heart of Nazi Germany to the Czechoslovakian border. That's the battle path of PFC Robert Sandor and the 87th Infantry Division during 154 days of action in the European Theater of Operations—154 days from December 6, 1944, when the 1st Battalion of the 345th Infantry Regiment, 87th Infantry Division moved in on Metz until May 8, 1945, when German Armies surrender unconditionally.[6]

Come July 1945, PFC Sandor disembarks from La Havre, France with the 345th and 347th Infantry Regiments and arrives in New York Harbor on the USS West Point (SS America) on the 11th. His mother, Emily is waiting for him at the docks. On the 14th, Sandor regroups with his infantry and together, they proceed to Ft. Benning, Georgia, to prepare for deployment to Japan.

On August 6, 1945, the first atomic bomb is dropped on Hiroshima. On August 9th, a second atomic bomb is dropped on Nagasaki. Then, on August 14, 1945, Japan surrenders unconditionally to the Allies, effectively ending World War II.

Wanting to do more for his country, Sandor reenlists in the United States Forces – Austria. Demobilizing from Ft. Devens, Massachusetts on November 13, 1945, Sandor's duty now is to protect the American side of the Nibelungen Bridge, in Linz, Austria, that serves as a Checkpoint Charlie from the eastern Russian zone. The Danube River becomes the demarcation line between the occupied territories of the Americans in Linz and the occupied territory of the Russians in Urfahr. Only those with personal documents are permitted to cross the bridge from one zone into the other.

[5] 87th Infantry Division pgs. 57 – 67
[6] Stalwart and Strong: The Story of the 87th Infantry Division

"You can do anything
You put your mind to doing"

~ Gertrude Kerschner ~

Post WWII - Linz, Austria

THE ATMOSPHERE IS ONE of noise, dust and work. The city is emerging from chaos. The wounds of war only makes the women stronger. Knowing that they survived gives them the strength to start over again. Trudel and her mother, Josefa, are ordered by the Allied Powers to participate in the postwar cleanup. For their laborious efforts, they receive a bowl of soup each every day from the American soldiers. Using their bare hands, their main job is to remove the bricks from fallen buildings. They are part of the chain of "Debris Women," who pass bricks out of the ruins into the streets where they are cleaned and stacked.[1] Wood and steel beams, fireplaces, washbasins, toilets, pipes, and other household items are collected, stacked, and reused. The women move the debris by wagons. They patch and fill the gaping holes in the streets. There are hundreds of women learning new masonry skills and working in all types of weather.

Trudel's sister, Anita, is captured by the Americans. Believing she is German, Anita is detained in a POW camp for women in Bamberg, Germany. She lives in constant fear for her life, in improvised conditions, sleeping outside in the mud, and only sustaining herself on rations enough to feed a mouse. To rid herself from lice, she stands in line with the other women and wait to be sprayed with DDT. Three months later, Anita proves to the Americans that she Austrian. It is only then that she is released and eventually reconnects with her family in Linz through the help of the International Red Cross.[2]

With post-war assistance from the Americans, Austria slowly rebuilds from the wreckage. The gradual normalization of life begins with the re-opening of a few businesses, the Linz radio station and the Upper Austrian postal system.

Taking a break from his checkpoint duties, Robert walks across the former Adolf Hitler Hauptplatz in Linz and into the St. Moritz Coffee Shop. He notices an empty chair in the back corner of the room. People stare as he walks in wearing his olive drab army uniform, carrying his M1903 Springfield standard issue infantry rifle strapped to his back. To them, he symbolizes the sovereignty of the Austrian people, because the United States Army proved itself ready to protect and rebuild their country. PFC Sandor leans his rifle against the wall in the corner of the room, pulls out a chair, and sits down.

Wearing her black server uniform, Trudel walks up to Robert and asks, "Was möchte Sie?"

"I cannot speak German," Robert replies.

---

[1] Trümmerfrauen
[2] Anita Leugner

Trudel is transfixed by his hazel eyes and warm smile. "Was you like to trink?" Trudel asks in her broken English.

"Coffee, light cream, and two sugars," Sandor replies. His hazel eyes gaze appreciatively upon her full body as she turns and walks away. A few moments later, she returns with his hot cup of coffee.

Robert and Trudel start dating. They spend time boating on the lake in Gmunden, hiking the mountains in Salzburg, and teaching each other their own native language. Over time, their relationship deepens. Robert transforms Trudel from a young server girl into a woman. For the first time in her life, Trudel is wearing mascara and eyeliner, rouge and lipstick. She dyes her black hair blond and wears her new two-piece business suit with nylon stockings Robert bought for her from the quartermaster house in Linz.

Trudel's brother, Franzel, and her sister, Anita, chaperon her everywhere while she is with Robert. They translate every word he says, even his marriage proposal.

On May 8, 1948, Robert is now a corporal. The Reverend Henry L. Durand, Chaplin, USA Army marry Robert and Trudel in the partially bombed out, twenty-thousand-seat Cathedral of the Immaculate Conception in Linz, officiated in the presence of Donald L. Smith and Heinrich Barth as witnesses.[3]

In 1950, the newlyweds move to the outskirts of Linz, in Langholzfeld to be near Trudel's sister and her young husband, Lorenz. Robert, who had served in the liberation of Austria, is now serving as a Corporal in the United States Forces Austria (USFA). He has since received his US Army Combat Infantryman Badge, Good Conduct Medal, World War II Victory Medal, and the European-African-Middle Eastern Campaign Medal, with two Battle Stars.

For the next six years, he is stationed in Linz where he works to rebuild the city's infrastructure. When the occupation of Austria ends in 1955, Robert and Trudel move to the picturesque town of Gmunden. Robert enjoys this time fishing for bass while Trudel enjoys this opportunity to sleep. In the afternoons, they take long walks up the Traunstein Mountain together with their little mutt named Max.

---

[3] Marriage Certificate of Robert and Gertrude Sandor

This Way to the United States

ON MAY 3, 1956, MR. AND MRS. SANDOR embark from the port of La Havre, France, on the luxury passenger liner the SS United States, bound for New York City. Trudel wears her black suit, high heels, and a full-length fox fur coat. Robert escorts his fine lady aboard wearing his suit and tie under his hand-loom herringbone overcoat. The matching hat and dark aviator Ray Ban sunglasses compliment his attire. In a wooden box, he carries their most valuable possession — a fine set of Austrian gold-rimmed crystal glasses. Near the gang-plank, the sign reads "This Way to the United States."

The couple makes their way to their cabin as Captain L. H. Alexanderson, U.S.N.R., prepares the ship for departure. The large brass whistle blows signaling their immediate departure. Robert and Gertrude stand by the railing and wave good-bye to the hundreds of people standing below. Everyone is in a jovial mood. Streamers fly and confetti falls. This great American Blue Riband record holder is setting sail to the new promised land of America, the land where dreams comes true. The mooring lines are cast, the massive brass whistle blows, and the fastest ship in the world begins her passage across the Atlantic. As the ship slowly pulls away from port, Robert and Gertrude kiss. The promise Gertrude had made to her dying father has finally come true.

Halfway through their journey the 53,330-ton, 990-foot-long ship runs head-long into a horrific Atlantic storm. The ship rocks through thirty-foot swells. Yet, even as wave after wave crashes over the bow, the captain holds his ship steady.

The next evening is smooth sailing. Robert and Gertrude attend the formal Gala Dinner. Dressed in their finest attire, they dine on smoked salmon, mush-room à la Française, and a chilled fresh cup of fruit Maraschino. Hors d'oeuvres consist of fried baby lobster tails in sauce rémoulade with coleslaw. The main dish is roast leg of South-Down lamb au jus with English mint sauce, corn on the cob, haricots verts from France, petits pois à la Française, Brussels sprouts, and the chef's salad with his special dressing. They finish their evening banquet with Vienna mocha layer cake, French ice cream, cheese (Stilton, Roquefort, or Brie) on toasted crackers.[1] Robert and Trudel enjoy the evening feast with the other passengers at their table. For the remainder of the night they are only one of two couples who dance in the grand ballroom. As the seas begin to settle, they stroll along the deck, and talk into the early morning hours.

Gertrude is determined to become a full American. After she was naturalized and received her full U.S. citizenship, she secured a job on the assembly line at

---

[1] SS United States Menu

Homelite in Norwalk, Ct. She saved all her money and with her husband, they purchased five acres of woodlands in the back woods of Greenwich, CT, right along the 14th hole of Tamarack Country Club.

In 1960, Robert purchases a dragline. Together with the help of his brothers and Trudel's co-workers from Homelite, part of the land is cleared and a two-acre lake is dug.

For the next four years, Robert and Gertrude build their new home.

On December 31, 1964, the Sandor family moves from their tiny apartment on Arthur St., in Pemberwick, into their beautiful new home. They ring in the New Year with their family and friends.

Gertrude is recognized in the community by her upbeat personality, her motherly affection, and her dedication to her family. During the winter months, Robert would take the kids outside and walk in the woods, skate on the pond, or ride the sleighs down the hills at the golf course. Trudel would make sure the fireplace is set and that there is plenty of hot coco to go around.

In the summer, family members, friends, and their children, would visit and spend hours fishing for bass or rainbow trout, boat, and swim in their lake. Every year, Robert and Gertrude would host the annual "Improved Order of Red Men – Mayn Mayano Tribe No. 46" BBQ and Clambake.

Trudel would share from her vegetable garden and tend to her many ducks, geese, chickens, Ginny hens, and two swans. On many occasions, her mother, Josefa, would come to America and visit the family. Josefa's universal duck call "Woolly, woolly, woolly, woolly, woolly," would become a familiar call heard and remembered the family members.

Many times, the family would drive along the scenic view of the Mohawk Trail on their way to Vermont and spend time with their children skiing.

On the holidays, Gertrude invited her elderly widowed friend, Edna Flynn, from Port Chester, NY, to enjoy a traditional turkey with all the trimming.

Gertrude is a devoted mother who continually encourages her children. She drove them to their piano lessons, recitals, Brownies, and Girl Scout meetings. Robert, her eldest, was a member of the Civil Air Patrol and took flying lessons. Many times, Cynthia and her mother would sit on the hood of their 1970 gold Oldsmobile station wagon and watch Robert's take offs and landings at the Westchester County Airport.

In the 1970's, Gertrude secured a position as a server in the cafeteria at American Can Company. Her outstanding work ethics were noticed by the CEO William May, who personally handled her promotion as Head Waitress in the Executive Dining Room. Within a year, Trudel was promoted again in the Head Server position for the Board of Directors. She exclusively served CEO May, his second in command, William Woodside, and Vice Chairman, Gerald Tsai, among others at all their private board meetings and party functions.

Trudel received final word from her mother that her two older brothers, Emmerich and Hans were officially M.I.A. in Russia. Their bodies were never found. She sends her mother an airline ticket and Josefa comes over to visit the family for an entire year.

Shortly after Josefa returns to Austria, Trudel receives a phone call that her mother was in a terrible accident. Josefa fell through the floor at the Bauer's family barn while she was stacking the hay. Trudel flies to Austria and spends the entire month at her mother's bedside. Reluctantly, she has to return home and go back to work.

On August 16, 1974, Trudel received a phone call from her sister, Anita, telling her that her mother had passed away. She flew back to Austria to attend the funeral.

Six months later, Trudel was diagnosed with breast cancer. She received chemotherapy and radiation treatments and thought she was healed until fifteen years later, the disease metastasized into bone cancer. Four months before Trudy's death, Cynthia, discovered her mother's personal journal from her time in Country Service Year Camp Seidorf. No longer afraid to tell her life story, Trudel spent her last moments sharing all of her personal memories from the time she was in the Bund Deutscher Mädel.

On the night of November 20, 1989, Trudel peacefully passes away at the Greenwich Hospital.

In January 1990, Cynthia flew her mother's cremated remains to Linz, Austria. Cynthia, along with the entire Kerschner family is accompanied by a 12-piece brass band. Over three hundred and fifty villagers pay their final respects to this remarkable woman. Trudel's ashes lay in the Kerschner family gravesite in Ob die Kirche, outside Kleinzell.

Robert passed away from stomach cancer on March 22, 1991.

In the summer of 1999, the Seidorf girls returned to visit their camp one last time. They are now in their mid-eighties. Steffi, Elli, and Maria live in Germany, and Nelly lives in Austria.

Trudel's sister Anita passed away on November 10, 2011, during the writing of this book. Trudel's brother Franzel died unexpectedly on July 20, 2013, from a massive heart attack while riding his bicycle. His death was a great loss within the Rohrbach and Kleinzell communities. His body was donated to the Vienna University for medical research.

Malgorzata Jackiewicz purchased Country Service Year Camp. It is open to the public as a bed and breakfast under the name Monte Cassino in Sosnówka, Poland.

Appendix A:

Brief History of the Hitler Youth

Much has been written about the Hitler Youth (HJ). Over the past decade, there has been a surge in demand for information about the girls' involvement within this organization called the Bund Deutscher Mädel (BDM) the League of German Girls.

The growth and success of the HJ and BDM organizations could not be appreciated without some reference to the history of the German Youth Movement. It started during the German Empire in 1896 for cultural and educational purposes. It consisted of numerous associations of young people, focusing on outdoor activities, including hiking and camping.

Young people of both sexes joined the youth communities, which later became known as the Young Hikers (Wandervogel). What had originally started out as a back-to-nature study group by grammar school teacher Herman Hoffmann Fölkersamb in 1895 would eventually evolve into the Hitler Youth, some twenty-seven years later.

On November 4, 1901, the non-political Young Hikers group was formerly established in Germany. These young boys were animated by their determination to express themselves, unfettered by the older generation. "They distinguished themselves by wearing shorts and hiking boots rather than the starched shirts and creased trousers of the middle class." They greeted each other with the religious salutation 'Heil.'" At that time, the greeting meant 'salvation' or 'to your soul's health.'[1]

The Young Hikers group was comprised of a few innocent, young boys from Steglizt (near Berlin), who longed for living a simpler life with nature as the focus of their group meetings. This was the birth of the "youth leading the youth."[2] Their activities included hiking, camping, evening meetings, lectures, and discussions. Much emphasis was placed on rediscovering and singing traditional German folk songs to reawaken the boys' pride in their heritage and traditions. The initial ethos was to shake off the restrictions, both society and parental, and to bond instead with nature and the land.

---

[1] Holocaust Education
[2] David Littlejohn, p.4

At a youth rally in 1913, the group made a proclamation called the Meissner Formula. This declaration defined their general policy of their inner freedom. It was a reaction against the complacency and restrictions of German middle-class life, with its prejudices and bourgeois mindset.

After the end of World War I the youth movement developed at an accelerated pace. Most prominent was the League of Youth, which partially replaced the original German Youth Movement.

Around the same time, the National Socialist German Workers' Party (NSDAP) formed their own youth organization that remained small until the late 1920's.[3]

On March 8, 1922, Adolf Hitler, not yet Chancellor of Germany, was gaining control of the fledgling NSDAP.[4] He announced in his own newspaper "The Folkish Observers," the establishment of the Youth League of the National Socialist German Workers' Party, which later became known as the 'Youth Storm Troop Adolf Hitler.'

In 1923, prior to Hitler's reign, a non-national, socialistic, pro-monarchic women's organization entitled Queen Louise League had been established. These sophisticated women strongly opposed democracy, welcomed German re-armament, and demanded the return of the former German colonies surrendered by the Treaty of Versailles. The Queen Louise League was modeled on the values and virtues of the former Queen of Prussia, Louise of Mecklenburg-Strelitz. The female members of this group idealized the Queen's feminine virtues, emulating her determination and her love for her country.[5] Memberships fell into three categories: one for women, one for adolescent girls, and one for the children.

In May of 1925, the Hiking Club-Vogtland, in Plauen, Saxony, merged with the Munich Youth League and became known as the Hitler Youth (HJ). The notorious anti-Semite Julius Streicher, then the NSDAP chieftain of Franconia and a close associate of Hitler, coined the term the "Hitler Youth." Hitler appointed him to the Party District Executive position of the Bavarian region. Streicher wielded immense Nazi propaganda power through his newspaper, "The Attacker" in which disparaging articles written demanded the extermination of the Jewish race. This newspaper was banned from the educational programs of the HJ.

In 1926, the first National Youth Leader of the HJ was Kurt Gruber. Gruber held this position until 1929 when Theodor Adrian von Renteln replaced him.

Although the HJ had borrowed much of its technique and some of its symbols from the old German Youth Movement, it added a nationalistic and decidedly militaristic note. In 1925, it became a junior branch of the Stormtroopers known as the Brownshirts. They were directly subordinate to the SA High Com-

---

[3] Nazi Party - History
[4] Dennis Weidner
[5] Queen Louise League

mand under the guidance of the young Hans Ulrich Klintzsch. This was the beginning of "the youth leading the youth" in the HJ. The movement, in its true fashion, was opposed to school, church, and home. This attracted many followers.

In 1928, some six hundred boys gathered at the first national HJ rally at Bad Steben, in Bavaria. The following year, the first Nuremberg Party Rally was held and over twenty-five hundred boys were present. In December the National Youth Leader, Kurt Gruber, held a meeting with the regional leaders of the HJ and agreed to set up a division called the "Sisterhood of the Hitler Youth" where fourteen-year-old girls could join and become members.[6]

In 1929, the National Socialist Schoolchildren's League was formed by Theodor Adrian von Renteln and was recognized as an official affiliate of the Hitler Youth Organization.[7] This organization unified the scattered remaining youth groups under one authority. Von Renteln would remain a Youth Leader until June 1932. He led the Combat League of the Commercial Middle Class and spearheaded the boycott of Jewish businesses.[8]

In July 1929, the public launching of the 'Sisterhood of the Hitler Youth' took place. Sixty-seven girls joined.[9]

By 1930, the HJ had nine hundred local groups in Germany. At the same time, the Sisterhood of the HJ was given the formal title of the 'League of German Girls in the Hitler Youth' (BDM – Bund Deutscher Mädel).

By April 1931, two new groups were established for the boys and girls ages ten to fourteen. These new groups were called the 'German Young Folk' (Deutsches Jungvolk DJ) for the boys and the 'Young Girls' League' (Jungmädelbund - JM), for the girls. By this time, total membership into the HJ had expanded to over fifteen thousand young people.

In May 1931, the Reich Youth Leadership "officially inaugurated the HJ Group Austria into their organization.[10] Even though Austria would not become a part of Germany until the Anschluss in 1938, members were given the privilege of wearing the same uniform as their counterparts in the Reich. It would not be long before the Austrian government would outlaw all existence of the HJ within its borders. Completely disappearing from public view, the group would eventually "re-emerge under a different guise," which was "merely covers for the pro-Nazi operations, operating under secret cells."[11]

Fueled by the Potsdam Rally in March 1932, membership in the HJ swelled to over one-hundred thousand youths.[12] Approximately 5,184 members were in the League of German Girls Proper (BDM), while 750 young girls belonged to

---

[6] David Littlejohn, p. 177
[7] Xufanc, "NSS"
[8] Adrian von Reteln
[9] David Littlejohn, p. 177
[10] David Littlejohn, p. 290
[11] Ibid, p. 291
[12] The History Place – Hitler Youth – Demise of Democracy

the League of Young Girls (JM). Elisabeth Greiff-Walden was appointed to the position of national leader of the BDM/JM with the title, Referent for Girls Matters in the National Leadership of the HJ.[13] By the fall of the same year, over fifteen-thousand additional girls became members. Though it had fewer members than the Hitler Youth, the league was marked by a growing attraction for female youths, since it appeared to satisfy certain needs of an ever larger number of adolescent girls."[14]

On January 30, 1933, Adolf Hitler became chancellor of Germany. This was a single-party dictatorship based on the totalitarian and autocratic ideology of National Socialism.

On May 20, 1933, the National Socialist Schoolchildren's League (NSS) officially merged with the HJ. This day was marked with a tremendous youth group celebration with Baldur von Schirach replacing Adrian von Renteln as the Hitler Youth Leader. Despite the fact that the Republican government temporarily banned the HJ, its ranks continued to swell under the leadership of Baldur von Schirach. Shortly thereafter, the Catholic and Left Wing Youth Movements were crushed and forcefully disbanded.

The Queen Louise League was dissolved and its members were integrated into the corresponding League of German Girls (BDM), and the National Socialists Schoolchildren's League (NSS).

On March 23, 1933, Germany's Reichstag passed the Enabling Act. With the stroke of a pen, President Paul von Hindenburg legally gave Adolf Hitler plenary powers to establish his new dictatorship.

On August 2, 1934, President Paul von Hindenburg died and Adolf Hitler became absolute dictator of Germany under the title of Der Führer.

The HJ was now complete and by December 1, 1934, the HJ was declared a Government sponsored Youth Organization having grown to over six million youths. These groups comprised of the Hitler Youth Proper (HJ), the German Youth (DJ), the League of German Girls (BDM), and the Young Girls League (JM).

The Decree of December 1, 1936, providing for Compulsory Youth Service not only legalized the existence of the HJ, but also destroyed the remaining youth organizations in Germany. Now, all children became the property of the state under the decree that contained three major points:

1. All German youth shall join the HJ.
2. The mission of the HJ is to train all German youths physically, mentally, and morally for national service in the spirit of National Socialism. School and home are subordinate to the interests of the State.
3. The Reich's Youth Leader is entrusted with all phases of the education of German youths and is responsible only to the Führer.

---

[13] Landjahralbum – The BDM before 1933
[14] Dagmar Reece, p. 31 - 32

The NSDAP gained an enormous influence over the youths. It will be their goal to educate them in Nazi ideology and prepare them for adulthood. The youths would become active members of society, at all times protecting and defending their country.

Once completed, the Hitler-Youth was finally organized into four main branches.

1. Hitler-Jugend Proper (HJ)—for boys ages 14–18
2. Deutsches Jungvolk (DJ)—for boys ages 10–14 who subsequently transferred into the HJ Proper
3. Bund Deutscher Mädel Proper (BDM)—for girls ages 14–18
4. Jungmädelbund (JM)—for girls ages 10–14 who subsequently transferred into the BDM Proper

The terms HJ and BDM are used loosely, and require a special note: strictly speaking, HJ refers to (1) and (3) above. In practice, however, HJ is widely used to cover both (1) and (2), and BDM is used to cover both (3) and (4). Further, the term HJ is used in a third sense, to indicate the entire Youth Movement (1)–(4).

On March 12, 1938, 98% of Austrians voted for annexation with Germany. Austria became Ostmark. It was reorganized into a National District before being divided into seven provinces under the administration of the NSDAP. This temporary reorganization was an attempt to resolve administrative disputes resulting from the overlapping jurisdictions and different boundaries in former Austria.[15] From here, the German Empire would increase from thirty-five to forty-two districts. Every child from the age of ten had to register and become a member of the HJ and BDM respectfully. Previously banned NSDAP organizations included some thirty-eight thousand underground secret Hitler Youths that reorganized and went back to wearing their uniforms.[16]

By 1939, the Hitler Youth was extensive and highly organized into forty-two districts on the national, regional, and local levels, which were overseen by the executive, administrative, and departmental branches.

The boys' DJ and HJ Proper divisions were divided into regiments, tribes, companies, platoons, comradeships, and files."[17]

The BDM paralleled the boys' organizational structure. It was divided into regions, districts, lower-districts, townships, regional groupings, troops, and dens.[18]

The National Youth Directorate (RJF) oversaw the command structure and controlled the policy as well as the administration of the entire HJ. The RJF was headed by the National Youth Leader and assisted by an Adjutant and a Chief

---

[15] Anschluss
[16] David Littlejohn, p. 293
[17] The Hitler Jugend
[18] Bund Deutscher Mädel - "Unit Structure"

of Staff. The National Women's Youth Leader controlled the JM and the BDM. She was directly responsible to the Reich Youth Leader of the NSDAP.[19]

Trude Mohr, a former postal worker, replaced Elisabeth Grieff-Walden as the Reich's Deputy of the BDM. Mohr resigned her position in 1937 when she married. She was replaced by twenty-seven-year-old Dr. Jutta Rüdiger, a personal acquaintance of Baldur von Schirach. Rüdiger reported directly to Schirach and Schirach reported to Adolf Hitler.

As a doctor of psychology from Düsseldorf, Rüdiger was more assertive. She resisted the efforts made by Gertrud Scholtz-Klink, the fervent head of the National Socialist Women's League, to gain control over the BDM. Klink was a good orator and her primary task was to promote male supremacy and the importance of rearing children. In one speech, Klink said that "the main mission of a woman is to minister in the home and in her profession to the needs of the life from the first to the last moment of a man's existence."[20]

The task of the BDM was to educate girls for companionship, honor, and faith. They were to be made conscious of their duty as German girls, to become good housewives, and to have as many children as possible.

The success of the girls' division of the HJ did not go without opposition from Gertrud Scholtz-Klink, who wanted absolute control over the BDM, but this never happened.

The subsection, Faith and Beauty Society was founded in 1938. The organization served as a tie-in between the BDM and the National Socialists Women's League, the women's wing of the NSDAP. Membership was voluntary and open to girls seventeen to twenty-one years old. The general idea was that girls should take part in working for the German community before they entered into the workforce or married and had children. Members of the League of German Girls' could not join the NSDAP until they reached eighteen years of age. [21]

In January 1938, Clementine zu Castell-Rüdenhausen, a countess and a member of the Franconian aristocracy, was the first woman appointed to lead the Faith and Beauty Society. Rüdenhausen was discharged when she married in 1939. Shortly before her twenty-second birthday, Austrian-born Annemarie Kaspar was appointed head of the Faith and Beauty Society. She was discharged when she married in 1941. In June 1941, Martha Middendorf replaced Kaspar who was discharged because she too married. In February 1942, Dr. Jutta Rüdiger took over and headed the organization along with leading the BDM until 1945.[22]

---

[19] The Hitler Jugend
[20] Gertrude Scholtz-Klink
[21] Chris Crawford
[22] League of German Girls

Appendix B:

The Landjahr Lager Program

Prior to entering into the BDM Proper, the Reich's Ministry of Science, Education, and Culture, specifically chose adolescent girls from the BDM to serve in the elite rural educational program called County Service Year Camp (Landjahr Lager).This was an eight-month long training program located in a rural environment far away from the family. This program was not the same as the mandatory Landdienst program, which involved four years of training in all phases of agriculture, part of which was conducted on a Model Training Farm.[1]

Landjahr grew out from much smaller programs that would eventually merge with the HJ.

Initiated in 1924, Landjahr was originally founded by Hals Holfeder as the Guardian of the Country.[2] The need arose when German nationalists called for the introduction of a general compulsory labor service because the majority of German youths were moving into the cities. This was affecting the ethnic composition in this region. To "fill the vacuum left by departing Germans, Slav workers had begun to move onto the farms and great estates."[3] It was feared that these migrant workers would become permanent settlers and turn the borderland of the German "Grenzland" into an extension of Poland, something that would not be tolerated by the German people. The Guardians of the Country was therefore created to oppose any encroachment upon their Germanic lands.

At the end of 1923 and into the beginning of 1924, notices were published in various publications calling for young German volunteers to take over the tasks assigned to the Polish agricultural workers. The benefits for the adolescents were twofold: first, it gave the young workers the opportunity to escape the fateful urbanization of city life, and secondly, it reduced the colonization of the Polish land in the east by the Slav workers.[4]

Holfeder's program was an effort to maintain the German population and economic stability of agriculture in East Prussia. Large German landowners had

---

[1] The Hitler Jugend p 3 - 11
[2] Dennis Weidner – Hitler Youth Activities: Landjahr
[3] David Littlejohn, p. 102-103
[4] Artamanen

regularly used seasonal agricultural workers from Poland to work on their land. This labor service sought to recruit youthful German volunteers who could give agriculture assistance in eastern Silesia and Saxony. Under the circumstance, the Guardians of the Country were but a small undertaking. It had little impact on the underlying demographic trends.[5] However, the movement grew and by the end of 1924, there were fourteen camps.[6]

The founding members of the Guardian of the Country were from various young people's leagues that included the Young Hikers together with the Catholic Quickborns, the Young German Order, and activists such as the Defense Association. Their intent was to lay down a new community using agricultural labor. Their movement became so strong in the eastern provinces that a well-structured organization evolved. It became very active in the eastern provinces of the Reich, especially in the Central and East.[7]

In April 1924, this first grassroots organization of urban youths started working the land. They established permanent communities within the region. Small groups of four to twenty people lived and worked together. They spent all their free time adventuring in the countryside. In the evening, they organized community discussions and sang traditional German folk songs. Their purpose was to contribute to the revitalization of rural culture and traditions.[8]

By 1926, the Guardians of the Country negotiated contracts with the local authorities and the owners of these large farms. By the time the negotiations were completed, over 2,300 Guardians were volunteering on 270 farms within the region. By 1938, there were over 1,452 camps with more than eighteen-thousand male members.[9]

At the height of its development, numerous conflicts arose and tore the foundation out from under the community. Instead of purchasing local farms as the members desired, the Guardians joined the NSDAP.

The main proponent of this absorption was Heinrich Himmler, who was for a brief moment a Guardian himself. Friedrich Schmidt, a member of the Dresden section of the NSDAP, then replaced the original founder Hals Holfeder.[10]

Shortly thereafter, the Guardians of the Country dismissed more than half of its staff. A new league was born, called the Guardian of the County League and Community Land for Labor Settlement. They adopted the Blood and Soil ideology and placed a high value on the virtues of rural living.[11]

By 1934, the Artamis-Bund was faced with insurmountable financial difficulties. It was completely absorbed into the Rural Service of the Hitler Youth.[12]

---

[5] David Weidner – Hitler Youth Activities: Landjahr
[6] Ibid
[7] Artamanen
[8] Ibid
[9] Ibid
[10] David Littlejohn, p. 103
[11] Ibid
[12] Artamanen

Since within the NSDAP party there was considerable support for the key concerns of the Guardians of the Country, they decided not only to continue the program, but also to expand it.

Gustrow in Mecklenburg was the first settlement and was transformed into Country Service of the Hitler Youth (Landdienst der Hitler Jugend). This new branch of the Hitler Youth aimed at sending urban lads for one year to a farm. This, it was hoped, would imbue them with a love of the land and, ideally, induce them to opt for it as a permanent way of life. At this time, Landjahr was not restricted to only Hitler Youth members. Other young men, if they wished, could participate. With the gradual absorption of almost the entire youth of Germany into the Hitler Youth, this provision later became meaningless.

Gustrow was formally dedicated to the Hitler Youth, becoming the very first Hitler Youth County Service Program. Adolf Hitler himself attended the celebrations in victorious splendor.[13] Landjahr Lager was born.

By the end of its first year of existence, the Landdienst had forty-five groups with a total of some 500 young men. The following year, 1935, this had risen to 240 groups with over 3,500 members. BDM girls were now included into the service. Expansion of the groups was rapid:

462 groups in 1936 (with 6,608 members)
1,175 groups in 1937 (with 14,888 members)
1,452 groups in 1938 (with 18,000 members)

By September 1939, Germany, the Soviet Union, and a small Slovak contingent invaded Poland. World War Two had begun. Country Service Year Camp expanded to over twenty-six thousand girls. It was under the direction of the Reich's Minister for Science, Education, and Culture and had to have the written permission of their parents to participate. They had to submit to a medical examination to assess their fitness for work, which amounted to between fifty-four and sixty-hours per week. These carefully chosen, responsible girls had to be physically fit, in good character, and ready to serve the German people at any moment. They left their home and family for a period of up to nine months (depending upon the location). They traveled to rural locations where they were taught life-building skills that would make them productive members of society when they reached adulthood at the age of seventeen.[14] In Country Service Year Camps were places of strict physical, intellectual, and moral education. Therefore, only those boys and girls chosen for Country Service Year, who had proven in school and in their Hitler Youth service that they possess the dependable character, the intellectual abilities, and the physical abilities to withstand the rigors of camp life, could attend. Country Service was similar to a finishing school.

---

[13] David Littlejohn, p. 103
[14] Ibid, p. 104

The educational plan of the Country Service year for girls included:

- Physical education: gymnastics, athletics, calisthenics, swimming, games, and dance.
- Medical service
- Musical education: singing, music theory, theatre
- National political education
- Practical and pre-professional education: kitchen work, housework, laundry, sewing and mending, childcare, gardening, farm work, and home economics.

The normal six-day workweek started at six o'clock in the morning and ended at nine o'clock in the evening.

Each group consisted of an average of sixty girls. The larger Host Country Service Year Camp had one-hundred girls.

By 1940, there were 1,753 camps totaling over 105,000 members. Each camp was under the direction of the Rural Service Sergeant who was directly responsible to the Hitler Youth Colonel or the BDM Lower District Leader.[15] Their symbol was an Odal rune pierced through the middle by a sword. The green and white triangular patch with the inscription "Landjahr" was worn on their left sleeve. Conscription into Landjahr was a great honor and privilege.[16]

---

[15] David Littlejohn, p. 103
[16] Franz Kerschner

Characters in Order of Appearance

Part I – Preparing to Become a Hitler Youth

Gertrude (Trudel) Kerschner – protagonist - 1927 – 1989
Anita (Anna) Kerschner – Trudel's sister – 1925 – 2011
Emmerich Kerschner – Gertrude's father - 1900 – 1931
Josefa Kerschner – Gertrude's mother - 1900 – 1972
Hans (Johann) Kerschner – Gertrude's older brother – 1922 - ?
Emmerich Kerschner – Gertrude's older brother – 1924 - ?
Franz Kerschner – Gertrude's younger brother – 1929 – 2013
Fräulein Dieter – Country Service Year Camp Troop Leader
Fräulein Albrecht – Country Service Year Camp – Camp Leader
Fräulein Grüber – Country Service Year Camp – Economic & Assistant Leader
Fräulein Erika Baron von Schmidt – Young Girls League Den Leader
Dr. Herbermeyer – Young Girls League Doctor
Frau Bauer – neighbor in Kleinzell

Girls in Trudel's Young Girl League
Gretchen Ackerman
Margarita Bauer
Gretel Fuchs
Hanni Gotlieb
Maria Klein
Erika Koch
Mitzi Rotheneder
Helga Schreiber
Irma Schumacher
Fräulein Brückner – Assistant Den Leader & Sports Instructor
Father Strobel – Kleinzell Parish Priest
Johanna "Hanni" Hinterleitner – Reisalpen Dairy Maid

Part II – Becoming a Member of the Hitler Youth

Herr Kunze – the Mayor of Kleinzell
Herr Adler – German Youth Den Leader
Herr Wulf – Hitler Youth Squad Leader

Characters in Order of Appearance

Part III – Country Service Year Camp

Ingrid Eberhart – Girl on Train/Gertrude's roommate
Barbara Achen
Herminie Azlsdorfer
Gabriele Bürgermeister
Elfie Fasser
Erika Hödlmaier
Sabine Jungmeier
Lotte Kirsch
Eleanor Mohler
Steffi Pucks – Gertrude's Roommate
Eleanor "Nelly" Mohler – Gertrude's Roommate
Maria Mikolasz – Gertrude's Roommate
Ellie Musial – Gertrude's Roommate
Anna
Kirsten
Liesel
Renate
Charlotte
Katarina
Aloise
Frau Else Torge – farmer's wife
Herr Bernhard Torge – farmer
Mayor Werner Blasius – Mayor of Hirschberg
Anna – little girl at puppet play
Marta – City girl from Upper Silesia
Magdalena – City girl from Upper Silesia
Sylvia – City girl from Upper Silesia
Dorota – City girl from Upper Silesia
Helli – City girl from Upper Silesia
Heidi – collection girl at Theatre
Frau Holle – Local weaver in Bad Wurzelsdorf

BIBLIOGRAPHY

"87th Infantry Division" © 1946 By Special Troops – 87th Infantry Division – Army & Navy Publishing Company, Baton Rouge, Louisiana

Adler, Horst. "Schweidnitz im Jahre 1937—Materialien zu einer Stadtgeschichte."http://www.horst-adler.de/Schweidnitz%20 1937. pdf. Pg. 9. Accessed: June 6, 2012

Adler, Horst. "Schweidnitz im Jahre 1941—Materialien zu einer Stadtgeschichte."http://www.horst-adler.de/Schweidnitz%20 1941.pdf. Pg. 8. Accessed: June 6, 2012

Anderson, Rachael Jane. "Lieder, totalitarianism, and the Bund Deutscher Mädel: girls' political coercion through song." © 2002 Rachael Jane Anderson. Faculty of Music, McGill University, Montreal, Canada.

"Anschluss." Various contributors. Wikipedia.org. http://en.wikipedia.org/wiki/Anschluss. Accessed: December 29, 2011.

"Ariosophy." Various contributors. Wikipedia.org. http://en.wikipedia.org/wiki/Ariosophy. Accessed: May 9, 2012.

"Artamanen." Various Contributors, Metapedia, Source: http:// fr.metapedia.org/wiki/Artamanen. Accessed: December 7, 2011.

"Assassination of Archduke Franz Ferdinand of Austria." Various contributors. Source: http://en.wikipedia.org/wiki/ Assassintion_of_Archduke_Franz_Ferdinand_of_Austria. Accessed: July 26, 2012.

"August 12, 1941." History.com. © 1996-2012, A&E Television Networks, LLC. All Rights Reserved. http://www.history.com/this-day-in- history/hitler-institutes-the-mothers-cross. Accessed: June 21, 2012.

"Aus Grauer Städt Mauren" Austrian Folk Song

"Austria." Various Contributors. Wikipedia.org. http://en.wikipedia.org/wiki/Republic-_of_Austria. Accessed: July 30, 2011

Badener Zeitung. "Die Geoffnung des Schutzhaues auf der Reisalpe." Oct. 15, 1898, No. 83, Pg. 3.

Bailey, George. Germans: The Biography of an Obsession. Avon, ©1978.

"Beer Hall Putsch." Various contributors. Wikipedia.org. http:// en.wikipedia.org/wiki-/Beer_Hall_Putsch. Accessed: August 1, 2011.

Bendersky, Joseph W. "A History of Nazi Germany: 1919 – 1945." 2nd ed. Burnham Publishers, 2000. Pgs. 24, 30. Accessed from: Nazism. http://en.wikipedia.org/wiki/Nazism#cite_note- 11 October 13, 2011.

Birke, Ernst. Personal e-mail dated June 24, 2012.

Bouhler, Philipp. Various Contributors. Wikipedia. http://en.wikipedia.org/wiki/Phillip_Bouhler Accessed January 15, 2012

Brachmann, Helga. "Personal Narratives—Why We Need Oral History."© 2003–2008 Chris Crawford and Stephan Hansen. Bund Deutscher Mädel: A Historical Research Page and Online Archive. (2003–2008) http://BDMhistory.com – Accessed: August 17, 2011

Bytwerk, Randall L. "Das danken wir dem Führer! (1938)." "We Owe it to the Führer." German Propaganda Archive. Calvin—Minds in the Making. © 1998 Randall Bytwerk. http://www.calvin.edu – Accessed March 17, 2012. All Rights reserved – Used by Permission

Bytwerk, Randall L. "Der Führer an das deutsche Volk Juni 1941." "The Führer to the German People: 22 June 1941." German Propaganda Archive. Calvin – Minds in the Making. © 2005 Randal Bytwerk. All Rights Reserved – Used by Permission

Bytwerk, Randall L. "Youth Ceremonies – Rites of Passage for the Youth" German Propaganda Archive. Calvin – Minds in the Making. © Copyright 1999 Randall L. Bytwerk. http://research.calvin.edu/german-propaganda-archive/jufeier.htm All Rights Reserved – Used by Permission

Bytwerk, Randall L. "Worldview Education for Winter 1938/39," German Propaganda Archive. Calvin—Minds in the Making. © 2006 Randall Bytwerk. http://www. calvin.edu

Buffington, Lina and Tamara Martinez, et. al. "The Educational Theory of Adolph Hitler: Hitler's Theory of Human Nature." New Foundation—2001— http://www.newfoundations.com/GALLERY/ Hitler.html. Accessed July 27, 2011.

Bund Deutscher Mädel: A Historical Research Page & Online Archive. © 2003–2008 Chris Crawford and Stephan Hansen. http:// BDMhistory.com. Accessed: August 17, 2011.

Camper, Casey. "87th Infantry Division Monuments" © 2017 Casey Camper - https://www.youtube.com/watch?v=dL2jktiigIk&t=23s

Carr, Adam. "Jutta Rüdiger." Wikipedia. http://en.wikipdia.org/wiki/ Jutta_R%C3%BCdiger. Accessed: September 16, 2011.

"Ceres (mythology)." Various contributors. Wikipedia. http://en.wikipedia. org/wiki/Ceres_(mythology). Accessed May 9, 2012.

Chanter, Alan "The Magnificent Queens." © 2004 – 2017 Lava Development, LLC. http://ww2db.com/other.php?other_id=44. Accessed: September 13, 2017

Crawford, Chris. Personal e-mail dated December 16, 2011.

Crawford, Chris. "History." Unpublished paper. December 20, 2011.

Crawford, Chris. "Jungmädelbund." http://www.en.wikipdia.org/wiki/Jungmadel – Accessed July 27, 2011.

"Cross of Honor of the German Mother." Various contributors. Wikimedia Foundation. http://en.wikipdia.org/wiki/Cross_of_Honor_of_ the_German_Mother. Accessed June 25, 2012.

"Das Lied der Getreuen—verse ungenannter Österreichischer Hitler Jugend aus den Jahren der Verfolgung 1933-1937." Edited by Baldur von Schirach. Added by: Dudeman5685@yahoo.com http://archive.org/dettails/DasLiedderGetreuen. Accessed May 29, 2012

"Das Mecklenburgische Landmädelin BDM—Werk 'Glaubeund Schönheit." Arbeitsrichtlinien für alle Mädel in der Arbeitsgemeinschaft— Bäuerliche

Berufsertüchtigung. Obergau und Landesbauernschaft Mecklenburg. Verantwortlich Untergauführerin Elli Hübbe, Jugendwart der Landes- bauernschaft Mecklenburg. © 1941 Auflage 3000 Druck Bever / Lange, Güftrow-Meckl.

Der Bannerträger (The Standard Bearer)—"Portrait of Adolf Hitler" by Hu- bert Lanzinger, circa 1935—oil painting on wood panel—US Army Center of Military History, German War Art Collection. Washington, D.C. http://www.ushmm.org-/propanganda/archie/ painting-the-standard- bearer/ - Accessed: December 15, 2011.

Der Hohenitsträger—#1/1939. "Jungendfeier—Lebenswende der Jugend." "Youth Celebration—Life Change for the Youth." Translator: Irma Nagengast Rosich. February 29, 2012. Oldsmar, FL. Library of Congress. Pages 23–28.

Der Stürmer – Various contributors. http://en.wikipedia.org/wiki/- Der_St%C3BCrmer). Accessed: March 3, 2011

"Deutschlandlied" Wikipedia. https://en.wikipedia.org/Wiki/Deutch land- lied - Accessed: September 17. 2011.

Dict.cc. English-German Dictionary. "Heil." http://www.dict.cc/german- eng- lish/heil.htm. Accessed: December 27, 2011.

"Donnerbüchse." Various Contributors. Wikipedia.org. http://wikipedia. org/wiki/DonnerbC3%BCchse. Accessed: March 21, 2012.

Dorson, Richard M. "Folklore and Folklife: An Introduction." The University of Chicago Press. Chicago, Ill. 1972. Pg. 16.

Douglas, Susan. "Bund Deutscher Mädel—Website Review." Roy Rosenzweig Center for History and New Media at George Mason University and the University of Missouri-Kansas City. © 2008.

DRGClass E 91. Various Contributors. Wikipedia.org. http://en.wikipedia. org/wiki/DRG_Class_E_91. Accessed March 29, 2012.

DRB Class 50 steam locomotive at the CFV3V, Treignes, Belgium. "Whistle." Trainfleet. http://www.youtube.com/watch?v=C0kOc-EnVmM – Accessed March 24, 2012.

DRB Class 50. Various Contributors. Wikipedia. http://en.wikipedia.org/wiki/
DRG_Class_50. Accessed March 21, 2012

Dubiel, Peter. Personal letter dated April 2, 2012. Berlin.

"Eichgraben." Marktgemeinde Eichgraben. Wienerwald Museum and
Carriage House Eichgraben. © FW Eichgraben. http://www.eichgraben.at/ -
Accessed March 28, 2012.

"Empress Elisabeth Railway." Various contributors. http://en.wikipedia.org/
wiki/Empress_Elisabeth_Railway. Accessed March 27, 2012.

"Esker." Wikipedia.org. Various Contributors. Access January 31, 2012

Europeana. "Brief von Werner Blasius von Hirschberg / Bürgermeister an
Gerhart Hauptmann | Hirschberg / Bürgermeister."
http://www.europeana.eu/portal/rec-
ord/2048611/data_item_sbb_kpe_DE_1a_8535_DE_611_HS_1909968.htm
l. Accessed February 6, 2016.

"European Green Woodpecker." Various Contributors. Wikipedia.org.
http://en.wikipedia.org/wiki/European_Green_Woodpecker - Accessed:
February 21, 2012.

Evans, Diane. Diane Evans Suite 101. "Hitler Youth: Thought-Control and
Brainwashing in Nazi Germany." http://diane-evans.suite101. com/hitler-
youth-thought-control-and-brainwashing-in-nazi- germany-a334644 – Accessed September 22, 2011.

"First Republic of Austria." Various Contributors. http:// en.wikipedia.-
org/wiki/Republic_of_Austria_%2819195E2%80%931934%29 – Accessed
July 30, 2011.

Foderà Serio, G.; Manara, A.; Sicoli, P. (2002). "Giuseppe Piazzi and the Dis-
covery of Ceres". In W. F. Bottke Jr., A. Cellino, P. Paolicchi, and R. P. Binzel
(PDF). Asteroids III. Tucson, Arizona: University of Arizona Press. pp. 1724.
http://www.lpi.usra.edu/books/ AsteroidsIII/pdf/3027.pdf. Accessed May 9,
2012.

"Franks." Various Contributors. Wikipedia. http://en.wikipedia.org/wiki/Franks. Accessed February 21, 2012.

"Frederick II, Duke of Austria." Various Contributors. Wikipedia. http://www.en.eikipedia.org/wiki/Frederick_II,_Duke_of_Austria Accessed February 21, 2012.

"Führer Proclamation to the German People: 22 June 1941, The." Translator: Professor Randall Bytwerk. "Der Führer an das deutsche Volk 22 Juni 1941," in Philipp Bouhler (ed.), Der großdeutsche Freiheitskampf. Reden Adolf Hitlers, vol. 3 (Munich: FranzEher, 1942), pp. 51 – 61.

"Gentiana verna." Various Contributors. Wikipedia.org. http://en.wikipedia.org/wiki/Gentiana_verna. Accesed February 20, 2012.

"German Austria." Various Contributors. Wikipedia. http://en.wikipedia.org-/wiki/German_Austria. Accessed: February 21, 2012.

German Militaria. "HJ Sleeve Insignia – N0002265 HJ Clothing Diamond." http://www.germanmilitaria.com/Political/photos/N002265.html - Accessed August 13, 2011.

"German Revolution 1918-1919." Various Contributors. http://en.wi-pedia.org/Germa_Revolution_of_1918%E2%80%931919 – Accessed July 29, 2011.

"Gutenstein Alps." Various Contributors. Wikipedia. http://www.en.wikipedia.org/wiki/Gutenstein_Alps - Accessed: February 2, 2012.

"Hanke, Karl." Various Contributors. Wikipedia.org. http://en.wikipedia.org/wiki-/Karl_Hanke. Accessed June 6, 2012.

Henle, Raymond, Director. "Oral History Interview with Clarence M. Young. July 19, 1971 at Sedona, Arizona." For the Herbert Hoover Presidential Library West Branch, Iowa and the Hoover Institution on War, Revolution and Peace, Stanford, California. 1972, Herbert Hoover Presidential Library Association, Inc. Pg. 3.

"Hirschberger Talbahn." Wikipedia.org. http://de.wikipedia.org/wiki/Hirsch-berger Talbahn. Accessed January 2, 2012.

Hitler Jugend, The —The Hitler Youth Organization – Basic Handbook Supreme Headquarters Allied Expeditionary Force—Evaluation and Dissemination Section G-2. (Counter Intelligence Sub-Division). Declassified April 23, 1973. Complied by MIRS (London Branch). Achive.org. http://www.archive.org/details/TheHitlerYouthdieHitlerjugendBasic-Handbook. Accessed July 28, 2011

"History of Austria." Various Contributors. Wikipedia. http://en.wikipedia. org/wiki/History_of_Austria. Accessed February 21, 2012.

History Place, The. – Hitler Youth – Demise of Democracy. http://www.historyplace.com/worldwar2/hitleryouth/hj-road.htm Accessed: March 4, 2011.

Hödlmaier, Gertrude. Personal Interview. November 2011. Linz, Austria.

"Hohenelbe." "Vrchlabi. History of the Town." © 2008, Městský úřad VRCHLABÍ http://www.muvrchlabi.cz/en/history/ Accessed June 14, 2012.

Holocaust Education and Archive Research Team. "Baldur von Schirach–Reich Youth Leader (Reichsjugendführer)" http://www. holocaustresearchproject.org/-holoprelude/bvs.html Accessed August 18, 2011.

Holocaust Education and Archive Research Team. "The Hitler Youth; Jungsturm Adolf Hitler." http://www.holocaustresearchproject.org/ holoprelude/hitleryouth.html. Accessed December 27,, 2011.

"Holy Roman Empire." Various contributors. Wikipedia.org. http:// en.wikipedia.org/wiki/Holy_Roman_Empire. Accessed February 21, 2012.

"Horst-Wessel-Lied." English version translated by Irma Nagengast Rosich. Note: This song is illegal in Germany and in Austria according to the German Criminal Code §86 and §86a, unless used for educational purposes -

"House of Babenberg." Various Contributors. Wikipedia. http://www. en.wikipedia.org/wiki/Babenberg. Accessed February 21, 2012.

Huesken, André. Photo of Dr. Jutta Rüdiger (1910-2001), deutsche Psychologin, Reichreferentin des Bund Deutscher Mädel (BDM). Anonyme Portraitaufnahme mit Autograph, ca. 1937, wahrscheinlich http://en.wikipedia.org/wiki/Jutta_R%C3%BCdiger#/media/File:Jutta_Rued iger.jpg Accessed: March 24, 2015.

"Hyperinflation in the Weimar Republic." Various contributors. Wikipedia.org. http://en.wikipedia.org-/wiki/Hyperinflation_in_ the_Weimar_Republic. Accesed August 1, 2011

"Interpretatio graeca." Various Contributors. Wikipedia. http:// en.wikipedia.org/wiki/Interpretatio_graeca#Roman_version. Accessed May 9, 2012.

Jackiewicz, Malgorzata. Owner of Monte Cassino where Landjahr Lager Seidorf is located in Sosnówka, Poland. Personal tour guide and interviews: November 3–9, 2011.

"Jungmädel-Dienst im Monat Mai 1939." Bayerische Ostmark. From the private collection of Stephan Hansen. Translated by Irma M. Nagengast-Rosich. © 2003-2008 http://www.bdmhistory.com

"Jungmädel-Dienst im Juni 1939." Bayerische Ostmark. From the private collection of Stephan Hansen. Translated by Irma M. Nagengast- Rosich.© 2003-2008 http://www.bdmhistory.com

"Jungmädeldienst." Reichsjugendführung, Berlin, February 1940. From the private collection of Stephan Hansen. Translated by Irma Nagengast-Rosich. © 2003-2008 http://www.bdmhistory.com

Jungmädel Führerinnen Dienst—January 1941. Gauverlag Bayerische Ostmark, Bayreuth, Germany. From the private collection of Stephan Hansen. Translated by Irma Nagengast-Rosich. January 4, 2012. © 2003 – 2008 bdmhistory.com

Kerschner, Franz. Author's uncle

Kershaw, Ian, "Hitler: A Biography," New York: W. W. Norton & Company, (2008) ISBN 0-393-06757-2.

"Landjahralbum." Jugend! Deutschland 1918-1945. http://www. jugend1918-1945.de/thema.aspx?s=3450&m=&v=4180. Accessed May 29, 2012.

Landl, Lotte. "12th Out of 13" ©Lotte Landl. Published by Book Pal.

Lanzinger, Hubert. Der Bannerträger (The Standard Bearer)—Portrait of Adolf Hitler. Circa 1935 – oil painting on wood panel – U.S. Army Center of Military History, German War Art Collection. Washington, D.C. http://www.ushmm.org/propanganda/archie/   painting-the-standard-bearer/ Accessed December 15, 2011.

"League of German Girls." Various contributors. Wikipedia. http:// en.wikipedia.org/wiki/League_of_German_Girls. Accessed July 27, 2011.

Leugner, Anita. Author's Aunt

"Leopold I, Margrave of Austria." Various contributors. http://en.wikipedia.org/wiki/Leopold_I,_Margrave_of_Austria - Accessed February 21, 2012.

Leppien, Annemarie and Jörn-Peter Leppien. Mädel-Landjahr in Schleswig-Holstein: Einblicke in ein Kapitel nationalsozialistischer Madchenerziehung 1936–1940. Schleswig-Holstein, Germany, Karl Wachholtz Verlag Neumünster GmbH. © 1989.

Lippenberger, Gertrude. Interview. December 24, 2012, Spring Hill, Fl.

Littlejohn, David. The Hitler Youth. © Agincourt Publishers, 1988.

"Mädel im Dienst—BDM-Sport." Reichsjugendführung. © 1934, Ludwig Voggenreiter Verlag Potsdam, Germany. Translated by Irma M. Nagengast-Rosich.

"Mädel im Dienst—Ein Handbuch." Reichsjugendführung. © 1934, Ludwig Voggenreiter Verlag Potsdam, Germany. From the private collection of Chris Crawford. Translated by Irma M. Nagengast-Rosich © 2003-2008 bdmhistory.com

McLeod, Hedwig. Personal recording of memories of Gertrude Sandor

"Migration Period." Various contributors. Wikipedia.org. http:// en.wikipedia.org/wiki/Migration_Period. Accessed February 21, 2012.

Morgenstern, Christian. The Lovely Earth. 1871–1914. See: Leppien, Annemarie and Jörn-Peter Leppien.

"Mostviertel." Various Contributors. http://www.mostviertel.info/d/ default.asp?id=81806&tt=MOST4_R46. Accessed March 27, 2012.

Natural History Museum. "Elder." http://www.nhm.ac.uk/nature-online/ british-natural-history/urban-tree-survey/identify-trees/tree- factsheets/c-to-e/elder/index.html. Accessed January 24, 2012

"Nazi Germany Timeline." Spartacus Educational. http://www.spartacus. schoolnet.co.uk/GERchron.htm. Accessed October 13, 2011.

"Nazi Party." Various Contributors. http://en.wikipedia.org/wiki/ Nazi_Party. Accessed March 4, 2012.

"Nazism." Various Contributors. Wikipedia. http://www.en.wikipedia.org/ wiki/Nazism#cite_note-11. Accessed October 13, 2011

Niederhuber, Gertrude – personal interview, Austria, November 2011

New World Encyclopedia Contributors. "Anschluss," New World Encyclopedia. Page ID: 690646, Date of last revision: April 10, 2008. http://www.new-worldencyclopedia.org/entry/Aschluss?oldid=690646 – Accessed September 16, 2011.

"Odal Rune." Delendaestziobot. Siddharreich—Loyalty is our Honor. © 2011. http://delendaestziobot.wordpress.com/2011/07/31/odal-rune. Accessed: May 29, 2012.

"Odin." Various Contributors. Wikipedia.org. http://en.wikipedia.org/ wiki/Odin. Accessed May 29, 2012.

"Opel Blitz—A Type—Mittlerer Gelandegangiger Lastkraftwagen offen." StrategyPlant.com. - ©1996-2009 IGN Entertainment, Inc. http:// www.strategyplanet.com/commandos/truck.html - Accessed June 20, 2012.

Onuska, Jeanne M. Personal interviews. June, 2012.

"Ötscher." Various Contributors. http://www.en.wikipedia.org/ wiki/%C3%96tscher. Accessed February 8, 2012.

Overy, Richard. "The Dictators: Hitler's Germany, Stalin's Russia." London: W. W. Norton. ISBN 0393020304.

Pannik, Maria. "Der Kleinzeller Chronik." http://kleinzell.gv.at –Accessed February 21, 2012.

Pine, Lisa. Education in Nazi Germany. The League of German Girls. Berg Publishers, New York, NY. © 2010, pg. 117.

Pine, Lisa. Nazi Family Policy—1933–1945. Berg Publishers, Oxford, New York. © 1997–1999.

"Protectorate of Bohemia and Moravia. Various Contributors." Wikipedia. org. http://en.wikipedia.org/wiki/Protectorate_of_Bohemia_ and_Moravia. Accessed March 29, 2012.

Proctor, Bob. "It's Not About the Money." CD. © 2009 BurmanBooks, Inc. Ontario, Canada.

"Queen Louise League." http://en.wikipedia.org/wiki/Queen_ Louise_League. Accessed December 27, 2011.

Randel, Mr. "How Fast Can A Little Boy/Girl Run." Yahoo answers. https://answers.yahoo.com/question/index?qid=20101113221556AAvg2jF, Accessed: January 31, 2016.

Reece, Dagmar. "Growing Up Female in Nazi Germany." Ann Arbor University of Michigan Press. © 2006

"Reisalpe Poem." Translated by Cynthia A. Sandor.

Reisinger, Gretel. Personal Interview. November 2011. Pöstlingberg, Austria.

"Republic of Austria (1919–1934)." Various Contributors. Wikipedia. http://en.wikipedia.org/wiki/First_Austrian_Republic - Accessed February 21, 2012.
"Republic of German-Austria – History." Various Contributors. Wikipedia.org. http://en.wikipedia.org/-wiki/German_Austria - Asscessed: July 29, 2011.

"Riesengebirgslied, Das." (The Riesengebirge Song—The Giant Mountain Song. Words by Othmar Fiebinger. Melody by Vinzenz Hampel.

Rosich, Irmgard M. Nagengast, Personal discussions – 2011 - 2012

Rotheneder, Mitzi. Personal discussions. 1989 - 2011

"Sagenhalle." Szklarska Poręba. "History—Kingdom of the Mountain Spirit." © 2008 Szklarska Poręba. http://www.szklarskaporeba.pl/ en/about-szklarska/history/the-kingdom-of-the-mountain-spirit. html – Accessed: June 11, 2012.

"Sambucus nigra." Various contributors. http://en.wikipedia. org/wiki/Sambucus_nigra. Accessed: January 24, 2012.

Samjeske, Werner. Personal e-mail dated: June 28, 2012.

Sandor, Cynthia A. "Europe to New York City on the United States—July 6, 1957" as contained in Braynard, Frank, and Robert Hudson Westover. 50th Anniversary Maiden Voyage Edition. S.S. United States—Fastest Ship in the World. ©2002 SS United States Foundation. Turner Publishing Company, Paducah, Kentucky. Pgs. 156–157.

Sandor Sr., Robert. Author's Father

Santrock, John W. "Socioemotional Development in Middle and Late Childhood: Friends." Life-Span Development, 7th Edition. McGraw- Hill College, Pgs. 247, 279, 307, 314, (1999).

Sautter, Reinhold. Hitler Jugend – Das Erlebnis einer großen Kameradschaft. Herausgegeben mit Genehmigung der Reichsjugendführung von Gustav Memminger. © 1942. Carl Röhrig—Verlag, Kom.-Ges., München 8.

Schirach, Baldur von. Wikipedia. "Vorwärts! Vorwärts! schmettern die hellen Fanfaren" ("Forward! Forward! Blare the Bright Fanfares"), Germany, 1933. http://en.wikipedia.org/wiki/Vorw%C3%A4rts!_ Vorw%C3%A4rts!_schmettern_die_hellen_Fanfaren. Accessed June 3, 2011. "Schneeberg (Alps)." Various contributors. Wikipedia. http://www. en.wikipedia.org/wiki/Schneeberg_(Alps). Accessed February 8, 2012.

Scholtz-Klink, Gertrud. Wikipedia. http://en.wikipedia.org/wiki/ Gertrud_Scholtz-Klink. Accessed December 27, 2011.

Schön, Winfried. "Schlesische Heimatforschung—Bewohner vor 1945 aus Seidorf, Kreis Hirschberg." http://www.wimawabu.de/Bergwacht/ Seidorf_Inter.pdf. Accessed April 3, 2012.

"Schuschnigg, Kurt." Various contributors. http:// en.wikipedia.org/wiki/Kurt_Schuschnigg. Accessed July 12, 2011.

Shea, J. "The Psychology of Uniforms." http://www.exploringbelieveability. blogspot.com/2010/12/psychology-of-uniforms.html – Accessed January 19, 2012.

Shears, Magdalena. Personal Interview. June 2012.

Shirer, William L. *"The Rise and Fall of the Third Reich"* (Touchstone Edition) (New York: Simon & Schuster, 1990)

"Sommerlage und Heimabendmaterial für die Schulungs und Kulturarbeit, Sommer 1941, Jungmädel," © Jungmädel, Schulungs-dienst der Jungmädel, (1941), p. 6 – 7.

"Sommersonnewende." ("Summer Sunshine Change") song written by Heinrich Gutberlet and Paul Dorscht. Public Domain. As contained in "Die Gestaltung der Feste im Jahres und Lebenslauf in der SS Family." 1933. Verantwortlich für den Inhalt: SS Abschnitt XXXIX, Prag. Pg. 55.

"Stalwart and Strong: The Story of the 87th Infantry Division" © 1944-1945 Stars and Stripes. Paris, France. Lone Sentry – Photos, Articles, & Research on the European Theater in World War II. © 2003-2007 LoneSentry.com.

"Szklarska Poręba." "Town History." © 2008 Szklarska Poręba. http:// www.szklarskaporeba.pl/en/about-szklarska/history/history-of-the-town.html - Accessed: June 11, 2012.

Thomason, M.F.A., Barbara. Personal discussions.

"Thor." Various contributors. Wikipedia.org. http://en.wikipedia.org/wiki/ Thor. Accessed April 28, 2012.

"Treaty of Versailles." Various contributors. Wikipedia.org. http:// en.wik-ipedia.org/wiki/Treaty_of_Versailles. Accessed July 26, 2011.

Triumph of the Will. The documentary of the Reich Party Congress, 1934. Produced by the order of the Führer. Created by Leni Riefenstahl. September 5, 1934. Accessed July 30, 2011.

Trueman, Chris. History Learning Site. "Nazi Education." (2000–2011) http://www.historylearningsite.co.uk/Nazi_Education.html - Accessed September 24, 2011.

"Trutnov." City of Trutnov—Official Website. © 2005–2010 Město Trutnov. http://www.trutnov.cz. – Accessed July 12, 2012.

"Über alles in der Welt." Various Contributors. Metapedia—the Alternative Encyclopedia. http://de.metapedia.org/wiki/ %C3%9Cber_alles_in_der_Welt. – Accessed June 18, 2012.

Vercamer, Arvo. "Organizational Structure" bdmhistory.com

"Völkisch Movement." Various contributors. Wikipedia. http:// en.wikipedia.org/wiki/V%C3%B6lkisch_movement. Accessed May 9, 2012.

"Walpurgis Night." Various Contributors. Wikipedia.org. http:// en.wikipedia.org/wiki/Walpurgis_Night. Accessed April 28, 2012.

Weidner, Dennis. "Hitler Youth Activities: Landjahr." Historical Boys' Clothing. 1999, http://histclo.com/youth/youth/org/nat/hitler/act/ha-jahr-htm - Accessed: December 7, 2011.

Weidner, Dennis. "Hitler Youth: Principles and Ideology." Historical Boys' Clothing. 1999. http://histclo.com/youth/youth/org/nat/hitler/prin/hj-prin.htm - Accessed October 14, 2011.

Weitzel, Fritz. "Die Gestaltung der Feste im Jahres und Lebenslauf in der SS Family." 1933. Verantwortlich für den Inhalt: SS Abschnitt XXXIX, Prag.

"Weimar Constitution – Provisions and Organizations of the Weimar Constitution – Section 1: The Reich and its States." Various Contributors. Wikipedia.org. Accessed July 30, 2011.

Weyrather, Imgard (PD Dr). "Muttertag und Mutterkreuz: der Kult um die "deutche Mutter" im Nationalsozialismus." Mother's Day and Mother's Cross: the cult of the "German Mother" in National Socialism. © 1993 Frankfurt am Main: Fischer Taschenbuch Verlag, ISBN 978-596-11517-4.

"Wir Mädel Singen. Leiderbuch des Bundes Deutscher Mädel." Herausgegeben von der Reichsjugendführung. 2 erweiterte ausgabe, 1938. Georg Kallmeyer Verlag/Wolfenbüttel und Berlin.

Wolf, Christa. "A Model Childhood." Translation: Ursule Molinaro & Hedwig Rappolt, New York: Farrar, Straus and Giroux, ©1980. Pg. 135.

WWII Troop Ships (c) 2007 Shayne E. Wallesch & Wendy J. Hochnadel. http://ww2troopships.com/ships/q/queenmary/cruiserecord1944.htm Accessed: September 23, 2017

Von Renteln, Adrian. Wikipedia. "Adrian von Renteln." http:wwen. wikipedia.org/wiki/Adrian_von_Renteln. Accessed December 28, 2011.

"Xufanc." Wikipedia. "National Socialist Schoolchildren's League." http:// en.wikipedia.org/wiki/National_Socialist_Schoolchildren%27s_ League – Accessed: December 20, 2011.

"Yggdrasil." Various contributors. Wikipedia.org. http://en.wikipedia.org/ wiki/Yggdrasil. Accessed May 31, 2012.

Zither Melodies—Welcome to Zither Melodies with Lotte Landl. True Austrian Zither and Songs CD. http://www.Lotte Landl.com. Accessed April 24, 2014.

"Zwergenkönig, der." ("The Dwarf King"). Austrian Folklore. This version adapted by Cynthia A. Sandor © 2011 Cynthia A. Sandor

D-DAY
CONNEAUT

Premier WWII Living History Event

AUG. ☆ CONNEAUT, OHIO

WWW.DDAYOHIO.US

9 780999 755006